D1104281

RISING FROM THE ASHES

RISING FROM THE ASHES

Survival, Sovereignty, and
Native America

Edited by William Willard,
Alan G. Marshall, and
J. Diane Pearson

UNIVERSITY OF NEBRASKA PRESS   LINCOLN

Library of Congress Cataloging-in-Publication Data
Names: Willard, William (Writer on anthropology),
editor. | Marshall, Alan G. (Alan Gould),
editor. | Pearson, J. Diane, 1941– editor.
Title: Rising from the ashes: survival, sovereignty,
and Native America / edited by William Willard,
Alan G. Marshall, and J. Diane Pearson.
Description: Lincoln: University of Nebraska Press,
[2020] | Includes bibliographical references and index.
Identifiers: LCCN 2019042717
ISBN 9781496219008 (hardback)
ISBN 9781496221056 (epub)
ISBN 9781496221063 (mobi)
ISBN 9781496221070 (pdf)
Subjects: LCSH: Nez Percé Indians—Government
relations. | Self-determination, National—Idaho. |
Phinney, Archie—Homes and haunts—Soviet
Union. | Anthropologists—Idaho—Biography.
Classification: LCC E99.N5 R57 2020 |
DDC 979.5004/974124—dc23
LC record available at https://lccn.loc.gov/2019042717

Set in Charis by Laura Buis.
Designed by N. Putens.

CONTENTS

ILLUSTRATIONS

TABLES

ACKNOWLEDGMENTS

J. DIANE PEARSON

Neither ode nor aria can express our gratitude to everyone who's been involved in this project for so many years. This is only the beginning; we thank William "Bill" Willard for his thirty-plus-year dedication to the study of the Nez Perce indigenous nationalist Archie Phinney and for Bill's unwavering devotion to American Indian survival and sovereignty. Bill, your passing in 2016 left huge holes in our hearts and in the halls of academe. We cannot begin to personally thank all the institutions, foreign countries, and intimate friends who lent Bill help; they are cited in the text, and Bill's photograph—taken while on a "mission" for Washington State University in 1992—is included in this book. Thank you, Dr. Trevor James Bond—now codirector of the Center for Digital Scholarship and Curation and associate dean for Digital Initiatives and Special Collections at the Washington State University Libraries—for the photograph and for all of your help throughout the years. Bill would be so proud of you, and our hearts grieve with you for the tears you shed at Bill's memorial while Alan G. Marshall sang a farewell song. Meanwhile, we forever thank Robert Keith Collins, associate professor and chair of the American Indian Studies Department at San Francisco State University, for arranging a gourd dance in Dr. Willard's honor following his death. Robert also erected a memorial display for Dr. Willard at SFSU; Rob, our gratitude is boundless.

Al Marshall personally submits: "My understanding of Nimiipuu (Nez Perce, or Numipu) people is strongly shaped by Samuel M. Watters, who kindly adopted my work; he is long deceased. This work also was influenced by other members of the Watters family, and the Conner and Red Elk families. Others who strongly affected this work include the Greene, Redheart, Wilson, Halfmoon, and Scott families. Many individuals also provided insights, among them Allen P. Slickpoo Sr. and Horace Axtell. Members of the Spalding Presbyterian Church and, more recently, the Spalding Longhouse have kindly shared their experiences with me. My thanks go to the Nez Perce Tribal Executive Committee (1972), which allowed me to conduct research among the Nimiipuu of the Nez Perce Reservation." We should add that any mistakes throughout this manuscript are those of the authors; our participants are a lot smarter than we are.

Additionally, our most genuine thanks to Dr. Tabitha "Beth" Erdey, cultural resources program manager at Nez Perce National Historical Park, for her tireless support and for the photographs and advice she provided from the Archie Phinney Collection. Patience is also one of Beth's virtues; we most certainly appreciate that! Once again, Dr. Steven L. Grafe, art curator at Maryhill Museum, has also been a generous source of information. He is a walking encyclopedia whose work reflects his tireless research; he didn't spend those years at the National Cowboy and Western Heritage Museum in Oklahoma City with his feet propped up on his desk! Neither did Allen V. Pinkham and Steven Ross Evans squander their tireless explorations of the Lewis and Clark pathways; thank you for sending me your exquisitely researched *Lewis and Clark among the Nez Perce: Strangers in the Land of the Nimiipuu* and Steve's *Voice of the Old Wolf*. These are invaluable resources; where else could I have learned about eagle and his feathers, miniature three-toed horses, and hunting woolly mammoths as I studied Nimiipuu peoplehood? And thank you, Professor Tom Holm, for expanding the peoplehood model of identity in your seminal book *The Great Confusion in Indian Affairs: Native Americans and Whites in the Progressive Era*. Those years of graduate school in Arizona and our friendship shine a bright light on my life and scholarship. I owe any cogent discussion of peoplehood to you.

Picking up on Willard's research for Archie Phinney in the former Soviet Union was difficult but not quite so impossible because of some very special people. As Al and I prowled our way through Russian archives (many of which are listed online now; of course, most of them are in Russian) we realized we needed translators and people on the ground in St. Petersburg (formerly Leningrad). In plain English, we needed help! That help came to us when we emailed Professor Sergei A. Kan, who teaches anthropology, Native American studies, Jewish studies, and Russian studies at Dartmouth College. This gracious man not only helped guide us to researchers in Russia and advised us about collections but was even so generous as to translate a bit for us. I could manage using Google Translator for one or two words, but that's about as good as that got. So, when Tabita Erdey gifted us with Archie Phinney family photographs taken in Russia that had Russian-language identifiers written on them, Professor Kan came to the rescue! I emailed him a scan of the photo and the writing, and he translated the notation into English back to me on email. He was even more accommodating with geographical information and more explanations. Thank you once again, Professor Kan!

We did, however, have to locate a full-service translator, since more files were available in Russia than when Dr. Willard had visited there in 1992. Frankly, the files exceeded our expectations. Fortunately, we found Renee (Stillings) Huh and the School of Russian and Asian Studies (SRAS) in Woodside, California; the SRAS offers great online translation services. Thank you, Renee; you were wonderful. Documents, files, anything needing a native Russian speaker went to you, and you took care of the rest. Thankfully, with Professor Kan's help and the SRAS translations, I was able to divorce Google Translator!

Luck was with us once again when we emailed Professor Kevin A. Yelvington at the University of South Florida. An anthropologist, Dr. Yelvington is studying the life and career of Dr. Jack Harris (who became an anthropologist at Columbia University). Lo and behold, Harris had been in Leningrad when Phinney was still there, during a very dangerous time. Dr. Yelvington shared archival materials, notes, and Harris's opinions of Leningrad—something we didn't have from Phinney because he was notoriously silent on that topic. Better safe than sorry in the USSR at that time; Harris wrote down his opinions only after his ship had left Soviet waters! So thank you, Kevin Yelvington, and I hope we were able to help you a bit with the Willard Collections at Washington State University.

Al and I also owe a particular debt of gratitude to the other scholars who have stayed with this project after Dr. Willard died. Hopefully, the book will be its own reward for your fine scholarship, which we are so proud to share. Chris Riggs, Brad Wazaney, Ben Colombi, and Jean Dennison: many, many thanks to all of you as we complete Dr. Willard's project. And Al, it's been a privilege to work with you. Your analytical work and your teaching abilities are amazing, and you write beautifully. Meanwhile, I really do wish you the very best luck salmon fishing!

INTRODUCTION

J. DIANE PEARSON

On Friday afternoon, January 15, 2016, my friend and colleague Rob Collins and I enjoyed a late lunch at Spenger's Restaurant in Berkeley, California. The new semester at UC Berkeley had just started, the academic week was wrapped up at San Francisco State University (SFSU), and we were prepared! We were enjoying a pleasant meal and relaxing conversation when the lights at our table went slightly crazy. Flashing, flickering on and off; yet, not another light in Spenger's even winked. We thought about defective wiring, waning light bulbs, an earthquake, mechanical problems. No one else seemed to notice anything; this was just for us. A few minutes later the lights returned to their previous dim, steady, calm state. Rob (who is Choctaw) and I (a *sooyáapoo* of Norwegian/Swedish Viking descent) had been discussing our Cherokee friend and mentor Dr. William "Bill" Willard at the time. Rob had been saying that Dr. Willard had given him some excellent advice about something at SFSU, where Willard had taught before going to Washington State University in 1976. And I had been talking about the "Rising from the Ashes" manuscript that Alan G. Marshall and I had agreed to coedit and coauthor with Dr. Willard. As friends sometimes do, we were also discussing our ancestors, such as Rob's great-grandfather, who had served with the Corps d'Afrique during the American Civil War. And Rob, who speaks Norwegian, was as usual not a bit surprised by my Scandinavian ancestors: Jan (Ian)

Bluetooth—a Norse Viking who painted his front teeth blue—and the Jonsdotter women, my female Viking relatives in Sweden. Not knowing that Bill was, at the moment, becoming a subject of this narrative, we also very much enjoyed exchanging some of his Cherokee ancestral stories, which he had so generously shared with us.

One of the first, and best, ancestral tales carried Bill's Cherokee ancestors and their dogs through Watauga Town (in present-day North Carolina) up onto the buffalo hunting grounds in West Virginia, Kentucky, and then on west through Indiana, Illinois, and out onto the very edge of the western plains. By the seventeenth century, following an eleven-hundred-year hiatus, American bison had resumed migrations into the southeastern portions of North America. Besides foraging for grazing areas, the buffalo sought the numerous salt licks that peppered what is now Kentucky and Virginia.[1]

As Bill told it, he remembered distant family stories about that salt, and that around 1735 (or perhaps even somewhat earlier) his Cherokee relatives had hunted buffalo (American bison) with dogs because they hadn't yet acquired horses! (According to various sources, the Cherokee had adopted horses from the sixteenth-century Spanish explorer DeSoto, or from nearby Native nations who had taken Spanish horses at the time.[2] Cherokee dogs were indigenous, though, and much older than DeSoto, Columbus, or imported European dogs.[3]) Continuing, Bill said, "The stories I recall tell of a large group of people; men, women and children in the summer hunt. The fall hunt was of men and women in good physical condition and health who could move fast ahead of the first big winter storm. They were described as traveling the same route every year, to the same part of the buffalo pasture."[4] His family finally settled into what eventually became Illinois, sometime before the Louisiana Purchase. According to reports submitted to Governor Luis de Unzaga y Amezaga, by 1775 the Cherokee had been settling in various parts of Illinois for at least forty years.[5] As the occupiers described them, these ancestral Cherokees lived in little "log huts" and raised small fields of corn, beans, and other vegetables that were tended by the women. They also participated in the very active trading markets for corn (and probably salt, as Bill had hinted) in Illinois and across the river in Missouri.[6] When the bison disappeared from that early area, Willard's kin moved into northwest Missouri, where the buffalo (American bison) still roamed.[7]

After the Civil War, when the buffalo had been hunted out in Missouri, the family moved into what is now Oklahoma, where the bison remained for a few more years. "Later," said Bill, "after the Cherokee Strip was opened by the federal government to homesteaders, they came to the same areas to file homestead claims on the land, where they had hunted buffalo until the buffalo didn't come anymore."[8] These Cherokee people were true to their earliest inclinations for survival and sovereignty: freedom, along with avoidance of restrictive colonialist policies and politics. Bill's family avoided any type of enrollment, whether French, Spanish, federal, or Cherokee.[9]

Willard's grandfather Peter B. Sharp, who had served in the Civil War with a volunteer Missouri Cavalry Regiment, refused to enroll the Sharp family in any federal or tribal program(s). Nevertheless, one day "when the word of allotment came out grandfather Peter saddled up his horse and was going to ride into the [Cherokee] agency to register for allotment." Having heard a rumor that Peter was going to enroll, the family uncles rode up on their horses, terribly upset, and said, "Absolutely no! Do not register. Unsaddle that horse and keep to ourselves." And that was just what Peter did.[10]

Bill had listened to these elders' stories, always told in the Cherokee language, when he was a little boy at his family's home in California. Their large family of about one hundred Cherokees had migrated to California to work together (probably as *gadugi*, the old-style Cherokee working groups) in the redwood forests and lumber mills. Bill's father even took him on a visit one time to rural California, where they saw a Bear Doctor. As Bill understood it, his father wouldn't let him get too close to the doctor because of the doctor's powers. Bill couldn't remember, or maybe he never knew, what or how his father knew about Dr. Sam, the grizzly Bear Doctor (who was probably either a Mono or Yokuts "bear shaman").[11] There was no doubt that after further memories surfaced, Bill understood that Dr. Sam could have turned himself into a grizzly bear at any moment.

Now, January 2019 marks the third year of Bill's journey to "the Sand Hills," as he always called the spiritual resting place. And we learned why the lights blinked just for us that day; that is, after we heard from Al Marshall and checked our credit card receipts for time and date. Either Bill, an unknown Bear Doctor, or some other spiritual power had been warning us in Berkeley. We didn't know that Dr. Willard, who lived in Pullman, Washington, had died that day until Al Marshall told us the sad news. So now, having said a more formal farewell to our friend with prayers, songs, an honoring gourd dance in memory of his military service and his early ancestors—one had signed the Treaty of Hopewell in 1785 (7 Stat. 18), and another had fought alongside General Jackson in the Battle of Horseshoe Bend in 1814;[12] his own grandfather Peter B. had fought in the Civil War—plus memorials at Washington State University and San Francisco State University in spring 2016, we bring to fruition with this manuscript two of his lifelong visions. We include Bill here as a participant as well as one of the coauthors.

Willard was always concerned with Native American survival, contemporary life within the U.S. colonialist empire, and sovereignty—such as that of the lives his ancestors had lived. He also focused on the life of the Nimiipuu (Nez Perce, also Numipu) anthropologist Archie M. Phinney, who was a world traveler, an indigenous nationalist, and later an official in the Bureau of Indian Affairs whose primary concerns were American Indian survival and sovereignty. To these ends, Willard published at least half a dozen important essays, one edition of the *Journal of Northwest Anthropology* devoted to Phinney, and articles written by Phinney himself. During Willard's tenure as coeditor of the *Wicazō Ṡa Review* and as a professor at Washington State University (beginning in 1976), he presented academic and professional data on Phinney to a global community, becoming an authority whose work inspired other scholars to incorporate Phinney's, the Nimiipuu's, and other American Indian survival narratives into a global academe. This is not at all improbable, for many of the Sharps had been members of the Deer Clan.[13] And among Cherokee Deer Clan attributes, such as being "good runners, ball players, clothes makers, [and] tanners," there is also a tradition of intellectualism.[14]

Long before "walking on" to the Sand Hills, Willard had incorporated his very good friend and colleague Alan Marshall as well as me in these aspirations. Willard also included his former students from Washington

State University, such as Ben Colombi and Brad Wazaney, as well as friends and colleagues in academia such as Jean Dennison and Chris Riggs. Marshall at Lewis and Clark State College and Willard at Washington State University became covisionaries who studied U.S. colonialism, American Indian survival, Native American sovereignty, and Phinney. Now, we bring to light a collective version of their dreams. Marshall's adumbration of mid-eighteenth-century Nimiipuu memory, land, loss, and language composes chapter 1; my exploration of Nimiipuu, Palus, and Cayuse peoplehood, survival, and spirituality during nineteenth-century U.S. expansion and federal incarceration are addressed in chapters 2 and 3. Collectively, our perspective on Archie Phinney and his dedication to education, indigenous rights, responsibilities, and sovereign Native Nations develops chapters 4 and 5. Riggs's description of American Indian citizenship before U.S. domination presents chapter 6; Brad Wazaney's examination of the Jicarilla Apache's self-actuated corporate model makes up chapter 7; and Ben Colombi's discussion of salmon, water, and Native nation building constitutes chapter 8. Anchoring the collection is Jean Dennison's twenty-first-century analysis of the indigenization of academic discourse, sovereignty, and Native-nation responsibilities and responses in chapter 9.

These topics are not only vital to studies of survival and sovereignty but also interwoven with Willard's dreams and visions, with Alan Marshall's adumbrations and visions, and, quite often, the work, life, and visions of Archie Phinney. Primarily, my own peoplehood work and history is reinforced and intertwined with Marshall's adumbration, ethnographies, linguistic expertise, and other publications. My work also includes Archie Phinney's linguistic studies and is closely tied to Sam Watters's advocation that Nimiipuu "make every step on the earth as a prayer."[15] And, of course, Native nations are interconnected by a deep, underlying commitment to their very existence and tradition, just as Archie Phinney was. He lived (and studied) Nimiipuu culture and language; he understood how difficult Native American survival was in a U.S. colonial world. As an adult employed by the Bureau of Indian Affairs, Phinney clamored for Native American voting rights, as Chris Riggs examines; he advocated sovereign recognition and nation building with an astute understanding of post–Dawes Act (allotment) failures and environmental degradations, as Ben Colombi presents; and he supported economic rehabilitations and success for Native American communities, as Brad Wazaney discusses. And with no small effect, Phinney predicted and aimed for the successes of sovereign, strong, and independent Native Nations such as the Osage of the twenty-first century, as Jean Dennison illuminates.

Alan Marshall also brings his mentor and friend, the late Samuel M. Watters (Nimiipuu), into this dialogue to "provide a snapshot from which we can see how the (Nimiipuu) generations since the mid-1800s have tried to deal with [the] on-going transformations" brought about by Euro-American colonization, settlers, and changing land-use patterns. Marshall and Watters's chapter 1 sketches the Nimiipuu cultural landscape and the beings that live there, thus identifying one source of Nimiipuu resistance to continued settler-colonial development. One other fascinating dimension of this chapter is Marshall's use of single- or two-word Numiputimt ("Numipu tongue" in the dialect spoken by Archie Phinney) linguistic translations that help the reader to understand many aspects of Nimiipuu life in their natal language.

Carrying forward Marshall's theme of changes "beyond the written record," chapters 2 and 3 address the peoplehood model of identity and Nimiipuu self-actuated survival during nineteenth-century U.S. expansionist wars and exile to federal prison camps. Now, as students of so many untold histories, we learn that the peoplehood model of identity, as laid out by Robert K. Thomas (a Cherokee scholar who expanded Edward H. Spicer's definition of cultural enclaves), consists of four factors—language, sacred history, ceremonial cycles (religion/spirituality), and place/territory (homelands)—that are "interwoven and dependent on one another." These factors form a "complete system that accounts for particular social, cultural, political, economic, and ecological behaviors" unique to indigenous peoples in specific territories. Thanks to expanded scholarship by our dear friend Professor Tom Holm, I extend the peoplehood model of identity in chapters 2 and 3 to reappraise the forced spiritual vacuities of U.S. expansionist warfare and confinement, the unique theological survivalist activities of the pre- and post-war Nimiipuu, and their incarceration in Kansas and Indian Territory. I also use this model to further delve into the enriched territorial, ceremonial, sacred, and other survivalist activities of these exiles as they lived out an appalling federal captivity between 1877 and 1885. Participation in truncated tribal ceremonials at Fort Leavenworth in Kansas, Sun Dances, horse races, gambling games, giveaways, and other ceremonials—and even their sacred and personal regalia—reminded the prisoners of Peoplehood's ancient lifeways as they joined meaningful Plains tribal activities at Quapaw, Ponca, Cheyenne and Arapaho, and Kiowa. In the aftermath of continued exile at Colville, Washington Territory, the peoplehood model of identity helps shed light on the Nimiipuu's continued ceremonial activities and Chief Joseph's lifelong determination to regain the exiles' stolen aboriginal homelands.

Next, we collectively utilize recently available data, extant scholarship, and archives in Russia and in the United States to discuss Archie Phinney in chapters 4 and 5, bringing Native American survival and sovereignty into the twentieth century. Such senior scholars as Professor Sergei Kan (Dartmouth) and Professor Kevin Yelvington (University of South Florida) have shared their current scholarship, personal advice, and data with us. New materials have been provided by archivists in Russia and translated by the School of Russian and Asian Studies (SRAS), while new photograph collections originally owned by the Phinney family, along with historical newspapers in Russia and in Lewiston, Idaho, have added depth and excitement to academic preparations. Following Willard's extensive research, the new data help to explain Phinney's education in the United States and his subsequent degree through the *kandidat nauk* (a degree equivalent to a PhD) in the USSR. This frames Phinney's ambitions to advance the lives of indigenous peoples by comparative anthropological research and Native nation building through his student days in the USSR and his participation in a global academe. Through his own travels to Russia and archives around the world, as well as his persistent research, Willard brought Phinney to the forefront of academia. Now, we explain the historical and theoretical underpinnings of Phinney's activities and education in the USSR, along with his travels throughout the former Soviet Union; we also highlight his relationships with his professors, student cohorts, and several unique historical personalities. To mention just a few, these include the Russian revolutionary, author, and anthropologist

Vladimir Bogoraz; Russian ethnographer and folklorist Nikolai Matorin; anthropologist and string-figure theorist Julia Averkieva; and the famed anti-British Indian revolutionary Virendranath Chattopadhyaya. We then follow Phinney's return to the United States in 1937 and his building of a successful career as an indigenous nationalist during his ascent through the Bureau of Indian Affairs. Phinney was heavily involved in FDR's Indian Reorganization Act (the Wheeler-Howard Act of 1934), as he promoted strong, independent American Indian nations, and he was a member of the group that founded the National Congress of American Indians. As a supporter of American Indian education, Phinney was also a tireless proponent of tribal constitutions and indigenous nationalism.

Expanding the concept of Native American rights and responsibilities, Christopher Riggs's chapter 6 evaluates types of citizenship celebrated by Native Americans and relates those ties to Alan Marshall's discussion of Nimiipuu tribal citizenship. Notions of American Indian citizenship before and after tribes found themselves within the boundaries of the United States are identified, analyzed, and critiqued based on Riggs's rich research base and thoughtful analysis. This thought-provoking discussion embraces a diverse collection of state and federal regulations and problems; it addresses a comprehensive, resource-rich sampling of tribal groups, Native Nations, communities, regulations, customs, and laws. Riggs confirms that indigenous societies had differing criteria for citizenship and that these citizenship rules, "plus the associated rights and responsibilities," resulted in a "primary allegiance to one's Native community." Following U.S. suppression, however, the federal government formalized tribal membership and defined the rights of those members—as part of national policies to appropriate land or to "civilize" American Indians—or moved to "terminate" Indian tribes by breaking them up and nationalizing their members. As Riggs rephrases, tribal citizenship was to become inferior to U.S. citizenship. Riggs underscores the idea that the "ongoing efforts by Native Americans to define tribal citizenship criteria and to exercise their voting rights" as U.S. citizens illuminate their ongoing struggle "to preserve a distinct tribal identity."

Brad Wazaney takes us into corporate Native America in chapter 7 with his analysis of Jicarilla Apache history and the development

FIG. 1. William Willard (*center*), WSU project cohort, Russia, 1992. William Willard Collection. Courtesy of Washington State University, MASC.

of their successful self-determined business model. Like many other American Indian nations, the nineteenth-century Jicarilla were placed on a remote reservation where they were expected to ranch or farm and somehow, perhaps, to survive. Unfortunately, the reservation wasn't especially suitable for cattle or farming, and by the early through mid-1900s life was often difficult. Treaties were made by the United States, scattering tribal bands. Meanwhile, poverty and lack of opportunity hounded the Jicarilla as they sought to provide for themselves, retain their cultural ways, and reinforce their peoplehood while surviving in a new economy. Then, subsurface oil and gas were discovered on Jicarilla holdings. Now, true to Professor Willard's initial request, Wazaney examines the progression of Jicarilla management from traditional tribal leadership to the current corporate-style management system. The Jicarilla were eager for the Indian Reorganization Act and did not need to be persuaded to accept self-governance. Yet, unlike standard capitalist corporate structures, the Jicarilla Apache have developed an economic system that redistributes public resources. The subsurface mineral resources on communal lands generate revenue and benefits to supplement the lives of all enrolled members. Much of the "success that the Jicarilla Apache have achieved is attributed to their ability to govern with limited interference from the Federal Government and their control over tribal resources." As Wazaney concludes, although many facets of Jicarilla society were "affected by conquest and further altered by the multitude of policies implemented in the name of acculturation, the basic fundamental values of cooperation and egalitarianism remain an intrinsic part of their economic system." And, while policies such as the Indian Reorganization Act in 1934 transformed the function of leaders within Jicarilla society, "their ability to adapt through cooperation remained strong." As Willard had planned, Wazaney—and history—indicates that the Jicarilla model could serve as a guidepost for other developing American Indian nations, since the intrinsic value in this and any other societal study "is in indicating problems and supplying alternative solutions."

As Alan Marshall prompts, another purpose of this manuscript is to "show how people maintain 'gemeinschaft,'[community] in the face of colonial forces." Incorporating many of Archie Phinney's ambitions and ideas, Benedict Colombi does just that in chapter 8. Salmon, clean water and cultural connections to water, history and homelands, economics, cosmology, language, and salmon nation building follow the Nez Perce (Nimiipuu) and other Northwestern Native Nations and organizations in their efforts to survive U.S. and global political, environmental, and economic devastation. Colombi reveals the historic roots of the Lewis and Clark Expedition, U.S. occupation, various land-loss mechanisms enacted by an expansionist United States, and acquisition of the Nez Perce homelands. He then brings to light how the Nez Perce, are building a sovereign "salmon nation" despite external globalizing forces. Colombi highlights the evolution of salmon and water as reserved rights, and he showcases strategies for indigenous self-governance and self-determination. Colombi's salmon nation building addresses creative solutions to many current salmon crises, and it may also help to "countervail environmental disasters" such as global climate change and large, restrictive dams. The projected "impacts of climate change" to salmon and water are addressed, as well as the "novel and innovative policies" tribal nations devise. "Salmon nation building," concludes Colombi, is a "process by which indigenous nations use tribally specific, cultural solutions to solve external problems of growth-oriented development."

Challenging sovereignty's assumed Eurocentric origins and the applicability of a sovereignty that "limit[s] Indigenous authority," Jean Dennison's seminal chapter 9, dealing with theory, history, sovereignty, and accountability, secures Professor Willard's vision into the twenty-first century. Our journey from memory, loss, and language; peoplehood, survival, and spirituality; corporate self-determination; American Indian citizenship; and globalization and salmon nation building culminates with Dennison's discussion on indigenizing the academy and notions of sovereignty. This "sovereignty," adds Dennison, "is currently theorized within the Osage Nation" as a path to tribal "accountability." Dennison, a citizen of the Osage Nation, also investigates history, Osage oratories, and ethnographic Osage data to explore the possibilities of indigenization. Indigenizing sovereignty, as Dennison reveals, means creating "a government that could be more accountable to the Osage people than the colonial government they had been under." Dennison posits Osage desires for accountability in sovereignty not as "fundamentally 'Western' in origin or inherently oppressive in nature but as a potential tool for building a stronger Osage future." Like the Jicarilla, the Nez Perce, and many other Native nations, the Osage are not alone in contemporary Native America. They are unique, however, because the Osage model provides another, more detailed potential guidepost for services to tribal citizens. As Dennison completes our manuscript, and as we say *wado* (thank you) to Dr. Willard, we close with two other important concepts put forth by Dennison: we hope to lead the way into the future with more research in order to "better understand" whether attempts at indigenizing sovereignty "can in fact lead to governments that are more accountable to the needs of their service populations." Hopefully, this can help to predict what role, if any, "the ongoing colonial process will play in disrupting these efforts." Or, as Dennison also suggests, this may offer a recipe for "accountability through practice."

NOTES

1. "Cumberland Gap," Denny-Loftis Genealogy (website), accessed November 21, 2017, www.ajlambert.com/history/hst_cg.pdf.
2. Mooney, *Myths of the Cherokee*, 182. By 1760 the Cherokee owned many excellent horses; in Mooney, *Myths of the Cherokee*, 82.
3. One of the oldest references to Cherokee dogs is included in Cherokee mythology; in it, dogs make tracks in the heavens, such as the Milky Way, "where the dog ran." Mooney, *Myths of the Cherokee*, 259.
4. William Willard, email message to the author, summer 2015.
5. In Starr, *History of the Cherokee Indians*, 38. Note: Starr misspelled the governor's name; this is the correct Spanish spelling.
6. Foreman, *History of Oklahoma*, 54–56. See Foreman further for an interesting discussion of the salt industry and Cherokee participation; Bill frequently mentioned salt and the importance of the commodity to his relatives.
7. William Willard, personal conversation with the author, January 15, 2014.
8. William Willard, personal conversations with the author, summer 2015.
9. William Willard, email message to the author, January 30, 2015.
10. William Willard, personal conversation with and emails to the author, summer 2015.
11. William Willard, personal conversations with the author, summer 2015. Willard told me that Dr. Sam was probably Yokuts in Willard, "Bear Doctors," 119.
12. "Cherokee Muster Roll from the Battle of Horseshoe Bend, March 27, 1814," accessed October 24, 2019, https://www.nps.gov/hobe/learn/historyculture/upload/cherokee.pdf.
13. Dennis Rainwater, "Names of Cherokee Indians and the Clans They Come From," Genealogy.com, October 22, 2011, http://www.genealogy.com/forum/surnames/topics/rainwater/2008; William Willard, personal conversation with the author, January 30, 2015.
14. Panther-Yates, *Cherokee Clans*, 16.
15. Marshall, "Fish, Water" 764.

BIBLIOGRAPHY

Foreman, Grant. *A History of Oklahoma*. Norman: University of Oklahoma Press, 1942.

Marshall, Alan G. "Fish, Water, and Nez Perce Life." *Idaho Law Review* 42 (2006): 763–93.

Mooney, James. *Myths of the Cherokee*. Washington DC: Bureau of American Ethnography, 1902.

Panther-Yates, Donald N. *Cherokee Clans: An Informal History*. 2nd ed. Cherokee Chapbooks 4. Phoenix AZ: Panther's Lodge, 2011. First published in 1923 by Warden (Oklahoma City OK). Page references are to the 2011 edition.

Starr, Emmett. *History of the Cherokee Indians*. Oklahoma City: Warden Co., 1923.

Willard, William. "Bear Doctors." *Cultural Anthropology* 10, no. 1 (February 1995): 116–24.

ABBREVIATIONS

APS   American Philosophical Society

ARBIC   *Annual Report, Board of Indian Commissioners.* Washington: United States Government Publishing Office, 1878, 1879

ARCIA   *Annual Report, Commissioner of Indian Affairs.* 1873, 1875, 1876, 1878, 1881, 1885, 1886. Washington DC: United States Government Printing Office

   Annual Report, Commissioner of Indian Affairs. 1873. H.R. Ex. Doc. 1, serial set vol. 1850. Washington DC: CIS

ARSW   *Annual Report, Secretary of War.* 1875–76. United States Government Printing Office, Washington DC

CIS   Congressional Information Service

LDCNP   Letters and Documents Concerning the Nez Perce

LROIA   Letters Received, Office of Indian Affairs

NAA   National Anthropological Archives, Smithsonian Institution, Washington DC

NARA   National Archives and Records Administration

NARA-PNWR	National Archives and Records Administration, Pacific Northwest Region
NCAI	National Congress of American Indians
NPNHP	Nez Perce National Historical Park Archives, Spalding ID
NPS	National Park Service
NWUA	Northwestern University Archives, Evanston IL
OHSAD	Oklahoma Historical Society, Archives Division
SPF ARAN	Arkiv Rossiskoi Akudemü Nauk (St. Petersburg Archive of the Russian Academy of Sciences)
USGPO	United States Government Publishing Office

RISING FROM THE ASHES

1 Nimiipuu at the Edge of History

ALAN G. MARSHALL AND SAMUEL M. WATTERS

This chapter provides insights into the life of Nez Perce people at the edge of history—in other words, lives beyond the written record of life in northwest North America in the mid-1800s. Only part of their lives and a little of their histories were observed and recorded in the writings of the settler colonists from the United States. So, with few exceptions published "Nez Perce history" reflects Euro-American reactions to, and interpretations of, Nimiipuu resistance against the immigrants to their land and the settler-colonists' increasing use of military and police power to enforce territorial control.[1] By sketching Nimiipuu life based on oral accounts, our interpretation of Nimiipuu life is at the edge of history.

This "edge of history" is the boundary of the known/unknown past as well as of temporal and spatial realities. The fragmented nature of written and oral records, which reflect the place and time in which the recorder made an observation, reflects the discontinuous character of "the frontier." The frontier has not disappeared, though it has continued to shrink and fragment. Nimiipuu oral accounts include places that Euro-Americans never visited and events that were unknown, and sometimes unrecognizable, to those newcomers.

Nimiipuu culture in the mid-eighteenth century was a symbolic pattern of landscape, objects, people, and habits that provided the means to meet the physical, social, and spiritual challenges of their homeland on the Columbia Plateau, in the northern Rocky Mountains, and over the northern Great Plains.[2] The use of these mazeways, or a habitus inclusive of the landscape, constituted their world—a taskscape.[3] Thus, their motivations and thoughts, often differing among individuals, about how to act in meeting those challenges arose from those physical, cognitive, emotional, and behavioral actualities.

This complex setting was already under considerable pressure by the time these peoples came onto the written historical horizon in 1805, when Lewis and Clark passed through the homelands of Nez Perce peoples. Some of these earlier pressures for change, such as the horse, enabled the expansion, intensification, and innovation of some sociocultural patterns at the expense of others. Other changes, such as a new disease environment contributing to constant population decline, were dangerous to the paths of life followed by Nimiipuu peoples. After Lewis and Clark all these changes increased in pace, intensity, and persistence as Nimiipuu were drawn into the developing world-system.[4] In brief, Nimiipuu in the mid-1800s were already in an apocalypse driven by disease, violence, hunger, social chaos, and ecological change.[5] These "stressors" were not wrought by distant forces but brought into Numipunm Wéetespe (Nez Perce Earth) by settlers who, through the use of force, literally "made the rough places smooth, and the crooked places straight."[6]

They continue to do so. Ongoing development by settler-colonists erodes the fundamental aspect of any dominated society: its relationship with "the environment." Nimiipuu culture is not found in this chapter, or in libraries, or in various media; it is found atop the mountains, on the prairies, in the valleys, and within the rivers. As "the land"—wéetes—continues to be altered, there are fewer and fewer Nimiipuu symbols, and there is less and less space and time in which Nimiipuu habitual action, feeling, worldview, and speech can occur. These changes cue the transgenerational trauma that Nez Perce people often experience. Many contemporary Nimiipuu continue to work to meet these continuing health, social, and cultural challenges by protecting and expanding that "traditional" spacetime.[7]

The purpose of this essay is to provide a snapshot from which we can see how the generations since the mid-1800s have tried to deal with these ongoing transformations. This suggestion of Nimiipuu culture at the edge of history is based on symbols, some of which have a continuing presence as discontinuous landscape, reduced and altered biota, and policed social life. It is the organization of these "traditional" aspects that provides the foundation and discipline of contemporary Nimiipuu life. These enduring symbols include (1) the physical aspects of "prereservation" time that remain in the midst of this ongoing change; (2) the experiences of a generation of elders in the 1970s, when I first conducted fieldwork among Nez Perce people, as well as continuing research with younger people;[8] (3) other ethnographic works; and (4) the land itself, which is changing in front of our eyes. Some implications of this "past" for the present are also outlined.

My (Alan Marshall's) fieldwork with Nimiipuu had some important "taphonomic" constraints on this image of mid-eighteenth century Nimiipuu culture. First, I was not there, nor were any of the people with whom I spoke. Nimiipuu with whom I spoke were always careful to attest only to what they had observed directly and were careful to identify when they were recounting others' descriptions from times or places where my interlocutors were not present. Second, my absolute age affects the information that is shared with me, and this has changed over the forty-five years during which I have interacted with Nimiipuu people. Third, our interactions varied depending upon my relative age and generational seniority or juniority. Fourth, my gender obviously strongly limited the issues discussed with me. Fifth, different geographic locations, for example, where interviews or interactions occurred, revealed different information. Sixth, the people with whom I lived and worked, my "family," also circumscribed the shared knowledge I was privy to. Lastly, as a *sooyáapoo*—a white person—I experienced constraints, particularly in public settings, on what information was shared with me. These constraints eased greatly with many individuals as I became more familiar to them; they also reveal strong traditional cultural values expressed by contemporary Nimiipuu in a variety of ways.

An outstanding, though unsurprising, impression I had about Nimiipuu is the unique character of each individual's, family's, and community's lives and knowledge. In other words, Nimiipuu life was, and continues to be, diverse and complicated. A brief example will illustrate what I mean. Today we buy our mass-produced shoes, made from industrially produced leather, metal, and plastic, at a store from someone whom we do not know, and those shoes indicate our social status and aspirations. The shoes are portable into many parts of the world. However, the shoes do not easily fit us—we must "break them in" or, perhaps more accurately, break our feet into them.

On the other hand, one's Nimiipuu "shoes"—ʔiléepqet—are handcrafted by one's women relatives from the hides of animal "friends" who sacrificed themselves to one's male relative's weapon; these animals came from places of which one has an intimate familial knowledge extending into time immemorial. Indeed, one may first have seen the animal in a dream. The ʔiléepqet fit one's feet from the moment they were completed. However, they are no longer portable into all aspects of the world in which Nimiipuu live, and the dissonance between ʔiléepqet and shoes—between Indigenous and non-Indigenous worlds—is palpable.

What this essay hopes to convey is the background to this complexity through the lens of people's place in the landscape.[9] In doing so, we can see the foundations of many contemporary issues among Nimiipuu, as well as part of the Nimiipuu motivation to persist. Perhaps, thus, the "soul-wounds" that many Nimiipuu express in a variety of ways and try to heal will become clearer to others.[10]

Who Are "the Nez Perce?"

"The Nez Perce," as Nimiipuu have become known administratively, was in the early 1800s an aggregation of "tribes" at the edge of history. Discussing the indigenous inhabitants of the region as though they were a single political, social, or cultural unit is therefore highly misleading, and I will use the term "Nimiipuu" to refer to the various politically independent, though socially interdependent, groups who spoke mutually intelligible dialects of Nimiipuutímt—the "Nimiipuu tongue." They lived in the regions known as Welʔíwe (Grande Ronde/Wallowa River Basin); Tamáanma (Salmon River) plus its tributaries; along the Kuuskúusxayx (Clearwater River) plus its tributaries; and along the Pikúunen (Snake River) plus its tributaries, from Pine Creek to Wawawai Creek. A significant minority of families spent several seasons of their lives living in *kúuseẏn* (the northern Great Plains) with their Cayuse, Sahaptin, Interior Salish, Kalispel, and Crow allies.[11]

While all Nimiipuu spoke Nimiipuutímt, there were at least two geographic dialects, identified by Kinkade et al.[12] However, my consultants indicated that one also could infer a person's origins more narrowly from their speech patterns.

Moreover, other languages were integral parts of Nimiipuu life. Many Nimiipuu were polyglots due to intermarriage and alliances with speakers of other languages, including dialects of Sahaptin, Cayuse, Interior Salish, and, perhaps, Lemhi Shoshone. Chinook jargon was part of the Nimiipuu's cultural capital; many Nimiipuu who traveled to Celilo Falls and beyond to fish and trade spoke Chinook jargon. Of course, the lingua franca of sign language was part of many people's abilities.

Ethnographers, linguists, and historians have elicited a variety of names for these peoples, commonly referred to as "bands."[13] Band names and territories shown in these sources are inconsistent. They appear to have changed somewhat over time, perhaps for political reasons and according to who is asked for information. In brief, Nimiipuu sociopolitical entities were context dependent and thus polymorphous. Today, the most inclusive self-referential name for these entities is some spoken variant of Niimiipuu.

In any case, the identities and origins of individuals and groups were rooted in "the land"—*wéetes*. *Wéetes* refers to the community of earth, water, plants, animals, sky, stars, and other beings, both human and non-human, in which Nimiipuu belong. The question, "Who are you?" was often answered in one of two principal ways: by naming one's grandparents or identifying the riverine village place—*téẃyenikees*—where one lived. These differences and similarities, and many others besides, reflect sociogeographical actualities, thus seeming to bear out the conviction of many contemporary Nimiipuu that they belong to "the land." This aspect is more fully outlined in the next section.

The land in which the Nimiipuu belonged was divided by the United States into present-day north-central Idaho, northeastern Oregon, southeastern Washington, and Montana during its territorial expansion into and political/social integration of this region. This division remains problematic for Nimiipuu; the division of the land divided the people as well.

The Land

Numipunm Wéetespe—"Nez Perce Earth"—is geographically diverse and biologically rich. Its geographic diversity, reflected in the diversity of speech, political, and other communities, supported about four thousand people in 1860.[14] In many ways the Earth disciplined the people; in order to survive, they had to accustom their bodies, actions, emotions, and thoughts to the seasons, resources, and so on.[15]

Their mid-1800s population reflected a decline in the Nimiipuu's numbers; "old-world" diseases had affected the people, possibly since the late 1600s.[16] Not only had the disease ecology of the region altered, other changes in the land were also already underway as new macroorganisms, artifacts, and social relations spread into the region and changed relationships among its inhabitants. Some of these new things and ideas were appropriated by Nimiipuu as their own; for instance, *sikem* (horse), *timáanit* (apples), and *kícuy* (metal). One must wonder, too, if at least some aspects of Christianity had not been culturally appropriated as well, especially following H. H. Spalding's sojourn in Nez Perce country between 1836 and 1847.

Regional topography is fundamental to the diversity of the region and to the diversity of the People. Elevations range from about 650 feet at the westernmost (most downstream) Nimiipuu village to 9000 feet and taller in the mountain heights of the Bitterroot Range along the eastern border, where some Nimiipuu camped in the late summer and fall. The region's mountains of metamorphic rock stand above a great loess-covered basaltic plateau averaging about 1900 feet in elevation. All are deeply dissected by the Snake, Salmon, and Clearwater Rivers and their tributaries.

The region lies in the rain shadow of the Cascade Mountains. In winter, the Bitterroots wring about fifty inches of precipitation from eastward-drifting maritime low-pressure systems after they have passed over the dry loess hills of the Columbia Plateau, which get less than twenty inches of precipitation each year. In summer, the region's climate is dominated by dry high-pressure systems. The maritime low-pressure systems produce cool and moist conditions, though they are often interrupted by warm, moist southwesterly flows—*yawínyeeye* (gentle wind/spirit)—and cold, dry northerly high-pressure systems, or *XálpXalp* (gusty, cold wind/spirit).

The montane region is deeply dissected by spring snowmelt. Snowmelt pulses enormous amounts of water down the deeply incised canyons of the Grande Ronde, Clearwater, Salmon, and Snake Rivers. Hells Canyon of the Snake River, between present-day Idaho and Oregon, is nine thousand feet deep; farther downstream, where the Snake River's gorge begins its cut across the basalt plateau, the canyon is about 1800 feet deep—its shallowest place in Nimiipuu land. The region thus experiences the "canyon effect": these deep canyons ameliorate winter's moist, cold weather and intensify summer's dryness and heat.

While near present-day Kamiah, Idaho, in the late spring of 1806, Meriwether Lewis commented on the relationship between the sharp elevation differences and weather contrasts, thereby noting, indirectly, the spatial and temporal patchiness ("diversity") of the environment. On 15 May, 1806, while at Camp Choppunish in the area, Lewis wrote:

> About noon the sun shines with intense heat in the bottoms of the river. the air on the top of the river hills or high plain forms a distinct climate, the air is much colder, and the vegitation [sic] is not as forward by at least 15 or perhaps 20 days. the rains which fall on the river bottoms are snows on the plain. at the distance of fifteen miles from the river and on the Eastern border of this plain the Rocky Mountains commence and present us with winter at it's utmost extreem [sic]. The snow is yet many feet deep even near the base of these mountains; here we have summer spring and winter within the short space of 15 or 20 miles.[17]

These dimensions of season, elevation, dissection, and slope aspect affected resource distribution, diversity, and complexity. Nimiipuu leaders had to know the places and timing of resource availability in order to make complex decisions in planning their family's journeys to the locations of minerals, plants, and animals. Since the resources available varied from area to area, "bands" had different rhythms to their lives. In this way, "the land" disciplined the Nimiipuu.

Nimiipuu groups traveled to assemble in their summer villages and camps to collect resources and make goods for their own use—or to exchange these for goods they could not gather in sufficient amounts. The warm, protected canyons provided places for winter villages, and the Nimiipuu returned to them as snow restricted their movement in the high country. There, the people could prepare for the following year's pulse of life. Of course, it is through these routines that individuals develop their own likes, dislikes, and identities in relation to others and to "the land."

The following brief "resource" lists are intended to impress upon readers (1) the specificity of the relationships between Nimiipuu and "the land," (2) the acuteness of Nimiipuu knowledge about "the land," and (3) the fact that no single person could embody all the knowledge, the motivation, or the full behavioral repertoire needed to produce all of the artifacts necessary for Nimiipuu individual, social, and spiritual survival. In short, these examples highlight the social nature of Numipunm Wéetespe—it was a community disciplined by the "Nez Perce Land."

Plants were significant for a number of reasons. Outstandingly, however, they are immobile, requiring people to move to specific sites in order to gather and process them.

Examples of "industrial" plants from different habitats include:

1. *Qéemu* (Indian hemp, dogbane) was used to make string and cordage. It was found along watercourses in the lower elevations.[18]
2. *Tóko* (cattail and bulrush) was used for matting and house coverings.
3. *Yéeye* (beargrass) was used for weaving, especially as decoration in "corn husk" bags.

Many food plants were managed by Nimiipuu through the use of fire.[19] Examples of food plants from different habitats include:

1. *Qeqíit* (snowdrops) is the earliest highly palatable plant to grow in the canyons; its corm, or "root," is still eaten with gusto. It was dried and stored for later consumption; when dried it is called *qáws*.
2. *Qáamsit* (biscuit root), another important corm found in profusion in many places, was eaten year-round after being dried and stored. Oftentimes, it was ground and stored as "biscuits."

3. *Qémes* (camas) was the signature food plant of the Nimiipuu. It is a lily with highly nutritious bulbs. Huge, dense stands were found in marshy meadows on the prairies and in the mountains. *Qémes* was steamed ("baked") in earth ovens. It was eaten year-round after being ground and formed into loaves called *ʔapa*. *Qémes* in this form was a significant trade item in the Plateau and the northern Plains.

4. *Cemíitx* (huckleberries) grow in great profusion in openings in the forested mountains; they were dried and stored for later use in a variety of ways.

5. *Lálx* (whitebark pine nuts) were found in the highest reaches of Numipunm Wéetespe; these were gathered and roasted for storage and later consumption.

Streams supported both anadromous and resident fish used for food and other purposes, such as:

1. *Léewliks* (four species of salmon) remain fundamental to Nimiipuu diets (Marshall 2006). These anadromous fish ascended virtually all the streams of Numipunm Wéetespe in huge runs that vary depending upon water conditions. The "chief" or "king" of these was *nacóʔox*, or chinook salmon.

2. *Héesu* (lamprey eels) are anadromous fish that arrived at *heesutoynu* (Asotin WA) during *heesuʔal* ("lamprey eel time"). They have since disappeared from this region.

3. *Qfilex* (sturgeon) are mysterious fish that live in the depths of the Snake River, in particular. They were sought for food but also highly regarded as a source of raw material for making an excellent glue.

4. *Qfiyex* (sucker) were a common source of food.

5. *Címey* (mountain whitefish) were a commonly used food source.

Terrestrial animals used for food and other purposes included:

1. *Wiséew* (elk) are in some ways the premier local source of meat; elk are highly sought after, perhaps because of their size. They also provided hides used for a variety of useful tools, clothing, and housing needs.

2. *Qoqáalx* ("buffalo"), as the American bison is referred to by most Nez Perce today, was also highly sought after by Nimiipuu. Once found in

small numbers in the Plateau area, Nimiipuu travel east of the continental divide to hunt them, sometimes in large multiethnic groups.[20] Bison provided meat (both for consumption and trade) and materials for tools, clothing, and housing needs.

3. *Sáaslaqs* (moose) are mostly solitary animals that provided meat and materials for tools and clothing.

4. *Tiṅúun* (mountain sheep, male) are a valued food source; their hides were prized for clothing, and the horns were made into highly sought-after recurved bows. No general term for "mountain sheep" is known.

5. *X̣áx̣aac* (grizzly bear) were hunted for both spiritual reasons and for food.

The abovementioned organisms are a few of the persistent members of the Nimiipuu community, and knowledge about them informed much of Nimiipuu life. Clearly, the land was not merely a backdrop for Nimiipuu activities. Instead, it became part of the people's bodies and society. It was part of their routines, motivation, memory, and self/group identity. It structured Nimiipuu life and disciplined its followers. Perhaps this is what some Nimiipuu referred to as *xollahxollah tamáalwit*: the hidden law.[21]

Besides the life-forms mentioned, "the land" itself formed the bedrock of Nimiipuu community. Some rock formations were well-known, serving as memorials and time-continuous "enculturational objects." These rock formations memorialize the actions of the land's original inhabitants, foremost of whom was/is ʔiceyéeye—Coyote—who shaped the present world and continues to influence events.

1. Heart of the Monster—near Kamiah, Idaho, this is where ʔiceyéeye saved all of the ancestors of today's animals from being consumed by a monstrous being.

2. Coyote's Fishnet—this talus slope on the lower Clearwater River is where ʔiceyéeye was fishing for salmon. He was taunted by others, which convinced him to throw his net down and head off over the Bitterroot and Rocky Mountains to go to "buffalo country," in present-day Montana.

3. Ant and Yellowjacket—this unique basalt rock formation is where two villagemates got into an argument over dried salmon; they came to

blows and wrestled. ʔIceyéeye was angered by their greed and conflict, so he transformed them into rock.

4. Coyote's Snowshoes—these are a pair of talus slopes on Potlatch Creek that memorialize ʔIceyéeye's chase of an elk during a winter hunt. The snowline was at this location, so he left his snowshoes here.

5. Sleeping Chief—in some accounts, this ridgeline near Lewiston, Idaho, is Coyote's son.

Besides these symbols, there were other important enduring symbols inscribed on the land by people and their ancestors—pictographs and petroglyphs. Hundreds of examples of these have been located, some in large concentrations.[22] A publicly known example of the latter is Buffalo Eddy on the Snake River above Asotin, Washington. Another type of enduring symbol are the rock cairns found throughout the high country.

The People's relations with these lasting signs are various and widely speculated upon. The signs may be "simple" artistic expression, or the petroglyphs may be the "records" of individuals' encounters with the spiritual world. Some individuals say that they are historical writings describing past events and claim to read them. Still another possibility is that some people used them for prophecy. Whatever their use or uses, they clearly remain important to Nimiipuu, and some are still visited regularly.

Other, far more mobile symbolic parts of the landscape were various spirits, ghosts, and monsters. Among the spirits, for example, are the "water elk" who lived near Lenore, Idaho; they were sometimes seen at dusk, dawn, or at night when they came out of their home in Pinkham's Eddy to graze; herds of these were found at various locations. "Monsters" included a one-horned serpent, which was last observed (to our knowledge) on the hillside across Potlatch Creek from Yeqéme village site. Another monster was a beach-ball-sized toad with a human head, who lived near present-day Ferdinand, Idaho. Finally, there were ghosts. A few, at least, were identifiable. For example, the ghost of notorious robber and murderer Cihu threatened people as they traveled up the Clearwater River near Agatha, Idaho, where Cihu met his end.

Other beings inhabited the region as well. ʔistiyehé, sometimes identified as "bigfoot," roamed the region and are still seen sometimes. S. M. Watters said that they followed a five-year north–south migration cycle in the Bitterroots, but they are seen throughout the region. Cawxcáwx, identified as "Little People," were found in the region as well. As elsewhere in the West, the men were well-armed and aggressive. At least some of them had their village(s) in the upper Asotin Creek drainage basin of southeastern Washington. Also, "stick Indians," or "Whistling Indians," were found in the forests of the region. These people were secretive. Sometimes they led lone hunters or berry pickers astray by whistling and kidnapped young people who strayed from their camps.

Lastly, there were *wéeyekin*. These beings were special because they had various powers that they could share with a human partner. Each one somehow epitomized a cognitive, affective, or behavioral characteristic of living beings and was much sought after, especially by boys. They lived in quiet places, often in deep pools in the rivers or lakes or on mountaintops; however, lone travelers could encounter one almost anytime. *Wéeyekin* are discussed more fully in the next section.

Permanent human-built places in the land related people to the land and to one another. Among these are winter village locations, summer village locations, and migratory routes. The terms for these are *téwyeni-kees*, *wispáykaas*, and *wísees*, respectively.

Each winter village had a name—for example, Yeqéme or Qemyexpu—peculiar to its (permanent) location. The winter village name identified not only the location but the people living there as well. So, a person or group of people would identify themselves as Yeqéme, for example, if they were asked, "Who are you? Where do you originate?" S. M. Watters stated that a *téwyenikees* might be unoccupied for a long time, even several generations. However, when it was reoccupied, the people there became, for example, Yeqéme.

Associated with most *téwyenikees* were a men's semi-subterranean sweathouse place and a women's semi-subterranean house place— *hʼiite-mees* and *ʼelwítees*, respectively.[23] The *hʼiitemees*, I (Alan Marshall) infer, functioned as "men's houses"; they were meeting and sometimes sleeping places for men. The *ʼelwítees*, I infer, was a "women's house" used not only as a menstrual and birthing "lodge" but also as a meeting and sleeping place. Both these buildings rapidly disappeared during the changes of the early 1800s. Later, a more impermanent structure called *wistítaṁo*, or the "traveling sweathouse," was used instead of the *híitemees*, and a small "teepee" separate from the village replaced the *ʔelwítees*. Another place associated with most villages was a *sáway* (graveyard). Some villages also had a *wéeyees*—a "guardian spirit winter dance floor." When people left to travel in the spring, summer, and fall, they stored gear in a *wikées*, or "cache," near the village.

Similarly, summer village places were named; these were generally known as *wispáykaas*. What distinguishes winter villages from summer villages is that the latter were bases for food production and processing. They were occupied for a shorter time than *téẇyenikees*, but like them these locations are permanently identified locations. Associated with many *wispáykaas* are a "traveling sweathouse place" (*wistéṁees*) and a menstrual/birthing place. People anticipated returning to these places, so they often left tipi poles and sweathouse frames hanging in trees so they would not rot. Other gear was often stored in a *wikées*, or cache pit. The things left behind were "respected" by others; that is, strangers to the place could not ethically use them. I heard complaints about *sooyáapoo* (Euro-Americans) not respecting this basic rule. Many families had several *wispáykaas*, which formed a *wísees*, or "migration route."

The fact that individuals and their coresidents identified themselves and were identified by their living spaces makes it the case, prima facie, that "the land" is Nimiipuu identity.

Growing into the Land

Community and personal identities were built from the bricolage of symbols concretized in a patterned landscape.[24] This enculturation is the internalization of experiences with the land channeled by social experience in the landscape. Some identities were inherited through consanguineal relationships, some were made through affinal relations, and others were discovered through "vision quests." In all cases, one's "place" in the land and society was created through personal effort and concretized in the things one made or used and in the narratives one told.

Everyone inherits a place through their family. All things were related in most Nimiipuu worldviews, and the use of human kinship terms for things sometimes occurred. This view is reflected, perhaps, in the identity of person with a community's physical location on the landscape. This, of course, initially depended on who one's consanguineal relatives were, especially one's parents and their parents. Elements of inheritance were one's birth family's *téwyenikees* and its *wispáykaas*. One's place also depended upon where one lived; postmarital residence was primarily patrilocal, but much variability existed.

Nimiipuu human consanguineal relatives (*himyúuma*) encompassed four ascending and descending generations—nine generations in all. Nimiipuu used a bifurcate collateral kinship terminology. In other words, relational terms for patrilateral consanguines were different from those for matrilateral consanguines.[25] Collateral relatives in the parental generation were distinguished from lineal relatives as well, and men and women were referred to by different terms. However, men did not distinguish their sister's children by gender.

In the grandparental generation, all men on the father's side were merged into a single term, *qálacaʔc*, as were the women, who were called *ʔéeleʔc*. Similarly, all male matrilateral relatives in the second generation were termed *pilaqáʔc*, while women relatives in that generation were termed *qáacaʔc*. Moreover, the terms for grandparent and grandchild were virtually reciprocal; one would refer to one's matrilateral grandmother as *qáacaʔ*, while she would refer to her grandchild as *qáacaa*. These relationships were especially significant, as is suggested by the reciprocal nature of the kinship terms. Grandparents, it seems, were often the primary caregivers for children, as the parental generation was often involved in active, sometimes dangerous, occupations. Moreover, several elders stated that a person would introduce him- or herself this way: "My grandparent is . . ."[26]

The principle of distinguishing collateral relatives did not apply to the third and fourth generations. All relatives in the third and fourth ascending and descending generations were merged into single terms: *póxpoqc* (great-grandparent/child) or *pítwit* (great-great-grandparent/child).

In one's own generation, all descendants of *pítwit* were merged as "older/younger brother" or "older/younger sister." "Older/younger siblings" were regarded as a social unit and rewarded and punished equally for the infractions of any member. Elders frequently recount stories of being "whipped" (often simply touched or brushed with a switch) by a *wéetuweet* or *weetuweetáyat*—"whipman" or "whipwoman," respectively—in a group with their same-gender siblings.[27] A common statement still is, "He made us kneel down in a line and whipped us."

Sibling terms were sometimes applied to non–blood-related friends, especially those living in the same places. And age- and gender-appropriate kinship terms were used for other friends as well. People "made" relatives. Special relationship terms existed for friends, though; these were an important part of "making a place," as discussed below.

Obviously, not all these siblings lived in the same *téwyenikees* as ego (anthropological usage), yet all were, ideally, proscribed as ego's possible marriage partners. Some issues related to this practice are discussed under the section on "making a place" below.

A person's place in the world, then, was partly inherited. The significance of kinship in the success of an individual and that of his or her brothers and sisters takes on wider implications when understood in terms of place. Each person develops a relationship with "places" across the landscape. Each *téwyenikees*, *wispáykaas* (traveling ground), *qinítees* ("root" ground), *tukéelees* (hunting ground), and *timánitees* (berry patch) is known only to some individuals who have developed a relationship with it. Thus, a person's success is dependent on knowledge held by his or her relatives. One gains knowledge of these places by growing up in them, and one's presence in these places is possible only through kinship relations; in the early stages of life those relations are primarily consanguineal ties.

Taking/Making a Place/Name
While kinship terms were used in most interactions, names were quite significant in formal or ceremonial situations. Some of these were places/names held by a family; these were commonly inherited after the death of the place/name carrier. The "resting" period for a name sometimes lasted for more than two generations. A strong feeling was that the place/name should be carried by persons of the same "genius": persons who carried the name should exhibit strong similarities in physiognomy, taste,

or behavior. When a place/name was passed down, the heir, who was obligated to uphold the place/name by continuing its fame, would memorize the attributes and actions of previous carriers and try to further and enhance them. In this way, history was made present.

But a person could also create a place/name. Some names came from a person's encounter with *wéeyekin*—a "guardian spirit." Famously, Young Joseph's Nimiipuu name—Hinmátoonyalatkáykt—resulted from his experience during a *wéeyek* (guardian spirit quest) above Wallowa Lake, Oregon. His later work to save Wal⁊wama—the Wallowa country/people—made his name lasting.

Building a Place

People literally build their place in the world over the course of their lives. A person "owns," or controls, only what that person makes. A person also has a say (or "tenure") in the disposition of any thing, place, or region that that person contributes to producing, constructing, or maintaining. Several significant points emerge from this perspective.

The first point is that each person, whether man or woman, can dispose of the "artifacts" they make "as they wish." For example, a man can give anyone he wishes the body or flesh of any animal or fish that he kills. Likewise, a woman can give the food she makes to anyone she wants to. Of course, if a man decides to give his kills to women other than his wife or unequally distributes it among his wives, he is likely to develop conflicts with her/them. Likewise, if a woman decides not to feed her husband with the food she makes, she is likely to develop a conflict with him. A man with multiple wives needs to be evenhanded in accepting food from each wife, however, for the same reasons. That is, such giving and taking is the work required for making and maintaining relationships.

The second point is that if one is part of a hunting party, one has a claim on any animals killed. Or, if one has helped build or maintain a fish trap, you have a say in the distribution of the fish caught there. If a person helps to maintain a sweathouse, he/she has a claim to its use. This principle applies to camps, villages, "root" grounds, and so on. This is the foundation of tenure, and continuing action is necessary to maintain one's relationship with the land and the others using it.

Those who are most knowledgeable, successful, and hardworking become people to listen to and copy over time, because they know the rhythms of the places in which they have experience. Their relationships with others—the land, people, and the spiritual world—become stronger and more widespread.

Transcending Spacetime

Building long-term relationships with others is fundamental to long-term well-being. In the case of the Nimiipuu, relations allow one to socially transcend space and time. One's group of consanguineal kin allowed access to the resources of a limited region. By marrying others, one rendered material, social, and spiritual access to other regions possible.

Year to year and decade to decade, a region's productivity varied. Moreover, some places were simply more productive for various reasons, some of them technical. For example, just above the confluence of the North Fork of the Clearwater River and the river's main stem is a place called Timímap. Timímap was one of the few places where a weir could be constructed on a large stream, and it was the most productive fishing site in Nez Perce country. Each year, as high water waned, the *lewteḱeneẉeet* (fishing leader) of that place watched the level fall on certain formations in the bedrock.[28] When the level was right, people from the surrounding villages would help build a *leqéelis* (fish weir) across the river following a general design adapted to that particular river location's streambed. As the fish were taken from the weir, the *lewteḱeneẉeet* distributed these to "the people." Making a relationship with this leader and members of that village was desirable for obvious reasons.

Marriages were arranged by elders, often by "grandparents." The calculus for arranging a marriage was complex. Compatibility between the marriage partners was fundamental, of course. A married couple was in some ways the basic unit of Nimiipuu life. The term for man (*háama*) presumed someone who was married. Without an active, determined wife (*ʔiwéepne*), a man could not succeed as a leader. Likewise, a woman could not succeed as a leader without an active, determined husband. Both must move in the same direction.

But the issue of compatibility extended far beyond the bride (*ʔapolámt*) and groom (*téemec*), since the relationship was not simply between them. Clearly, the relationship was also between the groom's siblings and the bride's siblings because of the mutual self-identity of sibling groups. Moreover, Nimiipuu followed sororate and levirate practices as well—when one's married sibling (of the same gender) died, one married their spouse. Men and women referred to their opposite gendered siblings-in-law as *pinúukin* and had a joking relationship with them. For example, when joking with his *pinúukin*, a man might call his brother's wife "*cikíiwn*." The "joke" was that upon the death of the connecting relative, the term for the same-gendered sibling's spouse would change to *cikíiwn*; sexual relations might begin, and marriage would be expected. Women referred to their husband's brother's wife (their potential cowife) as *peʔékstiwee* and to their husband's other wife (or wives), as *peʔéks*, terms which carry connotations of conflict. Men called their wife's sister's husband *híkáytiwaa*, which has the connotation of persons joined by eating from the same dish.

Men referred to their wife's brothers as *tiwéeye*, which has connotations of being bound together. Women referred to their sisters-in-law as *cíiks*. These relationships were friendly yet respectful.

Women held political, social, and spiritual power in Nimiipuu life. For this reason, a woman's family had a continuous claim to their in-laws' goods. A man's wife's brother always had a claim on whatever a man had. Stories of a man's *tiwéeye* dropping by and leaving with some valuable personal item are not uncommon.[29] Thus, compatibility and marriage was between sibling groups as much as between bride and groom.

Compatibility even beyond sibling groups was an issue in choosing marriage partners for one's grandchildren. Significant relationships were established between other members of their families, and compatibility was important for one's children as well. For example, the groom's mother's sister and the bride's mother's sister (both referred to as "*péeqex*") entered into an important long-term relationship as well. The substance of the relationship was mutual visitation and "sharing" of food, clothing, and other valuables. These relationships were formally acknowledged during an exchange in which members of the bride's family first placed the women's goods in front of themselves and their equivalents from the groom's family placed piles of the men's goods in front of themselves opposite the bride's relatives. Then, the participants exchanged places. This initial exchange might then grow into a lifelong relationship.

That said, the exchange was unequal; the men's goods were relatively "pitiful." That is, according to some of my teachers, the gifts of the bride's family (including the bride herself) were always more valuable than those of the groom's family, and this put the groom's family in debt. It seems that wife takers were at a "disadvantage" to wife givers, as we have seen in the relationship between *tiwéeye*.

There were differences in ceremonies associated with marriage. Some were more socially/politically significant than others. The more significant the marriage, the longer and larger the exchange. Significant exchanges took place over several weeks or months, with the bride's family giving first and the groom's afterward. Also, the more "distant" the alliance the more significant it was. That is, a widely recognized, well-connected family would literally and figuratively marry farther away than those less well-known.

This was probably most true for individuals who were scions of important families. Less powerful families, perhaps because they were less well-known, found it more or less difficult, depending upon their reputation, to attract marriageable spouses for their children from families with no known consanguineal connections. Scandal, however, did not attach to a marriage unless it was with children who shared grandparents. Very weak families married close relatives; such people were sometimes called, among other terms, *wéetunix*, or "worthless." Their poor reputations sometimes led to accusations of cache robbing and other transgressions.

In a world of kinsfolk, everyone was related through a network of rights and duties of privilege and obligation. These were branded on a person willy-nilly. Exercising and fulfilling these could be wholehearted or not. Friendliness had much to do with this, and this was, in a way, independent of kinship relations; a kinsperson might not be a friend.

Friendship with nonrelatives was extremely important, and there were other "alliances" made between members of the same gender as well. These relationships, substantiated through presence and presents, were more or less intense. The level or intensity of affection was acknowledged through a series of metaphorical terms perhaps indicative of the basis for affection. Aoki identifies four terms that my teachers independently confirmed: *qú'tiwee, síikstiwaa, láwtiwaa,* and *yelép.*[30] He offers glosses similar to the ones I elicited.

"Friendship" extended into the spiritual world as well. These friendships were made through *wáaẏat*—a "vision quest." This relationship with a "guardian spirit"—*wéeyekin*—was ideally the closest friendship a person had; the behavioral requirements a guardian spirit demanded superseded all others. Nevertheless, *wéeyekin* were highly desired.

Senior consanguineal relatives are important as caregivers and educators. Concern for the "coming generations" was a responsibility and duty. And success in building a place required more than mere technical competence. Helping juniors to find their place through the revelation of a physical/spiritual place in the "land," thus providing them with more than mere technical competence, was a fundamental right and privilege of being a senior person. This help involved as much physical, emotional, and cognitive training as any other pursuit.

The place is figurative as well as actual, and like other places it is based on relationships—in this case a relationship with a "guardian/ tutelary/spirit or genius," or a *wéeyekin*. A *wéeyekin*, commonly referred to as "power" or "partner" in English, is the source of a person's wisdom, desires, and technical abilities to accomplish something. There are many *wéeyekin* of any kind; they are, in a way, individuals. Some are "stronger" than others, and each may have somewhat different abilities. So, a person could refuse an unwanted *wéeyekin* if he or she were well-trained.

Generally speaking, each person was trained to relate to at least one *wéeyekin*, though the particular process described here is more characteristic of boys, perhaps, than girls. Initially, physical training was necessary, and it continued throughout a person's youth. Physical training included, in particular, bathing or swimming in cold water. This began when the child was as young as three or four years old and continued daily, year-round, whenever possible. This was coupled with sweatbathing in the *hitítamno* (semi-subterranean sweathouse) or *wistítamo* (camp sweathouse).[31] Of course, this activity also involved considerable emotional training, as swimming in cold water, especially in cool or cold weather, is uncomfortable at first, as is sweatbathing. Besides overt instruction simply by being there and listening to conversation among senior individuals, usually of the same gender, a child would receive instruction from grandparents, uncles, aunts, and others as to what to look for and what to do when the child encountered a *wéeyekin*.[32] The seeker had to be very careful, because a person is, naturally enough, attracted to beauty and wealth.

A girl or boy could encounter a *wéeyekin* at almost any time he or she was alone, as when going on some errand. So, she or he had to be prepared to accept or refuse the relationship. I have heard a few personal stories of such encounters. One such occurred when a boy about ten years old was going to care for horses. As he was going along, the boy was struck down by a burst of yellow and green colors, which resolved itself into a spray of earth from a rapidly digging badger (*síikʔi*), and then a well-dressed man appeared and began to speak to him. The boy was frightened and refused the relationship.

He refused the relationship for two reasons: first, *síikʔi* spirits have a reputation for being angry (*xiyáap*), jealous (*kées*), and greedy (*kitíwi*); second, obviously wealthy individuals also carry the reputation of being too proud (*cílii*). If the boy had accepted the relationship, he would have accepted those traits and "powers" as well.

More commonly, others formed partnerships with *wéeyekin* as a result of a vision quest—a *wéeyek*—to a known vision-quest site.[33] These were usually located at high points in the landscape or in a river.

Wéeyekin—as I understand the phenomenon—are different from one another and have homes. That is, they are independent beings. Some bear powers, for example, are stronger than others, and their human partners reflect that strength. Moreover, this bear partner might give this kind of power to his friend, while another bear might give a different kind of power to that bear's friend.

Individuals with *wéeyekin* were called *wéeyeknin* and became these spirit powers during the winter guardian spirit dances (*wéeyekweecet*). These were held in a *kuhetiníit*, or "longhouse," which was set up over a *wéeyes*, or "guardian spirit dance floor." I (Alan Marshall) have never seen one of these dances.

When All Is Said and Done

Relations with people after their death become attenuated but do not end. It seems that something of each person survives in a parallel world with dimensions like our own. The terms for "ancestor" include ʾanoqónma (firstcomers) and titílu (forefathers); some also used the term soqútma, or "nurse tree." These ancestors sometimes interact with people of this dimension. In the past, at least, visits between these worlds apparently took place; sometimes ancestors would come here, other times people would go there. In brief, these ancestors continued to maintain an interest in their descendants and to mentor them when possible. These visits resulted in prophecies, sometimes in the form of songs.

Caring for the Land/People

It should be clear that the power of Nimiipuu came from the land. On the one hand, they depended upon particular places at particular seasons for their physical sustenance, their social contacts, and their spiritual life. On the other hand, they took an active role in altering their environment through their various activities—root digging, hunting, fishing, and the use of fire. Getting these things done, influencing the course of events, is power.

The way people got things done constitutes political life. Political institutions, of course, were not separate from other institutions, principally the family and village. Even for the largest groupings, it was through the efforts of related families grounded in multiple téwyeni-kees that task groups were formed.[34] From this community, leaders of various kinds emerged to direct and complete various tasks. Common leadership roles and the terms for them include: mioxatmíoxaat (village leader), miyóoxat (war leader), tiwéet (medicine leader), lewtekeneweet (fishing leader), taawtakanawáat (hunting leader; food distributor), and wistemelwiyeet (travel leader).

The emergence of leaders depended upon the common will and advice of "elders," who identified the group's leader in the community.[35] The support of both influential men and women was essential in recognizing a leader's legitimacy. Elders' decisions were based on several elements:

1. Tradition: Who is the potential leader's family? What is its connection to the land? Does the family have a history of successful leadership? What is the potential leader's name or reputation?

2. Morality: Does the person know what he or she is doing? Does the person work hard and persistently; Is the person always "rustling around," as S. M. Watters said? Is the person committed to the community's well-being rather than to personal aggrandizement? This can be seen from a person's generosity, both materially and "spiritually," not only with family but also with nonfamily members and even strangers.

3. Charisma: Do the person's efforts result in plentiful outcomes? Does the person speak convincingly and beautifully? Do the person's words intentionally or unintentionally mislead people?

All these dimensions are related to the person's spiritual power (*wéeyekin*). In brief, a person established authority through actions that were recognized by the most influential people in the community.

The productivity of a family's traditional use areas is fundamental to successful leadership because it affects the outcomes of their efforts to make food, clothing, medicines, and other goods. The family is significant because if it is composed of hard workers, their productivity is higher as well. Hardworking persons who produce plentiful goods demonstrate a strong connection to the land, almost certainly resulting from a strong *wéeyekin*, and they have thus made the first demonstration of a moral life. A second step in demonstrating leadership is carrying through on their social obligations by sharing their wealth and abilities. Refusing material support or help in the face of another's need—to be greedy, or *kitíwi*—was an immoral act. A leader must be able to contribute to the community by convincing others to share as well and by settling disputes with the leader's own wealth.

Sometimes a person becomes a leader when no decision appears to have been made; instead, a leader seems to emerge from several likely candidates. In such instances, influential elders simply follow the suggestions or actions of the leader. Equally, leaders apparently lose their "positions" without any apparent decision, as influential people cease to pay attention to the erstwhile leader and follow another.

At other times, a conscious decision is clearly made through negotiations among the elders. Councils occurred when there was high probability of conflict or open contention. This obviously happened under conditions of change caused by the decline or death of a popular leader. Change was also often called for following a series of unsuccessful ventures, as people lost confidence in leadership. Under these conditions, the embattled leader was often accused of some moral failing or of misleading the people.

Group dissolution occurred through the same process, but it was the most severe and least desirable outcome of unresolved conflict. In such cases, people simply went their own ways, some with their own followers to establish new camps or villages, and others following different leaders to their camps and villages. For example, a family in which a marriage between a closely related "brother/sister" reputedly occurred left their natal village and established the village of Nikíse on the Clearwater River. Indeed, one wonders if part of the reason there were unused village locations was the flux of groups; as a group grew too large for the village site or lost its cohesion in some other way, some former members would move to unused village sites. Similarly, as separate groups developed cohesion, they would merge into the same location, perhaps leaving one village site unoccupied.

Differences in goals did not necessarily result in bitter difference, however; a preference for hunting in one area rather than another resulted in two hunting parties, each with a person who knew where to hunt and who oversaw the distribution of the kill. As these differences persisted, however, new, regularly occurring task groups would form.

As certain people became better known, they would attract more followers and would need to take care of more people. This required increasing the productivity of their families, which could be done in several ways. For men and women, one way involved having more spouses, cospouses, and children. However, this required increased effort to supply a larger household with more raw materials from hunting and fishing. Moreover, social relations among spouses became more complicated with more spouses. Husbands had to be more productive and evenhanded with wives, staying attentive to their differences and their children. For women, the challenges included (1) getting along with cowives (*pe'éksti-wee*), (2) childcare, and, often, (3) living in a new community, with their husband's village and its seasonal travel pattern. Some of these issues were mitigated by sisters marrying brothers—hence, the practices of levirate and sororate marriage.

The families who embody these values have children who are highly sought after as marriage partners. Indeed, the more prominent the family in this regard and the more widespread their reputation, the wider their network of "trading partners" and the more stable their resources. They become nodes in the redistribution of "goods" such as food, horses, and wealth items, thus attracting still more allies.

The complexity of Numipunm Wéetespe as captured by Hinmátoon-yalatkáykt (Chief Joseph) in the following statement:

> The earth was created by the assistance of the sun, and it should be left as it was . . . The country was made without lines of demarcation, and it is no man's business to divide it . . . The earth and myself are of one mind. The measure of the land and the measure of our bodies are the same . . . Understand me fully with reference to my affection for the land. I never said the land was mine to do with as I choose. The one who has the right to dispose of it is the one who has created it.

Saving the Land/People

This developing New World is vastly different from the past world of the Nimiipuu. Different concepts of tenure have excluded Nimiipuu from large tracts of land and destroyed long-cared-for root grounds, fishing and hunting grounds, berrying grounds, and so on. Farming has altered the chemistry and structure of the soil and destroyed the homes of *símqaa*, the giant Palouse earthworm. Road building has destroyed many of the memorials where Coyote shaped the Nimiipuu world. The by-products of everyday industrial and agricultural life increase the bright orange lichen that spread over petroglyphic and pictographic memorials of the ancestors in the Snake River canyon. The very air, rain, soil, and water are different, changed by altered human relationships within the natural, social, and spiritual world.

"The Earth"—*wéetes*—has been fragmented, and thus Nimiipuu have been fragmented culturally, socially, and individually. Families are often in disarray. These are the "soul-wounds" they suffer.

It is true that Nimiipuu are changing as they move into offices and cubicles from the fishing sites, the root-digging grounds, the hunting grounds, the berry patches, the trails and campsites. This change cannot do anything but alter their toolkits, actions, feelings, and thoughts. And this change creates conflicts in their bodies and identities, in their societies and culture.

But they enter these new places in order to protect what remains of their ancestors' legacy, to reclaim and revitalize what has been taken. The profound issues of these generations are land ownership, water, fish, and wildlife—and how to protect these. In other words, caring for "the Earth" and restoring, insofar as it is possible, the pattern of life found in kinship and the more-than-human community. This goal—to rise from the ashes—is seen in a variety of actions ranging from environmental restoration and land management to jurisdictional/legal issues and language "preservation."

NOTES

1. Josephy, *Nez Perce Indians*. Josephy's work is the most thorough for the 1804–77 period. Many histories have been written about the 1877 Nez Perce War, which looms large in western American history. Much of Nez Perce history focuses on the war or on Chief Joseph. Post-1877 history is sparse, though growing.

2. The term "landscape" is used in many contested ways. Here I follow Ingold: "In short, the landscape is the world as it is known to those who dwell therein, who inhabit its places and journey along the paths connecting them." Ingold, "Temporality of the Landscape," 156.

3. For a discussion of the mazeway concept, see Wallace, "Revitalization Movements," 266; cf. Hallowell, *Culture and Experience*. For a discussion of the concept of habitus, see Bourdieu, *Outline of a Theory*. "Taskscape" is defined in Ingold, *Temporality*, 158. These authors emphasize the role of experience in shaping cognition. Samuel M. Watters, too, emphasized their material dimensions. That is, his way of training Alan Marshall was to take Alan on his travels through the world, following his trails through "the maze" to important places to conduct important activities using everyday tools. Knowledge, Watters believed, was demonstrated in doing.

4. Wolf, *Europe and the People*.

5. Bodley, *Victims of Progress*.

6. This paraphrase of Luke 3:5 was made several times in 1972 and 1973 by Samuel M. Watters.

7. Borda, "Peoples' SpaceTimes," 624–34.

8. Marshall, "Nez Perce Social Groups."

9. The theoretical perspective on culture, society, and polity used in this essay is well expressed in Friedman, "Globalization, Class and Culture," 636–56.

10. Duran et al., "Healing," 341–54; Woodward, "*Nimiipuu*: The Story of the Nez Perce," *Idaho Statesman*, September 22, 2006.

11. Anastasio, *Southern Plateau*.

12. Kinkade et al., "Languages," 49–72.

13. Walker, "Nez Perce," 420–38; Spinden, "Nez Percé Indians," 173–75; Aoki, *Nez Perce Grammar*.

14. Walker, "Nez Perce," 433.

15. Taylor, *Biological Time*.

16. Jones, "Old World Infectious Diseases," 1–26.

17. Moulton, *Journals*, 262.

18. Indian hemp, or dogbane, was until recently regarded as a noxious weed and therefore "controlled" by cattlemen (it is poisonous to animals) and farmers (who regard it as an invasive weed). It virtually disappeared from this region but has been recovering slowly since it was removed from Idaho State's noxious weed list.

19. Marshall, "Unusual Gardens," 172–87.

20. Anastasio, *Southern Plateau*, 130–36.

21. Curtis, "Nez Perces," 8:16.

22. Boreson, "Rock Art," 12:611–19; Keyser, *Indian Rock Art*; Leen, "Inventory of Hells Canyon."

23. This term is sometimes translated as the term for winter village, village, or *téẃyenikees*.

24. Lévi-Strauss, *Savage Mind*, 16–18.

25. Nimiipuu used different terms for the same alter (anthropological) when referring to them or addressing them. I will use the referential kinship terms in this discussion.

26. "*(I)nimqaláacaaʔc* Jonas Watters *hiwes*," or "Father's father is Jonas Watters." One bound morpheme is elided in polite conversation; the initial "i-" sound self-refers to ego and almost always should not be spoken.

27. "Whipmen" and "whipwomen" were important figures. Respected elders, they were called in from a different household or living place to expound "the law" and/or administer physical punishment; physical punishment was rarely applied by direct caregivers.

28. These rocks were excised from the bedrock when Dworshak Dam was built in the early 1970s; it was set into concrete at a visitors center for present-day generations to see.

29. Personal spiritual items, however, were inalienable. Moreover, a person would be "crazy" even to touch them. Exemplifying this is an *ʔipéetes*, an item made by someone at the behest of a spirit power.

30. Aoki, *Nez Perce Dictionary*, 600, 638, 314, 942.

31. Throughout the Plateau cultural region, "sweathouse" is the term used instead of "sweatlodge," the term used in other regions.

32. Walker, *Conflict and Schism*; Walker, "Nez Perce Sorcery"; Coale, "Notes on the Guardian," 135–48.

33. Spinden, "Nez Percé Indians," 247–50; Coale, "Notes on the Guardian"; Walker, *Conflict and Schism*, 19.

34. Anastasio, *Southern Plateau*.

35. Walker, *Conflict and Schism*, 10; Humphreys et al., "Nez Perce Leadership Council," 135–52.

WORKS CITED

Anastasio, Angelo. *The Southern Plateau: An Ecological Analysis of Intergroup Relations.* Moscow: Alfred W. Bowers Laboratory of Anthropology, University of Idaho, 1985.

Aoki, Haruo. *Nez Perce Dictionary.* In *University of California Publications in Linguistics* 122:1280. Berkeley: University of California Press, 1994.

———. *Nez Perce Grammar.* Berkeley: University of California Press, 1970.

Bodley, John H. *Victims of Progress.* Lanham MD: Altamira, 2008.

Borda, Orlando Fals. "Peoples' SpaceTimes in Global Processes: The Response of the Local." *Journal of World-Systems Research* 6, no. 3 (2000): 624–34.

Boreson, Keo. "Rock Art." In *Plateau*, edited by Deward E. Walker Jr., 611–19. Vol. 12 of *Handbook of North American Indians*. Washington DC: Smithsonian Institution, 1998.

Bourdieu, Pierre. *Outline of a Theory of Practice.* Translated by Richard Nice. New York: Cambridge University Press, 1977.

Coale, George L. "Notes on the Guardian Spirit Concept Among the Nez Perce." *Internationales Archiv für Ethnographie* 48, no. 1 (1958): 135–48.

Curtis, Edward S. "The Nez Perces." In *The North American Indian, Being a Series of Volumes Picturing and Describing the Indians of the United States, the Dominion of Canada, and Alaska*, edited by Frederick Webb Hodge, 8:3–78. Norwood MA: Plimpton, 1911.

Duran, Eduardo, Bonnie Duran, Maria Yellow Horse Brave Heart, and Susan Yellow Horse–Davis. "Healing the American Indian Soul Wound." In *International Handbook of Multigenerational Legacies of Trauma*, edited by Yael Danieli, 341–54. New York: Plenum, 1998.

Friedman, Jonathan. "Globalization, Class and Culture in Global Systems." *Journal of World-Systems Research* 6, no. 3 (2000): 636–56.

Hallowell, A. Irving. *Culture and Experience.* New York: Schocken Books, 1967.

Humphreys, John, Kendra Ingham, Courtney Kenner, and Theresa Sadler. "The Nez Perce Leadership Council: A Historical Examination of Post-Industrial Leadership." *Journal of Management History* 13, no. 2 (2007): 135–52.

Ingold, Tim. "The Temporality of Landscape." *World Archaeology* 25, no. 2 (Winter 1993): 152–74.

Jones, Peter N. "Old World Infectious Diseases in the Plateau Area of North America during the Protohistoric: Rethinking Our Understanding of 'Contact' in the Plateau." *Journal of Northwest Anthropology* 37, no. 1 (2003): 1–26.

Josephy, Alvin M., Jr. *The Nez Perce Indians and the Opening of the Northwest.* New Haven CT: Yale University Press, 1965.

Keyser, James D. *Indian Rock Art of the Columbia Plateau.* Seattle: University of Washington Press, 1992.

Kinkade, M. Dale, William W. Elmendorf, Bruce Rigsby, and Haruo Aoki. "Languages." In *Plateau*, edited by Deward E. Walker Jr., 49–72. Vol. 12 of *Handbook of North American Indians.* Washington DC: Smithsonian Institution, 1998.

Leen, Daniel. "An Inventory of Hells Canyon Rock Art." Enterprise OR: Hells Canyon National Recreation Area, Wallowa-Whitman National Forest, 1988.

Lévi-Strauss, Claude. *The Savage Mind.* Chicago: University of Chicago Press, 1966.

Marshall, Alan G. "Fish, Water, and Nez Perce Life." *Idaho Law Review* 42, no. 3 (2006): 763–93.

———. "Nez Perce Social Groups: An Ecological Interpretation." PhD diss., Washington State University, 1977.

———. "Unusual Gardens: The Nez Perce and Wild Horticulture on the Eastern Columbia Plateau." In *Northwest Lands, Northwest Peoples: Readings in Environmental History*, edited by D. D. Goble and P. W. Hirt, 173–87. Seattle: University of Washington Press, 1999.

McWhorter, Lucullus Virgil. *Hear Me, My Chiefs!* Caldwell ID: Caxton, 1983.

———. *Yellow Wolf: His Own Story.* Caldwell ID: Caxton, 1983.

Moulton, Gary E., ed. *The Journals of the Lewis and Clark Expedition, March 23–June 9, 1806.* Lincoln: University of Nebraska Press, 1991.

Slickpoo, Allen P., Sr. *Noon Nee-Me-Poo (We, the Nez Perces).* Lapwai ID: Nez Perce Tribal Printing, 1973.

Spinden, Herbert Joseph. "The Nez Percé Indians." *Memoirs of the American Anthropological Association* 2, no. 3 (1908): 167–274.

Taylor, Bernie. *Biological Time.* Newberg OR: EaPress, 2004.

Walker, Deward E., Jr. *Conflict and Schism in Nez Perce Acculturation.* Pullman: Washington State University Press, 1968.

Wallace, Anthony F. C. "Nez Perce." In *Plateau*, edited by Deward E. Walker Jr., 420–38. Vol 12 of *Handbook of North American Indians.* Washington DC: Smithsonian Institution, 1998.

———. "Nez Perce Sorcery." *Ethnology* 6, no. 1 (1967): 66–96.

———. "Revitalization Movements: Some Theoretical Considerations." *American Anthropologist* 58, no. 2 (1956): 264–81.

Wolf, Eric R. *Europe and the People without History.* Berkeley: University of California Press, 1982.

2 Nimiipuu Peoplehood, Survival, and the Indian Territory

J. DIANE PEARSON

On October 5, 1877, an estimated 398 Nimiipuu as well as their Palus and Cayuse allies surrendered to the U.S. Army at Bear Paw, Montana.[1] A four-month-long "flight or fight" defensive war with the United States that began on June 17, 1877, was thus ended. They had not reached safety in the Judith Basin, Montana, nor had they gained sanctuary in Canada. And in spite of Colonel Nelson A. Mile's promise to return them to their homelands next spring, they were now homeless. As General Oliver O. Howard and Colonel Miles affirmed, most of the war leaders and war chiefs, including Toohoolhoolzote, Ollokot, Looking Glass, and other senior leaders and statesmen were dead.[2] These deaths were in addition to the ninety-six younger men, women, children, and elder fatalities recorded by the Nimiipuu schoolteacher James Reuben.[3] Facing almost overwhelming odds, younger leaders including Young Joseph, Yellow Bull, and Húsus Kute (Palus) had opted to surrender to Colonel Miles. Other leaders such as White Bird, who placed absolutely no trust in the United States, escaped to Canada. And those who surrendered did so with specific stipulations guaranteed by Colonel Miles. Committed to peace with the United States, the Bear Paw surrender accord guaranteed the prisoners' almost immediate return to Idaho.[4] Miles had promised that the prisoners would be returned to the Nez Perce–Lapwai Reservation in the spring, or as soon as weather permitted a move from Montana. As Miles would later defend, senior military authorities had overridden his decision; they would move the prisoners farther away to Fort Abraham Lincoln, and then again to Fort Leavenworth, Kansas.[5]

Now, following ethnohistorian Alan G. Marshall, who addressed the many changes experienced by the Nimiipuu "beyond the written record of life in Northwest North America," this study addresses the language, sacred histories, ceremonies, and sacred territories of these surrendered Nimiipuu and their peoplehood.[6] The peoplehood model of identity, defined by American Indian scholar Robert K. Thomas (Cherokee), clarifies how these several hundred persons influenced their survival as federal captives. It also explains their unremitting desire to avoid permanent federal incarceration in Kansas or Indian Territory and to actuate their return to their Columbia Plateau homelands.[7]

The peoplehood model of identity, as laid out by Thomas (who expanded Edward H. Spicer's definition of cultural enclaves), consists of four factors: language, sacred history, ceremonial cycles (religion/spirituality), and place/territory (homelands) that are "interwoven and dependent on one another." These factors form a "complete system that accounts for particular social, cultural, political, economic, and ecological behaviors" unique to Indigenous people in specific territories. The four factors of peoplehood "intertwine, interpenetrate, and interact" as they illustrate why so many of the white man's ideas, such as mechanistic land concepts, Christian doctrines, the U.S. Army, prejudiced federal officials, and the might of Congress failed to destroy the resistant Nimiipuu. The factors of peoplehood illustrate why these Nimiipuu were adamant about whom they were, where they belonged, and the fact that federal removal from their sacred homelands (Numipunm Wéetes—"Nez Perce Earth")[8] was a key motivator spurring them out of captivity.[9]

Language (Nimiipuutímt) in almost all of the Nimiipuu quotations in this study is nearly always expressed through an interpreter. Many of the conversations were, however, recorded through different interpreters and by people who maintained many different relationships with the Nimiipuu. When these various translations are examined in light of their social and historical circumstances, the theologies and activities of peoplehood emerge. These captives remembered and celebrated their sacred histories in many ways. They were also aware that they formed a new, sacred history in the making; they were a living captivity narrative. Leaders made point after point to federal authorities who threatened death and permanent expulsion from their sacred homelands; as their captivity wore on, some also communicated with the press, with Congress, with local businesspeople, and various federal representatives in especially meaningful dialogues.[10] These, then, are some of the ancestors whom, according to Alan G. Marshall, contemporary Nimiipuu "reclaim" as they "revitalize what has been taken."[11]

Peoplehood also illuminates the "organic, living, and spiritual nature" of the Nimiipuu that is "part of their heritage." As Robert K. Thomas, Tom Holm, Diane Pearson, and Ben Chavis specify, "particular territories are always mentioned in sacred histories, and quite often creation and migration stories specify certain landmarks as being especially holy." Burials, shrines, health and well-being, plants, water, earth, animal parts, and theologies "live in the expectation of divine intervention and the creation of more sacred places." The peoplehood model of identity contin- ues; "homelands are often considered holy lands, and even when groups migrate or are removed from original territories the people continue to attach great meaning to them."[12] In this case, the Nimiipuu prisoners understood that forced separation from their homelands meant the lack of spiritual/religious freedom, federal extermination or neglect, and, quite often, death. But in every possible instance, these prisoners expressed their theologies and spiritualties even as they became federal captives. They participated in inter- and intragroup ceremonials such as truncated winter ceremonials and mourning ceremonials; they even managed to engage in beloved interactive spiritual activities such as horse racing and gambling.

Holm, Pearson, and Chavis also propose that Thomas's peoplehood model of identity has "vast explanatory potential . . . [that] reminds us as scholars that human societies are complex and that Native Americans entwine everyday life with religious practice" and a view that "human beings are part of, rather than an imposition on, their environments." While no single "element of the model is more or less important than the others . . . we remember that the environment is an aspect of peoplehood." Or, as Marshall puts it so well, "Nimiipuu culture is not found in this chapter, or in libraries, or in various media; it is found atop the mountains, in the valleys, and in the rivers."[13] As we see throughout the Nimiipuu's period of federal captivity between October 1877 and May 1885, the "holistic matrix" of peoplehood "reflects a much more accurate picture of the ways in which" the Nimiipuu acted, reacted, "passed along knowledge, and connected with the ordinary as well as the supernatural worlds."[14] The peoplehood model of identity helps us understand Young Joseph, Yellow Bull, and other prisoners who repeated this mantra throughout their lives: they had made an official federal agreement that assured them of their return to the Columbia Plateau. These were the homelands that were considered sacred; even linguistically, the suffix "-pu" (also "-pa" and "-po") identified the Nimiipuu as people *of* and not *from* a place. For example, to be Tisayaxpo was to be one of the "people of the granite rocks." The Nimiipuu were also *of* Umnapu (East Kamiah), Tsaynaspu (Kooskia), Tawapu (Orofino), and *of* Tamanmapo (Salmon River).[15]

Condensing Nimiipuu ethnohistory in time, we find that these people and their ancestors have inhabited their Columbia Plateau homelands for thousands of years.[16] As ethnohistorians Allen Pinkham and Steven Evans explain, the Nez Perce—"Real People—have been in their Columbia Plateau homelands for time-out-of-mind: "Within the framework of legend, myth, oral history, and written history—in other words, in every dimension vital to a description of human beings in relation to place— the Nez Perces have always been where they remain today." They also trace their tribal memory deep into the prehistoric past; based on the "large hairy beasts" described in Nez Perce stories, Nimiipuu "knew of these animals, such as the wooly mammoth and the miniature three-toed horse, which were slain and eaten by the tribe's ancestors." These stories, and other stories of "exploding volcanoes and darkened skies," place the Nimiipuu in their homelands almost seven thousand years ago or earlier.[17] These sacred histories reaffirmed Nimiipuu origins, and shared ceremonials reinforced individual, family, band, and community relations and spiritual ties. These sacred homelands provided subsistence, health, and places of worship, spiritual guidance, and access to personal, spiritual, or communal power.[18] This peoplehood bound the Nimiipuu spiritually, culturally, socially, and physically.

Survival—A Critical Moment in History

The peoplehood model of identity helps us understand the survival mechanisms of the captive Nimiipuu during a critical time when they were being vanquished from their Columbia Plateau–homelands. Although this study is not particularly about warfare, destruction, and hopelessness, a historical review is necessary to accurately place the captives at Fort Leavenworth, Kansas, on November 26, 1877. Following intense negotiations, most of the acknowledged Nimiipuu leaders had signed their first treaty with the United States in 1855 (12 Stat., 957); after gold was discovered on the Nez Perce Reservation in 1860, five of these bands did not recognize or sign a subsequent treaty with the United States in 1863 (14 Stat., 647). These five "nontreaty" bands were Joseph's (Wallowa) band; White Bird's (Lahmtahma) band; Looking Glass's band; the Palus band from the Lower Snake River, led by Húsus Kute and Hahtalekin; and Toohoolhoolzote's group from above the Salmon and Snake Rivers.[19] As the Nimiipuu resister/survivor Yellow Wolf recalled, "None of our chiefs signed that land-stealing treaty."[20] Without their involvement in this treaty or the obligations implied by consensual decision-making, treaty-based participants and federally recognized "treaty chiefs" created by the 1855 treaty were pressured into selling most of the nontreaty homelands to the United States.[21] By 1867, when the treaty of 1863 was ratified, these assaults on Nimiipuu peoplehood had reduced their sacred, aboriginal land base by more than 13.5 million acres. Most of the nontreaty bands were now considered homeless or expected by the treaty to remove to the Nez Perce Reservation in Lapwai.[22] The treaty of 1863, as Verne Ray reported from the U.S. Court of Claims, also "took mostly the lands of Joseph's band, entirely west of the Snake River."[23] Agricultural and stationary lifestyles had been implemented, and Christian and non-Christian separatism had been established.[24] Federal officials, including U.S. Indian agents, superintendents, and commissioners, were substituted for traditional governance figures; Christian ministers, missionaries, and schools were institutionalized.

James Reuben, Archie Lawyer, and Luke Philips (a Nimiipuu student) further explained many other unpleasant life changes: "The white man is responsible for all the Indian outbreaks. White man has wronged the

FIG. 2. Joseph Too-we-tak-hes, chief of the Nez Perce Indians, May 29, 1855. Illustration by Gustav Sohon. Catalog: 1918.114.9.58. Washington State Historical Society, Tacoma WA.

Looking-glass
Apash-wa-hay-ikt
Chief of the Nez-perce Indians

3½

FIG. 3. Looking Glass Apash-wa-hay-ikt, chief of the Nez Perce Indians, June 9, 1855. Illustration by Gustave Sohon. Catalog: 1918.114.9.51. Washington State Historical Society, Tacoma WA.

red nations in every respect—he has moved on to his camping places without his consent—he has swindled him out of his home by cheatings and sharp practices—he has abused him and he regarded him as beasts of the mountains and did treat him accordingly. When the Indian sees the treatment he receives at the hands of whites, he feels the pain, and sees also that there is no hope for the future. The ground under his feet liable to be taken any day." American Indians such as the Nimiipuu could, Reuben continued, either get out of the way and accept "beggary" or die. Then the white man sends them away; "You go somewhere and be kicked about—steal, beg or starve, be treated like dogs and be shot down, nobody cares for you anyway, how you be treated." Like in Wallowa Valley country, Reuben understood that the white man now had the property and the Indians must be gone.[25] A few months later, the Reverend Archie Lawyer (Nimiipuu) summed up the long-term situation in a letter sent to President Chester A. Arthur: "Some one [sic] has to give an account to God for lives lost since we have been forced to die and suffer."[26] Luke Philips, the teenaged son of an Indian Territory exile who was enrolled at Carlisle Indian Industrial School in Pennsylvania, supported Reuben and Lawyer: "The white men abused and pushed these Indians from the birth-place of their fathers. Before those wars they were self supporting [sic] . . . They raised thousands of cattle and horses and had friendship with the white settlers. But they were driven out from their country . . . they would never see their verdant hills or winding rivers again."[27]

The decade following the ratification of the 1863 treaty was fraught with difficulties. Separatist political and religious influences increased along with an influx of federal officials, teachers, pioneers/settlers, and Christian missionaries.[28] While the bands that had not signed the treaty of 1863 tried to remain in their homelands, older traditional leaders such as the senior Chief Joseph (Tuekakas, who died in 1871) and the elder Looking Glass (Apash Wyakaikt, or Flint Necklace, who died in 1863) were gone. Younger men, including the aforementioned leaders' sons—Ollokot, the younger Joseph and Looking Glass (Allalimya Takanin)—were left to address changing federal relationships, shifting intratribal relationships, and increased federal pressures to accede to treaty provisions established in 1863. As their fathers had done before them, these leaders protected their homelands and peoplehood.

The old men had trained their sons well. The younger Joseph stated in 1879, "I deny that either my father or myself ever sold that land [Wallowa Valley]." Joseph continued, "It is still our land. It may never again be our home, but my father sleeps there, and I love it as I love my mother."[29] This was the peoplehood's position, which the younger Joseph had already clarified at an earlier meeting with federal commissioners, Indian agents, and army officers on November 11, 1876, at Lapwai, Idaho. "The earth was his mother," said Joseph. "He could not consent to sever his affections from the land that bore him. He asked nothing of the President. He was able to take care of himself."[30]

Joseph spoke, in accord with the Wéset (Seven Drums) religion and similar theologies that the earth is humanity's sacred Mother.[31] (Also pronounced "Washaat," the Wéset religion is also sometimes referred to as "Dreamers.")[32] Revitalization theologies such as these teach that the earth must not be disturbed, damaged, sold, or changed for commercial use. As Wanapum Dreamer Prophet Smohalla taught, "Earth is our mother," and people must "not take the land" or convert it to individual property; "Earth and its gifts [are for] all to share."[33] This sacred aspect of peoplehood also held that believers "seek great truth in lonely places."[34] In other words, the sacred homelands were necessary for successful vision quests. Professor Deward Walker explains this more fully: Plateau people such as the Nimiipuu cherished sacred geographies in which "portals to the sacred" offered devotees such as vision quest participants opportunities to experience another world.[35] This was a world of exceptional blessings and opportunities. Sacred homelands also provided special places for winter dances and feasts where people were brought together "with their guardian spirits."[36]

Nimiipuu scholar Archie Phinney further explained that many of the sacred winter villages were located primarily along the Snake, Clearwater, and Salmon Rivers in the Nimiipuu homelands. Phinney's linguistic research emphasized the importance of the winter villages as centers of peoplehood's sacred histories and ceremonialism. He taught that a language involves the stories of the people who speak that language, in addition to the complex relationships between sacred histories, language, and music. Most important, these relationships were reaffirmed each year by the Nimiipuu in their sacred winter villages. Families shared songs that were unique to their histories; power songs, historical songs, and spirit and dance songs that also related Nimiipuu histories. There were drumming songs, medicine or healing songs, holy songs, songs that honored the elements, and courting songs. Songs that honored all life, told of the past, and told of all of the earth's creatures, and recorded histories. In effect, families and bands that congregated in the winter villages reaffirmed their sacred histories.[37] As Alan Marshall concludes, the winter villages were places for the people to "prepare for the following year's pulse of life," thereby learning their relation to others and to the land.[38] Related families and small bands usually wintered in the same villages each year, and members of groups who had wintered in the eastern buffalo-hunting grounds of present-day Montana often snowshoed across steep mountain passes to visit these winter villages.[39]

Winter ceremonials held in these villages formed the backbone of the Nimiipuu winter spiritual calendar. Each winter village embraced a sacred, powerful area where guardian spirit or vision quest dances were held. Peripheral to residential areas of the villages, the sacred areas were cleaned and prepared for the ceremonials and dances by a qualified spiritual practitioner. This person made the necessary preparations for the ceremonials, built the mat lodges, conducted the dances and ceremonies, and took down the lodges when the dances ended.[40] The ceremonials and dances were held in continuous sessions for days, weeks, or even months. Winter spirit dances, individual dances, initiation dances, novice dances, audience dances, initiate feasts, and weather dances were some of the ceremonial forms conducted in the winter villages. Bringing together the Nimiipuu and their guardian spirits, the dances provided Nimiipuu practitioners an opportunity to reaffirm their powers with their communities. Men and women who had gained special powers displayed these powers at the winter dances; these individuals were often destined to become tribal religious leaders. Only a few people "mastered the difficult steps" to become a medicine person who had the "supernatural powers . . . (to) understand many things."[41] For the Plateau-area Nimiipuu (and their allies), these winter villages and the "sacred portals" did not exist—nor had they ever existed—in Kansas or Indian Territory.

Limited Spirituality, Peoplehood, and Lives: "Making Do"

The path to these incarcerations began in June 1877, as the nontreaty bands were being hunted by the U.S. Army.[42] They engaged in eleven conflicts staged across more than fourteen hundred miles of the American West before their struggle ended forty miles south of the Canadian border on October 5, 1877. From there, the prisoners were sent to Fort Leavenworth, Kansas. And there, on November 26, 1877, 418 of the more than 700 men, women, and children who had left their Columbia Plateau homelands that summer began a devastating new existence.[43] For the prisoners about to be incarcerated in Kansas and Indian Territory, there would be no vision quests, no sacred areas, and no winter villages so essential to their spirituality, peoplehood, and lives. There would only be places or ceremonies where they might "make do" or opportunities to join other Native nations in their spiritual celebrations.

Meanwhile, life developed rather strangely in the Fort Leavenworth, Kansas prison camp. The exiles were inundated by tourists, military officers and soldiers who controlled their lives, newspapermen, and Presbyterian missionaries.[44] Even would-be educators from the Bureau of Indian Affairs (BIA) were present.[45] The exiles tolerated the tourists, rejected the missionaries, and refused to abandon their young men to Captain Richard Henry Pratt and the Hampton Institute in Hampton, Virginia. They also made sure the visitors understood that the Nimiipuu were dedicated to peace. The press focused on Joseph, who usually responded favorably to their inquiries—he even gave one influential reporter a sample of his signature, reassuring Perry (a reporter) and the American public that he although he did not speak their language, he understood their ways.[46] Joseph learned to communicate his peoplehood to the American press, though he always spoke through an interpreter in Nimiipuutímt, his natal language.

While life in the prison camp was very difficult, the prisoners expressed their peoplehood in numerous ways, as best they could. One significant item of this expression was Joseph's visual record of the war and the Nimiipuu homelands, reported in the *Leavenworth Times* on December 4, 1877.

Developed by Joseph, this visual aspect of peoplehood was reminiscent of the handmade maps he and his brother Ollokot carried. Displayed at an April 20, 1877, conference with the United States, Ollokot's map framed the iconography of Nimiipuu peoplehood. Wallowa Lake was displayed as a single inked line showing the boundaries of the lake, with a "fish drawn in the center." Deer populated the mountains, and the Wallowa River was a "zigzag line with trees here and there along its length." The wagon road was indicated by "a double column of very small (half) circles running the entire length of the valley." The incomplete circles were "actually small horse shoes indicating the impress of the shoe upon the soft earth." The figures resembled Egyptian hieroglyphs, and the map also recalled another tragedy of the past, when a white man had killed an American Indian.[47] The brothers' maps disappeared after Ollokot was killed at Bear Paw that October in 1877, and General Howard was supposed to have taken Joseph's map.[48] Joseph must certainly have had his brother in mind, as he employed the same visual arts at Fort Leavenworth.

Within the first week of his incarceration at Fort Leavenworth, Joseph completed a comparable visualization of the brothers' peoplehood on a large tree in front of his government-issue tent. First, he peeled a strip of bark from the tree; then, he painted and carved letters and figures that told of the recent war and of Nimiipuu peoplehood onto the exposed wood. The base of the cleared surface was "filled with a long row of the Indian lodges," like those the Nimiipuu had occupied in their Columbia Plateau homelands. "Above these," continued the reporter, "were horses, birds, wolves, dogs and men all represented in such a manner as to convey the idea that they are all closely connected." And above all these elements, Joseph included some type of informative "petition" of "deep significance to the Indians, who all seem to be able to read it, and understand its import."[49] This representation of connectivity is central to Nimiipuu philosophy, as is the understanding that "humans are a link in the chain that binds together all of creation."[50] The visual aids of peoplehood's homelands may have entertained tourists and newspaper staff, but they were essential messages to the heartsick prisoners. The tree art helped the captives reaffirm their far-away sacred homelands and record the wartime additions to their sacred history at this most distressing time. Its visualized interconnectedness also reminded them of their reliance upon their peoplehood and upon each other.

Visions of the sacred histories of Nimiipuu peoplehood also adorned several of the prisoners' tipis. Often referred to as "medicine tipis," these old buffalo-hide dwellings were frequently painted with "symbolic figures and ornaments." Although we don't know which designs decorated these tipis, or to whom they belonged, we do know that these painted tipis were especially sacred items that the exiles had managed to save from the war. Such tipis were usually owned by "just a few . . . distinguished families."[51] The reporter offered a brief but fairly astute description of how the leather tipis were constructed: "The lodges are circular in form and of a conical shape. The skins which form the walls, or wall, are sewn together entirely with buckskin in bands or strips." He also noted that the dwellings were weatherproof and that the skins around the smoke hole had been "blackened by the smoke" of many fires. "In some of these lodges," he noticed that there were "furs of the finest description owned by the more wealthy members of the tribe." In other tipis, infants were suspended in their cradleboards "much like," the reporter said, other people would "hang pictures on the wall."[52]

Several of these symbolic, hand-painted dwellings were soon reinforced at Fort Leavenworth, along with other sacred items the prisoners had conserved. These included horse regalia, strings of bells, and sacred eagle feathers used to enhance mourning ceremonials held at Fort Leavenworth during December of 1877.[53] Since there were no Nimiipuu winter villages and sacred dance grounds in Kansas, truncated December ceremonials attempted to reassure survivors of their ceremonial/spiritual peoplehood. More than 150 Nimiipuu prisoners participated in sacred chants, drumming, curing rituals, storytelling of valorous deeds, mourning rituals, and revelations from before-the-war vision quests.

One such event was led by a *tiwét* (spiritual leader) on Sunday, December 9, 1877. As a local reporter describes, "about 100 seated men and women [prisoners] ranged in two lines near the walls," as other participants and guests entered the large canvas army tent. The somber participants were profoundly involved; chanting and singing, they ignored the curious visitors. All the while, more prisoner–participants arrived quietly from throughout the camp. Standing in the center of the gathering, the *tiwét* spoke a few words in Nimiipuutímt. He then "rang a small bell which he held in his hand and the entire party began to chant."[54] Consistent with Smohalla, the Wanapum Dreamer Prophet, the *tiwét* suggested that the "sound of the bell" [was the] "sound of the heart."[55] "Qualal Qualal rings like the heart . . . it comes from the heart," said the *tiwét*.[56] Many of the women also wore ankle adornments made with tinkling bells.

All of the participants waved handheld plumes; some were single feathers and others large plumes, such as those that decorated horse-drawn hearses. The plumes, which often consisted of swan or eagle feathers, waved back and forth as they carried messages "between the physical and spiritual worlds."[57] The trumpeter swan was noted for its spiritual connection with the heavens.[58] Eagle, according to Pinkham and Evans, contributed "his feathers as a reminder and symbol of bravery, spirituality, and many other things."[59] Now, three men sat in the center of the tent, where they struck small "tom tom"–like drums with sticks.[60] Drums, said Evans, "sounded out the heart and desires of the people as they performed sacred dances."[61] Feathers, bells, drums, and songs were among the peoplehood's sacred ceremonial items that were also—somehow—preserved during the war.

Once the introductory song was complete, several men rose and spoke in Nimiipuutímt; they then sang another chant. This chant and all of the other songs were followed "by a long, low wailing, sound" as everyone raised their "right hand[s] toward heaven." A form of spiritual supplication, this was followed by a woman who asked a special prayer or blessing.[62] After addressing her issues, George Washington led another lengthy chant and dance. When Major Junius W. MacMurray reported on the Dreamer services he had attended in Washington State in 1887, he could just as well have been describing the sounds at Fort Leavenworth. The Native women sang, as he recalled, in "shrill," high, "weird . . . voices" as the "drums beat in unison." "Occasional silences" were broken by "men's oratory [and] by ringing hand bells followed by drums," and, again, more "weird chanting." Seven drummers also played an "ear paralyzing orchestra."[63] Another actual visitor to the prisoners' camp a few months later was also impressed by the "wild and sweet" nature of a chant sung by Nimiipuu women during a curing ceremony. Singing almost continuously, a male *tiwét* who was seated near the patient's feet occasionally projected into the "rhythmic music of the women" his "masculine howl, which was partly *solo obbligato* and partly an independent observation of his own." Meanwhile, elderly women tried to keep intruders out of the medicine tipis; to the reporter, all of the grief, songs, and chants "seemed like a death-wail of the Indian."[64]

Expressed at full voice, these chants, songs, prayers, and drums were never bashful; this was the music that, as Archie Phinney reminded us, "honored all life."[65] It reassures that although we cannot literally "hear" these long-ago songs, chants, and drums of Nimiipuu peoplehood, we know that whenever and wherever possible, these divine activities were not taciturn; this history was not silent. Meanwhile, the sounds and songs— the "ululations" of curing—were heard almost constantly throughout the camps by late spring, when malaria and other illnesses, such as infectious eye diseases, plagued the exiles.[66]

When questioned by the Fort Leavenworth reporter, the elder *tiwét* expressed his syncretic notion of religion, ceremonialism, and peoplehood. First, he admitted that he was also a Catholic. Then he said, "You white man, another Black man, me Indian, but all same heart, good heart, all feel same to Him," pointing upward. The service, which lasted until late that evening, involved the sacred ceremonies and histories of people-hood that were expressed in the aboriginal language of their peoplehood, Nimiipuutímt.[67]

Two weeks later, the same reporter witnessed a memorial ceremony that was celebrated by Joseph's camp. "The dance was held," said the reporter, as "a token of respect to the memory of one of the most valued chiefs," who had been killed at Bear Paw. The unnamed chief may have been Ollokot, because his brother Joseph was central to this ceremonial; though there were several other "valued chiefs" also killed at Bear Paw, Joseph was the only celebrant clearly identified during this ceremony, although many other exiled men prayed, danced, and sang that day. "Joseph made the occasion one of great importance at the camp" and was "arrayed in magnificent style."[68] In accordance with the practices of the Nimiipuu, it is unlikely that Joseph would have repeated the name of the deceased man. Using descriptive phrases in lieu of the man's name, Joseph left it to the reporter and the public to define the honoree.[69] Alan Marshall clarifies this practice: "As to names; at present folks who strongly identify as 'traditional' avoid using the deceased's name for a year or so. . . . The name can be used in conversation after that. . . . At some point, though, a descendant will seem to display some salient feature of the deceased; that person will then 'receive' the name. Or, someone will be given the name in order to 'preserve' it. . . . The problem for Nimiipuu in those days (ca. 1877) was that the population was declining, and traditional patterns were disrupted." As Marshall concludes, there were too few "descendants to fill the titles and the replication of physical, behavior, and 'cognitive' traits was/is difficult in the new order."[70]

In the interim, horses borrowed from Army officers for the ceremonials were outfitted with sacred equine regalia that had somehow, almost miraculously, been preserved. Several types of animal pelt, such as those seen in the leather tipis, shrouded the horses; "some were almost covered with skins of various animals," while "long strings of bells and bead work" (that reminded the reporter of "circus horse" regalia) decorated their necks. Another handsome black horse, loaned by an interested army officer, was clad in some kind of sacred regalia that may have been made especially for that type of occasion. That horse, ridden by one of the older male captives (who was also unnamed to the press), led a parade of mounted riders around the outer perimeter of the camp, accompanied by the women's robust, grieving "cries" and "wails." All of the horses' tails were adorned with blessed eagle feathers; the ceremony continued throughout the day. These regalia too, had been preserved during the war; though the exiles had lost many tons of camp equipages, personal items, and in countless cases just about everything they owned—including the clothes on their backs—these secreted sacred items of peoplehood took precedence. Joseph then explained to U.S. Army Captain Ilsley that "if his heart was taken out, it would show the truth he was asserting, that the tribe had always had and that he hoped when, if he should ever return to his country, he would be able to show that he had told the truth." As he would do for the rest of his life, Joseph reiterated his love of his homeland and his peaceful intentions.[71] Modified winter ceremonials and funerals continued throughout the winter and spring, but the large mourning and memorial services were not repeated.

The United States Negates Its Bear Paw Accord;
Peoplehood Calls the Exiles Home

By the following July 1878, conditions in the Fort Leavenworth camp had dramatically deteriorated. Several hundred prisoners suffered from malaria, and the U.S. Army was tired of operating the camp. Consequently, in spite of the surrender agreement, the Bureau of Indian Affairs and the War Department decided to send the exiles farther east to the Quapaw Reservation in Indian Territory. Facing the intense heat of a Kansas summer, extreme filth, and so many people sick with malaria, the prisoners were taken by train to Baxter Springs, Kansas, on July 21, 1878.[72] The next evening they were relocated to Modoc Reservation at the Quapaw Agency.[73] No homes or preparations awaited them there, where the Indian Bureau and Indian Agent Hiram W. Jones became their new jailers. Quapaw was a nightmare of federal neglect, U.S. Army guards, semistarvation, and infectious diseases.[74] Within a matter of months forty-three prisoners had died, mostly from malaria and federal neglect. Agent Jones left them without medications, shorted their rations, and left them without shelters for months at a time. At least two hundred of the exiles suffered malaria infection without access to quinine or other effective treatments.[75]

Federal officials still planned to make the prisoners permanent residents of Indian Territory, expecting that through this, the prisoners ought to now become students, farmers, ranchers, and Christians. On that note, the Board of Indian Commissioners sent Clinton B. Fisk and William Stickney to Quapaw to interview the captives and to purchase another, permanent, reservation for them near Quapaw. Stunned by conditions in the prison camp, the commissioners were amazed when Joseph and the other exiles would not select a new reservation. They also refused to remain in Indian Territory; Joseph emphasized their homelands position by showing them his personal written copy of Miles's surrender accord. Miles's agreement was now part of a sacred history that would be—and is still being—quoted many years into the future. As Stickney reported of their August 12 visit, "We found Joseph averse to the idea of remaining in the Indian Territory."

Stickney mentioned that Joseph and the other headmen, "at every interview, strongly resisted our every argument in favor of the selection of permanent homes in any place excepting in their old hunting grounds in Idaho."[76] Peoplehood called the exiles home; they desperately needed the sacred, healthy environments of their Columbia Plateau homelands.

By August 14 when the commissioners signed a purchase agreement with the Confederated Peoria and Miami to acquire a seven-thousand-acre reservation, Joseph and the other leaders showed no interest and avoided a pivotal meeting with the commissioners. In a letter to Joseph, the commissioners warned that the exiles would be moved to the new reservation as soon as possible.[77] This did not, however, happen exactly as the federal authorities had planned. The prisoners did not obey Acting Commissioner of Indian Affairs William Leeds's instructions of August 12, when Leeds told Indian agent Jones, "You will at once inform the Nez Perces that they are to remain permanently on the Quapaw Reservation and that they must calculate to go to work and support themselves."[78] Then, a letter written at Fort Leavenworth by the interpreter Arthur I. Chapman was reprinted in the *New York Times*. The American public, Indian rights activists, and federal bureaucrats learned that Joseph was "very much dissatisfied" with conditions in the Indian Territory.[79] And on September 17, Commissioner of Indian Affairs Ezra Hayt denied another of Joseph's repeated requests to visit Washington DC. Commissioner Hayt was coming to deal with the Nimiipuu, or so he thought.[80]

The week before Hayt arrived at Quapaw, members of a joint Congressional Committee interviewed Joseph and a local businessman on October 7, 1878, in Seneca, Missouri. Following the businessman's testimony, Senator Thomas Clay McCreery (Kentucky) asked Joseph if he had anything else to say. "I am very glad to express myself to you chiefs," said Joseph through the interpreter; "Today you will find out what I think—This is my heart I am about to express—I am going to give my conclusions from what I have seen in this country." Joseph continued to be extremely clear: "I think very little of this country. It is like a poor man, it amounts to nothing. I see that it is not very productive; that it is not a productive country; I see this with my own eyes."[81] Asked several times who Joseph thought should control the Indian Bureau, Joseph replied that no one should control

American Indians. Everyone should be citizens of the United States, be free to "come and go when they please" and "be governed all alike. . . . Liberty is good and great . . . Those are my ideas."[82] Joseph's peoplehood included equal rights for American Indians.

One week later Commissioner of Indian Affairs Ezra Hayt and Commissioner E. W. Kingsley from the Board of Indian Commissioners arrived at Quapaw. They intended to convince the prisoners to accept the seven-thousand-acre reservation chosen by Stickney and Fisk. They met in council with Joseph, Yellow Bear, and twenty of the camp leaders at the Quapaw Agency. The Nimiipuu expressed their peoplehood in Nimiipuutímt, while the English speakers followed the interpreter. The first order of business presented by the prisoners was a review of the surrender accord; they again insisted that federal authorities had violated this agreement. They were being held illegally, and they complained that the removals to Kansas and Indian Territory had also ruined their health. Hayt insisted that it was too dangerous to return them to Idaho, but Joseph pursued recognition of the surrender accord. As he said in the terms of peoplehood's sacred homelands, their "one great desire was to be returned to their homes in the west."[83]

The Sacred Nature of Water

Faced with inexorable resistance, Hayt ended the council. He and Kingsley then inspected the reservation. Yielding to the prisoners' insistence that they faced certain death and that there was no water on the new reservation, the commissioners wanted to find another reservation. Joseph and the prisoners understood this lack of water in terms of their sacred homelands and through beliefs that the commissioners did not comprehend. The exiles knew that water was the most "vital" of "all the moving elements." As Pinkham and Evans reflect, "Streams and rivers were the threads that held life together. . . . Waters were the most powerful and mysterious moving force, the one which bound the sky to the earth."[84] They continue, "Water was critical to both physical and spiritual lives . . . spring water and water from the streams and rivers themselves, was the ultimate medicine, the ultimate visible tangible power available." In their words, "Water is a mysterious, regenerating power substance." Proof of this was, as they say, the "dependence of all life on the milk of the mother earth."[85] The Nimiipuu "knew the rivers [such as the Clearwater, lower Snake, and mid-Columbia] were a part of themselves, emotionally, mythologically, and spiritually."[86] Alan Marshall adds, "The Nez Perce word 'water' still carries these strong spiritual connotations; it is still regarded as medicine because it has healing properties."[87] The lack of swiftly flowing rivers, mountain streams, and the salmon-laden waters of their homelands further alienated the exiles from their religious beliefs and their homelands.

Húsus Kute (a Palus cocaptive) and Joseph still refused to transfer to another reservation. But in the event that they decided to move, it would be a consensual group discussion and decision. Hayt thought that Joseph would change his mind: "When he [Joseph] gives up the hope of returning to Idaho, I think he will choose the location I have named."[88]

By November 17, the prisoners had still not accepted the proposed relocation when another Congressional Committee visited Quapaw. Headed by Congressman John J. Patterson (South Carolina) and Senator Lafayette Grover, the former governor of Oregon, the committee came to investigate the Indian agent for fraud and to silence Joseph's steady complaints. Joseph addressed Patterson and Grover through the interpreter, reiterating his peoplehood position: "I object to this country." Then, he repeated a long, morose litany of the many deaths and illnesses his people suffered, the abrogation of the surrender agreement, and the unhealthy nature of the new country. Again and again, Joseph insisted that their lives depended on their return to their homelands. "I see nothing here. It is not a rich country. It is not a healthy or a good country at all," repeated Joseph, while Grover tried to redirect the conversation.[89] Joseph reaffirmed that their survival was predicated upon peoplehood in a healthy environment. Grover even acknowledged that Joseph's band had not participated in the treaty of 1863. But, the former governor added, the "Great Father" (i.e., the U.S. president), recognized majority rule, a concept that was basically unknown to Joseph. Consequently, the president insisted that the Nimiipuu had sold the Wallowa Valley. In Grover's words, "The Great Father said the Nez Perces had made the treaty, and you must obey it."[90] Joseph reminded Grover that

Joseph's band had never taken anything generated by the treaty of 1863 and that their Wallowa Valley homeland had been sold without their permission. He brought up the sacred territories of peoplehood again as he said, "That land raised us. Would we want to part with it? That is what makes us love our lands, because we grew up upon it."[91] Hayt, however, continued to press the exiles for a decision about the move to the west.[92] And as he had done at Fort Leavenworth, Joseph expressed his displeasure to local newspapermen.[93] He made his point (and the peoplehood focus of the exiles), as reported in the *Empire City Echo* on December 18, 1878: "Joseph is much dissatisfied with the new location assigned his people near the Qua Paw agency."[94]

Following several denied appeals for Joseph to visit the U.S. president, Reverend Alfred B. Meacham (former superintendent of Indian Affairs for Oregon and an Indian Rights activist) finally arranged with the Secretary of the Interior for Joseph, Yellow Bull, interpreter Ad Chapman, and Superintendent/Clerk H. H. Arthur to visit Washington DC in January 1879.[95] The complaints, newspaper articles featuring Joseph's requests, and interviews had borne fruit. During their well-publicized visit, Joseph and Yellow Bull lobbied President Rutherford B. Hayes for their freedom, petitioning at least forty senators and congressmen.[96] Their audience included U.S. Army generals such as Nelson Miles and Benjamin Butler, Commissioner of Indian Affairs Ezra Hayt, Indian rights organizations, and the Board of Indian Commissioners.[97] The Nimiipuu understood the rights of peoplehood and critical federal promises.

One special evening, Joseph addressed eight hundred federal authorities, reporters, commissioners, and Indian rights advocates at Lincoln Hall. With Yellow Bull standing nearby, Joseph remained on message. They clarified their nonparticipation in the treaty of 1863. They argued for their return to the northwest, and they reiterated the broken surrender accord and their subsequent incarceration.[98] As Joseph said through the interpreter when he made another speech at the Christian Missionary Conference in Washington by the Board of Indian Commissioners, "Since I was large enough to understand anything I have tried to learn the ways and the hearts of the people I have met, and I think God gave me a heart and brain to understand the world. I have not a deceitful heart. I have met many of the representatives of the government."[99]

As one reporter who attended Joseph's speech at Lincoln Hall recalled, Joseph clearly relayed his peoplehood:

> He began by an affectionate reference to his father, and to his views, which were to be always at peace. He told of the several councils to prevail upon his father to surrender the lands they held, and of his adamant refusal, for it was their country and like a mother, if he sold it for blankets and beads, his children would grow up and have no place to live . . . He recited the story of the fight from the time the war was declared until he surrendered to Miles and Howard; how they had broken faith with him, hurrying him from post to post . . . and closed with this simple remark, "This is my story and here I am."[100]

Supplemental Expressions of Peoplehood

While Joseph, Yellow Bull, and Húsus Kute were dealing with federal officials, they and many others also found supplementary expressions of their peoplehood. This was in spite of Indian Agent Hiram Jones, who was determined to eradicate American Indian ceremonialism and religions. As historian Velma Neiberding revealed, "If Agent Jones was harsh with the Nez Perces he was [also] harsh with the Senecas, who continued to carry on the Long House worship of the Handsome Lake doctrine, and with the Shawnees, who persisted in their ancestral Bread and Green Corn dances. Not only this, as if flaunting the Agent's wishes, they held these 'heathen' dances on Sunday."[101] Insofar as the historical records indicate, the Nimiipuu did not participate in these dances, but they surely knew about them; there are no secrets in small communities. And the Nimiipuu did express many other aspects of their ceremonial peoplehood. Besides several Christian Nimiipuu from Idaho who interacted with other Christians in the area such as the Wyandotte Quakers, many men and women participated in curing rituals administered by Nimiipuu *tiwéts*.[102] There were so many people suffering from malaria that the songs of curing, songs of death and mourning, ceremonies, and prayers were almost constant.[103] Whenever possible, the exiles expressed their peoplehood in other familiar ways.

Again, as Neiberding learned from the Ottawa man Guy Jennison, the Nimiipuu were recognized by their new neighbors as great "gamblers . . . [who] like good horses." Other than the mules and twenty-five teams of American-horse mares assigned to them just before they were moved again in June 1879, none of the Nimiipuu's own horses had survived the journey to Quapaw.[104] But the exiles never forgot the spiritual peoplehood of their relationships with horses, gambling, and races. "At Quapaw," Neiberding continued, the "Modocs and Nez Perces held horse races of 'great interest' to all tribes in the agency and much against the wishes of the agent . . . [who] deplored gambling and betting that went on among the Indians."[105] Yet horse races and the attendant gambling brought the joy of these spirit animals back into exiled lives. As Nez Perce cultural specialist Nakia Williamson explains, horses and the activities connected to them are extremely important. "Our connection to the horse is a very powerful thing to us and a very real thing." Williamson recalls that the horse joined the Nimiipuu before the year 1700.[106] At that point, horses "became a part of us and we became a part of them."[107] Horses were partners in war and peace and cocelebrants in tribal ceremonials.[108] As Pinkham and Evans point out, horses form vital spiritual "links between humankind and the rest of the natural world."[109] "Seeking spiritual guardianship in equestrian skills was warmly embraced . . . This is illustrated by the emergence of the many horse-related" guardian spirit powers.[110] These sacred powers, expressed through races and associated games of chance, reinforced Nimiipuu peoplehood. Horse races in their beloved homelands were often huge public events that involved intertribal festivals, gambling, and many other ceremonials of peoplehood.[111]

As for the Nez Perce, their story was another sad postscript to the war. The Army destroyed several thousand of the Nez Perce horses during the fighting.[112] Then, of the seven hundred Nez Perce horses taken to Fort Keogh by the army, three hundred were awarded to Cheyenne scouts employed by the army. The rest of the captured horses were meant to have been held for the Nimiipuu when they were returned to Idaho in the spring. Instead, claiming that the animals were too exhausted, injured, young, spirited, or difficult to handle, the army slaughtered most of them. Joseph himself had been allowed to take his own favorite horse as far as Bismarck.[113] Believing that the army was shipping the exiles home in the spring, Joseph was extremely upset when the prisoners were sent to Kansas instead and he was forced to sell that animal in Bismarck.[114] Lieutenant General Philip Sheridan excused these activities, saying, "Colonel Miles under the authority vested in him could accept the unconditional surrender of those Indians only, and if he made any such promises as it is claimed he did, that the captured animals, equipment, and camp equipage should be returned to the Indians, or that they should be permitted to return to Idaho either with or without escort, such promises were made without a shadow of authority."[115]

As bad as conditions had become at Quapaw, by April 23, 1879, the captives still had not agreed to relocate to another reservation in western Indian Territory. Even after having been moved twice since their captivity, in denial of their surrender agreement, their continued insistence on their peoplehood did not abate. They still spoke their natal language. They still celebrated the ceremonials and spiritualism of peoplehood whenever possible. And they desperately wanted and needed to return to their homelands, no matter what federal officials demanded; no matter what politicians in Washington DC did—or did not, promise; no matter what large audiences and newspapers saw and heard. The Nimiipuu, as illustrated by the peoplehood model of identity, remained strong in their sense of peoplehood. For a while, Húsus Kute and his Palus followers balked at the suggested move. They had been promised a speedier return to their homelands if they had stayed and become Quakers. Others were unsure of any promises that Joseph and Yellow Bull might have made in Washington DC.[116] As usual, though, in-camp governance was based on intense group discussions held on April 23 and 24. Then, while anxious federal officials telegraphed their worried supervisors in Washington DC, the captives decided to stick together. Their sense of peoplehood prevailed. They would all move once again—this time to a reservation in the western Indian Territory.[117] Following this next move, the exiles would participate in Sun Dances and other "medicine dances" just as those religious ceremonials were about to be banned by the United States.[118] As the Nimiipuu elder Samuel M. Watters reminded Alan Marshall, the exiles would "make every step on the earth a prayer."[119]

NOTES

1. McWhorter, *Hear Me, My Chiefs*, 499.
2. Tom Hill, in Curtis, *North American Indian*, 171; Oliver O. Howard, "Telegram to Division Headquarters from the Field," October 8, 1877, *ARSW* (1878), 1:633, 1878.
3. James Reuben, "History of the Nez Perce War," MS, MG5369, 1883, Special Collections, University of Idaho, Moscow.
4. Nelson A. Miles, "Extract from Annual Report," *ARBIC* (1887), 59–60.
5. John Pope, "Nez Perce Population Statistics at Fort Leavenworth," December 4, 1877, NARA, microfilm 666, Records of the Adjutant General's Office, Nez Perce War File, Washington DC. For a historical discussion of the captivity experiences, see Pearson, *Nez Perces*, 77–145.
6. See chapter 1 of this volume.
7. Robert K. Thomas, in Holm, Pearson, and Chavis, "Peoplehood," 12.
8. See chapter 1 of this volume.
9. Robert K. Thomas, in Holm, Pearson, and Chavis, "Peoplehood," 12.
10. Holm, Pearson, and Chavis, "Peoplehood," 13.
11. See chapter 1 of this volume.
12. Holm, Pearson, and Chavis, "Peoplehood," 14.
13. See chapter 1 of this volume.
14. Holm, Pearson, and Chavis, "Peoplehood," 15.
15. Pearson and Harrington, "Numipu Winter Villages," 48; Primary data from Archie Mark Phinney Papers, Bureau of Indian Affairs, Northern Idaho Agency, 1926–49, boxes 4-11, RG75, National Archives, Pacific Northwest Region, Seattle WA.
16. See chapter 1 of this volume.
17. Pinkham and Evans, *Lewis and Clark*, 10.
18. Holm, Pearson, and Chavis, "Peoplehood," 7–12.
19. Evans, *Voice of the Old Wolf*, 12.
20. Ray, "Ethnohistory of the Joseph Band," 190.
21. Flanagan, "Invalidity of the Nez," 87.
22. See Kappler, ed., *Indian Affairs*, 2:702–6.
23. Ray, "Ethnohistory of the Joseph Band," 192.
24. Flanagan, "Invalidity of the Nez," 86–88.
25. See chapter 1 of this volume; James Reuben, "Letter to Col. A. B. Meacham, March 10, 1880," *Council Fire*, June/July 1880.
26. Rev. Archie Lawyer, "A Memorial, from the Synod of Kansas of the Presbyterian Church, Asking for the Restoration of the Nez Perce Indians to their Home in Idaho Territory, September 30, 1881." Winfield KS: Courier Job Printing House.
27. Luke Phillips, "Letter in the *Morning Star*," February 1885.
28. See Walker, *Conflict and Schism*, 123–24.
29. Chief Joseph, "An Indian's Views," 425–34.

30. Chief Joseph, in Josephy, *Nez Perce Indians*, 487, 488.

31. Aoki, *Nez Perce Texts*, 125–26.

32. Alan G. Marshall, conversation with the author, August 31, 2017; Edward S. Curtis, in Ruby and Brown, *Dreamer Prophets*, 72, 223n2. From Curtis, *North American Indian*, 7:64.

33. Smohalla, in Relander, *Drummers and Dreamers*, 96, 104, 139, 280.

34. Smohalla, in Relander, *Drummers and Dreamers*, 35.

35. Deward E. Walker Jr., "Introduction, Sacred Geography in Northwestern North America," 1–6, American Indian Heritage Foundation, Indians.org, accessed August 30, 2017, http://www.indians.org/welker/sacred.htm.

36. Slickpoo and Walker, *Noon Nee-Me-Poo*, 61.

37. Archie Phinney, in Pearson and Harrington, "Numipu Winter Villages," 47–51.

38. See chapter 1 of this volume.

39. Archie Phinney, in Pearson and Harrington, "Numipu Winter Villages," 47–51.

40. Marshall, *Nez Perce Social Groups*, 23, 24.

41. Slickpoo and Walker, *Noon Nee-Me-Poo*, 54, 55, 58, 59, 61.

42. Evans, *Voice of the Old Wolf*, 12.

43. John Pope, "Nez Perce Population Statistics at Fort Leavenworth," December 4, 1877, microfilm 666, Records of the Adjutant General's Office, Nez Perce War File, NARA, Washington DC.

44. Samuel Baker, W. M. Burr, Manly Breaker, et al., "Report of Missionary Societies, Presbyterian Home Missions for the year 1878," ARBIC (1879), 88.

45. Richard Henry Pratt, "Speedy Civilization and Education of the Nez Perce Prisoners," June 24, 1878, microfilm 666, Records of the Adjutant General's Office, Nez Perce War File, NARA, Washington DC; Pearson, *Nez Perces*, 222, 223.

46. "A Perfect *fac simile* [sic] of the Autograph of the Noted Chieftain as Voluntarily Written and Given to a Times Reporter," *Leavenworth Times* (Leavenworth KS), December 18, 1877.

47. Parnell, *Battle of White Bird Canyon*, 94, 97.

48. McWhorter, *Hear Me, My Chiefs*, 157.

49. The reporter could not determine the nature of the writing in Joseph's message; it may have been Joseph's own calligraphy or, less likely, written by Joseph in Nimii-puutímt. As Steven Evans notes, Sam Lott (Nimiipuu) advised that Oliver O. Howard was incorrect in insisting that Joseph and his brother had attended a missionary school. Joseph, according to Evans, had not attended school and therefore probably did not write in his natal language. Evans, *Voice of the Old Wolf*, 123; "Camp Joseph; A Short Visit to the Nez Perces above Fort Leavenworth; Chief Joseph Leaves a History behind Him on a Tree," *Leavenworth Times* (Leavenworth KS), December 4, 1877.

50. Museum Management Program, Nez Perce Museum Collections, National Historical Park National Park Service, U.S. Department of the Interior, accessed June 11, 2016, https://www.nps.gov/museum/exhibits/nepe/spirituality.html.

51. "Nez Perce Architecture, Housing Types," University of Idaho, September 4, 2016, http://www.webpages.uidaho.edu/arch499/nonwest/Nez_Perce/ht_hide_tipi.htm.

52. "The Nez Perces are Visited by 5,000 People from the Country on Sunday; Their Religious Services as Witnessed by a Times Reporter," *Leavenworth Times* (Leavenworth KS), December 11, 1877; Pearson, *Nez Perces*, 85–86.

53. "The Nez Perces; A Dance in Memory of the Warrior Who Was Killed at the Battle of Bear Paw Mountain," *Leavenworth Times* (Leavenworth KS), December 23, 1877; Pearson, *Nez Perces*, 85–88.

54. "Nez Perces are Visited."

55. Smohalla, in Relander, *Drummers and Dreamers*, 85.

56. Smohalla, in Relander, *Drummers and Dreamers*, 84.

57. Trafzer and Beach, "Smohalla, the Washani," 313.

58. Thompson, *I Will Tell*, 92.

59. Pinkham and Evans, *Lewis and Clark*, 3.

60. "Nez Perces are Visited."

61. Evans, *Voice of the Old Wolf*, 43.

62. Dubois, *Feather Cult*, 33.

63. MacMurray, "'Dreamers' of the Columbia," 242.

64. "Among Captive Indians; Scattered Remnants of Tribes, a Visit to the Nez Perces and Modocs," *New York Times*, November 8, 1878.

65. Archie Phinney, in Pearson and Harrington, "Numipu," 47–51.

66. "Among Captive Indians." One old man suffered from eyes "purging thick amber and plum-tree gum." Presumably, this was not the only serious eye infection, since antibiotics had not yet existed and the prisoners were forced to live in filthy circumstances.

67. "Nez Perces are Visited."

68. "Nez Perces; A Dance."

69. Alan G. Marshall, conversation with the author, April 12, 2016.

70. Alan G. Marshall, conversation with the author, April 12, 2016.

71. "Nez Perces; A Dance."

72. John McNeil, "Report to Commissioner of Indian Affairs," July 24, 1878, RG75, NPS, NARA, LROIA, Quapaw Agent, Lewiston ID.

73. Sending the prisoners to the Modocs was apparently an early plan; it was submitted to President Rutherford B. Hayes in January 1878. See Rutherford B. Hayes, "Extract from the Annual Report of the General of the Army for 1877," in S. Ex. Doc. 14, at 9 (1877) (Washington DC: USGPO).

74. "Tables of Statistics," 286, *ARCIA* (1878).

75. "Indian Archives Files, Quapaw Agency, Indian Territory: Charges against Indian Agent Jones." Letters, December 10, 1879, to August 14, 1880, QA4, OHSAD, Oklahoma City.

76. Clinton B. Fisk and William Stickney, "Report of Visit of Commissioners Fisk and Stickney to Colorado and Indian Territory," August 30, 1878, *ARBIC*, 47–51; Pearson, *Nez Perces*, 121.

77. Fisk and Stickney, "Report," 47–51.

78. William W. Leeds to Agent Jones, August 12, 1878, Quapaw Agency, Indian Territory, materials from July 5, 1878, to November 25, 1878, OHSAD, Oklahoma City.

79. Ad Chapman, "The Nez Perces and the Modocs, Nez Perces Camp, Quapaw Agency, IT, August 29, 1878," *New York Times*, September 8, 1878, 9.

80. Ezra A. Hayt, "Telegram to Agent Jones," September 17, 1878, LDCNP, Quapaw Agency, Indian Territory, July 5, 1878–November 25, 1878, OHSAD, Oklahoma City; Hayt, in Pearson, *Nez Perces*, 118, 119, 129, 130, 138, 145, 147–50.

81. Chief Joseph and H. H. Gregg, "Testimony," in *Testimony Taken by the Joint Committee Appointed to Take into Consideration the Expediency of Transferring the Indian Department to the War Department*, 45th Cong., 3rd sess., S. Misc. Doc. 53, at 77–86, serial set vol. 1835, 1879 (October 7, 1878), CIS, Washington DC; Pearson, *Nez Perces*, 131, 132, 143.

82. Joseph and Gregg, "Testimony," October 7, 1878, Washington DC; Ollokot, in Oliver O. Howard, *Nez Perce Joseph*, 55.

83. E. M. Kingsley, "Report on His Visit to the Indian Territory," October 15, 1878, ARBIC (1879), 50; Click Relander, *Drummers*, 84.

84. Pinkham and Evans, *Lewis and Clark*, 2.

85. Pinkham and Evans, *Lewis and Clark*, 12.

86. Pinkham and Evans, *Lewis and Clark*, 38.

87. Marshall, "Nez Perce Water Rights," 770.

88. Ezra T, Hayt, "Commissioner's Annual Report, Chief Joseph," November 1, 1878, ARCIA, i–xlv, xxxiv.

89. John James Patterson, "Testimony Taken by the Subcommittee of the Committee on Territories, at the Camps of the Nez Perces, Seneca, Missouri," 45th Cong., 3rd sess., S. Rep. 744 at 810–13, serial set vol. 1839, 1878 (November 17, 1878), CIS, Washington DC.

90. Grover, in Patterson, "Testimony Taken," 811–12.

91. Joseph, in Patterson, "Testimony Taken," 812.

92. Ezra A. Hayt, "To Agent Jones, What Is Joseph's Decision," November 23, 1878, LDCNP, Quapaw Agency, Indian Territory, July 5–November 25, 1878, OHSAD, Oklahoma City.

93. "Baxter Springs Items," *Empire City Echo* (Baxter Springs KS), December 5, 1878.

94. "Baxter Springs Items," *Empire City Echo* (Baxter Springs KS), December 5, 1878.

95. Meacham, "Nez Perce Joseph," 22; Sewall S. Cutting, M. E. Strieby, John C. Lowrie, Benjamin Tatham, and Samual L. Janney, *Journal of the Eighth Annual Conference with Representatives of Missionary Boards, Held at Washington, D. C., January 15, 1879* (Washington DC: USGPO, 1879), 123, 126; "Chief Joseph on His Way to Washington," *Chicago Daily Tribune*, special dispatch, *St. Louis Tribune*, January 10, 1879, 2.

96. "Arrival of Chief Joseph," *Washington Post*, January 14, 1879, 4.

97. James M. Haworth, "To Ezra Hayt, CIA, Removal," April 23, 1879, LROIA 1824–81, Quapaw Agency, Indian Territory, 1870–1880, microfiche 1–4995, reel 708, RG75, NARA, Washington DC.

98. "Chief Joseph on His Way to Washington," *Chicago Daily Tribune*, January 14, 1879; "Arrival of Chief Joseph," *Washington Post*, January 14, 1879; "Broken Pledges," *Washington Post*, January 18, 1879, 1; "Chief Joseph as Lecturer," *New York Post*, January 18, 1879, 1; "Correspondence," *Friend's Intelligencer* 35, no. 49 (January 25, 1879): 775–76; Meacham, "Nez Perce Joseph," 22, 23; Meacham, "Letters in Reference," 47; Sewall S. Cutting, Reverend, Secretary, Baptist Home Missionary Society, M. E. Strieby, John C. Lowrie, D. D., Secretary, Board of Commissioners for Foreign Missions, Presbyterian Church, Benjamin Tatham, Society of Friends (Orthodox), and Samual L. Janney, D. D., "Journal of the Eighth Annual Conference with Representatives of Missionary Boards, held at Washington DC, January 15, 1879," *ARBIC*, 115–28.

99. Joseph, in Sewall S. Cutting, Reverend, M. E. Strieby, John C. Lowrie, et al., 126.

100. Chief Joseph, "Broken Pledges," *Washington Post*, January 18, 1879. It should be noted that this speech was probably "adapted and modified by a sympathetic white editor," as recorded by Evans in *Voice of the Old Wolf*, 20; Pearson, *Nez Perces*, 152–56.

101. Neiberding, "Nez Perce at the Quapaw," 26n13.

102. Asa C. Tuttle, "Union Meeting, Wyandotte Church," *Baxter Springs Times* (Baxter Springs KS), February 20, 1879.

103. Bob Sands, in Neiberding, "Nez Perce at the Quapaw," 24, 25, 26; "Among Captive Indians."

104. Neiberding, "Nez Perce at the Quapaw," 23; James M. Haworth, "Report to Commissioner of Indian Affairs, Ezra A. Hayt, Quapaw Agency, Removal to the Ponca Agency," June 25, 1879, RG75, LROIA, NARA: Quapaw Agency, Washington DC; H. Whiteman, "Nez Perce Arrivals, Report," August 31, 1879, *ARCIA*, 75, Washington DC.

105. Neiberding, "Nez Perce at the Quapaw," 23, 24.

106. See chapter 1 of this volume.

107. Nakia Williamson, in Jack McNeel, "'Horse Tribe' Documents the Nez Perce, the Appaloosa, and More," *Indian Country Today Media Network*, April 28, 2012, http://indiancountrytodaymedianetwork.com/2012/04/28/horse-tribe-documents-nez-perce-appaloosa-and-more-110542. For many more horse-acquisition stories, see Pinkham and Evans, *Lewis and Clark*, 14–24.

108. See fig. 4 in Thompson, *I Will Tell*, 32.

109. Pinkham and Evans, *Lewis and Clark*, 14.

110. Pinkham and Evans, *Lewis and Clark*, 15.

111. Chalfant, "Aboriginal Territory," 104.

112. McNeel, "'Horse Tribe' Documents."

113. Ad I. Chapman, interpreter, "To Ezra A. Hayt, CIA, Regarding Nez Perce Horses, Saddles, Equipment, etc.," December 13, 1878, microfilm 666, reel 340, Records of the Adjutant General's Office, Nez Perce War File, NARA, Washington DC.

114. "Joseph's Gone," *Bismarck Tribune* (Bismarck, ND), November 23, 1877, p. 1, cols. 5 and 6, 1–5.

115. P. Sheridan, in George McCrary, "To Ezra A. Hayt, CIA, Regarding his Letter December 28, 1878, Nez Perces Horses and Equipment at Fort Keogh," April 22, 1879, microfilm 666, reel 340, Records of the Adjutant General's Office, Nez Perce War File, NARA, Washington DC.

116. LROIA Quapaw Agency, Indian Territory, microfiche 1-4995, reel 708, RG75, NARA, Washington DC.

117. James M. Haworth, USIA. "To Ezra Hayt, CIA, Removal Council with Nez Perces," April 23, 1879. Washington DC: NARA, LRIOA, Quapaw Agency, Indian Territory, m/f 1–4995, reel 708; James M. Haworth, USIA. "To Ezra Hayt, CIA, Removal Council," November 24, 1879. Washington DC: NARA, LROIA, Quapaw Agency, Indian Territory, m/f 1–4995, reel 708; Pearson, *Nez Perces*, 147–64.

118. See chapter 3 of this volume.

119. Samuel M. Watters, in Marshall, "Nez Perce Water Rights," 764.

BIBLIOGRAPHY

Aoki, Haruo. "Nez Perce Texts, Chief Joseph's Speech at Carlisle Indian School," *Linguistics* 90, no. 90 (1979): 1–133.

Chalfant, Stuart A. "Aboriginal Territory of the Nez Perce Indians." In *Nez Perce Indians,* by Stuart A. Chalfant, Verne F. Ray, and United States, 89–110. New York: Garland, 1974.

Curtis, Edward S. Vols. 7 and 8 of *The North American Indian.* On the Nez Perces, Walla-walla, Umatilla, Cayuse, and the Chinookan Tribes. Boston: John Andrew & Son, 1911.

Dubois, Cora Alice. *The Feather Cult of the Mid-Columbia.* Menasha WI: George Banta, 1938.

Evans, Steven. *Voice of the Old Wolf.* Pullman: Washington State University Press, 1996.

Flanagan, John K. "The Invalidity of the Nez Perce Treaty of 1863 and the Taking of the Wallowa Valley." *American Indian Law Review* 24, no. 1 (1999–2000): 78–79.

Holm, Tom, J. Diane Pearson, and Ben Chavis. "Peoplehood: A Model for the Extension of Sovereignty in American Indian Studies." *Wicazō Ṡa Review* 18, no. 1 (Spring 2003): 7–24.

Joseph, Chief. "An Indian's Views of Indian Affairs; Interview Given at Washington." *North American Review* 128 (April 1879): 412–44.

Josephy, Alvin M., Jr. *The Nez Perce Indians and the Opening of the Northwest.* New York: Houghton Mifflin, 1997.

Kappler, Charles J, ed. *Indian Affairs: Laws and Treaties.* Vol. 2. Washington DC: USGPO, 1904.

MacMurray, J. W. "The 'Dreamers' of the Columbia River Valley, in Washington Territory." *Transactions of the Albany Institute* 11 (1887): 242.

Marshall, Alan G. "Fish, Water, and Nez Perce Life." *Idaho Law Review* 42 (2005–6): 763–93.

———. "Nez Perce Social Groups: An Ecological Interpretation." PhD diss., Washington State University, 1977.

———. "Nez Perce Water Rights Settlement Article: Fish, Water, and Nez Perce Life." *Idaho Law Review* 42 Idaho L. Rev. 763, 2006, pp. 763–93.

Meacham, A. B., ed. "Letters in Reference to Return of Chief Joseph and Speech at Lincoln Hall." *Council Fire* 2, no. 3 (March 1879): 47.

———. "Nez Perce Joseph; Visit to Washington, DC." *Council Fire* 2, no. 2 (February 1879): 22–23.

McWhorter, Lucullus V. *Hear Me, My Chiefs! Nez Perce History and Legend.* Caldwell ID: Caxton, 1983.

Neiberding, Velma. "The Nez Perce at the Quapaw Agency, 1878–1879." *The Chronicles of Oklahoma* 44, no. 1 (Spring 1966): 22–30.

Parnell, W. R. *The Battle of White Bird Canyon.* New York: Doubleday, Page, 1907.

Pearson, J. Diane. *The Nez Perces in the Indian Territory: Nimiipuu Survival.* Norman: University of Oklahoma Press, 2008.

Pearson, J. Diane, and Peter Harrington, Cartographer. "Numipu Winter Villages." *Journal of Northwest Anthropology* 38, no. 1(Spring 2004): 46–51.

Pinkham, Allen V., and Steven R. Evans. *Lewis and Clark among the Nez Perce: Strangers in the Land of the Nimiipuu.* Washburn ND: Dakota Institute Press of the Lewis and Clark Fort Mandan Foundation, 2013.

Ray, Verne F. "Ethnohistory of the Joseph Band of Nez Perce Indians: 1805–1905." In *Nez Perce Indians*, by Stuart A. Chalfant, Verne F. Ray, and United States. New York: Garland, 1974.

Relander, Click. *Drummers and Dreamers.* Caldwell ID: Caxton, 1956.

Ruby, Robert H., and John A. Brown. *Dreamer Prophets of the Columbia Plateau.* Norman: University of Oklahoma Press, 1989.

Slickpoo, Allen, Sr., and Deward E. Walker Jr. *Noon Nee-Me-Poo (We, the Nez Perces): Culture and History of the Nez Perces.* Lapwai ID: Nez Perce Tribe of Idaho, 1973.

Thompson, Scott M. *I Will Tell My War Story: A Pictorial Account of the Nez Perce War.* Seattle: University of Washington Press, 2000.

Trafzer, Clifford E., and Margery Ann Beach. "Smohalla, the Washani, and Religion as a Factor in Northwestern Indian History." *American Indian Quarterly* 9, no. 3 (Summer 1985): 309–24.

Walker, Deward E., Jr. *Conflict and Schism in Nez Perce Acculturation: A Study of Religion and Politics.* Pullman: Washington State University, 1968.

3 Nimiipuu Peoplehood, Survival, and Relocation
Strangers in a Strange Land
J. DIANE PEARSON

The Nimiipuu called Indian Territory Eeikish Pah—"the Hot Place." Or, as Alan G. Marshall explains it, the Nimiipuu understood their incarceration in Kansas and Indian Territory from 1877–85 as a "sojourn through Hell."[1] For approximately 390 Nimiipuu, Cayuse, and Palus allies who were removed from Quapaw, Indian Territory on June 6, 1879, to a new prison–reservation in western Indian Territory, this meant almost six years of continued captivity. Detained since October 1877 in federal facilities such as Fort Leavenworth, Kansas, and at Quapaw, the prisoners were fully relocated to what became known as the Oakland Sub-Agency (now Tonkawa, Oklahoma) by mid-June 1879.[2] Like the thousands of white homesteader "Boomers" moving into the Quapaw Strip, the prisoners were transported by wagon train.[3] Unlike the Boomers, though, this was no Western movie in the making, no romanticized magazine that praised the "hardships of the homesteader" or his "part of building up the Great West."[4] This was a sixty-five-wagon train carrying at least two hundred very sick American Indians who were being imprisoned more than 1,500 miles from their sacred Columbia Plateau homelands. The prisoners were also suffering from uncontrolled malaria infections, heat, injuries, and exhaustion. Two people died during the nine-day relocation, including one very old woman and one young man.[5] The Boomers and their families were free and excited to find new homes, but the Nimiipuu and their allies were still federal prisoners in every way, and they had never agreed to remain permanently in the Eeikish Pah. They remained there as the result of the disregarding of a federal surrender agreement by almost everyone except for the Nimiipuu and their allies. The Boomers came in anticipation of new lives, homes, farms, and financial advancement; the exiles were desperate to return to the sacred homelands of their peoplehood. And they truly were in the Eeikish Pah; almost immediately after their relocation, record-setting heat and droughts plagued Indian Territory for five long years.[6]

The move to Oakland had been intended to improve physical conditions for the exiles, according to federal officials. They had fought a tragic defensive war with the United States; now, the exiles were supposed to become students, farmers, and reconstructed Christians in accordance with Indian Bureau "civilization" strategies.[7] They were also supposed to give up their seemingly unreasonable desire to return to their Columbia Plateau–area homelands in favor of permanent residence in Indian Territory. But the situation at Oakland was no improvement over that in Quapaw or Fort Leavenworth; no housing, no preparations, and no other facilities awaited them. Malaria and other diseases continued as lethal predators. In the words of Indian rights activist Dr. M. Cora Bland, who visited the prisoners, "They wept in their hearts" when they remembered their "far away home by the beautiful 'Winding Waters . . . that home from which they were so wrongfully driven and which they never hope to look upon again."[8] One of the key factors of their peoplehood was central to so much grief: there were no Nimiipuu sacred places, no vision quest sites, and no Nimiipuu sacred plants or animals in the Indian Territory.[9] This, plus all of the deaths, diseases, and other disasters of warfare and captivity, wore heavily upon the exiles, as former U.S. Superintendent of Indian Affairs for Oregon Alfred Meacham commented upon meeting Joseph that fall in 1879: "How changed, indeed, his [Joseph's] fortunes since we saw him in 1870." In 1870, Joseph's band had been rich in land, horses, and cattle, and had still enjoyed the freedoms of their homelands. The people had been "happy and hopeful." "Now," Meacham continued, Joseph "is poor, a pensioner, an exile, a captive, a homeless man, his people dying around him almost every day, strangers in a strange land."[10] Or, as Joseph soon told Hiram Price, the Commissioner of Indian Affairs, "Every day of my life I am, and as long as I live, I will be discontented in this country." "I have two wishes," he continued, "one to be allowed to return to my country, the other to die."[11] Joseph also hoped that the Great Father (the U.S. president) would hear his plea and grant his people relief and release.

Unexpected Infusions of Ceremonial Peoplehood

Regardless of what federal authorities had planned, Oakland provided unexpected infusions of ceremonial peoplehood and a most unexpected mechanism for intertribal communication. First, the Indian Bureau supplied horses, plows, seeds, and other agricultural materials in order to turn the prisoners into agriculturists. Then, just before the prisoners left Quapaw, guided by the American Indian Teamster Act of March 1, 1877 (19 U.S. Stats. 291), federal officials taught the exiles how to drive freight wagons, manage wagon mechanics and engineering, and participate in wage-labor employment.[12] Following the guidelines of the American Indian Teamster Act, federal officials paid American Indian teamsters to haul almost all their possessions to all of the reservations, Indian Bureau hospitals, Indian Bureau schools, and other federal Indian facilities within the United States.[13] Now, accessible new neighbors and manageable distances would also favor the Nimiipuu; Oakland was only 39 miles from Arkansas City, 54 miles from Winfield, and 102 miles from Wichita. The Nimiipuu were just 15 miles from the Ponca, about 85 miles from the Cheyenne and Arapaho Agency, and nearly 190 miles from the Kiowa, Comanche, and Apache Agency. These tribal nations, plus the Pawnee, Comanche, and Nimiipuu, all picked up their federal supplies in Kansas.[14] The flour mill was in Arkansas City. The largest railroad depot was in Wichita, and many merchants in Winfield also supplied Indian Bureau contracts. Everything had to be picked up and freighted by wagon train back to the reservations. Area merchants were eager for the Indian trade.

The unexpected consequence was that the Nimiipuu, Palus, and Cayuse met their fellow tribesmen along the freighting routes and in the towns of Kansas. These meetings occasioned fellowship and shared information that certainly included news of tribal nations' ceremonials. For the Oakland prisoners, the Teamster Act was a vehicle of intertribal communication that they had not had at Quapaw. Another unexpected consequence of the Teamster Act was that it afforded the exiles a greater degree of freedom. For example, after the prisoners were issued the "American Horses" at Quapaw, Joseph's participation was markedly evident, such as on the day the Oakland teamsters drove through Arkansas City, Kansas, in mid-November 1879. The newspaper editor recalled that Joseph was a "handsome man" who rode a "very fine looking horse" as he led twenty wagons and the new Oakland teamsters on their way to pick up freight at the railroad depot in Wichita, Kansas.[15]

This was only a few months after Nimiipuu arrival at Oakland; by then, the Oakland teamsters were picking up freight in Wichita, Winfield, and Arkansas City. So were all of the other tribal teamsters. Hundreds of wagons rolled along the various trails of Kansas and Indian Territory, especially during the months of June, July, and August, when new Indian Bureau contracts were opened for delivery. In one instance during the week of July 21, 1880, the Oakland teamsters joined long lines of wagons driven by Osage, Kaw, Pawnee, Cheyenne, Arapaho, Kiowa, Wichita, and Comanche teamsters at Searing's Flour Mill in Arkansas City. Lines formed and waited in place overnight while the flour mill loaded the Indians' wagons around the clock.[16] (These Native American teamsters hauled more than 120 tons of flour from Searing's that month.) Interpreters went everywhere, and according to Alan Marshall, many Nimiipuu also spoke American Indian sign language, the lingua franca of the plains.[17] So while the teamsters waited in line, drove, rode, tended their horses, and camped, they most assuredly communicated with each other. Some of the most active Oakland teamsters included Joseph, Yellow Bull, Yellow Head (John Walker), Húsus Kute (Palus), Frank Buzzard, Powder Horn Owl, Sup-poon-mas (Charley Moses), "Solitoso," John Hill, and Feathers around the Neck (Frank Thompson).[18] When the exiles joined the cycle of Indian Territory ceremonials and Sun Dances, most of these teamsters participated in those events.

Joining Indian Territory Ceremonials—Peoplehood Extended

The exiles joined a ceremonial cycle at Oakland that revolved around "medicine dances," or Sun Dances, for many of the tribal nations that they met while hauling freight. Most of the ceremonials were held in the summer, though the Cheyenne and Arapaho also held winter dances. In fact, the Nimiipuu joined the winter dances in January 1881—along with the Kiowa and Arapaho at Cheyenne—and then returned the following June to participate in the full two-week round of Cheyenne Sun Dances. These dancers included Yellow Bull, Joseph, Red Elk, Tisca, Charley Moses, Wolf Head, "Rose Bush" (Tim-sus-sle-wit), and others, plus several Christian Nimiipuu, one of whom was James Reuben, a Nimiipuu school teacher.[19] The majority of these ceremonial expressions of peoplehood lasted one or two weeks and, as Professor Tom Holm puts it, "reaffirmed each tribe's place in the world." Most of the ceremonials involved entire communities, featured non-Christian theologies, and during the exiles' era, welcomed visitors from throughout the Indian Territory and Kansas. The dances and ceremonies were complex renditions of religious beliefs that Holm reaffirms "involved a sacrifice to symbolize the humility of mankind before the Great Mysteries of the world." "This part of the ceremonial," continues Holm, "was never done to demonstrate imperviousness to pain but to sacrifice the flesh as the most important and sacred offering a human being can make." Various tribal societies were responsible for each part of the complex ceremonial, songs, feasts, and dances. Many of the associated dances were social dances, special society dances, or other public performances. The self-sacrifice and vision-seeking events were often held in private lodges or enclosures. Like the Ponca Sun Dance in May 1880, these lodges were usually closed to outsiders, although the "pledgers" were held in special regard "for their willingness to undergo self-sacrifice for the continued health and prosperity of the tribe as a whole."[20] That particular dance, which was held only a few miles from Oakland, involved fifty-one central poles and as many self-sacrificing supplicants.[21]

Another reason the Nimiipuu knew about the ceremonial cycle of the western Indian Territory was newspaperman Cyrus M. Scott from Arkansas City. For several years Scott had attended tribal dances throughout the Territory, and he joined many of the social dances while hunting, racing horses, or just snooping around. As Scott became acquainted with the Nimiipuu, he encouraged them to participate in Sun Dances. Hoping to recruit more help with his state-sponsored activities, he also told them something else: that he was a spy for Governor St. Johns of Kansas.[22] The day Scott met the prisoners' wagon train when it arrived from Quapaw on June 14, 1879, Scott began encouraging Nimiipuu relationships with their new neighbors.[23] Unknown to Scott, and probably to everyone else in the area, was that the Nimiipuu were also "dancing" Indians. Many exiles knew from the Wanapum Dreamer Prophet Smohalla's words: "Those in the sky [when] they hear it [songs and dances], they know we are preparing to dance the Washat and they will come down to dance with us."[24] These "dancing" exiles would also understand and respond to the peoplehood of songs, theologies, and other manifestations of the sacred "medicine" or Sun Dances associated with these Plains people.

This lack of knowledge is not particularly surprising, since even scholarly experts such as anthropologist Leslie Spier would eventually also assert that the Nimiipuu had never Sun Danced.[25] The Nimiipuu did, however, practice a very old peoplehood ceremonial near Walla Walla, in present-day Washington State, that strongly resembled Sun Dance. As anthropologist Deward Walker clarified, "Alice Fletcher confirms the existence of a ritual pole" when describing an old Nez Perce dance "in the summer around a pole." "What the pole stood for, I was unable to learn," continued Walker, but it was "accounted unsafe for a person to touch this pole, as to do so irreverently would cause death." Walker learned that the dance took place on the prairie near Walla Walla and may have been a "Cayuse ceremony in which the Nez Perces shared." Walker notes that "the gathering at this dance was later made use of by the traders, and it was said that it became an occasion of great ceremony." He mentions that this included ritual flags, and that other ceremonies also used a central pole.[26] The powerful, sacred central pole; the summer timing for the dance; the dances and ceremonies around the central pole; the flags; and other markers on these poles are also common to Sun Dance. Neither was the timing of the dances unusual to the Nimiipuu. The Nimiipuu's old ceremonials occurred during two periods of the year. In the summer, certain ceremonials were common during the longest days of the year; the dances in the winter villages took place around the winter solstice.[27]

Most of the Indian Territory ceremonies involved the acquisition of hunting power, personal power, healing powers, special medicine bundles, or spiritual powers.[28] Spiritual help and interaction were essential to survival, and these ceremonies provided the communal platforms of spirituality critical to peoplehood. Many of the Sun Dances also paid special homage to buffalo (actually American bison but commonly referred to as "buffalo," or "*qoʠáalx̣*," in Nimiipuutímt).[29] The Kiowa ceremonial could not be held without a buffalo, so as these animals vanished from the Plains during the 1880s, the Kiowa Sun Dances declined as well. No Kiowa Sun Dances were held in 1880, 1882, and 1884.[30] The June 1881 Kiowa dance, however, was delayed until August, when they finally located one buffalo bull. Then, when no buffalo responded to a medicine man's call in summer 1882, the dance was not held that year.[31] The next year, Joseph and forty prisoners from Oakland returned for the great Kiowa, Apache, and Wichita Sun Dances. The prisoners danced with Kiowa and Apaches at Semat P'a, then participated in the Kiowa ceremonials north of Rainy Mountain Creek.[32] At least four Kiowa calendar keepers memorialized the 1883 ceremonial as the "Nez Perce Sun Dance" (or, as Candace Greene notes, the "Nez Perce Come Again Kado").[33] The Anko calendar features a man at the Sun Dance pole who had cut his hair in the Nimiipuu style, and the *Set-t'an* calendar shows a man at the medicine lodge wearing the striped blanket and hairstyle preferred by Nimiipuu men.[34] In addition to these sources, Greene has since published the wonderfully detailed Silver Horn Kiowa calendar, while other Kiowa descendants have shared their personal calendars with art historian and Plateau specialist Steven L. Grafe.[35]

The Silver Horn calendar even documents a previously unknown Nimiipuu presence at Kiowa in 1882, even though no buffalo had answered the medicine man's prayers that year. That Nimiipuu visitor was marked by his particular hair style rather than identified by name, but Silver Horn displayed a carefully crafted ermine (a weasel that turns white in the winter) aligned along the back of his head. The handsome young man is not dancing, and the Sun Dance central pole is not prepared for the ceremony. His eyes are wide open, and his mouth is expectedly silent; he is not singing. He is proof, however, that the Nimiipuu were there that year, in expectation of the sacred dance. The next year, 1883, Silver Horn featured an Oakland Sun Dancer who did participate when that ceremonial was held. This is not the same man pictured in the 1882 calendar. He is older and larger; his mouth is open, singing; his body reflects movement, such as that in dance participation. The Sun Dance central pole is prepared for the ritual in this picture, and the man is fully engaged in the ceremonial.

We do know that the core group of dancers from Oakland consisted of about forty people, but we do not know all of their names. Two of the regular Sun Dancers who wore weasel-tail garments, however, were Joseph and his almost constant companion Yellow Bull. There certainly may have been other Nimiipuu, or Palus cocaptives, wearing weasel too. Like Joseph, some of these men had saved their sacred ceremonial regalia when almost everything else had been lost during the war. Joseph managed to retain at least one weasel-trimmed war shirt; we know this because he posed for a photograph wearing the shirt at Fort Keogh in 1877.[36] He was also seen wearing the shirt a few weeks later in Bismarck, Dakota Territory. As one newspaperman described Joseph's attire, "his dress was composed of a hunting shirt of buckskin profusely embroidered with blue, red, and white beads. On each shoulder was embroidered a square block of beads, resembling the epaulettes of an army officer and all around his shoulders and breast were pendant long white fur tassels, presenting an elegant appearance."[37] Cyrenius Hall even painted a portrait of Joseph wearing that shirt the next summer at the Fort Leavenworth prison camp.[38] As Steven L. Grafe advises, we don't really know what meaning Joseph (or other men) attached to the weasel tails other than that "they appeared within a Plateau-wide tradition of using ermine skins."[39] After examining the photograph of the shirt, Alan Marshall explains how the weasel and rabbit skins were composed in Joseph's shirt. "Those are ermine 'tails,' but not just the tail," said Marshall, of Joseph's shirt; "they are the tail plus a strip of the hide that ran from the tail to the head. Sometimes these were composites of various kinds." At other times, "they were the remaining flank strips with black fur from some other animal attached." They could also consist of a "strip of white fur from some animal, (e.g., a winter coated snowshoe hare) plus black fur from some animal," and "the black-tipped ear from a 'rabbit' or hare was [also] used for the tip."[40]

Another Exciting New Dimension

Candace Greene also recorded another previously ignored and exciting new dimension of the 1883 Kiowa dance's participation. According to the Kiowa man Little Bluff—whom Greene also studied—one of the dancers was someone who was not Nimiipuu but combed his hair like them. The mention by Little Bluff and the depiction of the dancer's hairstyle in the Silver Horn calendar complement the historical record. This dancer is not the man in the 1882 Silver Horn calendar, nor is he pictured in either the Anko or Set-t'an calendars. The man in this Silver Horn drawing wears an intricate plaited hairstyle, which may point to Húsus Kute.[41] Húsus Kute was a Dreamer Prophet.[42] That said, the hairstyle could also indicate a different Dreamer Prophet; there were several in the camp, including the man who became known as "Star Doctor." However, Star Doctor (also known as Pahalawasheschit, or "Old Man Star") ran away and was never recaptured, and the other unnamed man had an arm and a shoulder severely damaged by war that were not pictured or mentioned in the calendar.[43] The Kiowa descendants' family calendar reinforces the Silver Horn calendar while emphasizing a Nimiipuu participant. That family calendar, which was not in the public domain at the time of this study, also features weasel-tail identifiers for the Nimiipuu who participated in 1883.[44] Most important, though, the combined memories of these calendars reinforce the presence and participation of both Nimiipuu and Palus at the Kiowa Sun Dances.

Giveaways at most of the dances usually involved all of the participants or special guests such as the Nimiipuu, who received twenty-seven ponies at the Arapaho dance in 1882.[45] Power was acquired through what was given, and giveaways were always accompanied with feasts, honoring songs, and dances. As Kiowa descendants mentioned, some of the Nimiipuu were so poor they literally had nothing to share, so they sold or traded special songs during reciprocal gift exchanges.[46] And as musicologist Loran Olsen found, one elderly Nimiipuu lady also recognized buckskin songs probably brought home from Indian Territory.[47] Certain ceremonies, such as the Ponca Sun Dance, also involved accoutrements like sun-reflecting mirrors, whereas other Sun Dance ceremonials, including that of the Kiowa, did not allow mirrors.[48] Charley Moses (Sup-poon-mas) holds one of those mirrors in a photograph taken of him in Arkansas City sometime between 1879 and 1885.[49] This mirror may actually place him at the Ponca Sun Dance in June 1880, during which many mirrors "flashed" in the sun.[50] Like Joseph and Yellow Bull, Charley Moses was another Oakland teamster and a known Sun Dancer.

Federal Authorities Eradicate American Indian Spirituality

Meanwhile, the Indian Bureau was trying to stamp out religious ceremonies such as Sun Dance and all other "medicine dances." That policy became official on April 23, 1883, when Commissioner of Indian Affairs Hiram A. Price issued a new federal directive titled "Rules Governing the Court of Indian Offenses." Following the Secretary of Interior's instructions, the Fourth Article directed the "ultimate abolishment" of the "sun-dance," the "scalp-dance," the "war-dance," and "all other so-called feasts assimilating thereto." Any American Indian taking part in these ceremonies could be punished by having their food rations withheld for ten to fifteen days. If they continued to dance and participate, they faced federal jail or prison. "Giveaways" were also banished by the federal edict.[51] According to Mennonite missionary Samuel S. Haury, federal officials and Christian missionaries wanted the regulations at Cheyenne and Arapaho in order to "break up tribal connections." "A great drawback to these and other Indians, who perhaps wish to abandon their old ways in order to make a good start in life, are their medicine dances," Haury claimed. Haury thought the dances should not be prohibited by force, "as they are dear and sacred to [the Natives] . . . though barbarous." Haury proposed that Christianity and agricultural development replace the ceremonials of peoplehood.[52]

Indian Agent Daniel B. Dyer at the Cheyenne and Arapaho Agency, however, wanted the dances stopped. Yet Dyer did not deny that dance participants were taking part in a significant religious event: "A strange sight is their 'medicine dance' their bodies naked from the waist up. A number of braves enter the 'medicine lodge.' They gash their arms and legs, and pierce holes in their chests, pass ropes through the holes and suspend themselves from the center of the lodge until their struggling tears the flesh loose." "Each one has a whistle," continued Dyer, and "they dance night and day without food or water until exhausted . . . These 'medicines' are a record of terrible suffering, endured with indomitable heroism, which sometimes ends in death." Dyer concluded by stating he thought their sufferings should be directed to a "better cause."[53]

When Indian Agent John W. Scott told the Ponca that their Sun Dance would be banned in June 1884, the leaders immediately protested that other agents had allowed the ceremony. Scott admitted that he had received no direct instructions to ban the ceremonies, so he would not ban the dance that summer. He did, however, warn dance permit applicants that next year the Sun Dance was forbidden and that he would use force to stop it.[54] He also told federal officials, "These tribes are addicted to certain heathenish customs, which while they do not particularly interfere with their progress toward self-support . . . are nevertheless barbarous and reprehensible, and must be given up before they can be considered fairly on the road to the civilization and status of the white man. The sun-dance is one of these." "It is gradually, I think," concluded Scott, "losing its more revolting features and I hope to be able to suppress it entirely."[55]

The exiles had arrived among these Sun Dance communities at a critical moment in history, just four years before the "Rules Governing the Court of Indian Offenses" and the publication of the federal ban for these ceremonies of peoplehood.

Graveyards, Bells, and Augmented Nimiipuu Memories

This was certainly an extremely difficult period of captivity for the exiles, who were so far from their own summer ceremonies, vision quests, winter villages, and dances. The substitute Sun Dances and attendant social dances, feasts, and ceremonials did not replace the sacred ceremonies of their own peoplehood and homelands. But for many of the detainees who recognized ceremonies that echoed the old dances at Walla Walla, these ceremonials augmented their spiritual, ceremonial peoplehood. In the meantime, the exiles expressed their own ceremonial practices when possible, such as in their grave markers at the Oakland cemetery. As Reverend George Spining recalled, he met Chief Joseph one day in late October 1883; Joseph was seated on a horse, silently contemplating the grave of a "wild Indian." Marking that grave was a bell tied to a long, limber pole that swayed and rang in the autumnal winds.[56] This bell was, Roderick Sprague explains, one of the "physical paraphernalia of a religious practice" attributed to the Wanapum Dreamer Prophet Smohalla.[57]

Dancers from Oakland followed the Sun Dance ceremonial cycle from Ponca to Cheyenne and Arapaho, down to the Wichita, to the Comanche religious dances, and on to Kiowa. The timing of the summer dances was favorable for the exiles; in accordance with federal mandates, their gardens were planted and their teamster activities well underway, affording them intertribal communication and other unexpected freedoms. They owned wagons and serviceable horses, something they really had not had until they were leaving Quapaw. And they were not watched as closely by federal soldiers as they had been at Quapaw.[58] Also, the federal government and the agents had not yet stopped the dances. The dancers almost always included Joseph, Yellow Bull, Red Elk (Yellow Bull's brother), and Es-pow-yes (Light in the Mountain—Yellow Bull's uncle). Es-pow-yes was a warrior and buffalo hunter, one of the "brave men with swiftest horses [who] were always at the front in war movements." He was also related to Joseph. In fact, Es-pow-yes had vigorously argued against the October 1877 surrender; he had never trusted the generals' promises.[59] Other dancers included Nick-co-lo-clum, Tim-sus-sle-wit (Rose Bush), Tisca (Pole Cat); Wolf Head, Charley Moses (Sup-poon-mas), Feathers around the Neck, Henry Rivers, Yellow Head, Húsus Kute, Three Eagles, Thomas Peters, Red Wolf, Crow Blanket, Captain Jack, Yellow Bear and Tuk-te-tna-tu-kayet. Even James Reuben, a Christian Nimiipuu schoolteacher from Idaho, joined the Cheyenne and Arapaho dances with Cyrus M. Scott in July 1882. Other men in that group were Tom Hill (a newly professed Christian), Wolf Head, Captain Jack, Yellow Bear, Jay Gould, Daniel Jefferson, Mat Whitfield, and Owhi—a Yakama cocaptive. Several of these men, such as Yellow Bear and even Húsus Kute, eventually converted to Christianity at Oakland; others did not. And as Cyrus Scott mentioned, they may have helped him spy for the governor. Scott did admit that he used Yellow Bull and Joseph to keep him informed of circumstances at the Cheyenne and Arapaho agency; this apparently concerned thefts of horses and dogs near the agency. Meanwhile, everyone hoped for peace with the Cheyenne.[60]

There were dances at Cheyenne and Arapaho in 1884, but the big Sun Dance at Kiowa was not held that year—they could find no buffalo.[61] At

Cheyenne and Arapaho, agent Dyer ranted against members of the Cheyenne Dog Soldier Society. Dyer hated the Dog Soldiers, who destroyed tipis, chickens, hogs, cattle, and crops of any Cheyenne who would not join the sacred peoplehood of summer dances.[62] These men, he said, ruled "with an iron hand"; in other words, they resisted federal policies of spiritual annihilation. The Kiowa Sun Dance of 1885 had been possible only because they had found one lone buffalo far out on the Staked Plains. Even then, the agent had hoped the dance would not be held following the death of the old spiritual leader who had usually conducted the dance. To the agent's dismay, a younger man came forward, and the ceremony was held.[63]

Some of the Oakland exiles may have joined the 1884 summer dances at Cheyenne and Arapaho, but, as mentioned, there was no Kiowa Sun Dance that year. Chances are that Joseph and Yellow Bull did not participate at Cheyenne, because federal officials had just announced that they would be returned to the Northwest that fall. Once that news was made public, the prisoners were preoccupied with leaving.[64] Meanwhile, excitement permeated Oakland. Governors, generals, Secretary of War Robert Lincoln, Secretary of Interior Lucius Q. C. Lamar, U.S. Indian Agents, Commissioners of Indian Affairs, Presbyterian officials and missionaries, and citizens had been arguing for years about what to do with the prisoners. Keep them all in Indian Territory? Send Joseph's people to the Colville Agency, Washington Territory, and welcome the Christians home to Lapwai, Idaho? Even Alfred Meacham, who claimed to be their friend and supporter, had advocated that the Nimiipuu must remain in Indian Territory. He blamed this on Joseph's peoplehood and religious theologies. Meacham felt that "Joseph's religious belief[s] and habits are opposed to locating. He must be made to understand that he is to settle down and go to work. His peculiar views upon religious matters are great obstacles to his civilization."[65] Meacham preached that the misfortunes that had befallen the Nimiipuu "will prove a blessing to them. . . . Had they remained in the Valley of the Winding Water [Wallowa], they being rich and proud, would have continued their old life until their brethren had outstripped them . . . [they] are now cut off from their old associations." Meacham's point of view mirrored basic Indian Bureau assimilationist policies: "the Nez Perces seem to be falling in line with other Indians and putting on working dress."[66] Meacham also represented the overwhelmingly pro-Christian theology pursued by the federal government, General Oliver O. Howard, and many other influential Americans. They detested the Dreamers and blamed them for the Nez Perce war, Nimiipuu resistance, and the earth-centric revitalization theologies that many of the exiles professed. "Smo-heller," [Smohalla, the Wanapum Dreamer Prophet] said Meacham, "is a freeborn man, a religious bigot . . . and the most difficult to manage."[67] Or, as Oliver O. Howard put it, the war had "needed prolonged, persistent pursuit and final capture to put to rest forever the vain hopes of these dreaming superstitious nomads."[68]

"Going Home," New Realities

Federal authorities finally appropriated twenty thousand dollars to cover relocation costs in June 1884. The exiles really were going to leave Indian Territory. Then came the dreadful news: Joseph's people would be sent to Colville, Washington Territory, and the Christians would be going home to Lapwai, Idaho. Joseph, Yellow Bull, and Indian Agent John Scott attended a mass meeting in mid-September to try to amend that decision.[69] Colville was no place of their peoplehood. They shared no sacred histories, language, or ceremonial traditions with that place. And again, they wanted to remain together. Then, in November, another disappointment: no one would be sent west until next spring.[70] The summer Indian Territory ceremonials had ended, and the prisoners would settle in for another winter of captivity.

Following a long, cold winter, agonies of expectation, and more federal promises, meetings, and dreams of home, 268 survivors were finally shipped west from Arkansas City, Kansas, on May 22, 1885. Five days later, when their train stopped at Wallula Junction, Washington Territory, federal authorities separated the exiles.[71] Yellow Wolf, a young warrior who had survived the prison camps, never forgot the day when the interpreter asked them, "Where do you want to go? Lapwai and be a Christian, or Colville and just be yourself?"[72] As Major C. T. Stranahan, former superintendent of the Nez Perce Indian Agency, confirmed that Yellow Wolf was absolutely correct when Stranahan himself had complained that "residence on the Nez Perce Reservation by the returned exiles could be had only by a declared abrogation of their Dreamer religion tenets."[73] At Colville, Washington Territory, 150 refugees continued in exile; 118 former prisoners were released to the reservation at Lapwai, Idaho.[74] Eleven of the known Sun Dancers went to Lapwai, and nine other Sun Dancers went to Colville.[75] The exiles had gone before the Indian Territory Sun Dances were held that summer.

Within weeks of their return to Lapwai, 80 of the 118 returnees officially joined the Presbyterian Church.[76] Yellow Bull, who had gone to Colville, would take an allotment at Red Rock Spring, Idaho, in 1891, the artesian well that was the place of his peoplehood.[77] "The strongest water," reports Alan Marshall, the "purest and most efficacious water, is found at water sources. So, water from springs and fountains is most highly regarded."[78] The sacred spring figured prominently in Yellow Bull's "vision"; dreams of the spring had comforted him when Yellow Bull was suffering from malaria while in Indian Territory. Yellow Bull remained at his home at Red Rock Spring until his death in 1919.[79] He is buried in the Lapwai Mission Cemetery in Spalding, Idaho.[80] As for the teamster Húsus Kute, the Sun Dancing Palus prophet who had gone to Lapwai as a Christian, he transferred to Colville to live the rest of his life near his old companion, Chief Joseph. Húsus Kute is buried on the Colville Reservation in Washington State.[81]

The Indian Territory "Medicine Dances"

In spite of the new federal ban, the sacred "medicine dances" in the Indian Territory continued whenever possible. Agent Dyer admitted the dances were sacred ceremonials, but he favored Christianity and wanted to stop all of the dances in 1885.[82] The next summer, Captain J. M. Lee of the U.S. Army, who was now agent at Cheyenne and Arapaho, asked both groups to delay their ceremonies until their crops had been harvested. Missionary Henry R. Voth supported this, reporting that the postponed dances attracted far fewer participants—between twelve and twenty young men—and that the truncated ceremonies had been of "short duration." The former ceremonies had often attracted between seventy-five to a hundred participants.[83] The situation was also difficult at Ponca. Indian Agent E. C. Osborne cared little about Ponca spirituality and took advantage of a difficult circumstance to stop the Sun Dance that year: the Ponca were extremely hungry. "They had run pretty short of provisions," wrote Osborn to Commissioner of Indian Affairs J. D. C. Atkins, and the "offer you made them of a feast in lieu of the dance, was too tempting to be rejected."[84] Two Ponca men literally came to blows over the lost ceremonial, one of whom suffered a broken arm. As Osborne watched a doctor set the injured arm, the extremely unhappy patient said that the "exchange of the sun-dance for the feast" had caused it all.[85] The Indian agent at the Kiowa, Wichita, and Comanche Agency thus reported that there was no Sun Dance at Kiowa that year, in 1886.[86]

Then, in 1887, the Kiowa found a temporary solution to the lack of buffalo. They purchased a buffalo from Charles Goodnight, a north-Texas rancher who knew many of the Kiowa and kept a small herd of domesticated buffalo. Anko did not mark that dance on his calendar; it was held more privately at the mouth of Oak Creek.[87] That sacrificed buffalo's sacred-peoplehood history lives on. Goodnight's herd became one of five foundational buffalo herds in the United States and Canada, and it was used to help repopulate Yellowstone National Park, the National Bison Ranges, Canada's National Parks, and the New York Zoological Society. In 1996, the owners of the JA Ranch donated the ancestral herd to the Texas Parks and Wildlife Department; the animals now roam the Caprock Canyons area. They and their ancestor's spirit remain in their aboriginal homelands.[88]

At Colville, 1890 marked the beginning of five difficult years of continued exile for the non-Christians. The Nimiipuu had not been welcomed by other groups.[89] Nor was Joseph especially popular with the federal agents. One agent in particular, Albert M. Anderson, found Joseph's attachment to his peoplehood particularly offensive. As Anderson said, "Chief Joseph himself is not in any way a progressive Indian . . . he is hostile to civilization, and he and his handful of warriors are the most backward of all the tribes on the Colville reservation." Anderson continued, "The Nez Perce are nonprogressive in their present state, immoral in their habits, and filthy in their customs."[90] While Joseph seemed pleasant in person, Anderson also thought he was highly overrated.[91]

The exiles were lonely. When they received letters or visitors from Lapwai, many became especially sad and longed for home.[92] This grief lasted for generations, as mentioned by the Palus descendant Andrew George, who was interviewed by Cliff Trafzer in 1980. George knew very little about his family's exile to Indian Territory because his mother and grandmother could never discuss those years. The experience was just too painful for them to relive.[93]

Meanwhile, Agency physician Edward Latham erroneously reported to federal authorities that the exiles practiced no religion.[94] Agent George H. Newman echoed this, saying that the Nimiipuu did not observe "any religious creed."[95] But the Nimiipuu did possess a deep spirituality and the sacred ceremonials of their peoplehood. The exiles, still considered American prisoners of war as reported by Professor Edmond Meany in 1901, celebrated their peoplehood whenever possible.[96] For instance, when Meany interviewed Joseph the week of June 21, 1901, Joseph still preferred living in his tipi, not far from the "Indian burial ground." And there, just as the exiles had done at Oakland, the graves were marked by "poles set in the ground with bells or feathers ornamenting the tops." Only now, as the bells sounded in this place of continued exile, it was Joseph who conducted all of the funerals.[97] As Meany learned, everyone "show[s] their respect for Chief Joseph by according him, without any questioning, the principal place of honor on all great celebrations or ceremonies."[98]

Joseph spent the rest of his life seeking the return of the Wallowa Valley homelands. In a letter dictated through an interpreter, Joseph told Professor Meany, "My old home is in the Wallowa Valley and I want to go back there to live. My father and mother are buried there. If the Government would only give me a small piece of land for my people in the Wallowa Valley, with a teacher, that is all I would ask."[99] This was made in the wake of Joseph's catastrophic visit to Wallowa the previous June, in 1900. Following several trips to Washington DC to lobby for a Wallowa Valley reservation, Joseph had been permitted to visit Wallowa and seek local approval for a federal reservation. Unfortunately, that would be Joseph's last visit to the place of his peoplehood, because citizen–settlers told him not to come back ever again.[100] Joseph restated his Wallowa Valley appeal on November 20, 1903, when he addressed the Washington State Historical Society in Seattle. "Today," he said through the interpreter, "'my heart is way off from here, far away . . . Today I would like to be back in my old home in Wallowa Valley. All my friends are there. My father is buried there. Some of my children are buried there." Joseph continued, "My only hope . . . in [my] declining years is that I may go home and die among my friends."[101]

Ten months later, Joseph was dead. He was said to have died of a broken heart, seated by the fire in front of his tipi.[102] The following June, in 1905, his old compatriots Yellow Bull and Es-pow-yes were central participants in the memorial service and dedication of a monument that officially honoring honored Chief Joseph at Colville, where he is buried. Both men were adorned with weasel-tail ornaments on their regalia.[103]

Peoplehood—Never Abandoned

In conclusion, the old exiles never abandoned their peoplehood. Regardless of the fact that Yellow Bull and others had learned to speak a little English, they relied on their aboriginal language, and Joseph always used an interpreter. They had survived a captivity that is now part of their sacred peoplehood history. Even during continued exile, no matter how sad they were, they never forgot the surrender accord and the United States' duplicity regarding that sacred agreement. Today, the Wallowa Band descendants are rehabilitating and reestablishing their presence in the Wallowa Valley homelands of their peoplehood.[104] As Trevor Bond reports in his doctoral dissertation, the Trust for Public Lands returned 10,300 acres of the Wallowa Valley to the Nez Perce in 1996. Not long after that, the Bonneville Power Administration purchased another 6,200 acres in Wallowa Valley for the Nez Perce, an amount vital to "restoration[s]" of Nez Perce peoplehood.[105]

In the face of incredible odds, the exiles never forgot their sacred homelands. Yellow Bull lived, and died, near his sacred spring. Joseph always knew that he truly belonged in his sacred homeland even though the citizens there had chased him away. He longed to be with his relatives in the Wallowa Valley. The exiles had celebrated their sacred spirituality and ceremonialism, participating in other, somewhat familiar ceremonies such as Sun Dances while in prison camps that limited their personal and religious freedoms. And in the end, Yellow Bull and Es-pow-yes prayed for their old friend at the Chief Joseph Memorial, clad in the sacred weasel-tail regalia that only they, in their peoplehood, truly understood.

The exiles' descendants never forgot their forebears' contributions to Nimiipuu peoplehood. In 1948—four decades after Joseph's passing, twenty-nine years after Yellow Bull's, and thirteen years after Yellow Wolf's—Agency Superintendent Archie Phinney and Tribal Secretary Joseph Blackeagle reiterated Joseph's peoplehood: "We know from Joseph's own recorded statements that he never gave up the Wallowa in his homelands." "This may be well understood," continued Phinney, "from his promise to Old Joseph, his father, never to give up the Wallowa." Blackeagle added that Joseph was forced onto a reservation "not of his choice and exiled to a country to which he had to adapt himself, much against his desires and wishes."[106] Both men also understood that the mistreatment of the exiles must remain a matter of public consciousness. Blackeagle repeated this position a year later on another occasion that was, again, hosted by Phinney. "The treaty of 1863 limited the Nez Perces to a specific area of the Columbia basin," said Blackeagle, "but Chief Joseph was no party to the agreement. Consequently, the Indian war of 1877 developed and resulted in the exiling of Chief Joseph to the Colville reservation."[107]

Despite everything, the old exiles never abandoned their peoplehood. And the Nimiipuu have not lost these sacred memories either.

NOTES

1. Marshall, "Review of *The Nez Perces*," 324.
2. James M. Haworth, Special Agent, "Report," June 25, 1879, NPS, NARA, RG75, LROIA, Quapaw Agency, Indian Territory, Lewiston ID; see also Pearson, *Nez Perces*, 145, 149, 166.
3. "Land Laws, June 5, 1872. No. 71, An Act–4th Article, Treaty of February 23, 1867, with Seneca, Shawnee, Quapaw, and other Indians," in *Public Land Laws Passed by Congress from March 4, 1869 to March 3, 1875* (Washington DC: Henry Norris Copp, General Land Office, 1875), 124; J. F. McDowell, "Quapaw Lands Being Opened for Settlement." *Baxter Springs Times* (Baxter Springs KS), May 1, 1879.
4. Spears, "Boomers of the West," 850–54.
5. James M. Haworth, "Report to Commissioner of Indian Affairs, Ezra A. Hayt, Quapaw Agency, removal to Nez Perce, Ponca Agency, Indian Territory, Statistics, population, dress, agriculture, schools," *ARCIA* (1879), 244. "The Ponca Agency," June 25, 1879,

LROIA, Quapaw Agency, NPS, Lewiston. The total population had dropped to 370 by August 1879, then to 344 the next year, and to 328 by August 1881. "Nez Perce, Ponca Agency, Indian Territory, Statistics, Population, Dress, Agriculture, Schools," *ARCIA* (1879), 232; "Nez Perce, Ponca Agency, Indian Territory, Statistics, Population, etc.," *ARCIA* (1880), 244; "Table of Statistics Regarding Population, Religion, and Education, Nez Perces, Ponca Agency, Indian Territory," *ARCIA*, H. Ex. Doc. 1 (47-1) serial set vol. 2018, 1881, p. 336, CIS, Washington DC.

6. Pearson, "Building Reservation Economies," 706.

7. See chapter 2 of this volume.

8. Bland, "Visit to the Indian," 133.

9. See Robert K. Thomas's peoplehood model of identity in chapter 2 of this volume.

10. Meacham, "Chief Joseph, the Nez Perce," 145–46.

11. Chief Joseph, dictated letter, "Appeal to CIA, to visit Washington, D. C. to meet with the President," June 4, 1881, LROIA Ponca Agency, doc. 9711, NARA, Washington DC.

12. Pearson, "Numipu Narratives," 39–40.

13. Pearson, "Developing Reservation Economies," 153–54.

14. John D. Miles, "Cheyenne and Arapaho Agency, Indian Territory, Annual Report," *ARCIA* (1878), 54; William H. Whiteman, "Ponca Agency, Annual Report," *ARCIA* (1879), 65; "Kiowa Population Statistics," *ARCIA* (1878), 285; "Pawnee Population Statistics," *ARCIA* (1879), 285–86; "Comanche Population Statistics," *ARCIA* (1879), 285–86; "Nez Perce Population Statistics," *ARCIA* (1879), 285–86.

15. "Nez Perce Going to Wichita, Freighting," *Arkansas City Traveler* (Arkansas City KS), November 19, 1879; Pearson, *Nez Perces*, 164–76.

16. "Indians in Town Last Week," *Arkansas City Traveler* (Arkansas City KS), July 21, 1880.

17. See chapter 1 of this volume.

18. Llewellyn E. Woodin, *December 31, 1883 Teamster Paychecks*, February 26, 1884, PA13, OHSAD, Oklahoma City.

19. William Whiting, "Permission to visit Cheyenne and Arapaho Agency for 15 Days," January 22, 1881, Archives Division, Oklahoma Historical Society, OHSAD, Oklahoma City; Cyrus M. Scott, "Territory News by C. M. Scott," *Winfield Courier* (Winfield KS), June 30, 1881.

20. Holm, *Great Confusion*, 34–35.

21. Dorsey, *Ponca Sun Dance*, 86–87.

22. Cyrus M. Scott, "Scouting for Governor of Kansas in Indian Territory; Nez Perce Assist Captain Scott in 1882," in Wortman, Wortman, and Bottorff, *History of Cowley County*, 48, 49.

23. Nathan Hughes, "Trip with Joseph Sherburne to See the Nez Perce Wagon Train," *Arkansas City Traveler* (Arkansas City KS), June 18, 1878.

24. The last prophet, Puck Hyah Toot, in Relander, *Drummers and Dreamers*, 153.

25. Spier, "Sun Dance," 459n8.

26. Walker, *Conflict and Schism*, 36, 38.

27. Wilson Wewa, R. Buck, R, Andrews A., and Slockish, S., "Washaat Religion of the Columbia Plateau," seminar notes, September 29, 2004, Washington State University, Pullman.

28. Hunt and Nye, "Annual Sun Dance," 340, 342, 346; Conlon, "Dance, American Indian," 2009; James Mooney, *Cheyenne Indians*, 403, 418; Donald J. Berthrong, *Cheyenne and Arapaho Ordeal*, 100, 81; B. Bonnerjea, "Reminiscences of a Cheyenne Indian, " 141; Spier, "Sun Dance," 453, 459, 460, 461, 477, 481–503.

29. See chapter 1 of this volume for Nimiipuu information on buffalo.

30. P. B. Hunt, "Kiowa, Comanche and Wichita Agency, Anadarko, Indian Territory, Annual Report, August 28, 1884," *ARCIA* (1884), 79.

31. Mooney, "Nez Perce Sun Dance," 256, 295, 344–47, 249, 352.

32. Mooney, "Nez Perce Sun Dance," 351, 154; Harrington, "Vocabulary of the Kiowa," 1; Pearson, *Nez Perces*, 238–44.

33. Greene, *One Hundred Summers*, 115.

34. Mooney, "Nez Perce Sun Dance," 351.

35. See Greene, *Silver Horn*. H Steve L. Grafe, personal communication with the author, September 2, 2004. Steve was director of American Indian Collections at the Cowboy and Western Museum in Norman, Oklahoma, when he shared this information with me.

36. Theodore Brasser, "Chief Joseph (1840–1904): Chief Joseph's War Shirt (circa 1877)," *The Coeur d'Alene Art Auction, Fine Western and American Art*, Coeur d'Alene ID: The Coeur d'Alene Art Auction, 2012, 130, http://cdaartauction.com/2012/lot/17359.

37. "Chief Joseph; the Captured Nez Perces Banqueted at Bismarck, the Walk and Appearance of Joseph to Pass Through St. Paul Tomorrow en route to Fort Leavenworth," *St. Paul Dispatch* (Saint Paul MN), November 23, 1877.

38. Tim Thorn, "Chief Joseph's War Shirt." Friends of Bear Paw, Big Hole, and Canyon Creek Battlefields, accessed March 30, 2016, http://www.friendsnezpercebattlefields .org/chief-joseph-s-war-shirt. In 1968 the U.S. Postal Department featured Hall's painting of Joseph wearing that shirt on a six-cent postage stamp.

39. Steven L. Grafe, personal communication with the author, April 22, 2016.

40. Alan G. Marshall, personal communication with the author, March 30, 2016.

41. Greene, *One Hundred Summers*, 115.

42. Trafzer, *Chief Joseph's Allies*, 7.

43. Relander, *Drummers and Dreamers*, 105. Star Doctor, also known as Pahalawasheschit, was in the prison camp for some time, but he eventually ran away. Another unnamed elderly Dreamer Prophet was also in the prison camp, but he had a permanently injured arm and shoulder, which is not displayed in these calendars.

44. Steven L Grafe, personal communication with the author, September 2, 2004.

45. Wortman, Wortman, and Bottorff, *History of Cowley County*, 194.

46. Steven L. Grafe. personal communication with the author, December 14, 2004.

47. Olsen, *Legacy from Sam Morris*, item 26.

48. George A. Dorsey, *Ponca Sun Dance*, 30; Mooney, "Nez Perce Sun Dance," 256.

49. Joseph H. Sherburne to Lucullus V. McWhorter, May 9, 1927, folder 255, McWhorter Collection, Special Collections Library, Washington State University, Pullman WA. See also photograph of Sup-poon-mas in Pearson, *Nez Perce*, 111.

50. "Ponca Sun Dance," *Arkansas City Traveler* (Arkansas City KS), June 2, 1880.

51. Hiram A. Price, *Rules Governing the Court of Indian Offenses*, April 10, 1883, 4, 5, Office of Indian Affairs, Department of the Interior, Washington DC; Daily, *Battle for the BIA*, 38.

52. Samuel S. Haury, "Cheyenne and Arapaho Agency, Darlington, Indian Territory, Annual Report," August 9, 1884, *ARCIA* (1884), 78.

53. Daniel B. Dyer, "Cheyenne and Arapaho Agency, Indian Territory, Darlington, Indian Territory, Annual Report," August 9, 1884, *ARCIA* (1884), 72, 73.

54. John W. Scott, *Ponca Sun Dance Banned by Ponca Agent*, June 6, 1884. Letters and documents concerning Nez Perce tribal and Individual Indian affairs, Pawnee, Ponca, Otoe, and Oakland Agency, Indian Territory, PA13, OHSAD, Oklahoma City.

55. John W. Scott, "Ponca, Pawnee, Otoe Agency, Indian Territory," August 15, 1884. *ARCIA* (1884), 85.

56. Reverend George L. Spining, "The Unhappy Nez Perces; Indians Confined on an Unhealthy Reservation," *New York Times*, October 29, 1883, 2; Pearson, *Nez Perces*, 162.

57. Sprague, *Aboriginal Burial Practices*, 218.

58. Grant Foreman, "Interview, Mrs. Emily Easeworth, Commerce, Oklahoma," Indian Pioneer History Collection, W. P. A. Project S. 149.

59. McWhorter, *Yellow Wolf*, 166, 223; McWhorter, *Hear Me, My Chiefs*, 216.

60. Cyrus M. Scott, "Scouting for Governor," 48–49.

61. Mooney, *Calendar History*, 352.

62. D. B. Dyer, "Cheyenne and Arapaho Agency," 71.

63. Mooney, "Nez Perce Sun Dance," 353, 354

64. "Nez Perce Eager to Leave," June 6, 1884, Letters and Documents Concerning Nez Perce Tribal and Individual Indian Affairs, Pawnee, Ponca, Otoe, and Oakland Agency, Indian Territory, PA13, OHSAD, Oklahoma City.

65. Meacham, "Nez Perces Joseph," 104, 105.

66. Meacham, "Nez Perces," 108.

67. Meacham, "Another Cloud Gathering," 82.

68. Oliver O. Howard, quoted in "General Howard: A Grand Public Reception Tendered the Gallant Officer on the Occasion of His Return to Portland," *Oregonian* (Portland OR), November 13, 1877. Howard also praised the beautiful new country now available for settlement, the advances of non-Native civilization, and the wonders of Mormon and other settlers entering the former Nimiipuu homelands: "We found no more beautiful and productive country than is afforded to your own the Willamette of Oregon, the Walla Walla of Washington, and the Camas Prairie lands near Mount Idaho."

69. "Appropriation for Removal of Nez Perce to Idaho," *Arkansas City Traveler* (Arkansas City KS), June 25, 1884; George L. Deffenbaugh, "Nez Perce Agency, Idaho, Annual Report," August 20, 1884, *ARCIA* (1884), 69–70; John W. Scott, "Permission from Commissioner of Indian Affairs to Convene a Board of Survey at Oakland Reservation; Value and Condition of Public Property," June 2, 1884, PA13, OHSAD, Oklahoma City; "Nez Perce Eager to Leave," June 6, 1884, Letters and Documents Concerning Nez Perce Tribal and Individual Indian Affairs, Pawnee, Ponca, Otoe, and Oakland Agency, Indian Territory, PA13, OHSAD, Oklahoma City; John W. Scott, "To Hon. H. Price, Commissioner of Indian Affairs, Nez Perce Very Excited about Going Home, James Reuben Has Visited Them," June 30, 1884, PA13, OHSAD, Oklahoma City; John W. Scott, "To Hon. H. Price, C. I. A., explains 'Colville' to Chief Joseph's Band," September 18, 1884, PA13, OHSAD, Oklahoma City; Brown, *Flight of the Nez Perce*, 429, 430.

70. John W. Scott, "Report, to H. Price, CIA, Nez Perce Very Disappointed Not Going to Old Home This Fall," November 1, 1884, PA13, OHSAD, Oklahoma City.

71. W. H. Faulkner, "Report, to the Honorable Commissioner of Indian Affairs, Nez Perce Removal to Lapwai and Colville," June 24, 1885, letter 14242-1885, RG75, LROIA, NARA, Washington DC; Pearson, *Nez Perces*, 283–87, 289.

72. McWhorter, *Yellow Wolf, His Own Story*, 290.

73. "Statement, Mr. G. D. Fleming, Clerk at Nez Perce Indian Agency, Idaho." In Yellow Wolf, *His Own Story*, 291–92.

74. Charles Monteith, "Nez Perce Agency, Idaho, Annual Report," *ARCIA* (1885), 71; Sidney D. Waters, "Nez Perce, Joseph's Band, Colville Agency, Washington, Annual Report," *ARCIA* (1885), 185, 186.

75. "Issues to Indians, Nez Perce, Oakland, IT," NARA, Washington DC: RG75; "1885 Census," Ethnic Studies Library, University of California, Berkeley; "June 30, 1885 Census, Nez Perce of Josephs Band, Colville Indian Agency, WT," NARA, RG75, Indian Census Rolls, 1885–1940, reel 49.

76. G. L. Deffenbaugh, "Nez Perce, Idaho, Annual Report." *ARCIA* (1885), 73.

77. Sue McBeth, in *Nez Perces since Lewis and Clark*, ed. Iverson and James, 97.

78. Marshall, "Fish, Water," 771.

79. Unidentified newspaper clipping, July 24, 1919, Willis and Marilyn Kimble Northwest History Data Base, Washington State University Digital Collections, http://content.libraries.wsu.edu/cdm/singleitem/collection/clipping/id/9892/rec/7. Yellow Bull died at his home in Red Rock Springs. The date was handwritten on the newspaper notice; Yellow Bull's burial headstone says "1920."

80. For Yellow Bull's headstone, photograph, and burial data, see "Chief Yellow Bull," Find a Grave, accessed April 23, 2016, http://www.findagrave.com/cgi-bin/fg.cgi?page=gr&GRid=54375477.

81. Trafzer, *Chief Joseph's Allies*, 40.

82. D. B. Dyer, "Cheyenne and Arapaho Agency, Annual Report," July 21, 1885, *ARCIA* (1885), 79.

83. J. M. Lee, "Cheyenne and Arapaho Agency, Annual Report," *ARCIA* (1886), 119; H. R. Voth, "Cheyenne and Arapaho Agency, Indian Territory, Annual Report," *ARCIA* (1886), 125.

84. E. C. Osborne, "Ponca, Pawnee, Otoe, and Oakland Agency, IT, Annual Report," September 10, 1886, *ARCIA*, (1886), 336.

85. Osborne, "Ponca," 136.

86. J. Lee Hall, "Kiowa, Wichita, and Comanche Agency, Annual Report. Anadarko, Indian Territory," August 26, 1886, *ARCIA* (1886), 131.

87. Mooney, "Nez Perce Sun Dance," 355.

88. David Bowser, "Last Free-Roaming Buffalo Herd in Texas Now behind Stout Fence; Internet Edition," *Livestock Weekly*, accessed April 4, 2016, http://www.livestockweekly.com/papers/99/05/27/whlbuffalo.asp. See also Russell Roe, "At Home on the Range Again," Texas Parks and Wildlife (website), March 2011, http://www.tpwmagazine.com/archive/2011/mar/ed_2/index.phtml.

89. Benjamin P. Moore, "Colville Agency, Washington, Annual Report," August 12, 1886, *ARCIA* (1886), 232, 234; R. D. Gwydir, "Colville Agency, Washington, Annual Report, Joseph's Band," *ARCIA* (1887), 206, 208.

90. Albert M. Anderson, "Colville Agency, Washington, Annual Report," *ARCIA* (1899), 354.

91. Anderson, "Colville Agency, Washington," 355.

92. Hal J. Cole, "Colville Agency, Washington, Annual Report," August 11, 1890, *ARCIA* (1890), 217.

93. Trafzer, *Chief Joseph's Allies*, 27. According to Trafzer and federal records, Andrew George's mother's name was "Ipnouw Sietsanm" and his grandmother's name was "Ananemart"; his grandfather and one of George's uncle had also been captives in Indian Territory.

94. Hal J. Cole, "Colville Agency, Washington, Annual Report," August 26, 1892, *ARCIA* (1892), 487; E. H. Latham, "Colville Agency, Washington, Physician's Annual Report," July 15, 1892, *ARCIA* (1892), 493.

95. George H. Newman, "Colville Agency, Washington, Annual Report," *ARCIA* (1896), 312.

96. Meany, "Chief Joseph," 45.

97. Meany, "Chief Joseph," 48.

98. Meany, "Chief Joseph," 49.

99. Meany, "Chief Joseph," 52.

100. McLaughlin, *My Friend the Indian*, 344, 346, 366.

101. Alan J. Stein, "Chief Joseph Watches a University of Washington Football Game and Gives a Speech in Seattle on November 20, 1903," January 01, 2013, essay 10286, HistoryLink.org, accessed April 15, 2016, http://www.historylink.org/index.cfm?DisplayPage=output.cfm&file_id=10286.

102. Josephy, *Nez Perce Indians*, 462.

103. Grafe, *Peoples of the Plateau*, 174.

104. "The Wallowa Band of Nimi'ipuu Return Home," *Indigenous Religious Traditions*, Indigenous Religious Traditions, Religion Department, Colorado College, accessed

September 19, 2017, http://sites.coloradocollege.edu/indigenoustraditions/sacred
-lands/3300-2/the-wallowa-band-of-nimiipuu-return-home/.

105. Bond, "Why Should We Have," 134, 135.
106. Archie Phinney and Joseph Blackeagle, "Indian Leaders Rap Criticisms on Moving
Body," *Spokane Daily Chronicle* (Spokane WA), March 9, 1948, 4.
107. Joseph Blackeagle, "Indians Assist in Anniversary," *Spokane Daily Chronicle* (Spokane
WA), March 4, 1949, 3b.

BIBLIOGRAPHY

ARCHIVAL SOURCES

American Indian Correspondence, letter 1, box D. Presbyterian Historical Society, Phil-
adelphia PA.
Annual Reports of the Department of the Interior. 58th Cong., 3rd sess., H.R. Doc. 5, pts.
1–2. serial set vol. 4798 (1903–4). CIS, Washington DC.
Census, Nez Perces of Joseph's Band, Colville Indian Agency, W T. Indian Census Rolls,
1885–1940, reel 49 (1885). NARA, Washington DC.
"Estimates, Removal of the Nez Perces from the Indian Territory." 48th Cong., 2nd sess.,
H.R. Ex. Doc. 88, serial set vol. 2302 (January 14, 1885). CIS, Washington DC.
"Leases of Land in the Indian Territory, Congress, Committee on Indian Affairs,
Hearings and Reports". 46–49th Congr. S. Doc (1880–86), microfilm reel 11,
Washington DC.
"Letters and Documents Concerning Nez Perce Tribal and Individual Indian Affairs." Vols.
PA13–14. Pawnee, Ponca, Otoe and Oakland Agency, Indian Territory, OHSAD, Okla-
homa City.
"Letters and Documents Concerning Nez Perce Tribal and Individual Indian Affairs." Vol.
QA4. Quapaw Agency, Indian Territory. OHSAD, Oklahoma City.
"Letters Received, Office of Indian Affairs, 1824–81." Quapaw Agency, Indian Territory,
1871–80. Reel 708, microfilm 1–4995, RG75, NARA, Washington DC.
"Letters Received, Office of Indian Affairs, Ponca Agency." Files 1881/9711, 1881/1452,
1881/9711, 1882-17594; box 98, files 1883-6796, 1885-11472. RG75, NARA, Washington DC.
Lucullus McWhorter Papers. Special Collections, Washington State University, Pullman.
"Memorial from Joseph's band of Nez Perce Indians, relating to claims for compensation
for lands in the Indian (now Oklahoma) Territory, and to other claims." 57th Cong.,
1st sess., S. Doc. 311 at 1–6, serial set vol. 4241. CIS, Washington DC.
"Memorial of the Nez Perce Indians residing in Idaho." 62nd Cong., 1st sess., S. Doc. 97,
serial set vols. 6108 (July 17, 1911). CIS, Washington DC.
"Nez Perce War File." Reel 340, microfilm 666, RG94, Records of the Adjutant General's
Office, NARA, Washington DC.
"Testimony Taken by the Subcommittee on Territories.". 45th Cong., 3rd sess., Report to
Accompany Bill S. 1802, S. Rep. 744, serial set vol. 1839 (November 17, 1878). CIS,
Washington DC.

Testimony Taken by the Joint Committee Appointed to Take into Consideration the Expediency of Transferring the Indian Bureau to the War Department. 45th Cong., 3rd sess., S. Misc. Doc. 53, serial set vol. 1835: 77–86 (1879). CIS, Washington DC.

PUBLISHED WORKS

Berthrong, Donald J. *The Cheyenne and Arapaho Ordeal: Reservation and Agency Life in the Indian Territory, 1875–1907.* University of Oklahoma Press, Norman OK, 1992.

Bland, Cora M. "Visit to the Indian Territory; Nez Perces." *Council Fire* 2, no. 9 (September 1879): 133.

Bond, Trevor James. "Why Should We Have to Buy Our Own Things Back? The Struggle over the Spalding-Allen Collection." PhD diss., Washington State University, Pullman.

Bonnerjea, Biren. "Reminiscences of a Cheyenne Indian." *Journal de la Société des américanistes*, n.s., vol. 27, no. 1 (1935), pp. 129–143.

Bowser, David. "Last Free-Roaming Buffalo Herd in Texas Now behind Stout Fence," *Livestock Weekly* (Internet edition), accessed April 4, 2016, http://www.livestockweekly.com/papers/99/05/27/whlbuffalo.asp.

Brown, Mark H. *The Flight of the Nez Perce.* New York. G. P. Putnam's Sons, 1967.

Conlon, Paula. "Dance, American Indian." *Encyclopedia of Oklahoma History and Culture.* 2009. https://www.okhistory.org/publications/enc/entry.php?entry=DA008.

Daily, David W. *Battle for the BIA: G. E. E. Lindquist and the Missionary Crusade against John Collier.* Tucson: University of Arizona Press, 2004.

Dorsey, George A. *The Ponca Sun Dance.* Anthropological Series 7. Chicago: Publications of the Field Museum of Natural History, 1905.

Gidley, Mick. *Kopet: A Documentary Narrative of Chief Joseph's Last Years.* Seattle: University of Washington Press, 1981.

Grafe, Steven L. *Peoples of the Plateau: The Indian Photographs of Major Lee Moorhouse, 1898–1915.* Norman: University of Oklahoma Press, 2005.

Greene, Candace S. *One Hundred Summers: A Kiowa Calendar Record.* Lincoln: University of Nebraska Press, 2009.

———. *Silver Horn: Master Illustrator of the Kiowas.* Norman: University of Oklahoma, 2001.

Harrington, John P. *Vocabulary of the Kiowa Language.* Bureau of American Ethnology, Bulletin 84. Washington DC: Smithsonian, 1928.

Holm, Tom. *The Great Confusion in Indian Affairs.* Austin: University of Texas Press, 2005.

Howard, Oliver O. *Nez Perce Joseph, His Lands, His Confederates, His Enemies, His Murders, His War, His Pursuit and Capture.* Boston: Lee and Shepard; New York: Charles T. Dillingham, 1881.

Hunt, George K., and Wilbur. S. Nye. "The Annual Sun Dance of the Kiowa Indians, as related by George Hunt to Lt. Wilbur S. Nye, U. S. Army Historian." *Chronicles of Oklahoma* 12, no. 3 (September 1934): 340–58.

Iverson, Peter, and Elizabeth James, eds. *The Nez Perces since Lewis and Clark.* Moscow: University of Idaho Press, 1993.

Joseph, Chief. "An Indian's Views of Indian Affairs; Interview Given at Washington, D. C." Introduction by Reverend William H. Hare. *North American Review* 128, no. 269 (April 1879): 412–33.

Josephy, Alvin M., Jr. *The Nez Perce Indians and the Opening of the Northwest.* New York City: Houghton Mifflin, 1997.

Marshall, Alan G. "Review of *The Nez Perces in the Indian Territory: Nimiipuu Survival.* By J. Diane Pearson." *Great Plains Quarterly* 29, no. 4 (2009): 324–25.

Marshall, Alan G. "Fish, Water, and Nez Perce Life." *Idaho Law Review* 42 (2006): 763–93.

McLaughlin, James. *My Friend the Indian.* New York: Houghton Mifflin, 1910.

McWhorter, Lucullus V. *Hear Me, My Chiefs! Nez Perce History and Legend.* Caldwell ID: Caxton, 1983.

———. *Yellow Wolf, His Own Story.* Caldwell ID: Caxton, 1940.

Meacham, Alfred B, ed. "Another Cloud Gathering in the Northwest; Smo-heller," *Council Fire* 1, no. 6 (June 1878): 82.

———. "Chief Joseph, the Nez Perce." *Council Fire* 2, no. 10 (October 1879): 145–46.

———. "Nez Perces Joseph." *Council Fire* 1, no 7 (July 1878): 104, 105.

———. "The Nez Perces." *Council Fire* 3, no. 7 (July 1880): 108.

Meany, Edmond Stephen. "Chief Joseph of the Nez Perce." Master's thesis, University of Wisconsin, Madison, 1921.

Mooney, James. *The Cheyenne Indians.* Arlington VA: American Anthropological Society, 1905.

Mooney, James. "Calendar History of the Kiowa Indians." In *Seventeenth Annual Report of the Bureau of American Ethnology to the Secretary of the Smithsonian Institution, 1895–96,* directed by J. W. Powell. Washington DC: USGPO, 1898.

———. "Nez Perce Sun Dance, Indian Territory, Summer, 1883." In Seventeenth *Annual Report of the Bureau of American Ethnology, 1895–96,* directed by J. W. Powell. Washington DC: USGPO, 1898.

Neiberding, Velma. "The Nez Perce at the Quapaw Agency, 1878–1879." *Chronicles of Oklahoma* 44, no. 1 (Spring 1966), 22–30.

Olsen, Loran. *A Legacy from Sam Morris, A Monograph for Use with Compact Discs I and II,* item 26. Seattle: Northwest Interpretive Association, 1999.

Pearson, J. Diane. "Developing Reservation Economies: Native American Teamsters, 1857–1921." *Journal of Small Business and Entrepreneurship* 18, no. 2 (Spring 2005): 153–54.

———. *The Nez Perces in the Indian Territory: Nimiipuu Survival.* Norman: University of Oklahoma Press, 2008.

———. "Numipu Narratives: The Essence of Survival in the Indian Territory." *Journal of Northwest Anthropology* 38, no. 1 (Spring 2004), 39–40.

———. "Building Reservation Economies: American Indian Agriculture 1858–1925." *International Journal of Entrepreneurship and Small Business* 4, no. 6 (2007): 706.

Relander, Click. *Drummers and Dreamers.* Caldwell ID: Caxton, 1956.

Spears, John R. "Boomers of the West." *Munsey's Magazine* 25 (April–September, 1901): 850–54.

Spier, Leslie. *The Sun Dance of the Plains Indians: Its Development and Diffusion.* Anthropological Papers of the American Museum of Natural History 16, part 7. New York: American Museum of Natural History, 1921.

Sprague, Roderick. *Aboriginal Burial Practices in the Plateau Region of North America.* PhD diss., University of Arizona, Tucson, 1967.

Thompson, Scott M. *I Will Tell My War Story: A Pictorial Account of the Nez Perce War.* Seattle: University of Washington Press, 2000.

Trafzer, Clifford E. *Chief Joseph's Allies: The Palouse Indians and the Nez Perce War of 1877.* Sacramento CA: Sierra Oaks, 1987.

Trafzer, Clifford E., and Margery Ann Beach. "Smohalla, the Washani, and Religion as a Factor in Northwestern Indian History." *American Indian Quarterly* 9, no. 3 (Summer 1985): 313.

Walker, Deward E., Jr. *Conflict and Schism in Nez Perce Acculturation: A Study of Religion and Politics.* Pullman: Washington State University, 1968.

Wortman, Richard K., Mary Anne Wortman, and William W. Bottorff, eds. *History of Cowley County Kansas, The Indians.* Vol. 2. Arkansas City: Arkansas City Historical Society, 1999.

4 The Education of Archie Phinney

WILLIAM WILLARD, ALAN G. MARSHALL, AND J. DIANE PEARSON

While Indian people are drifting toward the complete loss of racial and cultural identity, and blindly clutching vapid fetiches [*sic*] of traditional Indian glories, my biggest achievement, I think, has been to preserve an Indian personality and integrity, having both meaning and *elan* in modern life. To have Indian blood in one's veins is of little moment when one does not know and feel the traditional Indian life, its language, ideology, folklore, etc.

—ARCHIE PHINNEY, IN GRIDLEY, *INDIANS OF TODAY*

"They buried Archie Phinney yesterday," reported the *Lewiston Morning Tribune* on November 3, 1949. The forty-five-year-old Nez Perce Superintendent of the North Idaho Indian Agency, who championed the Nez Perce language (Nimiipuutímt), Nez Perce sovereignty, and indigenous nationalism, as well as advocated for American Indian education, was gone. Father Cornelius E. Byrne, from the Society of Jesus (SJ), who sang the requiem mass and delivered the eulogy, remembered Phinney "[as] a man who dedicated his life to his work, and this work was his people"; Byrne stated further that Phinney "had developed himself by his own God-given talents, not to prove to them what they could accomplish, but to develop the qualities that would be a contribution to his nation and his people. He did not seek to make himself a white man."[1]

These testimonials describe a self-aware indigenous leader who profoundly affected American Indian life during a period that historian Charles F. Wilkinson describes as the beginning of the rise of Indian Nations.[2] Dr. Archie Mark Phinney's leadership role in the "blood struggle" of revitalizing tribes is not widely known, even among Nez Perce people. But William "Bill" Willard (Cherokee) was fascinated by Phinney's resilience; he understood the social and cultural barriers Phinney had to surmount, the physical dangers he faced, and the temptations he resisted. To Willard, Phinney made a "hero's journey":

> [Phinney's life] is the story of a man who left his home in a remnant of the Nez Perce homeland (*Numipum Weeƚes*) in Idaho to begin an odyssey across the United States and the Union of Soviet Socialist Republics and back again . . . He was a tough, determined survivor who lived up to his Nez Perce warrior name of Red War Club . . . there is a set of themes which are more than evident in his achievements.
>
> They are:
>
> 1. His life-long maintenance of a duality of personal roles and activities, where ever he might be.
> 2. A readiness to venture into new places, among new people, to seek new knowledge.
> 3. A development of skills necessary to lead groups toward successful goal realization.
> 4. An ability to survive and accomplish his goals in very risky environments.
> 5. An awareness of being under surveillance and coping with being tracked by official agencies tasked with the function of surveillance.[3]

Perhaps Phinney fascinated Willard because the latter saw something of himself in Phinney's life history when Willard happened upon Phinney's tracks in the spring of 1977. It was then that Willard set out on his own journey to trace Phinney's significant scholarship, activism, and Indigenous nationalism.

Tracing Phinney

Phinney's contributions to the rise of American Indian nations were mostly unrecognized when Bill Willard came to Washington State University at Pullman in 1976 to establish an American Indian Studies program. To do this, Willard sought the support of regional tribal governments in order to forge an academic program that would sustain tribal students and their communities rather than detract from them. He started this process immediately upon arriving at the university. His basic question to tribal councils or education committees was, "What can I do for you?" He posed this question, so very unusual for academics of the time, to the Nez Perce Tribal Executive Committee (NPTEC—the executive board of the modern tribal government whose formation Phinney spearheaded) at Lapwai, Idaho, in the spring of 1977. It was met with studied silence by the members of the Executive Committee. Finally, Allen P. Slickpoo Sr. told Willard, "There was a man who did a lot for this tribe while he was alive. But younger people don't know who this man was, so maybe you could so some research about him. Then, you could write something that the youngsters could read."[4] This Nez Perce champion who was fading from memory was Archie Mark Phinney, anthropologist, linguist, PhD, Bureau of Indian Affairs (BIA) superintendent, and indigenous nationalist.

Although Willard knew almost nothing about Phinney at the time, he liked Slickpoo's proposed project. "Sure, I can do that," Willard responded. Nodding, the other eight members of NPTEC agreed: "That is what you are going to do." They all felt that the coming generations should know about a leader who forwarded Nez Perce sovereignty during very hostile conditions.

Then, Slickpoo showed Willard around the tribal offices, introduced him to several people, and visited the old BIA offices. There, they met a gentleman who was retiring that same day. When he learned about Willard's new project, he pointed to a door at the end of the hall: "See that door down there? This was Phinney's office when he was superintendent." Willard "looked hard" at that door, thinking to himself, "Could that door be the key to Phinney's history?"

The retiree went on to tell Willard, "Many people have seen Phinney here in this hallway, going into his office or coming out. About a week ago a woman who works in another office on this hallway came in one night to get something ready for the next day, and she saw a man in the hall. She thought he looked familiar, but she couldn't think of his name. The man nodded, she replied, 'Hello,' and he went into the office at the end there and closed the door."

The next day she asked several other people who the man she had seen the night before was. She had seen him but could not place his name. When she described him, someone told her, "That was Archie Phinney. Go look at that big photograph in the library. He is the white-haired man standing right in the middle of the NPTEC of that time. That is where you have seen him before."

"I don't think she has ever come into the building after hours again," said the retiree.

Willard recollected, "I have always thought that Phinney returned to complete work and projects that he had not had time to finish."[5] He also found that Phinney's biography was far less straightforward than he had initially imagined.

Thus was Willard's project of a lifetime launched; the more he learned, the more he wanted to know, and in some ways the more elusive Phinney seemed to be. As Willard scoured archives in Seattle, Philadelphia, Washington DC, Chicago, Spokane, New York, Pullman, and any other place where he could find relevant materials, there was always more to learn. Archie Phinney was an incredibly active, extremely productive individual with wide-ranging experience spanning his birthplace in Culdesac, Idaho; New York City; Stalinist Yakutsk; and Latin America.

Years later, in August 1992, Willard participated in a conflict resolution seminar held in St. Petersburg, in the Russian Federation.[6] While there, Willard visited the Russian Academy of Science's (RAS) Museum of Anthropology and Ethnology (MAE), which is housed in the Kunstkammer.[7] Fascinated by their ethnological collections and displays, he enjoyed the mannequins arrayed in the "Native dress" of ethnic groups subject to the former Tsarist Empire. As Willard toured the displays, another exhibit featuring non-Tsarist peoples amazed him; its central figure was a mannequin dressed in a complete set of Plains-style buckskin clothing, moccasins, and a large feathered warbonnet. Willard could learn nothing about the regalia from anyone at the MAE. Continuing his research in the United States, Willard learned that Archie Phinney had donated the entire ensemble to the MAE.[8] Willard never could determine who had constructed, owned, and supplied the MAE ensemble to Phinney.[9]

Willard found other traces of the Indigenous American leader moving through the great political confrontation of the Industrial Age. This sometimes-violent ideological conflict deeply influenced Phinney's career as an Indigenous nationalist. On the one hand, socialists and communists tried to recruit him to their cause(s) in order to extend their philosophies into Indian Country.[10] On the other hand, those who opposed those forces tried to vitiate Phinney's influence through innuendo and accusations of subversion.[11] Proponents of these European-originated ideologies could not imagine that their ideas and consequent policies did not suit Indian Country or that social progress, based in Native tradition and led by Indigenous people, was both possible and necessary. This then, was the dream Phinney sought throughout his life.

Archie Phinney—Crafting a Career

Twelve years before going to his final rest, Archie Phinney clarified his thoughts about American Indian education and Nez Perce culture and language while working in the USSR on his candidate of sciences degree in history.[12] A champion for education and Indigenous nationalism, Phinney illuminated the effects of schooling on most American Indian youngsters. His essay shows that Phinney was ahead of his time in thinking about the intersection of race, class, and ethnicity. While in Leningrad, he wrote,

> Many young Indians in recent times have been going to faraway federal Indian nonreservation residential schools where they become more estranged from the life of the tribe than those who attend local public schools. But regardless of the kind of schools these young Indians attend, whether public, federal or mission, their elementary training fits them only to take a low place in the rural white-Indian community, to which they are consigned by the circumstances of their racial and economic position. Though many now aspire to a higher education, their chances for completing such education are limited by the lack

of financial means, and those few who may finish higher schools can look forward only to the gloomy prospect of joining the rearguard of the white American youth in its dismal search for opportunities to apply its education.

He wrote further,

Experience has shown that the higher the education of an Indian today, the sharper the contradictions confronting him and the sorrier his fate. This educated, younger generation of Numipu is achieving a condition wherein it must face the adversities of exploitation and class antagonism, not as their forebears struggled against open transgression, but as an element corresponding to the white American proletariat.[13]

These observations grew from his generation's experiences at school.

Yet, Phinney had used his education to further and expand Nimiipuu identity and life. Somehow, he had gone beyond the commonplace, deadening educational experiences of Native American children that he described. As a youngster, Phinney was sent to public schools in Lapwai and Culdesac, Idaho, rather than Christian mission schools or federal Indian boarding schools. He was successful there; for example, in 1936 he won first prize in the Idaho State Public School spelling tournament.[14] We do not know who may have encouraged Phinney in his educational pursuits—perhaps the local Jesuit priest, a school guidance counselor, his mother and father, or many others. Whatever encouragement he may have had, it is clear that young Phinney was determined to turn schooling to his community's advantage.

Phinney therefore chose to attend college following his high-school graduation.[15] His commitment emboldened him to approach the local BIA superintendent Oscar Lipps to find a way to attend college. Lipps called a friend who was, at that time, Chancellor of the University of Kansas. Between the two men, they arranged an academic scholarship for Phinney, but Phinney lacked funds for living expenses. So Lipps contacted administrators at the Haskell Indian School, also located in Lawrence, Kansas, who offered Phinney room and board in exchange for working nights and Saturdays. Since there were still uncovered expenses, Phinney cut wood

FIG. 4. Archie Phinney, varsity baseball team, University of Kansas, ca. 1920. Courtesy of the National Park Service, Nez Perce National Historical Park, Archie Phinney Collection.

for the rest of the summer to purchase his clothing and a train ticket to Kansas.[16] This Nez Perce son and grandson—and proud great-grandson of the old frontiersman and trapper Colonel William Craig—was going to college.[17]

Phinney was a dynamo at the University of Kansas (KU), majoring in sociology while emphasizing coursework in anthropology.[18] He earned excellent grades even while living and working at Haskell Indian School and traveling to KU. His grades earned him a place in Alpha Kappa Delta, the International Sociology Honor Society. He lettered twice on the Jayhawkers baseball team (1925 and 1926), starting out as a utility player in 1925 as a walk-on before settling in as the school's ace pitcher during his senior year. These athletic accomplishments earned him membership in the "K" Club, KU's letterman organization.[19]

Upon earning his baccalaureate degree from the University of Kansas in 1926, Phinney moved to Washington DC to work as a BIA statistics clerk. At the same time, he launched his graduate studies in linguistics with two well-known linguists, Truman Michelson at George Washington University and J. N. B. Hewitt at the Bureau of American Ethnology. Michelson was an international authority on Algonquian languages, and J. N. B. Hewitt had conducted extensive studies on the related languages he categorized as "Shapwailutian": Nez Perce, Yakama, Klamath, Modoc, and Palus.[20] Phinney published several papers with Hewitt, including "Grammatical Notes on the Language of the Nez Perce" (1926) and a paper concerning "Nez Perce or Numipu Legends" (1927).[21]

Determined to advance his interests in linguistics, Phinney hoped to become one of Franz Boas's students at Columbia University in New York. In a letter to the eminent professor, Phinney made his case for matriculation: he had majored in anthropology at the University of Kansas and he had expanded those studies through linguistics with Michelson and Hewitt. He also mentioned that he spoke Numiputímt and was familiar with the Yakama language. Phinney explained to Boas, "[I would like an] arrangement through you whereby I could assist in your department with Indian language study within my particular sphere, and also study under you in some of your classes."[22] The only thing that held him back was his need for employment.

Boas discouraged Phinney because he could not offer the latter suffi-cient funding.[23] Even so, Phinney resigned from the BIA in the summer of the following year and moved to New York in 1928 to lobby Boas. Once in New York, he attended New York University while supporting himself during the school year with a part-time job at the Bureau of Community Research and Service working with recent Italian immigrants. Phinney also spent his summers as a counselor at a boys camp and a golf instructor.[24] Still, he kept petitioning Boas.

Boas finally relented, somewhat. In an *aide memoir* (dated March 18, 1929) headed, "Archie Phinney-Anthropology," Boas wrote: "He is quite intelligent and has fair knowledge. I am trying to train him to become an investigator, particularly of his own tribe. I think I can find funds for his support during the coming year."[25]

Phinney enrolled at Columbia for fall semester in 1929, while Boas obtained $1200 from the Committee on Research on American Indian Languages to fund Phinney's return to Idaho to collect Nimiipuutímt lin-guistic and ethnographic data.[26] Phinney made regular written progress reports to Boas during this time, occasionally mentioning his frustrations in recording *titwáatit*.[27] For example, Phinney wrote, "The sad thing in recording these animal stories is the loss of spirit—the fascination fur-nished by the peculiar Indian vocal tradition for humor. Indians are better storytellers than whites. When I read my story mechanically I find only the cold corpse."[28]

This remark parallels the objections many traditional Nimiipuu raise, even today, to recording stories, songs, and other arts—the living pres-ence of these arts cannot be recorded; therefore, any such recording is a misleading shadow. As for ethnographic data, Phinney wrote, "The ideas I have encountered regarding institutions before the coming of the whites seem fragmentary and obscure but you may be able to dope out some-thing," thus presaging later anthropological objections to the reliability of "memory culture."[29]

He returned to New York City in January 1930 with a thousand pages of handwritten linguistic notes and began working on his projects. Phin-ney's plan was to produce a book of *titwáatit* texts and to rewrite the study of Nimiipuutímt grammar begun by Jesuit missionary Joseph Cataldo, sJ.[30] He worked on both of these projects diligently. It remains unclear how he supported himself during this time, though Boas apparently provided a small stipend and a place for Phinney to work in an office shared with Frederica de Laguna at Columbia University. In her biography of de Laguna, Catherine McClellan relates that de Laguna fondly recalled Phinney, remembering him as a young man who "smoked fragrant *kinni-kinnick* and entertained her with wonderful Indian stories, dramatically voicing the parts of the different characters in them."[31]

However, Phinney's plans for a Nimiipuutímt grammar fell by the wayside in favor of his primary interest: "In four years spent at Columbia [1928–32], he further specialized in ethnology and historical processes in race and culture contacts, particularly interesting himself in Indian Reservation life."[32] Franz Boas encouraged this focus, which brought together several of his own interests and forwarded Phinney's studies of indigenous administration.

Boas was an academic and a significant public intellectual with strong progressive/socialist leanings.[33] Among his wide-ranging interests was rekindling the research of the Jesup North Pacific Expedition (JNPE) to the northwest coast of North America and to eastern Siberia (1897–1902), of which he had been the scientific director. Another concern was the administration of Native peoples in the United States. These interests Boas held in common with Russian anthropologist Vladimir Bogoraz.[34] Bogoraz was a strong influence in developing Russian ethnology, ethnography, and—especially—their applications to indigenous administration among "the small peoples of the North."[35] Bogoraz participated in the JNPE between 1900 and 1901, and he remained working at the American Museum of Natural History in New York City until 1904, when he returned to Russia. The two men maintained their professional relationship through the following years, during which Boas unsuccessfully consulted with Bogoraz about reanimating the JNPE.

Moreover, both wished to promote American–Russian anthropological cooperation through scholarly exchanges between the American Museum of Natural History and the Museum of Anthropology and Ethnology (MAE) of the Russian Academy of Sciences (RAS) in Leningrad, USSR. At least one student from the USSR, Julia Averkieva, had come to the United States to study at Barnard College and work with Franz Boas, while Boas and others were considering whom to send to the USSR.[36] It seems that Boas, at least, felt that such academic exchanges would proceed in a manner usual to the Western academy.

However, the October Revolution and political developments consequent to Vladimir Lenin's rise to power radically revised the purposes, academic organization, and leadership of the social sciences in the Soviet Union. They were harnessed to further the political and economic incorporation of non-Russian national groups into the USSR during this time. The task of the social sciences was to describe national groups so that scientific communism could be applied to them, thereby promoting them to communist republics. This policy was known as "Korenizatsiya."

Korenizatsiya was developed at the Twelfth Party Congress in 1923 to mitigate Great Russian chauvinism. The Russian word translates as "putting down roots," implying the nativization or indigenization of Soviet governance. The policy was aimed at creating and training a governing communist cadre within each nationality while preserving each nation's languages and other symbolic national identifiers in communist education and governing institutions. For many groups without a literary tradition, such as the "small peoples of the North," this process also included developing a written language. Associated with the MAE, the Committee of the North, of which Bogoraz was a member, was charged with this effort.

Following Vladimir Lenin's death in 1924, Stalin consolidated his power by eliminating his opponents. He then replaced Lenin's New Economic Policy (NEP) and initiated his first Five Year Plan in 1928. Thus began the "Great Transformation."[37] Among the many actions this change involved were the collectivization of agricultural lands and the elimination of "richer" peasants (dekulakization) through arrests, deportation, and execution. This campaign caused widespread disorganization in food production and distribution, causing famines. The outcomes of the Great Transformation, however, were not clear to many people outside of the USSR.

The Great Transformation fundamentally altered the administration of the "small peoples of the North," and its effects quickly extended into the MAE.[38] At an "infamous conference of Moscow and Leningrad ethnologists" conducted in April 1929, the revolution sidelined the Committee of the North and the old guard at the MAE, including Bogoraz; their work in ethnology was declared a "surrogate bourgeois social science," and they were required to reform their thinking to reflect Marxist sociology and history.[39]

Ethnography was not abandoned but became a subfield of history, an evolutionary or historical study of stages in the dialectical social development of the modern world. One of the uses of the new *ethnografiya* was in "national delimitation," or the creation of well-defined national territorial units in which Korenizatsiya could be implemented.[40] Moreover, the methods of *ethnografiya* changed greatly.[41] This project would be carried out by brigades of ethnographers rather than by independent researchers, the latter approach now deemed a hallmark of bourgeois anthropology. How much Boas, a premier proponent of "bourgeois social science" in the eyes of Soviet social scientists, was aware of this revolution in thought, method, and organization remains unclear.

Nikolai Mikhailovich Matorin, one of the recorders of the conference and a proponent of the new order, became the director of the MAE in October 1930.[42] With his appointment, Matorin instituted in the MAE a new ideological and theoretical order that was in line with scientific communism.[43] Reflecting this change, the new academic organization inhabiting the Museum was renamed the Institute of Anthropology and Ethnography (IAE) of the Academy of Sciences of the USSR, and it was placed under the Institute for the Study of the Peoples of the USSR (IPIN). The IAE remained headquartered in the Kunstkamera. In this new form, the IPIN and IAE, led by a brigade of ideologically "pure" academics, purged their ranks of bourgeois influences and concentrated their studies on "the noncapitalist development of the 'backward' peoples of the USSR and the 'construction of their new culture' as well as on 'unmasking the anti-Marxist and anti-Leninist trends in the pre-revolutionary Russia and contemporary western ethnology."[44]

Seemingly without Boas's knowledge, Phinney had seized his educational future by arranging with Nikolai Matorin to study Soviet minority policy at the MAE by mid-1931. Matorin became aware of Phinney's desire to study minority policy in the USSR through Julia Averkieva. This is revealed in a letter signed, "The Museum Director" (i.e., Matorin), written to Boris Evssevich Skvirsky, the USSR representative in Washington DC:[45]

> The Museum of Anthropology and Ethnography of the Academy of Sciences of the USSR informs that when museum researcher Comrade Averkieva was in America in 1930, she had an occasion to meet young (American) Indian Comrade Phinney who was working at Columbia University under the supervision of Professor Boas. Comrade Phinney manifested a great desire to visit the USSR, in order to see directly the construction of socialism and especially the development of national minorities in the USSR.
>
> The Museum of Anthropology establishes its consent to invite Comrade Phinney to the Academy of Science of the USSR for the stipend reserved by the Human Resource Department of the Academy of Science of the USSR.[46]

Phinney's invitation was a surprise to Boas. He and Edward Sapir had been discussing students to recommend to the MAE for a "Russian Fellowship"—most likely this very one, since no other was being offered. The two, most likely, had not considered Phinney. Boas waited until October 1932 to inform Sapir of this development: "I failed to reply to your question in regard to a Russian Fellowship. There is nothing being done in regard to that matter at the present time. The Museum in Leningrad has invited, without any suggestion on our part, an Indian, Archie Phinney, to go there and he is on his way now. I presume the principal idea is that he will see what they are doing with the Siberian natives."[47]

Despite his apparent disappointment, Boas worked during the months prior to Phinney's fellowship to enable the latter's success. The "Russian Fellowship" fully supported Phinney, housing him in the Aspirant Student residence in the historic home of the MAE on the bank of the Neva River, paying for his traveling expenses and meals, and awarding him a cash stipend.[48] However conditions in the Soviet Union were not immediately clear to either Boas or Phinney; perhaps the latter had been influenced by news of the "Soviet famine" of 1931–32.[49]

A four-way correspondence between Phinney, Boas, Matorin, and Averkieva developed as they tried to clarify the situation. Phinney asked

Matorin about the "conditions of his fellowship" in the USSR but received no satisfactory answer.[50] Boas wrote Matorin in November 1931 that he could get no information from either Skvirsky or "Amtorg's"; they apparently had little information to share.[51] Both Boas and Phinney tried to clarify this through Skvirsky.[52] Still, the position remained cloudy as far as Phinney and Boas were concerned. In a letter dated February 8, 1932, Boas complained, "Although Madam Averkieva has intimated the conditions under which he is to work, I want to know officially what is expected of him and how he is to subsist while in Leningrad. Mr. Phinney has to work for his living here, and while he will have in the fall enough money to pay for his passage he will have nothing else and will have to rely upon whatever is offered to him."[53]

There was also confusion as to how soon Phinney would travel to Leningrad. In a letter dated May 4, 1932, addressed to "Papa Franz" Boas, Julia Averkieva wrote, "Is Mr. Phinney getting ready for coming to USSR? We are waiting him. Mr. Matorin asked me to write to you an official letter about the conditions of his stay here. You will get it soon. Here I can assure you that his conditions here will be not bad. Aspirant of Academy of Science is [unreadable] person, and his conditions are not so bad. I am disappointed by [struck out] his worries about the conditions of his stay here. They are quite unnecessary."[54] Boas replied, "Phinney is intending to start by the end of the summer. I think he is quite right in wanting to know exactly what is expected of him and what the Academy want to do for him."[55] Clearly, despite no satisfactory resolution of this issue, Phinney continued his plans to go to the MAE. Significantly, too, no one seems to have made any exit plans for Phinney.

Why would Phinney have been so interested in Soviet policy regarding national minorities at this particular moment? Of course, American Indians were intimately familiar with the failures of U.S. Native policy, and awareness of the crisis had reached Congress through the report, *The Problem of Indian Administration* (also known as the "Meriam Report") by the Institute for Government Research (later known as the Brookings Institution).[56] In searching for solutions to these intractable issues, Americans observed the social and political developments in the USSR with great interest; many regarded the Soviet Union positively as a great social experiment.[57]

The "national question" in the USSR and government policy aimed at dealing with it is universally complex. The Tsarist regime found it troublesome at best. Continuing conflict with ethnic groups in the Caucasus and Transcaucasia made it salient to the Bolsheviks as well, so much so that Lenin assigned Stalin to study the issue.[58] In 1917 V. Ulianov (Lenin) and Josef Dzugashvili (Stalin) promulgated the "Declaration of the Rights of the People of Russia,"[59] in which four principles were enumerated:

1. The equality and sovereignty of the peoples of Russia.
2. The right of the peoples of Russia to free self-determination, even to the point of separation and the formation of an independent state.
3. The abolition of any and all national and national-religious privileges and disabilities.
4. The free development of any and all national minorities and ethnographic groups inhabiting the territory of Russia.

During the 1920s and early 1930s these principles were supposedly realized in the Soviet policy goal of Korenizatsiya. Perhaps influenced by the progressive climate at Columbia and by Averkieva, Phinney composed a now-lost paper on U.S. Indian policy, which he gave to Boas.

After reading this paper, Boas was enthusiastic about Phinney's approach to "Indian policy," finding himself in agreement with Phinney's ideas about Native administration. Their agreement was so strong that Boas sent a copy of "a paper" written by Phinney to then–Commissioner of Indian Affairs (CIA) Charles J. Rhoads; the paper forwarded the idea that Native cultures would persist despite efforts to transform Native people into "good citizens," and that successful "Indian policy" would build upon those cultures and languages rather than trying to supplant them through assimilation.[60]

The basic idea of self-determination expressed by Phinney led Boas and other progressives to think that he would benefit from learning how the Soviet government integrated non-Russian groups in the former Russian empire into the new Soviet state. As he wrote later (after John Collier had been appointed Commissioner of Indian Affairs), Boas presumed that Phinney's experience at the MAE under the tutelage of his friend Vladimir Bogoraz would prepare Phinney for a leadership position in the BIA when he returned to the United States.[61] Boas and Phinney sought the support of Rhoads, and Phinney visited Rhoads in Washington DC in early 1932. Rhoads was not so enthusiastic about the idea. Phinney described his meeting with Rhoads in a letter to Boas: "Regarding the Commissioner of Indian Affairs, he was very mildly interested in the thought of examining the Soviet methods of dealing with their aboriginal groups. He showed an obvious prejudice and ignorance of policies and conditions there. He said their system (general political scheme) is wrong, and that of course condemns their method of handling their native groups."[62] Despite these officials' resistance to his ideas, Phinney had found his professional life's direction in this position. He set out to develop it further at the MAE.

At the MAE/IAE—Learning a New Ethnography

Phinney was well met when he finally arrived in Leningrad in November 1932 for a planned two-year study. However, some details of his residency were not settled upon his arrival. He wrote Boas: "When I arrived here the representatives of the Museum were very friendly to me. Despite the fact that I had been expected several days no arrangements had been made so far as living quarters and board are to be had here. Matters here cannot be done with dispatch yet they prefer to do it later than beforehand. Consequently I find myself temporarily housed, unable to unpack my baggage, expecting momentarily, for almost a week now, to move to permanent quarters. On the other hand they [Mr. Matorin and others of the Academy] are most gracious about entertaining me."[63] And so began five years of study in the USSR that sharpened Phinney's interests in Native political movements and Indigenous governance, apparently with the expectation of a position with the BIA when he returned to the United States.

Phinney was immediately immersed in a very different curriculum and in the ongoing revisions of Russian anthropology. In the same letter to Boas, he wrote, "They held innumerable meetings—student meetings, faculty meetings. I've been to half a dozen already, and they talk for hours about plans. Later on, perhaps, I can participate intelligently to this sort of thing so I will make arrangements to become adjusted in my own way." He further observed, "I gathered at once that I must make my approach to Russian ethnography through two paramount positions—Morgan and

Marx. I seem to have plunged suddenly into the functioning and practical aspects of that new methodology. I suppose I shall continue to see Russian life confusedly until I get my proletarian glasses."[64]

Perhaps to clarify Phinney's direction at the Museum, Boas wrote to Matorin:

> I imagine that one of the most valuable things he [Phinney] can learn with you is the policy that you pursue in regard to Siberian native tribes. The problems that confront you there are about the same that confront our Government in relation to the American Indian tribes, although the tremendous rapidity of settlement in the West has made the problems in some regions seem almost hopeless. I still believe that a wiser policy may rescue some of the still existing tribes. I feel certain that Phinney might learn a great deal in this respect that would be of great use when he returns here. He is deeply interested in the welfare of his people and would take to this matter with great interest.[65]

Shortly after Phinney's arrival Matorin clarified the situation in a letter (written in German) to Boas saying that Soviet ethnography had benefited from studies outside the USSR, and that the very concrete ethnographic work done to build a socialist state in the USSR must be properly considered by other social scientists. Matorin was very happy to accept Boas's personal student for a two-year term of study, just as Boas had guided Julia Averkieva. Matorin was personally supervising Phinney's education, which would focus on the study of the revolution's "sociological principles, the construction of national cultures in the USSR, and their successful implementation."[66] Continuing, Matorin expressed that Russian language studies were essential and that the staff was there to help him in this. Further, Matorin would have Phinney accompany ethnographic expeditions and lecture about Nez Perce culture to Museum assemblies. Matorin went on to suggest avenues for further scientific exchanges.

Nonetheless, Phinney saw his first task as completing his linguistic book, titled *Nez Perce Texts*.[67] He therefore gave priority to the final editing and worked "day and night," as he mentioned in a letter to Boas, through the month of May 1933, until the final draft was in the printer's hands. This work, his academic studies, and settling into the new social order of Leningrad was terribly taxing for him; Phinney described in the same letter, "The medical people examined me last week and report to the Acad. of Sciences that I have a nervous condition from over work and now they are trying to ship me off to a rest sanatorium."[68] One wonders how Phinney felt about this recommendation; on most U.S. federal Indian reservations, a sanatorium, including the one in Lapwai, was viewed as a charnel house.

Regardless of this recommendation, Phinney remained in Leningrad to work. He studied, wrote to Collier about a possible position, began to review printer's proofs of his book, continued to develop the "best possible program for Nez Perces," and worked to finish his study of Russian national minority policy. He looked forward to developing a comparative study of Russian policy among the "small peoples of the North" and British policies for the hill tribes of India.[69] In the meantime, he worked on learning the Russian language.

Whatever his feelings about going to a sanatorium, he finally went to a fashionable spa in Kislovodsk, Stavropol Krai, later that summer. Two photos of him at a nearby tourist attraction called "Red Rocks" show him smiling, in the company of an unidentified young woman and another couple.[70] Even then, he had coursework, three reports to "the museum" on U.S. Indian reservations, more printers' proofs to review, and the Russian language to learn.[71] There, too, was where he may have met Agnes Smedley, a significant figure in the American Progressive movement and the international Popular Front; they became friends until Smedley left the USSR in 1934. Phinney also worked on some other projects in the USSR; he even participated in an academic anthropology movie while in the USSR. According to social scientist and Russian specialist Dmitry V. Arzyutov, Phinney was filmed as he explained Nimiipuu linguistic gestures in the Nimiipuutímt language.[72]

There were several people available to Phinney at the Museum who were especially qualified to help him learn to speak Russian. One of them was Julia Averkieva, recently returned from New York and Barnard College, who remained in familiar contact with "Papa Franz" for several years. Also, Americans Emanual Gonick and Roy Franklin Barton were already being employed by the Museum when Phinney arrived. A third

FIG. 5. Archie Phinney (*left*) and Emanuel Gonick at a spa in Kislovodsk, Russia, in 1933. Courtesy of the National Park Service, Nez Perce National Historical Park, Archie Phinney Collection.

American, Lucy Knox, was also there for a time before moving on to work for the *Moscow News.*[73]

But Phinney seemingly had difficulty with the Russian language. On February 4, 1933, Averkieva wrote Boas, "Of course Archy's [*sic*] hardships in Russian are great, but our aspirants who live in the same house with him teach him."[74] Averkieva was unimpressed by his progress in Russian. She mentioned this again in another letter dated October 9, 1933: "We already begin our study but he is somewhere wandering on the Caukases, and had not yet send even sign of his existence. Of course he could not do much in the last year too on account of his language which is going on very slowly on account of his American frend [sic] with whom he talks all time in English and who is his interpreter too."[75] The date of Phinney's return from the officially sanctioned rest cure is unclear; he might still have been in Kislovodsk when Averkieva wrote to Boas.

"The Conditions Here Are Not the Best"

Phinney adjusted to life in the USSR and at the MAE, but the details of his adjustment are understandably vague. The MAE was renamed the Institute of Anthropology and Ethnology (IAE) because it was being reorganized in line with the new theoretical principles of scientific communism. Vladimir Bogoraz was under great pressure from younger, more ideologically correct anthropologists such as Averkieva.[76]

The USSR was being strongly policed. Stalin's "Great Purge" (1934–39), perpetrated by the Soviet People's Ministry of Internal Affairs (NKVD), was in the making and intensifying. Phinney alerted Boas, "The conditions here are not the best but I get things adjusted [and] am getting along well enough . . . they ransack my mail."[77] Phinney learned that the NKVD surveilled everyone for deviation from Stalinist ideology; being found guilty of the latter could lead to terrible fates.[78] Thus, he was always careful in his letters to Boas not to mention names, any individual's activities, or the specifics of places he visited. Perhaps this contributed to the slightly "bizarre lack of informative communication between the two men," as noted by Willard.[79]

Additionally, Phinney had "a suspicious passport problem;" he was robbed of his passport, money, and official papers by a knife-wielding thug on a streetcar in Moscow in December 1933, an incident he reported to the police.[80] There was no U.S. mission to Russia at the time.[81] When he reported the loss again to the newly appointed U.S. Ambassador in the spring of 1934, he was accused of selling his passport "for one thousand roubles," and had not been issued a new one as of May 12, 1934.[82] Such problems were often a prelude to "investigation," coercion, and, possibly, subsequent arrest by the NKVD.[83] Just being a non-Russian resident in the USSR was dangerous whatever one's politics, and many people were disappearing into the gulags.[84] Agnes Smedley, however, took the loss of Phinney's passport seriously enough to lobby the prominent progressive Roger Baldwin to help resolve the issue.[85] After leaving Moscow in April she telephoned and then wrote to Boas about her concerns, suggesting that Boas use his influence to help resolve the problem.[86]

Perhaps, as he himself indicated, Phinney was not very worried, and Boas's response to Smedley is not in any of the records that we found. However, he must have written or cabled Phinney, because Phinney wrote to Boas on September 6, 1934, "The reports you had concerning my difficulties—losing my money and American passport were true but I was never particularly worried about it. I received a new passport in the course of time." When Phinney received his replacement visa remains unknown.

Phinney also participated in the Anglo-American Institute held in Moscow at the First University of Moscow. This summer institute was organized by the Institute for International Education "to offer courses on many aspects of Soviet civilization. Moreover, the courses are given in English, there being few Americans who could understand Russian. The interest in the new regime in Russia that prevails in the United States is made evident by the fact that some two hundred persons attended this summer session, more than is true of any other foreign institution. Moreover, they included college professors, research students, teachers and undergraduates."[87] Phinney's role in the Institute is unknown, but he is featured standing in the front row in a photograph of the Institute's participants at the Third House of the Soviets.[88]

Circumstances in Leningrad at that time were described by Jack Harris, a student of Melville Herskovits's who visited Leningrad and the IAE over seventeen days in October 1934. After being expelled from the USSR, he wrote a twenty-two-page letter to Herskovits while safely aboard a ship at sea, describing meetings with Bogoraz and Roy F. Barton as well as social conditions in the city.[89] Harris noted, "I wanted to write you from Leningrad but did not because of the rigid censorship of the mails. The country is decidedly war-conscious. The streets are full of Red Army men, singing swinging squadrons of them. War tanks lumber by in the streets and above, planes continually roar. I was there during the air-raid preparedness period. Every possible medium is utilized toward instructing the people what to do in the event of an air attack. Pamphlets, lectures, newspapers, movies, and most practical—sham attacks."[90] Phinney, however, made no mention of these activities in his letters to Boas.

A few weeks after Harris left Leningrad, the city's party boss, Sergei Mironovich Kirov, was assassinated on December 1, 1934.[91] Stalin used Kirov's assassination as a pretext for intensifying his purges of political enemies, especially members of the Communist International and associates of Leon Trotsky.[92] Nicolai Matorin suffered a terrible fate for his associations with this group. He was expelled from the Communist Party on December 1, then arrested in late December 1934. He lost his directorship at the IAE and his teaching position in 1935.[93] Phinney made no mention of this in letters to Boas either, despite maintaining at least a professional friendship with Matorin, who had sent Phinney an autographed photograph of himself taken in November 1934.[94]

Nor did Phinney mention his new academic supervisor and academic mainstay Virendranath Chattopadhyaya, familiarly known as "Chatto."[95] Chatto directed Phinney's studies of the "national question." Phinney continued to have difficulties with the intricacies of the Russian language and insisted on reading at least some of the theoretical literature in English.[96] Because of this difficulty, Chatto instructed him in the Russian language and translated for him.[97]

Phinney had, nevertheless, found his "proletarian glasses." Those glasses were certainly required for his many lectures; he spoke at the Institute of Anthropology and Ethnography, the Institute of Language and Thought, and the Institute of History and Philosophy. Navigating the reefs of both ideology and language must have been difficult. As Phinney wrote to his mother and father, he also found lecturing in the Russian language a "daunting task." He reassured his parents, however, that his research was going well.[98]

But Phinney did not spend all of his time traveling, working, or worrying about the ongoing revolution. He also took opportunities to enjoy cultural events. For example, while in Moscow in 1934, he attended the ballet and opera with his new friend Agnes Smedley.[99]

Travels in the USSR

Phinney was allowed to travel in the USSR even though bourgeois ethnographic research had been proscribed.[100] Phinney took advantage of his position at the IAE to travel in the USSR, from the Arctic to the Caucasus and on to Central Asia on the China–Mongolian frontier, thus verifying Soviet national minority policy on the ground. In 1934, and again in 1935, Phinney went to the Kabardino–Balkarskyia Associated Soviet Socialist Republic in the Caucasus Mountains. In 1935 he traveled further to the Nagorno Altaiskayia Oblast in Central Asia, which borders the Chinese province of Xinjiang. He may have also traveled to the Buryat Oblast beyond the Altai Mountains and east of Lake Baikal.

Only this sketchy record of Phinney's work in the USSR has been found. Although we know where he visited, we found no list of investigations, no mention of the institute or agency sponsors, and no identification of who received any reports at the IAE or in Phinney's own collection. Some of these may still be in Moscow or in other Russian files. Two months after working on some unidentified project in Moscow, Phinney wrote to Boas on September 6, 1934, stating, "I am getting my material in shape for a complete report on the National Minorities Policies of the Soviet Government."[101] Willard, we assume, could only suppose by comparative analysis what Phinney observed and thought about the regions he visited.

In the Nagorno Altaiskayia Oblast Phinney was likely interested to see the thirty-one thousand Oirat Mongols, herders of camels, yaks, horses, sheep, goats, and reindeer. Their situation was similar to that of the Navajo and San Carlos Apaches in the 1920s; the Navajo were dependent on herds of sheep, goats, and horses, while the San Carlos Apaches relied on a collective herd of cattle. A second similarity was the appropriation of favorable agricultural and grazing lands by settler colonists, who outnumbered the Indigenous population. Further, the Oirat Mongols were subject to the direction of the local Communist Party bureaucracy headed by a district secretary, all of whom were Russian—a situation like those of the Navajo and San Carlos Apache, who were under the control of nonnatives in the BIA.[102]

Phinney visited the Kabardino–Balkar region twice to study local government; as yet, we have found no further record of those visits. However, Anna Louise Strong was there about the same time as Phinney, and she published a lengthy description that provides some context for Phinney's experiences.[103] The Kabardins were herders, whereas the incoming Russians occupied mostly tillable lands. Strong recorded that the local bureaucracy was Russian except for the party secretary. And in the still-more-distant Altai and Caucasus Mountains, local governments were driven by nonnative bureaucrats who had to complete five-year plans as directed by Moscow.

These relationships were all too familiar to Phinney, who understood the BIA and reservation structures. There may have been differences in the official ideologies and population numbers, but the difficulties affecting ethnic minorities and Indigenous people in the USSR and in the United States both resulted from conquest and colonial domination.[104]

Early in his studies Phinney recognized that the USSR policy on national minorities and its implementation through Korenizatsiya did not provide an answer to Indigenous nationalism and economic development in the United States. Phinney wrote to Boas on August 19, 1933,

> I am not optimistic about the value of the Russian method as a thing applicable to the US Indian reservations. My study so far has been somewhat limited to those larger groups that were already in a good position to accept full autonomy. The Russian policy is sound enough and effective here but devised to operate within the range of a new set of economic relationships—economic relationships which on one hand the Indian Bureau [BIA] isn't likely to consider for Indian tribes and on the other are not at once attainable by a moribund reservation group. I will find out, however, what if anything has actually been done to deal with natives who live under the least favorable circumstances. I get from what I read and from what is constantly told to me, too many

facts about phenomenal development of native groups that were from the beginning rather well constituted socially and economically and not enough facts about the social rehabilitation or regeneration of tribes that haven't achieved an economic status consistent with the soviet industrialization plans.[105]

Phinney published only one article, in the 1935 edition of the journal *Pacific Affairs*, with some indication of his travels and interests in Native governance and tribal development in the USSR.[106] In this comparative study of Native peoples as well as their degradation and regeneration during the Tsarist government and USSR policies following 1917, Phinney addressed developing local governance, medical care, education, economies, and Indigenous language education among the Chuckchee, Eskimo, Tungus, and Koryak people. Reflecting his general caution about criticizing the USSR, the article focuses on progress and change for Indigenous people.

Phinney had been in the USSR for his planned two-year stint, and he was anxious to leave Leningrad and the USSR. But he had no money to make his way home and asked Boas for funds.[107] Despite his best efforts, Boas replied, "You are probably aware that our funds have been very hard hit by the 'depression' and I must confess I do not know where to turn."[108] Phinney wrote back that even though he had "procured his ticket and visas," Boas's letter had given him pause. He wrote, "In my indecision the Academy of Sciences finally prevailed upon me to remain here for another year."[109] The subsequent two pages of this letter discuss Phinney's interest in the Indian Service and in Nez Perce work.

In his last known letter to Phinney, Boas wrote in reply: "Will you please let me hear from you from time to time. I will try to keep your name before Washington."[110] Phinney's professional connection with Boas was expiring, as the latter was about to retire from his professorship at Columbia. And Boas's connection with the Russian Academy, already weakened by changes there, truly ended with the death of his friend and colleague Vladimir Bogoraz on May 11, 1936.[111] In fact, about a thousand university students, including Phinney participated in Bogoraz's funeral. Speeches made there further clarify the impact of Stalinism on Phinney's experiences in the USSR. As Roy Barton described the funeral to Boas in 1940:

The Academy of Sciences turned out to meet the body and escort it to the Kazansky Cathedral, which now houses his Museum. It was brought back in a little car hitched to the rear of a passenger train. From the station it was loaded on a caisson drawn by a truck. We marched behind it with two or three brass bands, about 1000 in numbers. The body lay in state for four or five days . . . The funeral proper occurred on the fourth or fifth day, with long speeches by akademiks and a few professors. These were all of the same type, as, indeed, all speeches in that country are. They praised devotion to his energy, his organizing ability, his mind for detail, his devotion to his science, but all condemned his "mistakes"—these were that he opposed giving an ignorant class absolute power, against perpetuating the old feudal system with merely the exchange of party men for the feudal lords and officials. They had to talk that way whatever they thought about the matter. In a way, it was perhaps better that he died when he did. The next years would have pained him at the least and "they" might have caught him in the way many other good men have been caught. He was never forgiven for having opposed the Bolsheviks during the Revolution—he was a Menshevik you know . . .[112]

Kandidat Phinney

The Russian Academy had, in the meantime, offered Phinney the opportunity to pursue a *kandidat nauk* degree at Leningrad State University (now St. Petersburg State University), the first step toward a professorship. Though professorship was never his goal in life, Phinney wanted to work in the Indian Service in order to improve the conditions of Native people, especially the Nez Perce. He felt that he was "marking time," as he intimated in his letter to Boas dated July 11, until he could do so. No wonder Phinney wrote to his mother and father in June 1936 that he longed to return to Idaho but did not know when he was leaving for home because he was "still snowed under with work." He wrote, "I have almost three months [*sic*] work yet to finish," but it will "feel very strange when I shall at least leave here." Phinney recognized that, "To make the change back to America will be a big step." He expressed no wish to go to New York or into academia. His Idaho homelands called to him; he missed the climate "and the quietness there that [he] need[ed]." He wrote further, "I have forgotten what it feels like to go hunting or fishing."[113] Phinney was overly optimistic; he remained in Leningrad for almost one more year.

Archie Mark Phinney presented his dissertation on March 19, 1937, and successfully defended it on April 25, 1937, earning the candidate of sciences degree. Titled "Customs and Folklore of the Numipu," the dissertation was divided into four sections: "Language," "Pre-History," "History," and "Mythology." It was translated into Russian for the presentation and retranslated into English for publication.[114]

Chattopadhyaya was one of Phinney's examiners, and he gave Phinney his full support. Historian Nirode Barooah carefully summarized and quoted a copy of Chatto's report about Phinney's dissertation, and the following quotations are drawn from this copy.[115] Significantly, Chatto wrote that Phinney had not made progress on the Soviet Union's national minority policy, as had been expected. This lack was explained by the fact that Phinney had known almost nothing about Marxism/Leninism; he thus had to overcome the social and political viewpoint of the "educated liberal American bourgeoisie," as well as come to terms with their role in creating the situation of American Indians. Phinney's dissertation, then, focused on Nimiipuu society. Despite its methodological shortcomings, the dissertation provided background for "practical work for the solution of the national question of the American Indians." As Chattopadhyaya put it, Phinney was a deserving candidate for the degree, and the former hoped that, after returning to his people, Phinney would actively practice the principles of Marxism/Leninism, which he had studied in the Soviet Union. Further, he would "contribute to making the Indian tribes more progressive as a revolutionary national minority under the red flag of the Communist International and the unconquerable banner of Marx, Engels, and Lenin."[116]

The dissertation has a number of odd characteristics that Willard noted when he compared its English and Russian versions. Although Phinney had studied the Russian language for at least a year before traveling to the USSR and had had at least three years of subsequent training "in country," he was still required to have an official Russian translation, over which he apparently had little control.[117] Whoever translated the document— probably Chattopadhyaya—"may not have known English very well."[118] Willard also found that "there is a great deal of misinformation on the history and culture of the Numipu" in the document, which is odd because Phinney was certainly cognizant of Nez Perce language, ethnography, culture, and history. Further, the basic ethnographic description "of Numipu culture is warped to fit Morgan-Marxist theory of the time-group marriage, primitive social equality, and group communism."[119]

But given Chattopadhyaya's kind tutelage as well as the ideological and other dangers inherent to the Great Purge, none of these contradictions may be "odd" at all. In his personal correspondence and single publication, Phinney produced nothing to offend the NKVD. So, in May 1937 Phinney's tenure at the IAE was completed; he left the Soviet Union that same month and was in the United States by July.

Chattopadhyaya's fate was less kind; he was arrested on July 17 and executed on September 17, 1937. His crimes were related to political differences with Stalinist ideology—Chattopadhyaya was an ardent supporter of the Communist International—and shared a close association with Sergei Mironovich Kirov, Stalin's most potent political rival.[120] According to Barooah, "It seems that Soviet authorities [had] pressured some of Chatto's students into denouncing him."

Phinney left just one substantial item as a trace of his presence at the IAE: the aforementioned suit of Nez Perce clothing and regalia. The gift was acknowledged in a telegram dated March 10, 1937, signed by Vice Director M. V. Makarov and Academic Secretary C. M. Abramson. This telegram reads, "To Archie Phinney. The Museum of Anthropology Archaeology and Ethnology of the Academy of Science of the USSR expresses to you its profound gratitude for the collection of clothes of the North American tribe (Numipu) that you have donated to the Museum."[121] There is certainly nothing threatening, pro-Communist, or Stalinist in this transaction. He had done what many students do to mark their graduations; Phinney had repaid an academic obligation in a time-honored manner with a special gift.

Clearly, Archie Phinney was well advanced in his "hero's journey," as Willard had thought. Phinney managed to maintain his Nez Perce identity while in the University of Kansas, Washington DC, New York, and Leningrad. These were dangerous travels for many reasons, especially as a foreigner in the uncertain political environment of the USSR, where Phinney was under constant surveillance. He had seen the failure of the Soviet system in dealing with "the small peoples of the North" and that the Soviet method of dealing with "the national question" was not transferable to the United States. Still, he came away convinced that the survival of the Nez Perces and other Native American groups in the United States depended on a strong common identity and organization.

NOTES

William Willard passed away before completing this and the subsequent chapter. J. Diane Pearson and Alan G. Marshall have edited his manuscript for this publication.

1. "Archie Phinney Quietly at Rest at Jacques Spur," *Lewiston Morning Tribune* (Lewiston ID), November 3, 1949, 14.

2. Wilkinson, *Blood Struggle.*

3. Willard, "A Hero's Journey."

4. Allen P. Slickpoo Sr. (WeeYux Timenin "Marked Leggings"; 1929–2013) did not take Nimiipuu language, culture, and history for granted. Raised and trained by elders in the Kamiah–Kooskia area, he actively pursued knowledge about Nimiipuu life with anyone who would share knowledge; in turn, he shared that knowledge with other tribal people and presented it to others through two books (*Nu Mee Poom Tit Wah Tit* and *Noon Nee-Mee-Poo [We, the Nez Perces]*). He did not take Nimiipuu sovereignty for granted, either. Elected to the Nez Perce Tribal Executive Committee (NPTEC) in 1955 at age twenty-six; he was by decades the youngest member. He served into the late 1980s. After his retirement from NPTEC, he served the Nez Perce Tribe in many capacities. He was director of the tribe's Cultural Resource Program until ill health forced his retirement in 1998.

5. This is one of many stories William Willard orally related to us, which we added as footnotes when we were writing this chapter. We share these stories with you, as he intended.

6. Lloyd D. Brown, "Group to Play 'Igra' Games," *Evergreen* (Pullman WA), July 14, 1992, 1, 8. With the formal dissolution of the Union of Soviet Socialist Republics (USSR), interest in the former Russian Soviet Federated Socialist Republic and in how to resolve conflicts as new institutions developed both grew. "Igra" was a game developed by Russian scientists to develop those skills. The game was shared with faculty at Washington State University.

7. The Kunstkamera is located in St. Petersburg, Russia. Peter the Great's (1672–1725) collection of "curiosities," both natural and artificial, was the foundation of this museum; the building housing it was completed in 1734. "The Kunstkamera (Museum of Anthropology and Ethnography)," Saint-Petersburg.com, accessed April 23, 2016, http://www.saint-petersburg.com/museums/kunstkammer-museum-antropology-ethnography.

8. Telegram to Archie Mark Phinney, March 10, 1937, RG75, Archie Phinney Papers, NARA–Pacific Alaska Region, Seattle WA.

9. Willard believed these regalia to be Nez Perce in origin. However, Nakia Williamson and Robert Taylor, Nez Perce experts on material culture at the Nez Perce Tribe's Cultural Resource Program, reject Willard's identification.

10. Barooah, *Chatto*, 308.

11. Price, "Archie Phinney," 21–32.

12. The candidate of sciences degree (*kandidat nauk*) is considered in the UNESCO International Standard of Education as equivalent to a PhD in the United States. It was introduced into the Soviet system in early 1934.

13. Phinney, "Numipu among the White Settlers," 32. The manuscript for this publication was written during 1936–37 in Leningrad.

14. Phiney, "Archie Phinney," in Gridley, *Indians of Today*, 99.

15. "Forty Years Ago, Culdesac High School, Graduating Class of 1922," *Lewiston Morning Tribune* (Lewiston ID), May 7, 1962, 4.

16. Willard, "Nez Perce Anthropologist," 5.

17. Cannell, *Intermediary*; Josephy, *Nez Perce Indians*, 172–73; Thomas J. Beall, "Recollections of Wm. Craig," *Lewiston Morning Tribune* (Lewiston ID), March 3, 1918, 8. Craig married a Nez Perce woman, Pa-tis-sah, in 1838. After the fur trade collapsed, he eventually made his way to the Lapwai Valley in 1840. He was such a strong ally of Nez Perce people that his ownership of 640 acres in the Lapwai valley was recognized in Article 10 of the 1855 Treaty with the Nez Perces. He is buried near Jacques Spur, Idaho.

18. At this time coursework in cultural anthropology was found in the Sociology Department. Sica, "Sociology," 605–23.

19. "Usher in Season Today," *Lawrence Journal-World* (Lawrence KS), April 13, 1926, 3; "K. U. Nine Opens," *Lawrence Journal-World* (Lawrence KS), August 14, 1926, 3.

20. Willard, "Nez Perce Anthropologist," 7; Boas, "Truman Michelson," 113–16; Swanton, "John Napoleon Brinton Hewitt," 287.

21. Voegelin and Harris, "Index to the Franz Boas," 5–43. Phinney and Hewitt, *Nez Perce or Numipu*; Phinney and Hewitt, *Grammatical Notes*.

22. Phinney to Boas, June 1927, box 4, RG75, Archie Mark Phinney Papers, Bureau of Indian Affairs (BIA), Northern Idaho Agency, file "1926 to 1949." RG75, NARA–Pacific Northwest Region, Seattle WA.

23. Boas to Phinney, September 20, 1927, Mss.B.B61, Franz Boas Papers, APS. https://diglib.amphilsoc.org/islandora/object/text%3A97924.

24. A photograph of Phinney with his summer camp golf team is in the NPNHP Archie Phinney Collection.

25. Boas to Phinney, March 18, 1929, Mss.B.B61, Franz Boas Papers, APS, https://diglib.amphilsoc.org/islandora/object/text%3A17852.

26. Willard, review of Nez Perce Texts, by Archie Phinney, *Wicazō Ša Review* 15, no. 1 (Spring 2000): 236–41.

27. *Titwáatit* are Nimiipuu histories of the Earth's most ancient days and original beings.

28. Phiney to Boas, November 20, 1929, Mss.B.B61, Franz Boas Papers, APS, https://diglib.amphilsoc.org/islandora/object/text%3A97824.

29. Phiney to Boas, October 10, 1929, Mss.B.B61, Franz Boas Papers, APS, https://diglib.amphilsoc.org/islandora/object/text%3A97823.

30. Willard, "Nez Perce Anthropologist," 5–20.

31. Frederica de Laguna, quoted in McClellan, "Frederica de Laguna," 767.

32. Phiney, "Archie Phinney," in Gridley, *Indians of Today*, 99

33. Boas was *Time* magazine's "Man of the Year" in 1936. "Anthropologist Franz Boas," *Time*, May 11, 1936, 19, 27. As an example of his progressive/socialist leanings, Boas was on the advisory council to the American Society for Cultural Relations with Russia, an organization affiliated with the USSR's All-Union Society for Cultural Relations with Foreign Countries (VOKS). See "Soviet Union—Society for Cultural Relations," Soviet Union Information Bureau, Marxists.org, accessed September 26, 2016, https://www.marxists.org/history/ussr/government/1928/sufds/ch24.htm. A review of other members of the advisory council illustrates the difficulty of understanding the Russian Revolution and the progressive movement in the United States through the lens of the Red Scare, Cold War, and contemporary politics during the 1920s and 1930s.

34. Bogoraz was an anti-Tsarist revolutionary who was imprisoned, then exiled to the Yakutsk region. There he began his work among the Chukchi (1889–99), publishing poetry, novels, and ethnographic works.

35. Kan, "'My Old Friend,'" 50–53. Bogoraz was in New York City from September to November of 1928 for the 23rd International Congress of Americanists and for academic studies. See also Slezkine, *Arctic Mirrors*.

36. Averkieva went to British Columbia, Canada, with Franz Boas in 1930 to work with the "Kwakiutl"—properly, the "Kwakwaka'wakw"—people; she studied string figures. Later she, along with her husband and two children, was somehow caught up in the maelstrom of Stalin's Russia in the 1940s and was imprisoned for five years. She returned to ethnography after being rehabilitated in 1956 and led a distinguished career.

37. The New Economic Policy, which created a mixed economy, was devised by Lenin and put into action in 1923 to replace the disastrous policy of war communism. The "Great Transformation" has a variety of synonyms, including the "Great Change" or "Great Turn"; these terms refer to the collectivization of the agricultural sector of the Soviet economy to create *kolkozy* and *sovkozy*, or collective- and state-owned industrial farms, respectively. These new agricultural organizations supposedly erased the social differences among agricultural workers, industrial workers, and "the small peoples of the North," creating an industrial proletariat. This new proletariat would, the Soviet ideologists imagined, create the surpluses necessary to fuel rapid heavy industrialization. They were initiated by Stalin's first Five-Year Plan in 1928. The policy apparently failed, as it was followed by food shortages and famine.

38. "The small peoples of the North" were primarily hunters, fishers, and reindeer herders with no common "national identity" at the time of this discussion. They were most similar to the remaining Native peoples of the United States. By 1932, however, "the small peoples of the North" became merely "backward" in the eyes of the government; their cultures were dismissed, and they were subjected to very strong yet only partly successful assimilative pressure from the Soviet government. See Slezkine, *Arctic Mirrors* for a thorough discussion of this issue in the Soviet Union.

39. Kan, "'My Old Friend,'" 44–45. See also Slezkine, "Fall of Soviet Ethnography," 476–84; Slezkine, *Arctic Mirrors*, 87–189; Gellner et al., "Soviet and the Savage," 595–617.

40. In this context, the terms "national" and "nationality" roughly refers to "ethnic group." Additionally, though, the term suggests that the ethnic group is at least capable of forming a unique "state." Because the "small peoples of the North" were not seen as fulfilling that criterion, they were increasingly ignored in this process.

41. Anderson and Arzyutov, "Construction of Soviet Ethnography," 183–209.

42. Matorin, it seems, was a "Red Professor": someone trained in the Institute of Red Professors of the All-Union Communist Party (Bolsheviks). Often without a strong academic background (some lacked a secondary education) but with strong loyalty to the regime, the Red Professors received strong ideological training and were "proclaimed Full Professors and put in charge of academic institutes, faculties and departments, or appointed as editors-in-chief of leading academic journals etc. Many qualified scholars of the 'old school' were declared '*bourgeois*' by these newcomers, which generally meant their expulsion from institutes and universities, often their imprisonment, exile or even execution (like Zolotarjov, Dolgikh and others)." Bondarenko and Korotayev, "In Search," 234.

43. The theory governing the personnel and organizational structure was "Japhetic theory," promulgated by the linguist Nicolai Yakovlevich Marr. Marr's theory, now debunked, applies the concept of class struggle to linguistics, and it became the official position of the Party. Matorin was a "Marrist."

44. Kan, "'My Old Friend,'" 56.

45. The United States and Union of Soviet Socialist Republics had no formal relations until 1933. Boris Evssevich Skvirsky worked for VOKS, an organization that gathered information about "cultural trends," sponsored contact among cultural workers and intellectuals, and managed societies favorable to the Soviet Union. In the United States that society was the American Society for Cultural Relations with Russia; Boas sat on its advisory board. Skvirsky became *charge d'affairs* at the Soviet Embassy in Washington DC when formal relations were established in 1933. He became suspect after eleven years of service in the United States. When he was recalled to the Soviet Union in February 1937, he was briefly posted to Afghanistan, recalled again, purged, imprisoned, then tried and executed July 8, 1941, for "participation in a terrorist organization and espionage."

46. LL. 56 560b., Ed.hr.12, Op.1 (1931), F.142, SPF ARAN, translated by Sergei Kan and SARS, Woodside CA; archival research, Dr. Svetlana Podrezova, St. Petersburg, Russia.

47. Boas to Edward Sapir, October 25, 1932, Mss.B.B61, Franz Boas Papers, APS, https://diglib.amphilsoc.org/islandora/object/text:106636.

48. Willard, "Nez Perce Anthropologist," 5–20.

49. Boas and Phinney's anxiety over "conditions" may have been stoked by conflicting reports of this famine, known as "Holodomor" in the Ukrainian Soviet Socialist Republic and in neighboring Kuban, where up to 7.5 million people died from its effects. The famine was more widespread than in the Ukraine, however, and many millions more died. Its cause was the collectivization of agriculture under Stalin's second Five Year Plan.

50. Phinney to Matorin, October 15, 1931, SPF ARAN, F.142. Op.1 (1931). Ed.hr.12, 96l, LL.74.

51. Boas to Matorin, November 23, 1931, Mss.B.B61, Franz Boas Papers, APS, https://diglib.amphilsoc.org/islandora/object/text%3A86744. "Amtorg," or "Amerikanskaia Torgovlia," was the American Trading Corporation, the first Soviet trade organization in the United States. Armand Hammer was a key figure in forming this trade group in 1924.

52. Boas to Boris D. Skvirsky, October 9, 1931, Mss.B.B61, Franz Boas Papers, APS; Phinney to Boas, January 21, 1932, Mss.B.B61, Franz Boas Papers, APS, https://diglib.amphilsoc.org/islandora/object/text%3A113193.

53. Boas to Matorin, February 8, 1932, Mss.B.B61, Franz Boas Papers, APS, http://diglib.amphilsoc.org/islandora/object/text%3A86745.

54. Averkieva to Boas, May 4, 1932, Mss.B.B61, Franz Boas Papers, APS, https://diglib.amphilsoc.org/islandora/object/averkieva-julie%3A-boas-1932-may-4.

55. Boas to Averkieva, May 19, 1932, Mss.B.B61, Franz Boas Papers, APS, https://diglib.amphilsoc.org/islandora/object/averkieva-julie%3A-boas-1932-may-19.

56. Meriam, *Problem of Indian Administration*.

57. Before the "Red Scare" of the post–World War II era, many scholars and policymakers were interested in Soviet minority policy regarding the ethnic groups within the USSR, of which there are more than 140. See Hula, "Nationalities Policy," 168–201; Kehoe, *Passion for the True*, 76; Darnell et al., *Franz Boas Papers*, 266.

58. J. V. Stalin, *Marxism and the National Question*, Marxists Internet Archive, https://www.marxists.org/reference/archive/stalin/works/1913/03.

59. V. Ulianov and Josef Dzhugashvili, "Declaration of the Rights of the People of Russia," Marxists.org, https://www.marxists.org/history/ussr/government/1917/11/02.htm. This declaration was translated into English and published in *The Nation*, December 28, 1919, and so was available to the American audience.

60. Smith, "Cultural Persistence," 266–71. Apparently, Phinney's paper was forwarded to the Superintendent of the Northern Idaho Agency—a "Mr. Upchurch"—who reviewed it somewhat unfavorably. Phinney wrote a detailed rebuttal to the review in a letter to the Commissioner of Indian Affairs, June 4, 1932, PI-163 E-121, Box No. 1, 00-1910-011 to 61156-1929-052, Fort Lapwai, 1907-39, Central Classified Files, RG75, NARA).

61. Boas to Matorin, January 12, 1933, Mss.B.B61, Franz Boas Papers, APS, https://diglib.amphilsoc.org/islandora/object/text%3A86746.

62. Phinney to Boas, January 21, 1932, Mss.B.B61, Franz Boas Papers, APS, https://diglib.amphilsoc.org/islandora/object/text%3A97827.

63. Phinney to Boas, November 13, 1932, Mss.B.B61, Franz Boas Papers, APS, https://diglib.amphilsoc.org/islandora/object/text%3A97829.

64. Phinney to Boas, November 13, 1932, Mss.B.B61, Franz Boas Papers, APS, http://diglib.amphilsoc.org/islandora/object/text%3A97829.

65. Matorin to Boas, January 12, 1933, Mss.B.B61, Franz Boas Papers, APS, https://diglib.amphilsoc.org/islandora/object/text%3A86746. Some miscommunication about what constituted "Siberia" was likely.

66. Matorin to Boas, December 15, 1932, Mss.B.B61, Franz Boas Papers, APS, https://diglib.amphilsoc.org/islandora/object/text%3A86749. This typescript letter was written in German; translation by Alan Marshall.

67. Phinney to Boas, November 13, 1932, Mss.B.B61, Franz Boas Papers, APS, https://diglib.amphilsoc.org/islandora/object/text%3A97829.

68. Phinney to Boas, May 22, 1933, Mss.B.B61, Franz Boas Papers, APS, https://diglib.amphilsoc.org/islandora/object/text%3A97837.

69. Phinney to Boas, August 8, 1933, Mss.B.B61, Franz Boas Papers, APS, https://diglib.amphilsoc.org/islandora/object/text%3A97838.

70. Archie Phinney Collection, Nez Perce National Historical Park, Spalding ID.

71. Phinney to Boas, August 8, 1933, Mss.B.B61, Franz Boas Papers, APS, https://diglib.amphilsoc.org/islandora/object/text%3A97838.

72. Arzyutov, "Samoyedic Diary," 345, 346.

73. Willard, "Nez Perce Anthropologist," 12; Kan, "'My Old Friend,'" 33–68.

74. Averkieva to Boas, February 4, 1933, Mss.B.B61, Franz Boas Papers, APS, https://diglib.amphilsoc.org/islandora/object/averkieva-julie%3A-boas-1933-feb-4.

75. Averkieva to Boas, October 9, 1933, Mss.B.B61, Franz Boas Papers, APS, https://diglib.amphilsoc.org/islandora/object/averkieva-julie%3A-boas-1933-oct-9.

76. Kan, "'My Old Friend,'" 55–57. Despite her commitment to Soviet ideals, Averkieva was sentenced to the gulag from late 1947 to the early 1950s. Kan, "'My Old Friend,'" 65n39.

77. Phinney to Boas, December 26, 1932, Mss.B.B61, Franz Boas Papers, APS, https://diglib.amphilsoc.org/islandora/object/text%3A97830. Jack Harris, one of Melville J. Herskovits's students, "jumped ship" from a cargo vessel in Leningrad. Before being expelled by the authorities Harris visited the MAE (by then called the Institute of Anthropology and Ethnography due to Stalinist reorganization) in September 1934. Harris wrote in a letter to Herskovits: "I wanted to write you from Leningrad but did not because of the rigid censorship of the mails." Folder 13, box 9, series 35/6, Melville J. Herskovits Papers, Northwestern University Archives, Evanston IL.

78. Manjapra, *Age of Entanglement*, 104.

79. In both an earlier draft of this chapter and discussions, Willard commented that Phinney's letters exhibited a "bizarre lack of informative communication" about his ethnographic work in the USSR. He thought that this was designed to pass the scrutiny of the secret police. However, most of the Phinney–Boas correspondence concerned Phinney's completion and publication of his book *Nez Perce Texts* and some financial issues. Once those projects were settled, the correspondence between the two declined and ended soon after Boas's retirement in the summer of 1937.

80. Agnes Smedley to Boas, May 28, 1934, Mss.B.B61, Franz Boas Papers, APS, https://diglib.amphilsoc.org/islandora/object/text%3A113294.

81. The United States had recognized the Russian Provisional Government in March 1917. Woodrow Wilson withheld unofficial as well as official recognition of the Bolshevik government following the October Revolution. Wilson also entered the Russian Civil War in support of the Allies against the Bolshevik Red Army. Two forces were dispatched in September 1918: the American North Russia Expeditionary Force (about 5000 troops) to Arkhangelsk and the American Expeditionary Force Siberia (7950 troops) to Vladivostok. Withdrawals of these forces began in June 1919.

82. Agnes Smedley to Boas, May 28, 1934, Mss.B.B61, Franz Boas Papers, APS, https://diglib.amphilsoc.org/islandora/object/text%3A113294.

83. Such was Roy F. Barton's experience. See Price, "Fear and Loathing," 5–7.

84. Tzouliadis, *Forsaken*.

85. Price, *Lives of Agnes Smedley*, 248. See also MacKinnon and MacKinnon, "Moscow, New York, and Shanghai." Smedley was a controversial figure in American and international politics. She may have met Phinney in Kislovodsk—where she, too, had gone for rest—in the late summer of 1933. Later that year and in early 1934 they met in Moscow and Leningrad, respectively. Smedley had a long-standing relationship with Virendranath Chattopadhyaya. Roger Baldwin (1884–1981) was a founder of the American Civil Liberties Union; initially a supporter of the USSR, he became deeply antipathetic to Stalinist/Soviet ideology and its sympathizers. See also Price, "Fear and Loathing," 3–8.

86. Agnes Smedley to Boas, May 28, 1934, Mss.B.B61, Franz Boas Papers, APS, http://diglib.amphilsoc.org/islandora/object/text%3A113294.

87. Duggan, "Fifteenth Annual Report," 11.

88. Archie Phinney Archive, Nez Perce National Historical Park, Spalding ID.

89. Harris presents a quite different view of the Leningrad seaman's "home" than the very positive one presented by reporter L. M. Houseman of the Moscow News. See L. M. Houseman, "Leningrad Has 'Home from Home' for Seaman," *Moscow News*, March 15, 1933, 7.

90. Jack Harris to Melville J. Herskovits, October 25, 1933, *Harris-Herskovits Correspondence*, series 35/4/13, Northwestern University Archives. For more information about Jack Harris, see Yelvington, "Jack Sargent Harris, Obituary," 537–39; and Yelvington, "A Life In and Out," 446–76.

91. S. M. Kirov was First Secretary of the Leningrad Regional Committee of the All-Union Communist Party (Bolsheviks), First Secretary of the Leningrad City Committee, a member of the Politburo, the Seventeenth Secretariat, and Seventeenth Orgburo at the time of his killing. Kirov was popular, and many believe that Stalin had arranged this murder of a potential rival.

92. The Communist International (Comintern), or Third International, lasted from 1919 to 1943. This international organization was aimed at world revolution overthrowing the bourgeoisie. It was in direct conflict with Stalin's implementation of Nikolai Bukharin's theory of "Socialism in One Country."

93. Kan, *Lev Shternberg*. Matorin was sentenced to five years in a labor camp, but in February he was returned to Leningrad. On October 11 the Military Collegium of the Supreme Court of the USSR tried and convicted him of an active role in the counterrevolutionary Trotskyite-Zinovievite Terrorist Center, which assassinated Kirov. He was executed right away.

94. Nez Perce National Historical Park, Archie Phinney Collection. The photograph picturing the balding Matorin behind a makeshift desk is inscribed, "To dear friend—first (American) Indian scientific worker in the USSR—from N.M. Matorin (photographed in Moldovia Autonomous Region during ethnographic expedition in the summer of 1934)—6 November 1934, on the eve of the October Revolution Day."

95. V. Chattopadhyaya was an Indian revolutionary and friend of Agnes Smedley, who had supported "Hindu nationalists" in California during the 1910s. "Chatto," as he was familiarly known, had emigrated to the USSR following Hitler's Machterbegreifung ("seizure of power") in 1933 and the purge of the German Communist Party (KPD). Chatto was not only a foreigner and KPD member but also a stalwart member of the Comintern, which made him triply suspect in the eyes of the Stalinist regime.

96. Barooah, *Chatto*, 308.

97. Barooah, *Chatto*, 307.

98. Archie Phinney, *Lewiston Tribune* (Lewiston ID), September 29, 1935, in Burbick, *Rodeo Queens*, 24.

99. MacKinnon and MacKinnon, "Moscow, New York, and Shanghai."

100. Kan, "'My Old Friend,'" 55. Perhaps Averkieva's complaint that Phinney was merely a tourist was related to this proscription; For what possible reason would one travel if one could not conduct research?

101. Phinney to Boas, September 6, 1934, Mss.B.B61, Franz Boas Papers, APS, https://diglib.amphilsoc.org/islandora/object/text%3A97847.

102. The information on the local governing body is contained in Anna Louise Strong's book *I Change Worlds*, written after her visit to Nagorno Altaiskayia about one year after Phinney's trip. See Strong, *I Change Worlds*. Strong was a well-known progressive activist and reporter who supported Communist movements. Expatriated, she lived in and reported about political and economic developments principally in the

USSR and China. She founded the English language publication *Moscow News* with Party approval in 1930. See Strong and Keyssar, *Right in Her Soul*.

103. Strong, *I Change Worlds*.
104. The Indian Service, commonly known as the BIA, was developed by the United States to augment the conquest, colonization, and control of American Indians. Acquisition of land, imperial powers, and domination of Native peoples were aided by the treaty system, the reservation system, and hundreds of federal statutes aimed exclusively at American Indians. Indigenous religions were suppressed, formal education was delegated to federal or Christian authorities, and most American Indians were denied the vote. The basic system remained unchanged until the reforms mandated by the IRA of 1934.
105. Price, "Archie Phinney, the FBI, and the FOIA," 25.
106. Archie Phinney, "Racial Minorities."
107. Phinney to Boas, April 26, 1935, Mss.B.B61, Franz Boas Papers, APS, https://diglib.amphilsoc.org/islandora/object/text%3A97850.
108. Boas to Phinney, June 5, 1935, Mss.B.B61, Franz Boas Papers, APS, https://diglib.amphilsoc.org/islandora/object/text%3A97819.
109. Phinney to Boas, July 11, 1935, Mss.B.B61, Franz Boas Papers, APS, https://diglib.amphilsoc.org/islandora/object/text%3A97851.
110. Boas to Phinney, September 9, 1935, Mss.B.B61, Franz Boas Papers, APS, https://diglib.amphilsoc.org/islandora/object/text%3A97820.
111. Boas, "Waldemar Bogoras," 314–15.
112. R. F. Barton to Boas, November 17, 1940, Mss.B.B61, Franz Boas Papers, APS, https://diglib.amphilsoc.org/islandora/object/barton-rf%3A-boas-1940-nov-17.
113. Excerpts from Archie Phinney to Mr. and Mrs. Fitch Phinney (his parents), *Lewiston Morning Tribune* (Lewiston ID), June 6, 1936.
114. Willard, "Nez Perce Anthropologist," 15.
115. Barooah, "Chatto," 308–9.
116. Barooah, "Chatto," 308. The fact that Chattopadhyaya publicly spoke positively of the Communist International shows that he was both principled and courageous—the Stalinists were purging them at the time.
117. Willard, "Nez Perce Anthropologist," 11.
118. Willard, "Nez Perce Anthropologist," 15.
119. Willard, "Nez Perce Anthropologist," 15.
120. Barooah, "Chatto," 320–24. See also Manjapra, *Age of Entanglement*, 104. Manjapra states, "During the purges, a campaign to prove his heterodoxy, and letters from some of his students, especially Archie Phinney, as well as from his ex-wife Agnes Smedley, accused him of being an Indian nationalist, not a 'true' Soviet." Through a researcher in Moscow's Russian State Archives of Socio-Political History, we were unable to find Phinney's letter in the archive cited by Manjapra.

121. Telegram to Archie Mark Phinney, March 10, 1937, RG75, Archie Phinney Papers, NARA-Pacific Alaska Region, Seattle WA.

BIBLIOGRAPHY

Anderson, David G., and Dmitry V. Arzyutov. "The Construction of Soviet Ethnography and the Peoples of Siberia." *History and Anthropology* 27, no. 2 (2016): 183–209.

Arzyutov, Dmitry V. "Samoyedic Diary: Early Years of Visual Anthropology in the Soviet Arctic." *Visual Anthropology* 29, no. 4–5 (2016): 331–59.

Barooah, Nirode K. *Chatto: The Life and Times of an Indian Anti-Imperialist in Europe*. New York: Oxford University Press, 2004.

Boas, Franz. "Truman Michelson." *International Journal of American Linguistics* 9, no. 2/4 (January 1938): 113–16.

———. "Waldemar Bogoras." *American Anthropologist* 39, no. 2 (April–June 1937): 314–15.

Bondarenko, Dmitri M., and Andrey V. Korotayev. "In Search of a New Academic Profile: Teaching Anthropology in Contemporary Russia." In *Educational Histories of European Anthropology*, edited by Dorle Dracklé, Iain R. Edgar, and Thomas K. Schippers, 230–46. New York: Berghahn Books, 2003.

Burbick, Joan. *Rodeo Queens: On the Circuit with America's Cowgirls*. New York: Public Affairs, 2004.

Cannell, Lin Tull. *The Intermediary: William Craig among the Nez Perces*. Carlton OR: Ridenbaugh Press, 2010.

Collier, John. "Restoration of the Red Atlantis." *Survey* 49 (October 1922): 15–19, 62–63.

Darnell, Regna, Joshua Smith, Michelle Hamilton, and Robert L. A. Hancock, eds. *The Franz Boas Papers*. Vol. 1. Lincoln: University of Nebraska Press. 2015.

Duggan, Stephen. "Fifteenth Annual Report of the Director." New York: Institute of International Education, 1934.

Gellner, Ernest, Olga Akhmanova, Frank B. Bessac, Yu V. Bromley, Tamara Dragadze, Stephen P. Dunn, J. L. Fischer, et. al. "The Soviet and the Savage [and Comments and Replies]." *Current Anthropology* 16, no. 4 (December 1975): 595–617.

Gridley, Marion E., ed. *Indians of Today*. Chicago: Indian Council Fires, 1936.

Hula, Erich. "The Nationalities Policy of the Soviet Union: Theory and Practice." *Social Research* 11, no. 2 (Summer 1944): 168–201.

Josephy, Alvin M., Jr. *The Nez Perce Indians and the Opening of the Northwest*. New Haven CN: Yale University Press.

Kan, Sergei. *Lev Shternberg: Anthropologist, Russian Socialist, Jewish Activist*. Lincoln: University of Nebraska Press. 2009.

———. "'My Old Friend in a Dead-End of Empiricism and Skepticism': Bogoras, Boas, and the Politics of Soviet Anthropology of the Late 1920s–Early 1930s." *Histories of Anthropology* 2, no. 1 (2006): 33–68.

Kehoe, Alice Beck. *A Passion for the True and Just: Felix and Lucy Kramer Cohen and the Indian New Deal*. Tucson: University of Arizona Press, 2014.

MacKinnon, Janice R., and Stephen R. MacKinnon. *Agnes Smedley: The Life and Times of an American Radical*. Ars Femina: Online Frauenbibliothek, accessed August 12, 2016, http://arsfemina.de/agnes-smedley/moscow-new-york-and-shanghai-1933 -1936.

Manjapra, Kris. *Age of Entanglement: German and Indian Intellectuals across Empire*. Cambridge: Harvard University Press, 2014.

McClellan, Catherine. "Frederica de Laguna and the Pleasures of Anthropology." *American Ethnologist* 16, no. 4 (November 1989): 766–85.

Meriam, Lewis. *The Problem of Indian Administration: Report of a Survey Made at the Request of Honorable Hubert Work, Secretary of the Interior, and Submitted to Him February 21, 1928*. Baltimore MD: Johns Hopkins Press, 1928.

Phinney, Archie. *Nez Perce Texts*. New York: Columbia University Press, 1934.

———. "Numipu among the White Settlers." *Wicazo Sa Review* 17, no. 2 (Fall 2002): 21–43.

———. "Racial Minorities in the Soviet Union," *Pacific Affairs* 8, no. 3 (September 1935): 321–27.

Phinney, Mark [Archie Mark Phinney], and J. N. B. Hewitt. *Grammatical Notes on the Language of the Nez Perces*. February 13, 1927. Manuscript 2338. National Anthropological Archives, Smithsonian Institution, Washington DC.

———. *Nez Perce or Numipu Legends*. February 13, 1927. Manuscript 2339. National Anthropological Archives, Smithsonian Institution, Washington DC.

Price, David H. "Archie Phinney, the FBI, and the FOIA." *Journal of Northwest Anthropology* 38, no. 1 (Spring 2004), 21–32.

———. "Fear and Loathing in the Soviet Union: Roy Barton and the NKVD." *History of Anthropology Newsletter* 28, no. 2 (December 2001): 3–8.

———. *Threatening Anthropology: McCarthyism and the FBI's Surveillance of Activist Anthropologists*. Durham NC: Duke University Press, 2004.

Price, Ruth. *The Lives of Agnes Smedley*. New York: Oxford University Press, 2005.

Sica, Alan. "Sociology at the University of Kansas, 1889–1983: An Historical Sketch." *Sociological Quarterly* 24, no. 4 (September 1983): 605–30.

Slezkine, Yuri. *Arctic Mirrors: Russia and the Small Peoples of the North*. Ithaca NY: Cornell University Press, 1994.

———. "The Fall of Soviet Ethnography, 1928–38." *Current Anthropology* 32, no. 4 (August–October 1991): 476–84.

Smith, Joshua. "Cultural Persistence in the Age of 'Hopelessness': Phinney, Boas, and U.S. Indian Policy." In *The Franz Boas Papers, Volume 1*, edited by Regna Darnell, Joshua Smith, Michelle Hamilton and Robert L. A. Hancock, 263–76. Lincoln: University of Nebraska Press, 2015.

Strong, Anna Louise. *I Change Worlds: The Remaking of an American*. New York: Henry Holt, 1937.

Strong, Tracey, and Helene Keyssar. *Right in Her Soul: The Life of Anna Louise Strong*. New York: Random House, 1984.

Swanton, John. "John Napoleon Brinton Hewitt." *American Anthropologist* 40, no. 2 (April–June 1938): 286–90.

Tzouliadis, Tim. *The Forsaken: An American Tragedy in Stalin's Russia.* New York: Penguin, 2008.

Voegelin, C. F., and Harris, Z. S. "Index to the Franz Boas Collection of Materials for American Linguistics." *Language* 21 no. 3 (July–September 1945): 5–43

Wilkinson, Charles F. *Blood Struggle: The Rise of Modern Indian Nations.* New York: Norton, 2005.

Willard, William. "A Hero's Journey: Prologue for the Odyssey of Archie Phinney." In possession of Alan G. Marshall, n.d.

——. "The Nez Perce Anthropologist." *Journal of Northwest Anthropology* 38, no. 1 (Spring 2004): 5–19.

Willard, William, Roy Franklin Barton, and Franz Boas. "American Anthropologists on the Neva: 1930–1940." *History of Anthropology Newsletter* 27, no. 1 (June 2000): 3–9.

Yelvington, Kevin A. "A Life In and Out of Anthropology: An Interview with Jack Sargent Harris." *Critique of Anthropology* 28, no. 4 (December 2008): 446–76.

——. "Jack Sargent Harris, Obituary." *American Anthropologist* 113, no. 3 (September 2011): 537–39.

5 Archie Phinney, Indigenous Nationalist

WILLIAM WILLARD, J. DIANE PEARSON, AND ALAN G. MARSHALL

In commemoration of his undying efforts concerning Indian Affairs, as a founder of the National Congress of American Indians, for his work as superintendent of the Northern Idaho Agency, and for his distinction in scholastic achievement, this memorial is hereby dedicated this 27th day of September, 1958.

—THE NEZ PERCE TRIBE

Archie Phinney had earned a *kandidat nauk* degree in history from the Russian Academy of Sciences in June 1937 after five years of study at the Institute of Anthropology and Ethnography in Leningrad. His studies focused on the Soviet Union's minority policy. Their "national" policy was crucial to the Bolshevik's consolidation of power over the collapsed Tsarist empire, which comprised a variety of nationalities, cultures, and ethnic groups that spoke a wide variety of languages and dialects. These diverse peoples regarded the Russians with some suspicion: Would specifically Russian interests subsume their own under the new government? Resolving the "national question" was essential to forming a Bolshevik government. Stalin, a Georgian national, was detailed to study the issue. In 1917 Lenin and Stalin forwarded a "Declaration of the Rights of the People of Russia" which promulgated territorial recognition, native-language use, cultural autonomy, and even rights of secession.[1] They may have hoped to convince the ethnic Others that the latter would have some measure of self-governance in the process of communist world revolution.

While many progressives in the United States imagined that the Soviet experiment would offer some solutions to social issues in the United States, Phinney found little hope on the ground in the USSR. Korenizatsiya—or "putting down [Soviet] roots"—was the method for carrying change forward. It was realized through institutions such as the Committee of the North and the Museum of Anthropology and Ethnography (MAE). Following Lenin's death in 1924, Stalin began consolidating power by suppressing proponents of internationalist and other visions of communism with his "One country, one socialism" policy. The policy of Korenizatsiya eroded and was functionally abandoned in the early 1930s. This conflict, which began in earnest about the time Phinney arrived in Leningrad, finally resulted in the "Great Terror." In it, at least some of Phinney's mentors—namely Nikolai Matorin and Virendranath Chattopadhyaya—were both "purged."

Archie Phinney returned to the United States shortly before Chattopadhyaya's arrest and execution in the summer of 1937.[2] Phinney was convinced that "the Soviet method" of dealing with minorities would not work in the United States.[3] Phinney's studies of Siberia apparently led him to believe that "the small peoples of the north" (the people most like the Nez Perce and other Native Americans) lacked a large population, relatively complex organization, and political solidarity—in short, a "national identity" as the Russians defined it—leaving them prey to the interests of the Russian central government, its representatives, and Russian newcomers. That government easily dismissed their lives in the rush to extract resources to support industrialization.[4] He also saw that the large, organized groups with strong national identities were considered a force to be reckoned with by the agents of the industrial state being developed by the Soviets under Stalin. Seeing the issues of American Indian lives in this light, Phinney set out to strengthen tribal organizations and develop a nationwide Native identity.[5] These developments, he believed, would make American Indians a political force to be reckoned with. But such developments were not necessarily well met by all Indigenous people, including many Nimiipuu.

Phinney's immediate problems upon his return were to readjust to life in the United States and to obtain a position in the Indian Service. In the background, the continuing conservative reaction against social unrest and the outbreaks of "popular front" movements following World War I mitigated Phinney's effectiveness.[6] Phinney's five-year sojourn in the USSR and his *kandidat nauk* degree made him suspect as a communist, and his career path was followed by J. Edgar Hoover's Federal Bureau of Investigation (FBI). Moreover, the Bureau of Indian Affairs (BIA) was regarded by many conservatives as a hotbed of communists, which added resistance to BIA-sponsored indigenous development.

John Collier Becomes Commissioner of Indian Affairs

The man who would become Phinney's boss, John Collier, had become Commissioner of Indian Affairs in 1933, when he introduced major changes to BIA policies by actuating the Indian Reorganization Act (IRA, or the Wheeler-Howard Act) of 1934. First outlined in 1922 by Collier in his article, "Restoration of the Red Atlantis," the IRA provided legislative guidelines for restructuring the BIA and the federal Indian reservation system.[7] Three policy guidelines were essential to the IRA: American Indian economic rehabilitation (especially of American Indian lands), tribal self-government and organization, and civil and cultural freedoms and opportunities for American Indians. The IRA provided for the adoption of tribal council systems and governments based on written constitutions that were approved by tribal elections. Tribes could also organize as corporations in order to manage the development of Indian-owned resources; tribal members also determined acceptance or refusal of the IRA by majority-rule elections.[8] Nevertheless, self-governance remained tethered to the federal government through the Secretary of Interior, who held final approval of tribal government decisions.

Collier had experienced unique opportunities to put his vision of the "Red Atlantis" forward. Having spent ten years as an Indian rights lobbyist, Collier was part of a select group that included Harold Ickes, whom President Franklin D. Roosevelt appointed Secretary of the Interior in 1933. Ickes, in turn, recommended Collier as Commissioner of Indian Affairs, which also ensured Collier's access to the president. Driven to change U.S. and inter-American policies affecting Indigenous people, Collier was a visionary and a ruthless radical who often turned the tables on his opponents.

Neither Franz Boas nor Felix Cohen were supportive of Collier's appointment.[9] Both had similar concerns: Collier ignored treaties and locally driven, historically sensitive development to focus on civil liberties, moving too quickly using a single governmental template. Boas—a long-time supporter of Phinney's, as mentioned—argued for "the importance for officials to understand Native law and Native customs, together with the Russian example of recognizing the rights and the ability of their Native peoples to develop in accordance with their own cultures."[10] Cohen outlined, in a letter to Boas, his concerns regarding the selection and performance of Collier as Commissioner of Indian Affairs and who would be best to advise him. He went on to express his disappointment that Phinney was in Russia and unavailable to work for the BIA on "work involving the drawing up of community charters and constitutions (based on a knowledge of the history—& [sic] culture of particular Indian tribes). It is in the latter field we feel Archie Phinney, with his anthrop. training & recent work on racial Minorities in Russia, may prove of real value." Cohen further asks for Boas's opinion regarding Phinney's "qualifications & ability for this particular kind of work."[11]

Collier was well aware of Archie Phinney's unique qualifications for working with American Indians. In a memorandum to Phinney (who was still in the USSR) dated August 9, 1934, Collier stressed, "There is a need of workers with anthropological training"; these people should have field experience "among the American Indians or other native people," and they must express a "genuine interest in the contemporary problems" of Native Americans. Following that, Collier reminded Phinney, "Professor Boas has spoken highly of your experience, ability, and interest."[12]

Phinney's description of his studies in the USSR helps to explain his selection by Collier.

My work has been mainly anthropological but I have given a great deal of time to the study of national minority policies as carried into operation in southern Russia and Siberia. As a matter of fact, one of the aims of Soviet ethnography is to define the processes of Soviet ethnography [and] to define the processes of social development as a basis for programs that will consolidate all possible forces for cultural and industrial development. Thus my work here has been doubly interesting.[13]

Phinney also reported in his civil service record that he was preparing studies of economic development and local governments, as structured by Soviet policies applied to the national minorities of the USSR, but there was nothing appropriate for referral to U.S. reservations. Neither the Caucasus, the Nagorno Altai, nor the Buryat Oblast were inhabited by "the Siberian native tribes," at least as American anthropologists conceived of Siberia; nor were the three parts of southern Russia. Yet these areas presented "native problems" for Russian domination then and even today. Phinney told Boas that he was studying local governance in all of these places.

Phinney had written to Boas in September 1934 that he appreciated the chance to work for the BIA. He had also received two more letters from Collier suggesting that he make a formal application to the BIA. "Regarding my efforts to get established in the Indian Service," Phinney told Boas, "I still have nothing definite to report." He had sent his application to Collier a month earlier with a brief letter stating his view of Indian problems and present programs as well as "indicating a definite line of work for which [he] consider[ed] [himself] qualified." Shortly after that, Collier's reply assured Phinney they knew all about him and were keen: "We want you in the Indian Service." Collier continued that he could not say yet what, or if, there would be a problem with the Civil Service, though he was optimistic: "I think we can elude it, as you are an Indian. When will you reach the United States?"[14]

Archie Phinney, Indigenous Nationalist

Once back in the United States, Phinney accepted an offer of employment from BIA director John Collier.[15] As D'Arcy McNickle had told John Collier on June 18, he thought it "rather amazing" that Phinney's early work had essentially anticipated the Indian Reorganization Act. "A person who has this quality of intellect," said McNickle, "it seems to me, could put his hand to anything and do a creditable job. There are too few such persons around."[16]

Dr. Archie Phinney was hired as an agent in the Reorganization Division of the Bureau of Indian Affairs (BIA). Phinney's primary goal was to advance Native control of Native American life. He worked on two fronts: the first was to develop an American Indian political organization that would represent all Native Americans in the United States, and the second was to establish a strong Nez Perce tribal government that would assert its sovereignty in order to stop the erosion of the land, language, and resources embraced by the Nez Perce homeland. President Franklin D. Roosevelt's reorganized BIA offered a federal bureaucratic platform for furthering these goals.

John Collier needed Phinney, with his stellar education and his many talents, in the Reorganization Division. Phinney was valuable for several reasons: he was an anthropologist who had fieldwork experience among "national minorities" in the USSR, an enrolled member of the Nez Perce Tribe of Idaho, and a graduate of the University of Kansas who held a doctorate-equivalent degree from Leningrad State University. No one else in the Reorganization Division had such a unique background. Like Phinney, every Reorganization agent was an enrolled tribal member except for two long-time BIA employees, Oscar Lipps and Joe Jennings. Another agent, D'Arcy McNickle (Salish Kootenai) had traveled abroad in England and Europe but had not conducted fieldwork.

The Reorganization Division, created to work with American Indian communities to restore the "Red Atlantis," had begun operation in July 1935.[17] Reorganization agents functioned as traveling field representatives supported by a small staff in Washington DC. Their mission was to help tribal governments become self-governing. The agents' job was to assist reservation Indians as they created tribal constitutions and bylaws, as well as to help with the preparation and interpretation of tribal charters. Agents were also expected to help guide corporations after the tribal charters were ratified and to facilitate any other related matters. Boas recommended Phinney to Collier because Phinney's studies in the USSR had focused on local governments and the governing of Indigenous peoples throughout the USSR. Boas was sure that Phinney could apply that knowledge within

American system(s) for Indigenous people. Phinney had begun work as a "Field Grade Agent 12" at the duty station in Minneapolis, Minnesota, by October 27, 1937.[18] His assigned work area covered the Great Lakes Region of Wisconsin, Minnesota, and Michigan.[19]

First among Collier's plans for the new Reorganization Division was the actualization of the Indian Reorganization Act through adoption of the newly devised tribal constitutions. The constitutions were meant to be accepted by tribal communities in majority-vote elections, but on November 17, 1934, the Nez Perce voted to reject the IRA; 214 voted for and 252 voted against the Act.[20] Both the preliminary discussions and the votes marked the diverse opinions and concerns about the IRA among the Nez Perce. Several reasons account for its failure: federal explanations of the IRA were inadequate (especially for the many Nez Perce who spoke no English), there was limited interest in a move to tribal self-governance, and many Christian Nez Perce resisted proposed religious freedoms for non-Christians. People worried that another dramatic change, the recalling of tribal allotments following the Dawes Act of 1887, would do more harm than good. Further, the federal government did not give the Nez Perce enough time to research and understand the changes; indeed, as Amos Powaukee suspected, more federal deceptions, such as those in previous federal treaties that had dispossessed their ancestors, were hidden in these very changes.[21] Language, land, and government were key components of the argument.

Toward Strong Self-Governance

Although he was stationed in Minnesota, Phinney urged the Nez Perce in Idaho toward strong self-governance. He intended that tribal autonomy would be housed within constitutional administrative, legislative, and judicial branches. Phinney's first opportunity for active participation in that movement came in 1939, when his brother George Phinney wrote him a letter. George, who was chairman of the Nez Perce Business Committee, had asked Archie to prepare a model constitution and bylaws for the Committee to examine. Phinney, who had done this in his own working area, did as George asked, drafted a model constitution, and sent it for the Business Committee's consideration. Phinney now became a catalyst for tribal change, working with the Committee toward a vote for a written constitution, albeit usually remaining offstage, such as in his letters to his brother George in 1939. For example, in June 1939, a letter laid out the problems Phinney anticipated in gaining acceptance from the general council for a strong Nez Perce tribal government. Phinney listed items for the Business Committee to consider:

1. The Nez Perce are to some extent antagonistic toward anything that suggests the I.R.A.
2. They do not, perhaps, understand that the right of an Indian tribe to organize and handle its own affairs antedated the I.R.A., and that there is no logical reason why the Nez Perce could not take advantage of their inherent right to practice local self-government.
3. In order to exercise any degree of self-determination, the Tribe must act through a well-knit tribal organization, which provides effective machinery for carrying out the functions of a tribal organization.
4. A tribal organization that does not provide for the active participation of the various communities and which places authority and responsibility only in a detached representative governing body has been found to be less successful than the more democratic forms of organization.
5. It is important, however, that the executive body be vested, with rather unlimited powers, subject only to an indirect control by the members of the Tribe.[22]

Phinney continued,

> In this proposed Constitution, I am suggesting that a tribal council with a definite composition be established in place of the general councils, which have existed in the past. I am suggesting this for the reason that the general council in my opinion, did not fully represent all the various Nez Perce communities, and at best was unwieldy, also there is no conception of a tribal organization in the relationship between the Tribal Committee and this general council. I consider it important that the Nez Perce should become aware of their tribal organization as a definite means of developing tribal activity and of expressing themselves. Therefore, while it might be simpler to have only a tribal

executive council of nine members to perform all of the functions of self-government, the large mass of the people felt themselves too far removed from the governing body, and yet upon occasions would still attempt general meetings to take action independent of their governing body. I believe that it will be only a rare occasion proposed in this Constitution that the tribal council will see fit to challenge the action of the Executive Committee, and that the regular thing will be for the tribal council to meet only once a year to elect the Executive Committee and to hear reports of the Executive Committee as to their achievements and their proposed programs. In other words, the set-up intends that the tribal council should become an advisory body that will have real importance because of its power to reverse decisions of the Executive Committee whether or not that power is ever exercised. Upon re-examining this proposed Constitution, I notice that no provision has been made for removal of Executive Committeemen and also for filling vacancies. It would seem reasonable to have vacancies filled by the Executive Committee itself. I would suggest that a two thirds majority vote of the tribal council be the manner of removing an Executive Committeeman. These provisions might be included in the Constitution under an article preceding the present Article V under the title REMOVAL from office. I hope that the efforts of the present Business Committee to have the Tribe adopt a Constitution will be successful, and that the Tribe will see fit to place real authority in the governing body. I suppose that there will be considerable opposition to any attempt at tribal organization. Most of the people should agree, however, that any kind of an organization will be better than their present one.[23]

Phinney reflected several principles in American Indian law that are embodied in the Supreme Court decisions known as the "Marshall Trilogy"; these principles are further explained by federal attorney Felix S. Cohen. "An Indian tribe," says Cohen, possesses all the "power of any sovereign state," and treaties and cessions "rendered the tribes subject to the legislative power of the US" but do not "affect the internal sovereignty of a tribe in regard to its powers of local government." Cohen states that "these powers are subject to qualification by treaties and express congressional legislation." "Full powers of internal sovereignty," concludes Cohen, "are vested in the Indian tribes and in their duly constituted organs of government."[24]

The Nez Perce Business Committee prepared and presented a constitution to the General Council at its annual meeting in 1940. Like the IRA, the 1940 Constitution and all other proposed constitutions until 1948 were voted down for similar reasons: Nez Perce land would be taxed, BIA agency supervision would be discontinued, there would be a loss of private property, and many were concerned that increased self-governance would relieve the BIA from its obligations to the Nez Perce. Though none of these conditions had existed in the model constitution (or in the IRA), an influential group of tribal voters may have misinterpreted the proposed constitution. According to IRA historian Robert Riley, there was also a general disinterest in self-government following 1940 (and the rejection of the IRA) that "dominated the political atmosphere of the [Nez Perce] Tribe until 1945."[25]

Phinney's work on the Business Committee's proposed constitution was but one instance of his devotion to community participation and the democratization of tribal governments. As Lawrence Kelly remarked, Phinney expressed many of the same concerns during his work with the Chippewa (of Minnesota, Wisconsin, and Michigan) in 1942. Phinney reported that while most tribal councils he had seen were functioning "wisely and efficiently" in the transaction of tribal business affairs, self-government had not yet succeeded in attaining that most important goal: "community or tribal spirit." Phinney observed that "most tribal councils function as instrumentalities of the Indian Service" rather than as representatives of Indian people. He also denounced what he termed the "democratic centralism" that kept "community participation in tribal affairs at a minimum."[26]

In 1942 Collier assigned Phinney to conduct BIA studies similar to those he had done in the USSR. His first assignment was to consult with the Iroquois; Collier wanted to know why they had rejected the IRA. Phinney had only one month to study tribal government at all six reservations and he chose to focus on the St. Regis Mohawk Tribe. Phinney had no time to repeat earlier, more in-depth studies of treaties and land cessions, even though they had a profound influence on the vote.[27] Nevertheless, Phinney sought to "avoid lifting the considerations of tribal government out of the wider contexts of legal status and jurisdiction."[28]

Using ethnographic methods, Phinney's study began with a primary participant and proceeded to other individuals until he had interviewed representatives of the various tribal factions. Phinney suggested the St. Regis adopt a tribal constitution "based on ancient political institutions of the Iroquois." He felt that the historical political monopoly that the state of New York had assumed over the St. Regis should be discontinued, leaving treaty relationships to the Federal government. Phinney also noted that comparatively few people participated in tribal elections and that factionalism had helped defeat the IRA. Another key point he raised was that tribal members should be educated about the IRA.

Phinney's St. Regis report generated no action. When the report was first sent to the New York BIA, instructions mandated that the document must not be copied. The New York office was told to forward the original document to the reservation-level BIA office, along with the same instructions not to copy the report. This time, it was suggested that an official copy would be sent at a later date. The single original was then forwarded to the state agencies involved with the St. Regis Mohawk Reservation and to the elected St. Regis chiefs, again with the same instructions. The last recipient sent the original report to the BIA central office in 1942. Since 1942, however, none of the reviewing agencies have located a copy in their files. Phinney's recommendations for reform were never implemented at St. Regis, although it appears that all of the St. Regis factions supported his efforts. The question of why the Phinney report was consigned to oblivion has been left to history.

After Phinney visited St. Regis in 1942 he met the prominent Iroquois historian Arthur C. Parker, whom he had first met at a conference in Ontario in 1939. Parker and Phinney discussed the situation at St. Regis (New York) and the development of a new national American Indian political organization.[29] Phinney supported an organization that would become a national American Indian political presence representing tribal constituencies and visible to Congress.

Several attempts to create an organization led only by Indigenous people had already occurred. Parker had been involved with one of them, the Society of American Indians (SAI) which existed from 1911 to 1923. The SAI was unique because its membership involved mostly middle-class professional American Indians, many of whom had attended the Indian Industrial School in Carlisle, Pennsylvania. Internal dissension eventually destroyed it. The other organization was the National Council of American Indians, which existed between 1924 and 1937. In contrast to the SAI, the National Council of American Indians involved mostly rural and reservation people. Two leaders of this first organization, Raymond Bonnin (Nakota) and his wife Gertrude Bonnin (Zitkala Sha, or Red Bird, Yankton Nakota/ Eastern Sioux), were the only members of the National Council of American Indians who had participated in the SAI.[30] The National Council of American Indians terminated in 1937 following Gertrude Bonnin's death.

Despite these failures, Arthur Parker remained interested in developing a national American Indian organization. Based on this common interest, Phinney and Parker began discussing the regeneration of a national American Indian organization that would include middle-class professionals and reservation people. Parker gave Phinney a review copy of the old SAI Constitution and bylaws and presented his views on what was necessary for such an organization to function sustain itself. The seed of the National Congress of American Indians (NCAI) was planted.

Most of the American Indians who formed the new National Congress of American Indians were stationed at the BIA Chicago office. Phinney sent instructions to the group through another federal employee, Charles E. J. Heacock (Lakota). Darcy McNickle, who was stationed at the Central Office, transmitted information from Collier and relayed details between Collier and Phinney; McNickle reiterated Collier's viewpoints during the early Chicago meetings. Meanwhile, Heacock thought that McNickle and Collier wanted to draw the tribal governments into the national organization. They believed that Indians and democracy would do well together and that "everything will enfold itself magically to the good." In order to assure a good organizational beginning, Heacock and Phinney felt that top-down control was essential during the early stages of its development.[31] Phinney, Heacock, and McNickle pioneered a national political organization that had no formal ties to the federal government, by networking with people in the Chicago BIA office and the Reorganization Division. Heacock brought the Chicago group together to discuss the organization they were planning, and Phinney and McNickle attended meetings when they could.

People without strong federal connections were gradually added to the network, including Osage novelist John Joseph Mathew (who was active in the Osage government), Henry Throessell (Tohono O'Odham tribal chairman, cattle rancher, novelist, and Carlisle Indian Industrial School graduate), and Father Phillip Gordon (Anishnabe Roman Catholic priest who had belonged to the SAI). Arthur C. Parker also participated, as did Henry Roe Cloud, another veteran of the SAI. Roe Cloud (Winnebago), a Yale University graduate, served as federal superintendent of the Umatilla Reservation in Oregon.

The network prepared to launch their new organization, which was constituted as the National Congress of American Indians (NCAI) in October 1943. Holding the first NCAI convention at the Cosmopolitan Hotel in Denver, Colorado, on October 15, 1944, eighty delegates from fifty tribes and twenty-seven states launched the organization.[32] By now, however, tension had grown between the tribal delegates and the federal employees. Many tribal delegates did not want BIA employees to serve as NCAI officers, regardless of the fact that the BIA people had developed the organization. A motion that federal employees could join NCAI as members but not serve as officers was put forth during the first meetings. Following a lengthy debate, the motion was defeated. The Blackfeet and Flathead nations hosted the next annual NCAI convention in Browning, Montana, in October 1945, during which McNickle and Phinney withdrew from the NCAI executive committee.

Before withdrawing from the NCAI executive committee, Phinney composed another manifesto in 1944, "The New Indian Case," in which he outlined his ambitions for the National Congress of American Indians. The five-page proposal called for American Indian revitalization as well as support for an "ethnic democracy" that "presumed the end of colonial exploitation, racial supremacies . . . and all other forms of race and class aversion." Phinney recommended tribal economic development and that federal and state governments be held responsible for reconstruction of the ruins of the past . . . not merely those of war but the devastations of history. Depredations wrought by the impact of civilization against the dignity and well-being of colonial and subject peoples [and that these problems must remain on the] world conscious. Damages to Indians as conditioned historically [concerned] diet, disease, inactivity and exposure, poverty and oppression, destroyed tribalism [and] reparations. Reparations must include substantial restoration of tribal lands, a crying need for excellence in education and an American Indian College, [and a] desperate need [for a program of] Indian preference that included American Indian employment in departments of Fish and Wildlife, the National Park Service, the U.S. Geological Survey, and the American Indian Service. The Indian Service [commonly referred to as the BIA] should be completely revamped, to remedy the defects of its organization and operation [under the guidance of] skilled American Indian involvement and support. [Phinney also demanded] a drastic revision in the Code of Federal Regulations.

As Phinney said about poverty and colonization, "Indian resources are inadequate on most reservations. It has been a continent lost but not civilization won."[33]

Meanwhile, in 1943 federal politicians who were indebted to western powerbrokers decided to terminate funding for the BIA Reorganization Division. The twelve people employed by the Reorganization Division seemed to threaten U.S. power-producing corporations, mining companies, trading-post operators, cattle companies leasing Indian land, and Christian missionaries, all of whom pressured members of Congress to destroy the Reorganization Division. As Charles Heacock reported on March 16, 1947,

> Another factor to aggravate the situation was that partial self-government for Indians meant that they were being given more control over their property. This created misgiving among western cattlemen, farmers, and others who from early times leased large amounts of Indian land and now feared that Indian control over their land might jeopardize their former leasing practices.[34]

About the same time, non-Natives also opted to avoid dealing with American Indians who could request return of federal deposits and assets due to the tribes from their contracts, land cessions, resource royalties, and—on the part of the missionaries—denial of American Indian freedom of religion. Trust funds resulting from treaties and federal agreements had been held in limbo since 1887; billions of dollars had not been repaid to tribal nations. (It was not until October 9, 2009, that President Barack Obama announced that the United States was finally settling the Trust Accounts lawsuit, *Cobell v. Salazar, et al.*, with the affected tribes for $3.4 billion plus an additional $60 million for education scholarships. The settlement may not have been a perfect solution, but Obama admitted that extending the lawsuits was itself a needless expense.[35])

A step ahead of his congressional opponents, Collier arranged for most of the Reorganization Division employees to become the superintendents of American Indian agencies. D'Arcy McNickle remained in the central office, Heacock was relocated to the Chicago office, and Phinney was finally transferred in 1943, at his own request, to the position of superintendent to the North Idaho Agency after short assignments at the Navajo Agency in Arizona and the Fort Totten Agency in North Dakota. Phinney's new headquarters was at Fort Lapwai, Idaho, on the Nez Perce reservation. Now that he was home in Idaho he would work toward a more strongly organized tribal government, reducing the influence of the General Council established in the 1927 Constitution and bylaws., The General Council strongly opposed this, so Phinney needed to build tribal support. In order to do this Phinney fostered Nez Perce self-government in his position as BIA superintendent through consultation with the Nez Perce Tribe's Business Committee and community development; initially he was only partly successful.[36]

This was a difficult time for Collier, Phinney, and IRA supporters; as Charles Heacock mentioned in 1946,

The foregoing [report] is given for describing a tense situation where suspicion, name calling, etc., were frequent. Congressional hearings on Indian affairs since 1933 are filled with considerable name-calling, charges, and countercharges. Mr. John Collier, former Commissioner of Indian Affairs and another sponsor of the Act mentioned [IRA], was under constant attack as well as most of the more articulate, who were directly associated with him. Mr. Phinney was perhaps one of the more articulate and colorful among employees associated with Mr. Collier.[37]

The Indian Claims Commission Act

Waiting for a strategic moment to make a significant move toward Nez Perce sovereignty, Phinney saw his chance on August 1, 1946, when President Harry S. Truman signed the Indian Claims Commission Bill. Passed into law on August 13, 1946, the Indian Claims Commission Act (605 Stat. 1060, 25 U.S.C.S. 70a et seq.) was meant to adjudicate claims of "any Indian tribe, band, or other identifiable group of American Indians" that were filed against the United States. The Act provides grounds for various tribal recoveries, including claims based on "unconscionable consideration" (low prices paid) for tribal lands. Now that there was a local rallying point directed at financial restitution for illegal takings of land and resources, Phinney leveraged the Nimiipuu toward a strong tribal government.

Superintendent of the Northern Agency

Phinney became superintendent of the Northern Agency in 1945 under the auspices of the 1927 constitutions and bylaws that had been established for three federal reservations in northern Idaho: Coeur d'Alene, Kalispell, and Fort Lapwai (Nez Perce). Following the expiration of treaty provisions and dictatorial BIA supervision of the reservations, the 1927 constitutions provided federal governance administered by an assigned area superintendent from the BIA. Shadow governments comprised of Business Committees (elected by a general council of tribal members and approved or rejected by the BIA superintendent) governed the reservations. The BIA superintendent called the Business Committee into session once a year; they elected new members of the Business Committee during these sessions. Business Committee members held no fiscal authority, and their decisions required final approval by the BIA superintendent.

Now that Phinney's official BIA position directly affected the Nez Perce, his mission to establish self-rule contravened their history of federal governance since the Treaty with the Nez Perces was ratified in 1859.[38] The

Nez Perce General Council had rejected attempts to establish a written self-rule constitution; an elected tribal government with executive powers; and minimal, indirect federal involvement. Alert for effective mechanisms of change, Phinney used the U.S. Indian Claims Commission (ICC) to advance his ideals. Signed into effect on August 1, 1946, by President Harry S. Truman, the U.S. Indian Claims Commission was designed to adjudicate American Indian claims against the federal government. For the Nez Perce, these claims considered reparations for thefts of gold and land during the gold rush years following 1863, as well as lands lost consequent to later treaties and agreements under the Dawes Act. Meanwhile, Phinney circulated news of the impending Nez Perce ICC claims among influential Nez Perce tribal members. Besides addressing tribal leaders throughout the Nez Perce community in meetings to explain proposed constitutional updates and changes, Phinney used the NCAI publication, the *Sentinel*—as he had done at Coeur d'Alene—and other personal platforms to urge change.[39]

It is not surprising that Phinney relied on publications and the press to forward his ideas. He was adept at using public appearances, newspapers, and national awards to draw attention to his policies. Speaking in Chicago before the League of American Pen Women and the Illinois Federation of Women's Clubs in February 1939, Phinney epitomized intertribal cooperation and aboriginal survival during Federation Day celebrations in the greater Chicago area. Reforms and race relations were on Phinney's mind:

> It is time for Indians everywhere to begin facing certain propositions which will determine the future of Indians. . . . It is important that a consideration of these matters should be entirely from the Indian point of view rather than from the angle of administrative expediency and government interest.[40]

Several months later, in August 1946, Phinney appeared on a star-studded "Education for All" panel sponsored by President Harry S. Truman in Minneapolis, Minnesota. In his message to the meeting of the American Federation of Teachers Union, Truman stressed, "Every child in the United States regardless of race, creed or color, is entitled to a good education in adequate schools staffed by well-paid capable instructors."[41] Phinney, who had served as Supervisor of Indian Education at Denver and for the Navajo Nation at Window Rock, spoke of his goals and presumably discussed his plans to establish an "Indian Service College" for American Indians. Phinney appeared with such luminaries as Dr. Albert O. Nier of the University of Minnesota; Dr. Floyd Reeves of the University of Chicago; Representative Frank P. Starkay of Minnesota; Frank Fenton, director of the American Federation of Labor; and Minneapolis mayor Hubert H. Humphrey (D-MN).[42] Two years later, in 1948, Phinney received the sixteenth Indian Council Fire Achievement Award; the Indian Council Fire was made up of Indians and others who promoted American Indian welfare. Previous winners of the award include Charles A. Eastman, Sioux physician; Maria Martinez, noted potter from San Ildefonso Pueblo; Henry Chee Dodge, Navajo Nation leader; Evelyn Yellow Robe (Rosebud Dakota Sioux), English Department faculty at Vassar College; and Ruth Muskrat Bronson (Cherokee) of Washington DC, an official of the NCAI.[43] Returning to Chicago to accept the prize, Phinney was recognized as "a powerful force in organizing in 1944 the National Congress of American Indians," "an educator," a "champion of the Indian's cause," an "economic and political reformer," and an intertribal diplomat.[44] As always, Phinney marked his interest in American Indian activities when he appeared with Whitney Powless, president of the Council Fire, at the Treaty Stone that marked the spot where the Potawatomi, Chippewa, and Ottawa had ceded their local properties to the United States in 1833.[45] Phinney maximized his successful relationships with Chicago-area leaders after his transfer to Idaho.

Constitutional Struggles

Back in Idaho, the Nez Perce Business Committee held another meeting on March 13, 1945, in which they considered replacing the 1927 Constitution with a self-rule constitution. A constitutional subcommittee consisting of tribal members Harry Wheeler, Joseph Blackeagle, and James Parsons was formed, and committee members were advised to work with Superintendent Phinney to develop a new constitution. "Tribal leaders," said Robert Riley, "hoped that their efforts to draft a new document would meet with more success than had been the case in 1940."[46] Several influences that affected acceptance of the 1945 Constitution involved inertia about

FIG. 6. Archie Phinney (*center front*), BIA superintendent, ca. 1946. Courtesy of the National Park Service, Nez Perce National Historical Park, Archie Phinney Collection.

self-governance and "considerable opposition" from a tribal faction led by traditionalist leader James McConville.[47] A skilled reservation politician, McConville had enjoyed close relationships with previous superintendents who supported the status quo.[48]

The next self-rule constitution was defeated by nearly 70 percent of the voters during a constitutional election on January 3, 1946; American Indian Federation (AIF) members and supporters opposed this constitution. As David Price learned from FBI records, "Phinney was greatly disappointed when the tribe did not adopt a self-rule constitution."[49] Phinney did not recommend another election at that time, because there was no reservation-wide demand for a revote.[50] As the FBI documented the election, one informant complained that provisions of the new constitution "would have resulted in the tribe members being unable to will their property to anyone outside the tribe . . . or the land would revert to the Nez Perce Tribe itself."[51] Another informant thought that the new constitution was "Communistic" and that, having married a non-Native woman, Phinney (or any other Nez Perce person who married outside of the tribe) "would under such an arrangement be unable to will the land to their wives or other relatives." The same person also thought that the new constitution was just another Phinney effort to include the tribe under the IRA which they had already rejected.[52]

If the opponents to a strong tribal government supported by a new constitution had succeeded for any length of time, the federal termination policy would almost certainly have been applied to all three of the northern Idaho reservations (including Nez Perce, Kalispell, and Coeur d'Alene), implementing fundamental changes in land ownership. For the smaller tribes, land would have been appraised and sold to the highest bidder (with the proceeds paid to individual enrolled tribal members), the federal trust relationship ended, state judicial jurisdiction imposed, state tax exemptions ended, all federal tribal programs discontinued, all special programs for individuals ended, recognized tribal sovereignty ended, and individual tribal members paid for their land.[53] But the fear of ending everything that federal recognition meant for enrolled tribal members, combined with the prospects of ICC rebates, BIA reform, and threats to liquidate the Lapwai agency, encouraged a shift in tribal perspective that was expressed in 1948. "A new constitution," said historian Robert Riley, "had to be adopted or else the whole tribal political structure would collapse."[54]

At the General Council meeting in 1948, council members accepted a written constitution with amendments and an elected executive council that held full administrative powers. Several ICC claims were also filed that year. Phinney coordinated the efforts of the Tribal Business Committee and several committee members who were elected to draft a new constitution. Tribal members worried that Phinney might devise a new constitution based on the failed IRA "without instruction from the tribal General Council."[55] Tribal members also worried that Phinney might contribute to land taxation, the loss of private property, and the removal of agency supervision. A majority of tribal members, however, "believed that pressure was exerted on the Tribe only because the Superintendent [Phinney] knew that without more definite and powerful tribal government, the Nez Perce would remain pawns in the hands of the Bureau of Indian Affairs."[56]

A simple majority of the Nez Perce electorate voted the new constitution into effect on April 30, 1948.[57] The constitution and attendant bylaws went into effect immediately, but by May 1949 tribal factionalism and the "complete Nez Perce political organization erupted in chaos and turmoil."[58] Discussions heated up, and neither Phinney nor the tribal governing body could suppress expressed hostilities. As a result, the General Council voted to annul the 1948 Constitution and bylaws on May 5, 1949. Stunned by the smallest vote in tribal history, Phinney sprang into action, telephoning upper-echelon BIA officials. Commissioner of Indian Affairs Collier determined that the vote was invalid, while various tribal factions continued to resist proconstitution elements. Tribal leaders and Phinney mobilized meetings and group sessions that garnered enough support to retain the 1948 Constitution and the bylaws.[59]

Phinney, the Nez Perce nationalist, had helped to provide the Nez Perce Tribe with a self-governing, land-based sovereignty platform that would support the long fight for ICC claims. The Nez Perce Tribe of Idaho filed several ICC claims resulting from past depredations and multiple treaty violations, which Phinney prefigured in his article, "Numipu among the White Settlers." Phinney addressed the loss of more than 13.5 million acres of land, $3 million of losses from illegal gold mining on the Nez Perce reservation; loss of the Montana hunting grounds as established by the Blackfeet Treaty of 1855 (Oct. 17, 1855, 11 Stat., 657, ratified April 15, 1856), and loss of access to Celilo Falls and other fishing grounds on the Columbia and Clearwater Rivers. The ICC finally settled the Nez Perce gold-mining claims on July 5, 1960, eleven years after Phinney's death. The Nimiipuu received $2.8 million for the loss of their Columbia River fishing grounds, $4.2 million for land preempted and undervalued during the gold rush, and $3 million for gold stolen from the Nimiipuu reservation; further, the Nimiipuu have recently reasserted their treaty-protected prerogative to hunt buffalo in Yellowstone Park.[60]

The Nez Perce Tribe was not the only one in the Northern Idaho Agency. The Coeur d'Alene tribe (Schitsu'umsh) and the Kutenai tribe of Idaho were also served by the Agency. But Phinney's role there was greatly constrained as he did not have tribal or family connections there. The Coeur d'Alenes were also creating a new government in the late 1940s and taking the lead in a significant legal action against the Internal Revenue Service. At the same time, the ICC was being established, and Phinney urged the Coeur d'Alenes to participate; he put them in contact with a law firm in Billings despite their discouragement about the process.

Charles Heacock described Phinney in March 1947: "[He was] a brilliant conversationalist and authority on Indians. He enjoys talking and a good argument. Frequently I have noticed that some are inclined to consider Mr. Phinney a so-called 'long-haired' anthropologist and impractical." "At any rate," Heacock continued, "with this disposition, some experience abroad, and well educated, he may seem to some overly aggressive 'for an Indian.' In the work of field agent . . . he cut quite a brilliant figure, but to others I do not think he was so popular."[61]

Do You Believe Mr. Phinney Is a Communist?

Recalling his experiences in the USSR, Phinney understood that local administrators face a unique risk in a centralized bureaucracy. Policies based on shifting ideological interpretations may realign with little or no warning. Suddenly the administrator, following current policy-approved courses of action, is at peril. In the USSR that included arrest by the NKVD, imprisonment, trial, exile to slave-labor camps, execution, and burial in mass graves. In the United States, the perils included FBI surveillance, FBI informant reporting, Congressional committee hearings, dismissal from federal employment, and the possibility of arrest, trial, and imprisonment. In both nation-states, administrators survived if protected by a high-level authority. In the USSR that authority rested with Stalin and the Politburo, while in the United States higher levels of authority were more diffuse. In the end, the administrator was dependent on the executive branch of the federal government; in Phinney's case, Secretary of the Interior Harold Ickes and Commissioner John Collier offered protection.

Phinney certainly knew that he needed protection, considering the fate of Nikolai Matorin. Matorin, who was so instrumental in bringing Phinney to the MAE/IAE, was dismissed from his official responsibilities, and he and his family were sentenced to a ten-year exile in Central Asia. Recalled to Leningrad in 1936, Matorin was tried again and sentenced to die; he was shot to death one hour after his sentence was pronounced. Phinney, who must have been horrified by Matorin's death, was also aware of the FBI's lifelong surveillance of Franz Boas. In 1943 FBI surveillance and informant reporting about Phinney began. FBI agents followed Phinney everywhere he was sent by the BIA. Their lead question was, "Do you believe Mr. Phinney is a Communist?"[62]

FBI surveillance of Archie Phinney did not end until Phinney's death in 1949. That surveillance resulted in an FBI-supported myth that was long-repeated by Phinney's opponents: "Mr. Phinney was a Communist."[63] Phinney's years in the USSR, his efforts to implement the IRA, and his plans to make the Nimiipuu self-supporting through cooperative tribal organization and corporate ownership would have provided excellent fodder for anti-Communist diatribes. Had Phinney lived longer as a federal employee, he would certainly have been called before U.S. Congressional loyalty and security hearings.[64]

Various American Indian informants left a trail of "Communistic" complaints about Phinney with the FBI. Phinney was accused of trying to communalize or communize the Fond du Lac Reservation in Wisconsin after working with that community to accept the IRA. As an unidentified informant said, "He had, himself, read extensively on Communism and had talked to several people he believed to be Communists from Kettle River, Minnesota, and after hearing Phinney, he firmly believed him to be advocating the practice of Communism, on the reservation, although he could recall no specific statements."[65] Informants, including one unidentified Nez Perce tribal member, also complained that Phinney had been educated in the USSR; they even asked that Phinney's services be terminated or that his plans to update tribal leasing systems be changed.[66] BIA employees who had worked with Phinney at Window Rock, Arizona; the United Pueblo Agency, New Mexico; St. Paul, Minnesota; and Butte, Montana were all questioned about Phinney's loyalties. Their answers varied from accusations of Communist tendencies to full support for Phinney as a non-Communist. Joe Jennings, Superintendent of the Cherokee Agency, maintained that Phinney "had the confidence of the Indians [of the Lake area] and Indian Service personnel alike and is a tireless worker."[67] No matter. Wherever Phinney went, the FBI was not far behind. His Russian education and purported Communist tendencies plagued his support for self-rule constitutions, tribal change, and consolidated local governments.[68] As anthropologist David Price understood, "in the end, the truth of Phinney's past Party membership mattered not at all[;] what did matter was Phinney's activism."[69]

Archie Phinney was never a member of the Communist Party, but his years in the USSR, combined with supposed Communist or Nazi influences within the BIA, tormented American politicians who opposed the IRA. Senators Patrick McCarran (D-NV), Arthur V. Watkins (R-UT), Dionisio "Dennis" Chavez (D-NM), and Burton K. Wheeler (D-MT) threatened the IRA. Representing non-Native constituencies that would benefit from restricted reservations, expanded mineral and resource development, increased cattle ranching on reservations, termination of American Indian treaties, and accelerated land loss on American Indian reservations, they controlled federal appropriations that funded BIA programs. Watkins became the driving force behind the American Indian Termination policy (House Concurrent Resolution 108) that intended to end all federal–tribal treaty obligations and relationships as well as any sovereign tribal relationships with the United States. Chavez used threats of Nazi involvement at the Navajo Nation to threaten Collier's career. Wheeler, who had organized the Wheeler-Howard Act, now favored repeal of the IRA and closure of the BIA, and Senator Patrick McCarran detested the IRA.

In a letter addressed to NCAI director Ruth Bronson (Cherokee), McCarran clarified his views about the NCAI and Collier. According to McCarran, Collier had established the NCAI in order to destroy another (and in his opinion more patriotic) organization, the American Indian Federation (AIF). McCarran pointed out that the House Un-American Activities Committee had discovered this conspiracy and had shown that the NCAI was a Communist front organization that received funds from the Jewish-American, ultraliberal Robert Marshall Civil Liberties Trust.[70] These red-baiting criticisms were also aimed at Phinney because of his Russian education, as well as his connections to the NCAI and to Collier.

McCarran did not mention that there was a strong pro-Nazi faction within the AIF and that the AIF had accepted funding from the Nazi German government until the beginning of World War II.[71] Neither did he point out that John Collier and Secretary of the Interior Harold Ickes had spent much of their time defending the BIA from Nazi incursions and pro-Communist accusations. For instance, when the German American Bund solicited California Indian support in 1938, Ickes and Collier responded in the *New York Times*. Collier attacked the Nazis: "In California, the Nazi bund is enrolling Indians and that is being exploited from Germany. It is a Nazi activity."[72]

Chairman of the House Un-American Committee Martin Dies Jr. (R-TX) accused the BIA of Communist involvement. Ickes denied Communist invasion of the BIA, and Dies countercharged that Ickes himself belonged to another "Communist front" organization, the American Civil Liberties Union (ACLU). In turn, Ickes denied ACLU membership and labeled Dies "the world's champion 'zany.'"[73] Meanwhile the Muscogee president of the AIF Joseph Bruner (1934–45) used the German American Bund as his personal vehicle to resist Collier and the IRA.[74] Amid accusations that Bruner collected trumped-up payments from American Indians and that the "AIF took money from its members with the understanding that it would persuade Congress to enact a bill paying them $3,000 as a final settlement on any claims they may have with the United States," the German American Bund trolled for American Indian members at their 1939 annual meeting in San Francisco.[75] Even Elwood A. Towner—mixed-blood Too-too-to-ney tribal member, attorney, and Nazi AIF member from Portland, Oregon (who called Collier a "Jew-loving Pink Red")—accused President Franklin D. Roosevelt of being Jewish and promoted anti-Semitism against Margold and other BIA employees.[76] McCarran and his allies used competing Soviet and German political ideologies to support their mantra: Collier was a Communist, and the IRA was a Bolshevik plot. These attacks were poisoned with an anti-Semitism that conflated fears of Communism and Judaism; meanwhile, two of the most visible Jewish employees in the BIA, Felix Cohen and Nathan Margold, were being targeted by anti-Semites.

Another nearly implacable obstacle directed at Phinney's network involved reservation politicians who were opposed to significant change. Preoccupied with dominating reservation factions and preserving their sub-rosa political roles with BIA superintendents, these people maintained their status as superintendents' secret informants. Many reservation politicians protected their local patrons' prerogatives, and in several instances they held ties to national political groups. Phinney had prefigured these problems when he wrote from the USSR in 1936,

> Apart from the question of class feeling there has arisen a divided political sentiment with regards to the activities of the Indian agency. While the agency has always attempted to curry favor with all tribes people and has, in the main, enjoyed the loyalty and cooperation of the Numipu tribal council, a minority group has arisen which believes that the Indian agency exercises too much influence on tribal affairs, since tribal business is conducted only under the auspices of the agency. This minority has organized and become a chapter of a national Indian organization called the American Indian Federation. The Numipu chapter is composed of both landed and landless Indians, and like its parent organization, pursues a reckless, unprincipled course absurdly reactionary. For example, this organization has been fighting the reforms of the new Indian Bureau Administration since 1932. This reformism represents the height of bourgeois liberality, yet this Indian Federation agitates against the new government programs on the score that the Indian Bureau is undermining "Americanism," introducing communism, affiliating itself with the American Civil Liberties Union etc. In general, however, the reactionary minority has exercised little influence among the tribes people at large.[77]

Phinney was prescient with his concern for the AIF and threats of Communism, but his intentions were clear: Phinney supported the IRA and, accordingly, American Indian constitutional governance.[78]

Traces of Soviet Russia

Phinney returned to the United States under a cloud of suspicion for being a Communist.[79] That suspicion continues despite the fact that Phinney's name appears on no Communist Party or Socialist Party membership lists, his few surviving letters reject Soviet minority policy as a model for U.S. Indian policy, and neither his public nor private papers use Communist slogans—not even the term "comrade."[80] The only evidence of his Communist sympathies seems to be that he had resided in the USSR. Nevertheless, the FBI and others have scoured Phinney's history for traces of Soviet Russia and Communism. Phinney did make a few public speeches about the USSR at the request of local organizations upon his return to Idaho in the summer of 1937. The Lewiston-area non-Native community was interested in his experiences in the Soviet Union.[81] He lectured on the topic to a general assembly of students at the Lewis-Clark Normal School, the Kiwanis Club, and the American Association of University Women.

Following his employment by the BIA, Phinney was silent about anything to do with the USSR. Charles Heacock, who became Phinney's close friend and colleague in the Reorganization Division, wrote,

> I have for periods of several weeks at a time seen a lot of Mr. Phinney, practically all our decisions and arguments involved Indian Service administration. He talked little of his experiences in Russia, so little in fact that as close as I was with him during these periods I can scarcely describe the nature of his assignment except that, insofar as I could gather, he was studying the customs of some of the more backward people in the remote area of Russia.[82]

As the U.S. confrontation with the USSR and "Red Scare" began taking form in January 1943, six years after his return to the United States, Phinney described his activities in the USSR in a loyalty report for the FBI:

> During five years in the USSR my work, arranged for conjointly by Columbia University and the Academy of Sciences, I came into direct contact with the life of backward national minorities in various parts of Siberia and Russia. Many of these tribes are, by genetic relationship and cultural affinity, the Siberian counterpart of American Indian tribes. My experiences among these peoples, covering about eighteen months, consisted of investigating problems of socialization and economic rehabilitation that have arisen in connection with the recent operation of the national minority policy of the government of the USSR. Aside from consultations with Russian scientists and officials, I carried on this work independently. When I was not in the field my time was devoted to the preparation of reports, monographs, etc., and to lecturing in institutions of the Academy of Sciences.[83]

Other than implying that the Bering Land Bridge theory of migration accounted for the peopling of North America, there was nothing seditious, threatening to the United States, or indicative of Communist proclivities in this statement to the FBI. Phinney also mentioned that he had worked as a clerk in the BIA School Division monitoring "the regulation of the rates and the amounts of tuition to which such schools were entitled to for Indian pupils in attendance" and that he had extensive experience as a Columbia University anthropologist.[84]

A public presentation sometimes cited as demonstrating Phinney's ties with communism and the USSR was made in October 1943, but its authorship remains in serious doubt. A typescript of a speech given to the Tsceminicum Club, an elite women's group in Lewiston ID, is found in Phinney's NARA file.[85] Though cited as expressing his procommunist views, it is hardly an endorsement of Marx, Lenin, Stalin, or socialism.[86] This eleven-page typescript provides a brief review of Marxist/Leninism, the theory of materialist history, and Russian history following the October Revolution. The goals and rationale for Stalin's dictatorship and policies (e.g., "Socialism in One Country") are outlined. A highly positive review of the "progress" of the USSR toward modernity is given. Finally, the author speculates about the Soviet Union's demands following the war and the potential conflict with democratic capitalist nations. At the end of the text someone, probably Phinney, had typed, "An address delivered before the Tsceminicum Club, Lewiston, Idaho, October 2, 1943."

The speech has been attributed to Phinney on this basis. However, an identical text was printed in the *Lewiston Morning Tribune* on October 3, with its author listed as prominent Lewiston attorney Eugene A. Cox.[87] The paper's editor noted, "The following is an address delivered yesterday by Mr. Cox before a meeting of the Tsceminicum club, one of the oldest women's clubs in Idaho." Given Phinney's silence about the subject once he was employed by the BIA and his awareness of FBI interest in him, it seems quite unlikely that the speech was his work; it was Eugene Cox's.

In brief, Phinney's efforts toward developing Indigenous sovereignty were not inspired by communist or Soviet ideologies, nor even Collier's goal of restoring the "Red Atlantis." Both of these were based on post-Enlightenment, even Romantic, visions of indigenous "communal" life.

The wide variety of Native social systems and cultures did not match these visions. Of course, no Native intellectual who studied the societies of the settler colonists occupying their lands could ignore the latter's ideologies, and Native intellectuals had to find ways to deal with them while reserving the power to direct their own futures.

Consequently, the exercise of Indigenous sovereignty fit neither of these dominant political systems. And, agents of both communist/socialist and liberal-democratic political traditions accused Phinney and others like him of being either a bourgeois counterrevolutionary or a communist, thus undermining their influence. After a detailed examination of Phinney's extensive FBI file obtained through the Freedom of Information Act (FOIA), David Price came to a similar conclusion.[88]

"I Was Simply Bogged Down"

Signs of overwork and a vague discontent followed Phinney's withdrawal from the executive board of the NCAI. Phinney told his friend, Superintendent Peru Farver of the Tomah Indian Agency, in Wisconsin,

> I am simply bogged-down in myriad petty problems about which you know well enough as a Superintendent, in fact I have given little or no attention to our National Indian Organization since the Montana meeting. Your presence was sadly missed at that Conference but it was only another grand splurge of bell-ringing, but it did generate considerable excitement among the Montana Indians. As you know, McNickle and I withdrew from the executive body, I know little about the activities of the executive group since that time.[89]

Charles Heacock furthered Phinney's position:

> I would say he labors under a terrific handicap because even at best an Indian Superintendent is perhaps among the most maligned of all our public servants. The only organization to which Mr. Phinney belongs, that I know of, is an organization made up of Indians over the United States called the National Congress of American Indians. It is an organization dedicated to promote Indian welfare. This organization interests itself in general Indian problems, including legislation

on Indian matters. It has a lobby and is also called upon to testify regarding legislation affecting Indian groups.[90]

The NCAI was launched, the Nez Perce self-rule constitution in the offing, and Phinney in his homeland. Still, Phinney supervised four reservations, directed the ICC claims process, and remained somewhat weary of the federal bureaucracy. Just eleven months before his mother's death in May 1947 (his father died four months later in September), Phinney mentioned of Agency affairs: "[They] are going a[l]ong smoothly enough but we hardly know which way we are headed." On Idaho, he reflected: "This is an ideal location but frankly I am getting a belly-full of playing nursemaid to the tribes. We have four reservations under this Agency and I am kept at the desk too much of the time."[91]

Between his roles as a father and husband, a bureaucrat who admittedly worked too hard, and a man submerged in the minutiae of the BIA, Phinney missed playing golf. As he confessed to Farver, he was still in his golfing prime but "not playing as much as [he] should like"—"Our season here is year around, but I am lucky to play once of a weekend." He promised, though, that he would be ready for his next golf game with Farver.[92]

Phinney was an energetic man with a difficult job. As Charles Heacock summarized, he was at the time superintendent of the "reservation from which he originates." Also, many were "skeptical that an Indian can succeed in a Superintendency, much less from his own reservation." "Offhand," continued Heacock, "I would say he labors under a terrific handicap because even at best an Indian Superintendent is perhaps among the most maligned of all our public servants."[93]

In the meantime Phinney had gained weight, his hair had turned white, and the boy who had loved hunting and fishing seemed somewhat disgruntled.[94] His parents' deaths also marked unhappy changes: Phinney's beloved mother Mary Lily Phinney (Wailatpu, and a monolingual Nez Perce speaker), his lifelong language teacher and guide, spent her final days in Phinney's Lapwai home. And his father, Fitch, who was quietly involved in Phinney's life, no longer played checkers at the local store in Culdesac, Idaho.[95]

Dr. Archie Phinney remained superintendent of the North Idaho Superintendency until suffering what may have been a cerebral hemorrhage on October 27, 1949. Stricken in his Lapwai office, Phinney passed away at St. Joseph's Hospital in Lewiston, Idaho. Memorialized in the October 30, 1949, edition of the *Lewiston Tribune*, Phinney was remembered as a man who was dedicated to the Nez Perce, an intellectual, and an able federal administrator.[96] Several days later, more than five hundred friends, relatives, and supporters bid Phinney a loving farewell during his funeral mass at St. Stanislaus Catholic Church. The funeral cortege was more than a mile long. Local schools were dismissed, and transportation to the funeral was provided. The Indian Boys Choir from Desmet Mission joined Father Bryne to sing the requiem high mass.[97] Among the many accolades he received for his accomplishments, Phinney was also recognized as a founder of the "National Congress of American Indians."[98]

Bill Willard did not attend the funeral, of course. But almost fifty years later, Willard visited Archie Phinney's grave near Jacques Spur, Idaho, where Phinney continues to watch over his homeland. Willard was privileged also to share his stories, records, research, and photographs with Phinney's daughter Mary Ellen. Just a little girl in 1949, she enjoyed the many new memories of her father.[99]

NOTES

Memorial Dedication Program—in honor of Archie Phinney, B.A., M.A., Ph.D. and Isaac M. Broncheau—Northern Idaho Indian Agency, Lapwai, Idaho—September 27, 1958. In possession of Alan G. Marshall.

1. Among the founding documents for this policy is V. Ulianov and Josef Dzhugashvili, trans. unknown, "Declaration of the Rights of the People of Russia," Marxist Internet Archive, https://www.marxists.org/history/ussr/government/1917/11/02 .htm. English translation previously published in *The Nation*, December 28, 1919. "V. Ulianov" was Lenin's birthname; Stalin's Georgian birthname was "Dzhugashvili." These men and some others took "party names" when they became active in the revolution. See also Lenin, "Theses on the National Question," in V. I. Lenin Collected Works, 19:243–51.

2. "Archie Phinney Return to Idaho from Russia," *Lewiston Morning Tribune* (Lewiston ID), June 20, 1937, 12. Among the speakers at this dedication were Don C. Foster, Portland BIA area director; the Honorable Howard Heckner, Idaho state senator; and the Honorable Joseph R. Garry, Idaho House of Representatives, president of the National Congress of American Indians, and president of the Northwest Affiliated Tribes.

3. Phinney to Boas, August 8, 1933, Mss.B.B61, APS, https://diglib.amphilsoc.org/islandora/object/text%3A97838.

4. The Committee of the North, of which Vladimir Bogoraz was a member, was ended just before Phinney arrived at the MAE/IAE.

5. We use Phinney's terms for the indigenous peoples of North America.

6. We use the term "popular front" in its broader sense, as referring to antisystemic movements.

7. See Collier, "Restoration." Collier served as Commissioner of Indian Affairs until 1945.

8. Phinney, "Numipu among the White," 21–42.

9. Smith, "Cultural Persistence," in *Franz Boas Papers, Volume 1*, 264. Kehoe, *Passion for the True*, 76.

10. Smith, "Cultural Persistence," 265.

11. Kehoe, *Passion for the True*, 76.

12. Archie Mark Phinney Papers, RG75, NARA-PNWR.

13. Phinney to Lipps, October 25, 1933, Archie Mark Phinney Papers, RG75, NARA-PNWR. By the time Phinney returned from the USSR, Lipps was one of two non-Native men assigned as at-large agents for the Reorganization Division.

14. Phinney to Boas, May 1934; Archie Mark Phinney Papers, RG75, NARA-PNWR .

15. Phinney, "Numipu among the White," 21

16. D'Arcy McNickle to John Collier, June 18, 1937, "Office of Indian Affairs, Personal History and Experience Record, Archie Phinney," 2, Archie Mark Phinney Papers, RG75, NARA-PNWR.

17. Collier, "Red Atlantis," 15–19, 62–63.

18. Willard, "Nez Perce Anthropologist," 13.

19. Franz Boas, Oscar Lipps, George Phinney—Phinney's brother and a member of the Nez Perce Business Committee—and other people employed in the Central Office of the BIA must have kept Phinney up-to-date on the IRA while he was in Leningrad. Unfortunately, those personal communications have not yet appeared in the public domain.

20. Riley, "Nez Perce Struggle," 82.

21. Riley, "Nez Perce Struggle," 80; Corbett B. Lawyer, in Riley, "Nez Perce Struggle," 81.

22. Riley, "Nez Perce Struggle," 91.

23. Riley, "Nez Perce Struggle," 91.

24. Cohen, *Handbook*, 122–25.

25. Riley, "Nez Perce Struggle," 96.

26. Kelly, "Indian Reorganization Act," 311.

27. Willard, "Nez Perce Anthropologist," 15.

28. Archie Phinney, "Tribal Government of the St. Regis Indians (Mohawk Tribe) of the State of New York," 1942, New York Indians Correspondence, box 6, RG75, NARA-PNWR. Excerpts from Phinney's report have been reprinted by Darren Bonaparte, "The Phinney Report of 1942," Wampum Chronicles, accessed November 5, 2019, http://www.wampumchronicles.com/toomanychiefs13.html.

29. Phinney, "Tribal Government."

30. Willard, "Nez Perce Anthropologist," 16–20.

31. C. E. Heacock to Phinney, January 18, 1944, Archie Mark Phinney Papers, memos by Charles E. J. Heacock, National Congress of American Indians, box 10 RG75, NARA-PNWR.

32. Wilkinson, *Blood Struggle*, 102–3.

33. Archie Mark Phinney, "The New Indian Case," MS, Archie Mark Phinney Papers, box 2, RG75, NARA-PNWR.

34. Charles E. J. Heacock, report, March 16, 1947, memos by Charles E. J. Heacock, Archie Mark Phinney Papers, National Congress of American Indians, box 10, RG75, NARA-PNWR.

35. McCarthy, "Bureau of Indian Affairs," 141–43. See also Charles E. J. Heacock, report, March 16, 1947, in Archie Mark Phinney Papers, National Congress of American Indians, memos by Charles E. J. Heacock, box 10, RG75, NARA-PNWR; Charlie Savage, "U.S. Will Settle Indian Lawsuit for $3.4 Billion," *New York Times*, December 98, 2009; see also Cobell v. Salazar, et al., Case no. 1:96CV01285 (D.D.C.), Civil Division Archive, U.S. Department of Justice.

36. The nine-member Nez Perce Executive Committee was established by the Nez Perce Constitution and bylaws of 1927. This constituted local governance at the Nez Perce Reservation until 1948.

37. Charles E. J. Heacock, report, March 16, 1947.

38. "Treaty with the Nez Perces, 1855," in Kappler, *Indian Affairs*, 702–6.

39. Fahey, *Saving the Reservation*, 157; see also Riley, "Nez Perce Struggle," 104–5.

40. Archie Phinney, in Szasz, "Listening to the Native Voice," 42–53; see also "Request for Report on Loyalty Data," January 14, 1943, Archie Mark Phinney Papers, box 34, RG75, NARA-PNWR.

41. Albert J. Gordon, "Education for All Urged by Truman, Agenda at St. Paul is Keyed to Social Implications in the Nuclear Age," *New York Times*, August 19, 1946.

42. Gordon, "Education for All"; Jeffrey Wollock, "Protagonism Emergent," 12; Crum, "Idea of an Indian College," 20; "Supervisor of Indian Education, etc.," March 1943–January 1944, "Office of Indian Affairs, Personal History and Experience Record," Archie Mark Phinney Papers, box 2, RG75, NARA-PNWR.

43. Irene Steyskal, "Indian Scholar Wins Award of Council Fire," *Chicago Daily Tribune*, September 19, 1948, R4.

44. Steyskal, "Indian Scholar"; "Indian Council Fire to Confer Award Tonight," *Chicago Daily Tribune*, September 24, 1948, B6; "Indian Award Winner Makes Pilgrimage to Famous Treaty Stone in Olson Park," *Chicago Daily Tribune*, October 3, 1948, 20.

45. "Indian Award Winner."

46. Riley, "Nez Perce Struggle," 105, 100.

47. Riley, "Nez Perce Struggle," 100, 105.

48. Field notes of an anonymous participant, William Willard's files, Washington State University, Pullman WA.

49. Price, "Archie Phinney," 25.

50. Archie Phinney, January 17, 1946, quoted in Riley, "Nez Perce Struggle," 107

51. Price, "Archie Phinney," 25.

52. Price, "Archie Phinney," 25–26.

53. "Public Law 280," *US Statutes at Large* 67 (1953): 588–90. Public Law 280, passed in 1953, was aimed at terminating the federal treaty and other relationships with Indian Tribes, and gave state governments the power to assume jurisdiction over Indian reservations, which had been excluded from state jurisdiction. The House of Representatives passed House Concurrent Resolution 108, supporting the Senate's action. For broad discussions of these Congressional actions, see Wilkinson, *Blood Struggle*; Wilkins, *American Indian Politics*. For current developments regarding Public Law 280, see "Public Law 280," Tribal Court Clearinghouse, Tribal Law and Policy Institute, accessed November 5, 2019, http://www.tribal-institute.org/lists/pl280.htm.

54. Riley, "Nez Perce Struggle," 109, 110, 112; see also Walker, *Conflict and Schism*, 125.

55. Corbett B. Lawyer, May 25, 1960, in Riley, "Nez Perce Struggle," 113–14.

56. Lewis B. Holt, May 27, 1960, in Riley, "Nez Perce Struggle," 114.

57. Riley, "Nez Perce Struggle," 116–17.

58. Riley, "Nez Perce Struggle," 121.

59. Riley's description is based on the following consultants' statements: Joseph Blackeagle, May 28, 1960, Lewis B. Holt, May 27, 1960, Richard Halfmoon, May 26, 1960, and Corbett B. Lawyer, May 25, 1960. Riley, "Nez Perce Struggle," 113, 122.

60. Pearson, "Numipu Land Loss," 37–42, 42–51, 62. As Pearson noted, "By the time that Phinney was preparing the evidence for the Indian Claims Commission, the U.S. court of Claims had already dismissed a Nimiipuu lawsuit that sought $18.5 million in losses related to use of the common grounds."

61. Charles E. J. Heacock, report on March 16, 1947, 2, memos by Charles E. J. Heacock, Archie Mark Phinney Papers, National Congress of American Indians, box 10, RG75, NARA-PNWR.

62. Price, "Archie Phinney," 28.

63. Two surviving Nimiipuu who had known Phinney repeated this statement to Bill Willard; both persons were closely related to anti-Phinney factions and had strong ties to the old Presbyterian treaty chiefs and other tribal members. Field research notes in Willard's personal collection, Washington State University, Pullman WA.

64. Janiewski, "Confusion of Mind," 101–12; see also Price, *Threatening Anthropology*, 195–96, 224; Franco, *Crossing the Pond*, 1–2.

65. Price, "Archie Phinney," 26.

66. Price, "Archie Phinney," 27.

67. Joe Jennings, memorandum, May 26, 1939, Archie Mark Phinney Papers, RG75, NARA-PNWR.

68. Price, "Archie Phinney," 20–32.

69. Price, "Archie Phinney," 31.

70. Philp, *Termination Revisited*, 105, 202, 208, 198–99; "Ask Indian Inquiry, Two Senators Tell of Complaints against Collier's Indian Bureau," *New York Times*, August 8, 1937, 37; see also Hasse, "Termination and Assimilation."

71. Philp, *John Collier's Crusade*, 200–202.

72. "Nazi Agents Accused of Recruiting Indians: Operations in California Charged as Ickes and Collier Renew Attacks," *New York Times*, November 24, 1938, 14.

73. "Nazi Agents Accused."

74. "Joe Bruner, Muscogee," in Littlefield and Parins, *Native Writing*, 226.

75. Bolt, *American Indian Policy*, 296nn64–66.

76. Philp, *John Collier's Crusade*, 201–2; see p. 202 for a photograph of Towner wearing full Nazi-decorated "American Indian" regalia and an American Bund member done up in a warbonnet. See also Philp, *Termination Revisited*, 154.

77. Phinney, "Numipu among the White," 21–42.

78. For another view, see Hauptman, "American Indian Federation," 378–402.

79. Price, "Archie Phinney," 21–32; Price, *Threatening Anthropology*, 195, 223, 374.

80. Balthaser, "'Travels of an American Indian,'" 385–416; Balthaser, *Anti-Imperialist Modernism*; Balthaser, "Colonies and Capital," *Jacobin*, November 16, 2016, https://www.jacobinmag.com/2016/11/native-americans-marxism-colonialism-nodapl-archie-phinney-means-nez-perce/; Barry Rigby, "Archie Phinney Was a Champion of Indian Rights," *Lewiston Morning Tribune* (Lewiston ID), July 3, 1990, 4, https://news.google.com/newspapers?id=Q3ZfAAAAIBAJ&sjid=fy8MAAAAIBAJ&pg=4335%2C850275.

81. The Northwest had a reputation for being friendly to the labor movement; frequent strikes, some violent, occurred in the miner's towns, fruit-picking camps, and logging camps in Washington and neighboring northern Idaho. An often-quoted toast was, "To the 47 States of the Union and the Soviet of Washington." This toast is variously attributed, most commonly to national Democratic Party leader and Franklin Delano Roosevelt's U.S. Postmaster General James A. "Big Jim" Farley. See Walt Crowley, "Washington State Politics — Its Past, Present, and Utterly Unpredictable Future," HistoryLink.org, April 5, 2003, http://historylink.org/File/5451.

82. Charles E. J. Heacock, March 26, 1948, Archie Mark Phinney Papers, box 10–11, memos by Charles E. J. Heacock, National Congress of American Indians, NARA-NWPR, RG75.

83. Archie Phinney, "Request for Report on Loyalty Data," January 14, 1943, Archie Mark Phinney Papers, box 3, RG75, NARA-PNWR.

84. Phinney. "Request for Report," 4. As requested, Phinney also reported that his mother and wife had been born outside the continental United States. His wife Ellen French, who was a British citizen, had been born in Scotland, and his mother,

Mary Lilly, had been born on the Nez Perce reservation. Even Phinney's personal relationships indicated his loyalty to Western democracies.

85. Archie Phinney, "On Understanding Soviet Russia," 1943, Archie Phinney Collection, box 2, RG75, NARA-PNWR.

86. Balthaser, "'Travels of an American Indian,'" 385–416.

87. Eugene A. Cox, "How to Understand Russia," *Lewiston Morning Tribune* (Lewiston ID), October 3, 1943, https://news.google.com/newspapers?id=87NeAAAAIBAJ& sjid=6i8MAAAAIBAJ&pg=1284%2C152489.

88. Price, "Archie Phinney," 21–32.

89. Archie Phinney to Peru Farver, April 19, 1946, 1, Archie Mark Phinney Papers, National Congress of American Indians, RG75, NARA-PNWR.

90. Charles E. J. Heacock, memos, Archie Mark Phinney Papers, National Congress of American Indians.

91. Archie Phinney to Peru Farver, April 19, 1946, 1.

92. Archie Phinney to Peru Farver, April 19, 1946, 1. According to the late Allan Smith, Phinney and D'Arcy McNickle met for the first time on a New York golf course. Phinney, the caddy, and McNickle (the golfer) recognized one another as fellow Native Americans and began a lifelong conversation (personal communication with William Willard, n.d.).

93. Charles E. J. Heacock, March 16, 1947, 2. Archie Mark Phinney Papers, box 10–11, memos by Charles E. J. Heacock, National Congress of American Indians, NARA-NWPR, RG75.

94. Archie Phinney, "Nez Perce Youth in Russia Longs for Native Idaho," *Lewiston Morning Tribune* (Lewiston ID), June 7, 1936, 9.

95. Antone Minthorn, field notes of conversation with William Willard, William Willard's papers, Washington State University, Pullman WA.

96. "Death Summons Archie Phinney, 45, Prominent Nez Perce Leader" obituary, *Lewiston Morning Tribune* (Lewiston ID), October 30, 1949, 4.

97. "Archie Phinney Quietly at Rest at Jacques Spur," *Lewiston Morning Tribune* (Lewiston ID), November 3, 1949, 14.

98. "Archie Phinney Quietly at Rest at Jacques Spur," *Lewiston Morning Tribune* (Lewiston ID), November 3, 1949, 14.

99. William Willard, personal conversations with J. Diane Pearson, 2014, 2015, 2016; "Phinney Rites Set Wednesday," *Spokane Daily Chronicle* (Spokane WA), October 31, 1949, 46.

BIBLIOGRAPHY

ARCHIVES

Franz Boas Papers, reel 35. American Philosophical Society, Philadelphia PA.

Memorial of Nez Perce Indians of Idaho on Claim for Payment for Land. Congressional Information Series, S. Doc. 97 (62–1) (1911), serial set vol. 6108. Microfiche, APS.

Balthaser, Benjamin. *Anti-Imperialist Modernism: Race and Transnational Radical Culture from the Great Depression to the Cold War.* Ann Arbor: University of Michigan Press, 2015.

———. "'Travels of an American Indian into the Hinterlands of Soviet Russia': Rethinking Indigenous Modernity and the Popular Front in the Work of Archie Phinney and D'Arcy McNickle." *American Quarterly* 66, no. 2 (2014): 385–416.

Bolt, Christine. *American Indian Policy and American Reform.* London: Academic Division, Unwin Hyman, 1987.

Cohen, Felix. *The Handbook of Federal Indian Law.* Washington DC: USGPO, 1941.

Collier, John. "Restoration of the Red Atlantis." *Survey* 49 (October 1922): 15–66.

Cowger, Thomas W. *The National Congress of American Indians: The Founding Years.* Lincoln: University of Nebraska Press, 2001

Crum, Steven. "The Idea of an Indian College or University in Twentieth Century America Before the Formation of the Navajo Community College in 1968." *Tribal College* 1, no. 1 (July 1989): 20.

Fahey, John. *Saving the Reservation: Joe Garry and the Battle to Be Indian.* Seattle: University of Washington Press, 2001.

Flanagan, John K. "The Invalidity of the Nez Perce Treaty of 1863 and the Taking of the Wallowa Valley." *American Indian Law Review* 24, no. 2 (1999): 75, 78.

Franco, Jere B. *Crossing the Pond: The Native American Effort in World War II.* Denton: University of North Texas Press, 1999.

Greenwald, Emily. *Reconfiguring the Reservation: The Nez Perces, Jicarilla Apaches, and the Dawes Act.* Albuquerque: University of New Mexico Press, 2002.

Hasse, Larry J. "Termination and Assimilation: Federal Indian Policy, 1943 to 1961." PhD diss., Washington State University, 1974.

Hauptman, Laurence M. "The American Indian Federation and the Indian New Deal: A Reinterpretation." *Pacific Historical Review* 52, no. 4 (November 1983): 378–402.

Holm, Tom, J. Diane Pearson, and Ben Chavez. "Peoplehood: A Model for the Extension of Sovereignty in American Indian Studies." *Wicazō Ŝa Review* 18, no. 1 (2003): 7–24.

Janiewski, Dolores E. "Confusion of Mind: Colonial and Post-Colonial Discourses about Frontier Encounters." *Journal of American Studies* 32, no. 1 (April 1998): 81–103.

Josephy, Alvin M., Jr. *The Nez Perce Indians and the Opening of the Northwest.* Boston: Houghton Mifflin, 1965.

Kappler, Charles J. *Indian Affairs: Laws and Treaties.* Vol. 2. Washington DC: Government Printing Office, 1904.

Kehoe, Alice Beck. *A Passion for the True and Just: Felix and Lucy Kramer Cohen and the Indian New Deal.* Tucson: University of Arizona Press, 2014.

Kelly, Lawrence C. "The Indian Reorganization Act: The Dream and the Reality." *Pacific Historical Review* 44, no. 3 (August 1975): 311.

Lenin, Vladimir I. *Lenin Collected Works.* Vol. 19. Moscow: Progress Publishers, 1977.

Littlefield, Daniel F., and James W. Parrins. *Native Writing in the Southwest: An Anthology 1875–1935*. Jackson: University Press of Mississippi, 1995.

McCarthy, Robert. "The Bureau of Indian Affairs and the Federal Trust Obligation to American Indians." *BYU Journal of Public Law* 19, no. 1 (March 2004): 141–43.

McClellan, Catherine. "Frederica DeLaguna and the Pleasures of Anthropology." *American Ethnologist* 16, no. 4 (November 1989): 767.

Pearson, J. Diane. "Numipu Land Loss following Archie Phinney's Research." *Journal of Northwest Anthropology* 38, no. 1 (2004): 42.

Philp, Kenneth R. *Termination Revisited. American Indians on the Trail to Self-Determination, 1933–1953*. Lincoln: University of Nebraska Press, 1999.

———. *John Collier's Crusade for Indian Reform*. Tucson: University of Arizona Press, 1977.

Phinney, Archie M. "Numipu among the White Settlers." *Wicazō Ša Review* 17, no. 2 (Fall 2002): 21–42.

———. "Racial Minorities in the Soviet Union," *Pacific Affairs* 8, no. 3 (September 1935): 321–27.

———. *Nez Perce Texts*. New York: Columbia University Press, 1934.

———. *Nez Perce or Numipu Legends*. February 13, 1927. Manuscript 2339. NAA, Washington DC.

Price, David. "Archie Phinney, the FBI, and the FOIA." *Journal of Northwest Anthropology* 38, no. 1 (2004): 25–28.

———. *Threatening Anthropology: McCarthyism and the FBI's Surveillance of Activist Anthropologists*. Durham NC: Duke University Press: 2004.

Ramsey, Jarold. *Coyote Was Going There*. Seattle: University of Washington Press, 1980.

Riley, Robert James. "The Nez Perce Struggle for Self-Government: A History of Nez Perce Governing Bodies, 1842–1960." Master's thesis, University of Idaho, 1961.

Strong, Anna Louise. *I Change Worlds: The Remaking of an American*. New York: Garden City, 1937.

Szasz, Margaret Connell. "Listening to the Native Voice: American Indian Schooling in the Twentieth Century." *Montana: The Magazine of Western History* 39, no. 3 (Summer 1989): 42–53.

Walker, Deward E., Jr. *Conflict and Schism in Nez Perce Acculturation*. Pullman: Washington State University Press, 1968.

Wilkins, David E. *American Indian Politics and the American Political System*. 2nd ed. Lanham: Rowman & Littlefield, 2006.

Wilkinson, Charles F. *Blood Struggle: The Rise of Modern Indian Nations*. New York: Norton, 2005.

Willard, William. "The Nez Perce Anthropologist." *Journal of Northwest Anthropology* 38, no. 1 (Spring, 2004): 5–20.

Wollock, Jeffrey. "Protagonism Emergent: Indians and Higher Education." *Native Americas* 14, no. 4 (December 1997): 12.

6 American Indian Citizenship, Past and Present

CHRISTOPHER K. RIGGS

In 2013 the Nooksack tribe in northwestern Washington State found itself embroiled in litigation over the tribal council's efforts to strip 306 individuals of their tribal citizenship. Many of those facing expulsion had resided on the reservation for over two decades. Many had exercised tribal fishing and hunting rights. Many had been tribal employees. Many had relied on the tribe for housing and medical services. Nooksack officials, however, argued that the individuals in question were being disenrolled because they had not been able to prove their tribal ancestry, a requirement for membership.[1]

Conflict over tribal membership is not unique to the Nooksack.[2] The Cherokee Nation of Oklahoma amended its constitution in 2007 to limit membership to those of "Indian blood," which effectively expelled about 2,800 persons descended from the "Cherokee Freedmen." The Freedmen were the ancestors of enslaved African Americans held by Cherokees in the nineteenth century, and the United States government had forced the tribe to extend them full citizenship rights in an 1866 treaty. The 2007 expulsion stripped the Freedmen of their right to vote in tribal elections as well as other rights associated with Cherokee citizenship. It also threatened the Cherokee Nation with the loss of millions of dollars of federal funds.[3]

The same year that the 1866 Cherokee treaty was signed, Carlos Montezuma was born to Yavapai parents in Arizona. Kidnapped as a child by the Pima and sold to a non-Indian photographer, he eventually ended up in Illinois, where he attended medical school and created his own medical practice. Montezuma also became a political activist who repeatedly criticized the federal government's treatment of Native peoples. He eventually applied to the United States government to be legally recognized as a citizen of the San Carlos Apache. His parents had settled on the San Carlos reservation in 1871; their graves were located there, and reservation leaders supported his enrollment. Federal officials in the Interior Department's Office of Indian Affairs (OIA), however, rejected his application in 1922, because Montezuma was a United States citizen. His criticism of the OIA—formally known as the Bureau of Indian Affairs (BIA) since 1947—was also a factor in his rejection.[4]

Introduction

Although perhaps only loosely related, the examples above illustrate the importance and complexity surrounding issues of citizenship—both tribal and U.S.—for Native Americans. Although its meaning is contested, citizenship is often understood to entail membership in a larger community (be it a country, state, tribe, or the like). It constitutes, as scholar Derek Heater puts it, "the social or political ties which hold an individual in community with his fellows."[5] It also involves the rights and obligations of community members and the sense of identity and belonging related to being a part of a community.[6] In regard to the former, for example, the right to a jury trial also entails the responsibility to serve on juries when called.[7]

Historians and other scholars have paid increasing attention to citizenship for indigenous peoples both past and present, tribal and American.[8] What was or is required to be a citizen of an Indian tribe or nation? Living on tribal lands? Being born to a tribal member? Having a certain percentage of Indian blood? What did it mean to be a tribal citizen? What rights and responsibilities did tribal citizenship entail? Who had the power to decide the answers to these questions? How were such rules affected by the growing power the United States had over tribes living within its borders? To what extent have tribes been able to determine their own membership? Would Native peoples within America's borders become

American citizens? If so, how would that citizenship be conveyed? Would tribal members even want United States citizenship?

Such questions are important because Native citizenship rules have dictated the well-being and the survival of individuals and their communities. Such rules impacted, for example, an individual's access to a group's material resources and protection. Citizenship also influenced a person's psychological health. As Patricia Riggs (Ysleta del Sur) explained, tribal membership dictated who may partake of "things that are dear, sacred and spiritual" to a particular people.[9] Citizenship rules helped to ensure—by fostering feelings of interconnectedness and a commitment to reciprocal responsibilities—that individuals would act in ways that ensured their community's long-term survival.

This chapter examines different definitions of citizenship for indigenous peoples in what became the United States. The first section describes continuity and changes in the rules governing tribal citizenship—especially after Native peoples found themselves within the territorial boundaries of the United States. Prior to contact, criteria for tribal membership typically included such components as kinship, culture, language, and geography. The United States recognized, at least in theory, that tribes were sovereign entities that had the right to determine their own membership. In practice, however, American efforts to acquire indigenous lands and assimilate indigenous persons into mainstream society severely disrupted and altered tribal citizenship rules. In fact, federal policymakers throughout the nineteenth century and well into the twentieth century envisioned ending tribal citizenship and replacing it with United States citizenship.

By the 1930s, federal policy had shifted away from assimilation and toward preserving tribes as politically and culturally distinct entities. Indian nations developed federally recognized governments and crafted criteria for membership. Although the federal government worked to influence tribal citizenship rules, Native peoples have adapted to federal efforts to dictate such rules. They have done so by creating membership requirements intended to protect their culture, political autonomy, and economic resources in the face of changing circumstances.

The second section examines the extension or imposition of United States citizenship upon Native Americans and the conflict over whether

Indians would enjoy the same rights as non-Indian citizens of the United States. For much of the nineteenth century, federal policymakers defined Indian tribes as separate, sovereign (or at least semisovereign) nations. As a result, tribes and their members had a unique status under federal law, and policymakers tended to see tribal and U.S. citizenship as mutually exclusive. By the early twentieth century, however, policymakers had increasingly come to believe that Indians were not ready for "full citizenship." Instead, they endorsed "dual citizenship," which meant indigenous persons would be citizens of both the United States as well as their tribes. The extension of citizenship did not automatically come with the extension of the same rights enjoyed by other citizens, such as suffrage. Nevertheless, most American Indians came to accept, if not embrace, dual citizenship. Some Native groups even fought to protect Indians' rights as U.S. citizens as a way of protecting the rights of Indian tribes against the threat of assimilation.

Such attitudes and actions are consistent with political scientist Diane Duffy's research on perceptions of citizenship among indigenous people in the United States. At one end of the spectrum are "indigenous nationalism" and "measured separatism." Indigenous nationalists see themselves as citizens solely of their tribe. Those in the latter category identify primarily with their Indian nation but also to some degree with the United States. In at least some ways, measured separatism constitutes an endorsement of dual citizenship: both tribal and U.S. citizenship. At the other end of the spectrum are "assimilative" and "co-opted or colonized" approaches to citizenship. In the case of the former, Indians see U.S. citizenship as superior to tribal membership, while Native Americans in the latter category do not see tribal citizenship itself as worthwhile. In other words, citizenship is conceived as being either exclusively tribal; dual (both American and tribal), with either the tribal or the American citizenship seen as superior; or exclusively American and not tribal.[10]

Duffy's categories have long been reflected in Native Americans' criteria for citizenship both before and after contact. Ultimately, Native Americans have found ways to craft or use such criteria in order to preserve distinctive tribal identities—that is, to foster or maintain a sense of indigenous nationalism or measured separatism. Indians have done so in spite of pressures from the United States to adopt an assimilative or co-opted/colonized style of citizenship.

This chapter on Native Americans and citizenship reflects the broader theme of *Rising from the Ashes*: indigenous peoples' adaptability and resilience in the face of significant difficulties and existential threats. For example, authors Alan Marshall and Samuel M. Watters explain in chapter 1 of this volume how mid-nineteenth century Nez Perce had to undertake a complicated set of political, social, and psychological actions to survive in the resource rich but complex physical environment of the Columbia Plateau. The challenges became infinitely greater when the United States and rival powers expanded into the American West. The results involved massive land loss, deaths from disease and violence, and campaigns to eradicate Nez Perce culture. Such developments devastated—but did not destroy—the Nimiipuu. They adapted to their new circumstances, incorporating and utilizing elements of mainstream American society in order to continue existing as a changed but distinct people. Their efforts embody a rising from the ashes.

The history of American Indian citizenship, past and present, echoes Marshall's theme of adaptation and resilience. Indigenous peoples developed and redefined their membership criteria as a way to survive in challenging environments. Such criteria nurtured a sense of belonging and established a collection of rights and reciprocal obligations necessary for group cohesion and survival; they provided a means to deal with internal and external conflicts, allowed for adjustments to be made in face of geographic concentration and dispersion, and so forth. Faced with threats to their existence and identity from the United States, tribes were forced to modify their membership requirements. At the same time, American Indians found ways to take the dominant society's conceptions of tribal and U.S. citizenship and use them in ways that allowed for the preservation of Native identities. In short, an examination of American Indian citizenship over time helps explain how and why Native peoples continue to exist as politically, socially, and culturally distinct entities.

Some caveats are in order. This chapter provides a general overview of a broad topic. It is not intended to offer a comprehensive description and analysis of all, or even most, of the many, varied, and complex definitions of tribal citizenship that have evolved over time. An effort has been made to include a representative sample of Native groups and geographic regions, but many peoples and places are not included. The intent here is to provide some selective examples to illustrate larger themes and ideas.

Tribal Citizenship

Overview

Prior to coming under the rule of the United States, American Indians held conceptions of citizenship that generally fell into Duffy's category of "indigenous nationalism."[11] Since most of Duffy's other categories are predicated upon the existence of the United States, they would not be applicable to precontact times. Indigenous peoples had a number of ways of defining membership or citizenship, typically with the means to incorporate outsiders. Such criteria were designed to preserve a distinctive identity, and they usually included culture, language, geography, and family.[12]

As the United States gained increased power over Native peoples by the nineteenth century, if not earlier, federal officials both intentionally and unintentionally influenced the tribes' citizenship requirements as well as the rights of tribal citizens. The Americans imposed ostensibly new criteria for determining and defining the rights of tribal citizens, such as race and blood quantum. They also tried to eradicate tribal citizenship and replace it with American citizenship alone, a move consistent with Duffy's idea of an assimilative or colonized citizenship. Even today, despite the general (albeit interrupted) trend in federal policy toward greater tribal self-determination since 1934, political leaders in Washington DC, have continued to influence the rules governing tribal membership. Nevertheless, Native peoples have found and continue to find ways to adapt to federal pressures and shape their own citizenship criteria. In so doing, they have preserved a degree of political and cultural distinction from mainstream American society. That is, tribes designed or adapted rules that were intended to promote either indigenous nationalism or measured separatism, to use Duffy's typology.

A comprehensive assessment of the polyglot conceptions of tribal citizenship and how these have changed across time and place is beyond the scope of this section. The intent here is to offer a descriptive overview of the diverse conceptions Native peoples had of citizenship, consider how actions by the United States disrupted but did not wholly destroy those conceptions, and argue that indigenous peoples worked to conceptualize tribal citizenship in a way that ensured Native societies' survival and preserved distinctive indigenous identities.

Tribal Citizenship in Precontact Times

Each indigenous society had its own ways of distinguishing between "us" and "them," thereby affirming its own unique sense of indigenous nationalism. Hualapai oral traditions, for example, held that the Creator determined that the people of what is today the Southwest would be separated by geography and language into separate groups such as the Hualapai, Havasupai, Hopi, Yavapai, and Maricopa.[13] Similarly, the Nez Perce story of "Coyote and Monster" tells how Coyote used pieces of a monster to create the Nimiipuu, Coeur d'Alene, Blackfeet, Cayuse, and other peoples, each with their own lands.[14]

Prior to and even after European contact, Indian societies typically had the authority to determine who was a part of their communities. Native peoples made that determination based on a variety of factors. Those factors included shared cultural, geographic, linguistic, and family ties, and they were designed to ensure the survival of culturally distinct societies.

Kinship ties stood out as an extremely important determinant of tribal membership among peoples such as the Dakota (or Santee) Sioux. As Dakota author Ella Deloria explained, "By kinship all Dakota people were held together in a great relationship that was theoretically all-inclusive and co-extensive with the Dakota domain. . . . Dakota camp-circles were no haphazard assemblages of heterogeneous individuals." All Dakotas were related to one another, and citizenship obligated each Santee to "obey kinship rules" and to "be a good relative." If such efforts were not made, "the people would no longer be Dakota."[15]

Like Deloria's people, the Cayuses, Umatillas, and Walla Wallas of the Northwest formed communities based on kinship ties. As authors Roberta Conner (Umatilla/Cayuse/Nez Perce) and William L. Lang put it, "these communities recognized their citizenship by relations." However, the groups distinguished their members based on territorial and cultural factors as well, such as the geographic location of villages, types of foods and herbs utilized, and village size.[16]

Similarly, Nez Perces emphasized membership based on geography, language, common cultural activities, and kinship relations. Nimiipuu bands consisted of extended families; these bands were identified based on the river drainage by which they resided and the Nez Perce name for the drainage areas.[17] As Marshall notes, kinship has historically helped Nez Perces to preserve a common identity, as they were dispersed far and wide to fish, hunt, and gather plants. Further, Marshall observes, "people, when asked what group they belonged to . . . answered with the name of their winter village site. The identification . . . was symbolized through the linguistic form . . . in addition to a geographic name."[18] Individual Nez Perce citizens had the right to refuse to comply with the wishes of their leaders but were obliged to help maintain fishing stations, participate in food gathering expeditions, and defend against enemy attacks.[19]

Native social groups had boundaries, but those boundaries could and did change over time. Migration, interactions among different communities, intermarriage, adoption, and the like all led to changes in the composition and nature of Indian communities. Events in what is today the American Southwest illustrate the point. The ancestors of the Pueblo Indians began moving into the region over a thousand years ago, seeking "better sources of food and a better environment."[20] Among other methods, they used songs to define their relationships to each other and to the land. During the thirteenth century, a drought helped drive the Towa to migrate from what is now Rio Arriba County to the area where the Jemez Reservation is today. The Towa's songs refer to lakes and canyons in Rio Arriba. Later, the Towa expelled some members, who then migrated southwest and joined another group, the Tampiros. The exiles eventually returned and were reintegrated into Towa society.[21] As Tessie Naranjo of the Santa Clara Pueblo has explained, migration profoundly shaped how Pueblo communities defined citizenship: "People have moved from place to place and have joined and separated again throughout our past, and we have incorporated it into our songs, stories, and myths."[22]

The Pueblo people were not the only ones whose identities were shaped by migration to the Southwest. Athapaskans from northwestern North

America left Saskatchewan by about 700 CE and moved into Montana and Wyoming, where they presumably met and intermarried over the next three centuries with peoples already there. At least some migrated into the American Southwest and became Apaches and Navajos (Diné).[23] According to accounts from the latter, as the Diné moved from what is now Colorado into New Mexico, they intermarried with Zunis and formed the sixth Navajo clan.[24] As historian Peter Iverson put it, "There is little debate about the ability of the Diné through time to incorporate other peoples into their ranks, to make them or their children into Navajos, with equal status and standing."[25]

Movement also shaped the evolution of Native American citizenship on the Plains. Western Siouan emigrants splintered and became the Mandan and Hidatsa of the northern Plains. A group of Hidatsas separated from their people and eventually became yet another separate community, the Absaroka (Crows). Schisms and amalgamations among the Ponca, Omaha, Osage, and Kansa peoples meant that some Kansa people became citizens of the Omaha tribe, some Osage people became citizens of the Ponca, and some Ponca people became citizens of the Kansa.[26]

Tribal Citizenship and the United States before 1934

As Indian nations came under the jurisdiction of nations that developed out of European colonies in the Americas, tribal citizenship requirements, rights, and obligations were affected. The experiences of tribes that fell under the domination of the United States illustrate the point. During the colonial and early national periods of the United States, Europeans and Euro-Americans recognized the existence of Native American political communities. However, they also tended to lump all indigenous North Americans into the racial category of "Indian."[27] The Supreme Court even ruled in *United States v. Rogers* (1846) that the term "Indian" was a racial classification distinct from tribal membership.[28] This was in spite of the fact that a number of Native societies had adopted non-Indians.[29]

Over time, the United States came to possess substantially greater power than the Indian peoples into whose lands the new nation expanded. The federal government's Indian policy emphasized taking land from the tribes and assimilating Native Americans into mainstream American society well into the twentieth century. In other words, government policymakers prior to 1934 tended to favor a conception of tribal citizenship akin to Duffy's categories of assimilative and co-opted/colonized citizenship. The ways in which policymakers worked to achieve those goals led them to more formally define tribal membership. For example, treaties frequently involved Indian nations ceding land in exchange for material goods (under duress), and the government's assimilationist efforts frequently entailed dividing tribal lands into individually owned plots. The distribution of money, goods, and land allotments led to the creation of formal membership rolls to define who was eligible.[30]

Although Indian tribes generally determined their own membership, federal officials sometimes used racial and blood-quantum criteria to define the rights of tribal citizens in the nineteenth and twentieth century. In treaties with the Winnebago and the Sioux from 1837, for example, tribal members had to possess a minimum of Indian blood to receive payments for ceded land. Further, the Supreme Court declared in 1846 that whites adopted into Indian nations were subject to federal criminal law, even though the United States had considered intra-Indian crimes to be under tribal jurisdiction prior to 1885. (This changed with passage of the Major Crimes Act of 1885, which extended federal jurisdiction over certain crimes committed in Indian Country.)[31]

A watershed in the federal government's formalization of tribal membership standards came with the General Allotment Act, or the Dawes Act of 1887, which grew out of the desire to assimilate Indians into mainstream American society and to acquire tribal lands. Named for Senator Henry Dawes (R-MA), the law allowed for the government to divide selected reservations up into individually owned allotments of land. Dawes and other supporters of the law believed it necessary to turn Native people into individual landowners in order to "civilize" them. The allotments would be held "in trust" by the federal government—meaning it could not be sold or taxed—for twenty-five years. The premise was that Native Americans would need that time to learn how to manage their property in a way consistent with the values of mainstream society. The act also allowed for the sale of "surplus" reservation land left over after eligible Indians had received their parcels. Further, it conferred United States citizenship upon allotted Indians. The sale of surplus land and the high number of allottees who lost their property reduced the Indian land base by about two-thirds between 1887 and 1934.[32]

To implement the law, federal officials developed membership rolls for each allotted tribe to determine who was eligible to receive property under the Dawes Act. The rolls listed the blood quantum of each member, and federal officials later used that to determine whether tribal members could be released from trust restrictions on their property (see below).[33] When making decisions about whom to include on the rolls, federal officials often disregarded tribal input. For example, in 1889, the OIA told government agents developing a membership list for the White Earth Anishinaabeg that they were free to ignore the wishes of tribal leaders.[34] When the Five Civilized Tribes (Cherokee, Choctaw, Chickasaw, Muscogee Creek, and Seminole) in what is now Oklahoma resisted allotment, Congress authorized the Dawes Commission—a presidential commission charged with overseeing the allotment of the tribes' land—to determine who would be included on the membership rolls.[35]

Nevertheless, as discussed below, tribal peoples had and have a sovereign right to determine their membership, and they often succeeded in determining which names to include on their membership rolls.[36]

Although the Allotment Act made no reference to blood quantum, officials considered the blood quantum of tribal members when determining whether to remove the trust status of individual allotments. This decision had significant effects on the rights of tribal citizens. As noted above, the original law provided for holding allotments in trust for twenty-five years. The Burke Act of 1906, however, amended the Dawes Act by allowing the government to remove the trust status before the end of the twenty-five years if an allotted Indian was deemed "competent" to manage his or her affairs. By the early twentieth century, policymakers decided that a lower quantum of Indian blood would mean that an individual was competent to manage his or her property. For example, between 1904 and 1908, Congress removed the trust status of all land belonging to members of the Five Civilized Tribes with less than one-half Indian blood. Those individuals between one-half and three-fourths Indian blood saw the trust protections removed on some of their property, while lawmakers preserved trusteeship on the lands of persons with a blood quantum of three-fourths or greater.[37] From 1917–20, Commissioner of Indian Affairs Cato Sells applied a variation of that policy nationwide. He removed the trust protections on property owned by "all able-bodied adult Indians of less than one-half Indian blood," because he felt such a blood quantum indicated that they were "competent" to manage their own affairs.[38]

The removal of trust protections from mixed-blood tribal citizens all too often led to them losing their property. This loss adversely affected tribal citizenship, especially given the emphasis on individual land ownership in the Dawes Act and in mainstream U.S. society. Among the Coeur d'Alenes, for example, it became very difficult, if not impossible, for individuals to participate in communal deer hunts and berry gatherings, which traditionally had been expected of tribal members.[39]

Growing dissatisfaction with allotment and other elements of Indian policy among the public and government officials led Congress to pass the Indian Reorganization Act (IRA) of 1934.[40] Also known as the Wheeler-Howard Act, the IRA stood out as a key piece of Indian affairs legislation during the "Indian New Deal" era of the 1930s and 1940s. During the Indian New Deal, federal policy shifted to emphasize, at least in theory, the preservation of tribes as politically and culturally distinct entities. The IRA ended allotment and established provisions for the creation of federally recognized tribal governments.[41] The law also provided a definition of "Indian" that included "all persons of Indian descent who are members of any recognized Indian tribe now under Federal jurisdiction, and all persons who are descendants of such members who were, on June 1, 1934, residing within the present boundaries of any Indian reservation, and . . . persons of one-half or more Indian blood."[42] More significant for tribal citizenship, the Interior Department's interpretation of the law reaffirmed that tribes had the sovereign right to decide their own membership criteria.[43] As seen below, however, the federal government continued to influence tribal membership rules.

Overview of Tribal Citizenship Requirements since 1934
Since 1934, tribes have organized federally recognized governments (either under the auspices of the IRA or through separate processes), and those

tribal governments have crafted a variety of membership requirements. A number of these reflected the criteria used in precontact times, such as geography (residency within the tribal community) and family ties (in the form of descent). In other cases, ostensibly new requirements such as blood quantum have been used. However, some tribes have adapted blood quantum as a way to preserve older conceptions of membership using new methods. Ultimately, Native peoples—in the name of indigenous nationalism and/or measured separatism—have adjusted to federal efforts to influence or dictate citizenship rules and crafted membership requirements intended to protect their cultures, political autonomy, and economic resources in the face of changing circumstances.

Criteria for membership varied and continues to vary from tribe to tribe. This is evident from tribal constitutions, many of which were created in the aftermath of the IRA's passage.[44] The 1936 constitution of the Fort McDermitt Shoshones and Paiutes (on a reservation that straddles the Nevada–Oregon border) combined family ties, geography, and blood: it stipulated that tribal citizens included those listed on the allotment rolls, their descendants who continued to live on the reservation, and all children of tribal members who possessed at least one-quarter Indian blood.[45] The Tohono O'odham (Papago), in its constitution of 1937, extended citizenship to those listed on the tribal census and to "all children of resident members." The tribal council could adopt children of tribal members born off-reservation if they possessed at least one-half Indian blood.[46] Under the Mississippi Choctaw's 1945 Constitution, to be a member one had to be listed on the tribal census of 1940 and have at least one-half Indian blood. Individuals born after the 1940 census needed to possess at least one-half Choctaw blood (not simply Indian blood) and be residents of Mississippi.[47] The Navajo Nation Council's membership resolution of 1953 stated that citizens would consist of all persons of Navajo blood listed on the tribal roll maintained by the BIA; individuals not listed but who possessed at least one-quarter Navajo blood were eligible for membership.[48] The Minnesota Chippewa Tribe provided in 1964 that membership would include persons listed on the annuity roll of 1941, children born to tribal members between 1941 and 1961, and children of at least one-quarter Minnesota Chippewa Indian blood born to at least one tribal member after 1961.[49] The 1975 and 1999 constitutions of the Cherokee Nation of Oklahoma stipulated that individuals included on the Dawes Act membership rolls and their descendants were tribal citizens.[50] In 1999, the Nez Perces restricted citizenship to those listed on the tribal membership roll of 1956, children of tribal members with at least one-quarter Nez Perce blood, and persons adopted into the tribe via a membership ordinance.[51]

Federal Influence on Tribal Citizenship Requirements

Federal policy has long held that Indian nations have the right to determine their own membership. In practice, however, the United States has sought to shape tribes' decisions in this area. For example, the federal government frequently pushed or forced tribes to adopt blood-quantum and lineage requirements. As noted above, officials used blood quantum to define the rights of Indians, such as maintaining or removing trust protections on allotments. However, the government also favored basing tribal citizenship on blood quantum and lineage. In part, this preference reflected the long-standing practice, described above, of government officials defining Indians as members of a racial group as well as of political organizations (tribes) with membership based on descent. Therefore, federal agents believed, one needed to have Indian blood and ancestry to be a member.[52] In addition, members of Congress and federal bureaucrats wanted to limit the number of tribal members to limit the number of people eligible for federal benefits.[53]

Therefore, Congress and the Interior Department encouraged, pressured, or forced tribes to adopt blood-quantum requirements. Between 1907 and 1917, government officials sometimes prevented individuals from being listed on the Colville Indian rolls because they lacked sufficient Indian blood.[54] In 1931 and 1934, Congress set minimum blood-quantum requirements for the Eastern Cherokee and the Menominee (one-sixteenth and one-quarter, respectively).[55] Tribes that organized under the IRA after 1934 had to submit their constitutions to the Department for approval; many tribes' membership requirements reflected the Interior Department's preferences.[56] Local BIA officials wrote the Navajo's aforementioned blood-quantum requirement and successfully urged the tribal council to adopt it in 1953. They argued it would allow the nation to limit claims to wealth generated from uranium mining, restrict the number of people entitled to benefits under the Navajo's treaty with the United States, and assist members with establishing their right to Social Security.[57] Congressional legislation restoring the trust relationship between the Ysleta del Sur Pueblo and the federal government in 1987 mandated that tribal members must be of at least one-eighth Native blood.[58] In the 1990s and early 2000s, the BIA resisted the efforts of the Lac Courte Oreille Band of Lake Superior Chippewa to replace blood quantum with lineal descent.[59]

Continuity and Change in Tribal Citizenship Requirements

Nevertheless, historian Mikaëla Adams notes that it would be a mistake to conclude that tribes were "simply the victims of federal Indian policy." Rather, indigenous peoples "actively worked within the constraints they faced" to craft membership requirements intended to protect their cultures, political autonomy, and economic resources in the face of changing circumstances.[60] That is, tribal peoples have sought, in general, to use citizenship requirements to preserve a sense of indigenous nationalism and measured separatism, to use Duffy's categorization. Native Americans have reached different conclusions about what requirements would best facilitate those goals, however.[61]

Residency

For example, residency requirements sometimes grew out of concerns that relying only on descent would allow off-reservation individuals to dominate reservation political life and lead to per-capita distribution of tribal income instead of using that income to provide services for reservation residents. Despite such concerns, Indian nations increasingly moved away from residency requirements beginning in the 1940s and 1950s. This shift stemmed from the fact that many people were compelled to leave their tribal communities because of poor economic conditions, off-reservation economic opportunities fueled by the Second World War, and the federal government's relocation programs.[62] As of 2010, only one Indian tribe has made residency a requirement for membership, although about a fifth of all tribes required one or both parents to have lived on the reservation at the time of a potential member's birth.[63]

Blood Quantum, Descent, and Culture

Tribes have also relied on a combination of culture, descent, and blood quantum to determine membership. In other words, while the United States government often pressured or forced tribes to adopt certain citizenship standards (see above), many tribes have adopted those standards of their own accord, using them to protect and promote their own interests. In some cases, tribes have crafted blood-quantum and descent membership requirements to prevent persons with little to no connection to a tribe from claiming citizenship just to receive benefits stemming from federal Indian programs (such as health care and education) or income-generating tribal enterprises (such as mining or gaming). In other cases, tribes adopted more expansive membership criteria in order to reunite families and to share resources with relatives.

The tribes' use of blood quantum has been and remains controversial. Some authors argue that the adoption of blood-quantum rules amounts to tribes abandoning traditional ways of defining their identity and adopting the dominant society's conceptions of Native Americans as a race.[64] Historian Alaina E. Roberts observed that some economically successful tribes appear to have adopted more restrictive blood-quantum requirements to "confine their newly won economic fortune to as small a population as possible."[65] Other critics argue that given the relatively high rate at which Natives marry non-Natives, blood-quantum requirements could significantly reduce the number of tribal members or even define some tribes out of existence over time.[66]

Other scholars, however, maintain that the tribes' reliance on blood quantum, in combination with descent, constitutes an adaptation to changed conditions rather than a wholesale departure from tribal traditions. Carole Goldberg writes that "biological relationship has always formed some part, often a significant part, of tribal belonging. Extended kinship groups or clans formed the basic units of nearly all tribal societies." Historically, "proper descendance is the key to tribal belonging, and a person possessing such descendance could far more readily establish membership than someone who did not."[67] Legal scholar Kirsty Gover argues that tribes have "borrow[ed] concepts of Indianness and Indian blood quantum from federal policy, but increasingly use these to construct and define a tribe-specific genealogic structure."[68]

Tribes have used blood-quantum requirements in some cases to limit their membership when that seemed necessary to defend their interests. Between the 1880s and 1930s, for example, the Mississippi Choctaw increasingly relied on blood quantum to determine its membership. Racist views were widespread within mainstream American society, especially in the South. That racial ideology greatly influenced Indian policy, as evidenced by the aforementioned ways in which officials used blood quantum in the implementation of the Dawes Act. The Choctaw played on that ideology by defining themselves by blood (specifically, "full blood")—as well as by culture and descent—in order to bolster their claims for federal support owed to the Choctaw under an earlier treaty and other United States laws. The Mississippi Choctaw also used racial criteria to distinguish themselves from two other groups. First, they created boundaries between themselves and African Americans in order to protect themselves from the virulent racial discrimination blacks faced. In fact, racist local OIA agents discouraged the Choctaw from associating with African Americans, and the agents refused to add children born of Choctaw–black unions to the tribal roll. Second, the Mississippi Choctaw differentiated themselves from people with little to no biological or cultural connection to the tribe but who sought enrollment for financial gain.[69]

Other Indian nations—such as the Flandreau Santee Sioux, the Confederated Salish and Kootenai of the Flathead Reservation, and the Navajo Nation—appear to also have used blood quantum as a way to make tribal citizenship more restrictive in the name of preserving tribal land and other resources.[70] The latter group, according to author Paul Spruhan, supported enacting a blood-quantum requirement in 1953 "to protect the Nation's limited resources" from those who "merely sought enrollment for financial benefit."[71] The Navajo Nation further limited membership by the use of various cultural standards. The Council allowed rejected applicants to appeal, but they would be judged on both blood quantum as well as other criteria such as residency, membership in a Navajo clan, and the ability to speak the Navajo language. The purpose of the non-biological criteria apparently was to limit the ability of the descendants of Navajos who had been enslaved by Anglos and Hispanics before the twentieth century and had lived away from the reservation for some time to become tribal citizens. The perception then seems to have been that these individuals had rejected opportunities to return to the reservation and were only seeking to return in the 1950s for financial benefits.[72]

In other cases, however, tribes endorsed citizenship criteria that expanded tribal membership—sometimes in defiance of federal officials—in order to share tribal resources with kin, to be inclusive of individuals with family ties, and to enhance tribal political power. Between 1907 and 1917, for example, the Colville Indians in Washington State held several councils to consider applicants for membership. The United States officials who supervised the process pressed the Colville to admit people based on blood quantum and descent in order to limit the number of people entitled to tribal resources and federal benefits. In some cases, the Colville went along with the government's wishes. In other instances, councilors defied the agents and voted to enroll individuals regardless of blood quantum if they had the proper "cultural orientation."[73] Sometimes, the "fervent desire to gather kin together" led council members to admit persons who had been living off-reservation but had family ties to one or more of the on-reservation Colville bands.[74] The Colville belief that "everyone is entitled to a living" compelled tribal representatives to admit those in need so that they could have access to reservation land and resources.[75]

The Cherokee Nation of Oklahoma opted not to rely on a minimum blood quantum. The rationale was that setting such a minimum would wrongly exclude deserving individuals from membership because there was not a reliable way to measure Indian blood historically. As noted above, during the Allotment Era, whether allotments were held in federal trust depended on the amount of Indian blood of each owner. Whether land was held in trust status was significant because it determined whether the allottees could sell their land or would have to pay taxes on their property. The Cherokee knew this and manipulated government officials' focus on racial criteria, according to former principal chief Ross Swimmer. Persons with a high Indian blood quantum who wanted to sell their allotments claimed a low quantum in order to be released from the trust restrictions; mixed bloods who wished to avoid paying taxes on their property claimed a higher level of Indian blood to preserve their land's trust status. In other words, there was (and is) no accurate way to determine a Cherokee's blood quantum based on the allotment rolls.[76] Therefore, the tribe has relied on descent instead. The Cherokee also rejected utilizing a minimum blood quantum because it would restrict their membership; at least some tribal members believed that a larger population would strengthen the tribe's political influence with the state and federal government.[77]

Concerns that overly restrictive requirements would result in descendants not being tribal citizens have prompted some Native nations to look at revising them in the twenty-first century. According to Hopi leader Le Roy Shingoitewa, his people have considered reducing their one-quarter blood-quantum requirement because intermarriage has resulted in fewer tribal members being able to meet that standard. Shingoitewa stated, "We want to ensure the longevity of our continued existence. . . . We're trying to make sure the Hopis keep growing and are maintained."[78] In 2013, the Utes of the Uintah and Ouray Reservation in Utah proposed reducing their five-eighth Ute blood-quantum requirement out of fear that not doing so would exclude many of the descendants of current members and lead to a reduction of the tribe's population.[79] In 2015, after considerable internal debate and discussion, the Ysleta del Sur Pueblo (Tigua) abolished its blood-quantum requirement for membership.[80]

Tribal Peoples and United States Citizenship

Overview

On June 2, 1924, Congress passed the Indian Citizenship Act, which stipulated "that all noncitizen Indians born within the territorial limits of the United States be, and they are hereby, declared to be citizens of the United States: Provided, That the granting of such citizenship shall not in any manner impair or otherwise affect the right of any Indian to tribal or other property."[81] The act endorsed the idea that Native Americans were members of two political communities: their tribes as well as the United States. This acceptance of "dual citizenship" for Indians represented a shift in the thinking of the time. Federal policymakers had traditionally held that United States and tribal citizenship were mutually exclusive and that replacing the latter with the former would facilitate the assimilation of Native peoples. Policymakers believed that Indians were members of separate, sovereign tribes and that their tribal existence had to be dissolved in order to incorporate them into mainstream American society. By the early 1900s, if not before, government officials had become increasingly skeptical that American Indians had the ability to fully assimilate into mainstream society and therefore came to accept the idea of Indians as only "partial" citizens. The act also constituted the culmination of a long, piecemeal process by which the federal government extended citizenship to Indians through various treaties and laws. However, the extension of American citizenship did not mean that Native Americans enjoyed equality with non-Natives, and discrimination against Indians continued. More than a few Native peoples opposed the imposition of United States citizenship, seeing it as a threat to their tribal sovereignty and identity. Other indigenous groups, however, endorsed the idea of dual citizenship and fought to protect their rights as American citizens in order to protect the rights of their tribes. Framed within the context of Duffy's typology, such groups used American citizenship rights to protect a measured separatism between tribal and mainstream American society.

Extending United States Citizenship to Native Americans in the Nineteenth Century

Throughout the nineteenth century, federal officials and other Americans concerned with Indian policy emphasized acquiring tribal lands and "civilizing" indigenous people. They saw the extension of citizenship as a way to achieve both goals. American Indians would be expected or forced to adopt the attributes of mainstream United States society. President Thomas Jefferson, for example, wrote in the early 1800s that as American Indians took up Euro-American–style farming and land allotments, Americans and Natives would "blend together" and "become one people." Indians would end up, ultimately, "incorporating themselves with [Americans] as citizens of the United States."[82]

Assimilation involved the extension or imposition of United States citizenship and the dissolution of tribal citizenship—and the unique legal status and protections that came with the latter—for those Native Americans who had become "civilized." In other words, the perception of government officials for much of the nineteenth century—and well into the twentieth—was that Native persons could not be members of both the American political community and a tribal polity. In the mid-twentieth century, that view would be called "Termination." American citizenship would replace tribal membership, which officials felt would benefit Indians. As the Commission of Indian Affairs explained in 1891, in a statement that reflected federal officials' attitudes for much of the previous century,

> There is no place within our borders for independent, alien governments, and the Indians must of necessity surrender their autonomy and become merged in our nationality. In requiring this we do not ask they concede anything of real value to themselves but only that for their highest welfare they abandon their tribal organizations . . . and accept in lieu thereof American citizenship and a full participation in all the riches of our civilization.[83]

The surrender of tribal membership would also supposedly "emancipate" individual Indians from federal "guardianship." Guardianship—also called the "trust doctrine"—referred to a distinctive set of federal laws and policies dealing with indigenous peoples that developed over the course of time. The trust doctrine was rooted in a variety of federal laws and court rulings—most notably the "Cherokee Cases" of *Cherokee Nation v. Georgia* (1831) and *Worcester v. Georgia* (1832). The former found that tribes were "domestic dependent nations" with a relationship to the federal government akin to that of a ward to its guardian. *Worcester v. Georgia* affirmed that tribes constituted separate political communities that possessed an inherent sovereignty that shielded them from state laws. In theory, guardianship protected Indians from being taken advantage of by unscrupulous persons, but it also limited Indians' freedom by allowing the United States broad authority over their lives. For example, holding land in trust made it less likely private individuals could swindle Indians out of their property, but it also limited what Native Americans could do with that property.[84]

Various nineteenth-century laws and treaties extended American citizenship to certain indigenous peoples in the context of the removal policy of the 1830s. Advocates of removal worked to compel or coerce tribes to relocate farther west. In some cases, federal agents offered Indians the chance to remain where they were if they accepted individual allotments of land, dissolved their tribal ties, and became U.S. citizens.[85] For example, treaties with the Choctaw in 1830 and the Cherokee in 1835 provided for the wholesale cession of tribal lands in the Southeast and removal to the Indian Territory but allowed individuals to remain in the Southeast if they accepted U.S. citizenship (or state citizenship, in the case of the Cherokees) and individual land allotments.[86] In 1839, the Brothertown Indians, in order to avoid being removed from Wisconsin, successfully lobbied Congress to pass a law making them citizens and allotting them their tribal lands.[87] However, by and large, advocates of these types of citizenship and allotment proposals anticipated the Native Americans would end up selling their property to non-Indians and relocating anyway. For most Southeastern Indian allottees, that was exactly what happened.[88]

Some tribal members in Kansas became U.S. citizens through federal laws, judicial decisions, and treaties in the mid-1800s. Treaties with the Wyandots (1855) and Ottawas (1862) declared that they had ended their tribal membership and had become American citizens because they were "sufficiently advanced in civilization."[89] Similarly, treaties made around the same time with the Potawatomi and Kickapoo allowed individuals to become United States citizens if they accepted land allotments, separated themselves from their tribe, and "adopted the habits of civilized life."[90] The Kansas legislature followed suit by extending citizenship to those Native Americans covered by the treaties, but it denied them voting rights.[91]

Certain states extended state citizenship to particular Native Americans if they had become "civilized" and severed tribal ties.[92] Massachusetts did that in 1869 when it granted citizenship to the Chappaquiddick, Christiantown, Gay Head, Herring Pond, and Mashpee communities. Unlike the Kansas law, the Massachusetts Citizenship Act allowed Native Americans access to the ballot box. Advocates were motivated, at least in part, by a concern over civil rights and equality. They tended to see American Indians as a racial minority and often viewed the political inclusion of indigenous persons as an extension of efforts to provide equal rights to African Americans. To that end, the Act abolished the tribes' distinct legal status, scotched the state's trusteeship of communal Indian lands, and allotted those lands. Supporters of the Citizenship Act believed these steps would provide greater economic opportunities for Indians as well as non-Indians who had intermarried into the tribes. State policymakers also understood that the Act would allow non-Indians to acquire Indian lands and "develop" them. Lawmakers were further motivated by a desire to do away with the tribes' cultural practice of allowing Native wives to own and manage the family's property. In sum, the Citizenship Act granted American Indians Massachusetts citizenship, eroded tribal identities and cultures, and increased the alienation of Native lands.[93]

Like the Massachusetts case, the extension of U.S. citizenship to the Pueblo peoples of the Southwest illustrated the economic and assimilationist motives behind such efforts. It also showed that the process of political incorporation often did not proceed smoothly and that the results could be ambiguous.

The Pueblo found themselves within the borders of the United States as a result of the U.S.–Mexican War of 1846–48. In that war, the United States seized Mexico's northern territories—including all or parts of New Mexico and California. The Treaty of Guadalupe Hidalgo of 1848, which ended the war, stipulated that any Mexican citizens who did not affirm that they wished to retain their political allegiance to Mexico within one year would be considered U.S. citizens. Pueblo Indians had been Mexican citizens, and not one of them officially declared that they wished to maintain that citizenship.[94] Hence, they would presumably have become Americans under the treaty. However, two decades after the war's end, their political status remained ambiguous. Pueblo Indians could sue in American courts, for example, but could not vote in American elections. Laws prohibiting the sale of alcohol to Indians did not apply to the Pueblos in the late 1860s, but—like other tribes—they were not free to sell their lands.[95]

District Court judges attempted to settle the matter in the case of *United States v. Lucero* (1869). At issue was an attempt to collect a fine from a non-Indian who had been living on Cochiti Pueblo lands in violation of a federal law that prohibited trespassing on tribal lands. The court ruled that the law did not apply because it had been intended for "wild, wandering savages" and not for settled agriculturalists like the Pueblo people. Further, under the terms of the Treaty of Guadalupe Hidalgo, they were

U.S. citizens, as they had been Mexican citizens at the time of the treaty's signing and had not declared they wished to retain allegiance to Mexico. The Supreme Court effectively confirmed the ruling in 1876.[96]

As with other instances involving the extension of citizenship to Native Americans at this time, the court rulings reflected non-Indians' economic interests and desire for assimilation. Evidence suggests that the New Mexico lawyers involved in the cases wanted to advance the interests of their land-hungry clients as well as further their own land speculation. Moreover, they wanted the Pueblo Indians as clients. All of that depended on the Natives being defined as American citizens.[97]

In addition, the rulings illustrated mainstream American social and political attitudes during the period that historian Elliott West refers to as the "Greater Reconstruction." During the 1860s and 1870s, federal officials faced significant questions about citizenship and the nature of political inclusion. The attempted secession by the states of the South raised the issue of whether Southern whites could reject their U.S. citizenship. The results of the Civil War forced the nation to determine the status of African Americans recently liberated from slavery. Westward expansion in the 1840s and 1850s raised the question of the place of Indian nations in the American republic. Ultimately, federal officials emphasized political incorporation: Southern whites would remain citizens, citizenship would be extended to Blacks and American Indians, and all would be expected to conform to mainstream American economic and cultural norms. If the political and economic incorporation of Native Americans required coercion, so be it.[98]

Ironically, even after the Supreme Court's ruling in *United States v. Lucero*, the federal government interacted with the Pueblo peoples as it did with other tribes, in many respects. For example, federal agents continued to be assigned to the nations; the United States funded activities related to farming, education, and the like; and Congress declared that Pueblo lands, like other tribal lands held in federal trust, were tax exempt. In other words, by the late 1870s, the Pueblo peoples had a de facto form of dual citizenship—that is, they were recognized as members of their own indigenous nations as well as of the United States.[99] That was formalized in 1913 when the United States Supreme Court, in *United States v. Sandoval*, ruled that the Pueblo peoples were under federal guardianship (see below).

Relatively few Natives became U.S. citizens under the piecemeal measures described above.[100] Those who did often faced substantial discrimination from whites, lost their property once federal guardianship was removed, or ended up being re-tribalized.[101] By contrast, the General Allotment Act (Dawes Act) of 1887 turned a sizable number of Native Americans into United States citizens. It extended citizenship to Indians who received a land allotment either under the act itself or through any other law or treaty.[102] In addition, citizenship was bestowed upon indigenous persons who took up "residence separate and apart from any tribe" and "adopted the habits of civilized life."[103] As author Nicole Tonkovich explained, to government officials the Allotment Act allowed non-Indians to acquire large quantities of "surplus" reservation land, and in exchange Native Americans "would be given a gift of inestimable value: American citizenship."[104] Approximately half of all American Indians became United States citizens through the Allotment Act.[105]

Extending United States Citizenship to Native Americans in the Twentieth Century

By the early twentieth century, however, federal officials increasingly doubted that indigenous persons were ready for citizenship. One government agent in the Northwest stated in 1905, "We are rushing the Indians too rapidly into a civilization and citizenship for which they have had little or no preparation."[106] A 1912 survey of OIA superintendents found that about 80 percent did not believe most Native Americans were ready for United States citizenship.[107] A number of factors accounted for these doubts. The growing acceptance of scientific racism in the late nineteenth and early twentieth centuries led many policymakers and other non-Indians to feel that Indians were so racially inferior that they lacked the capacity to fully assimilate. The development of the modern anthropological concept of "culture" during the same period prompted many government officials and scholars to the conclusion that assimilation would take much longer than initially hoped. Therefore, Indians were unfit for "full" citizenship, as they would either take advantage of it or would be exploited by non-Indians seeking to control their property. Government officials concluded that Natives deserved "partial citizenship." Indians would be made U.S.

citizens, but tribal citizenship would be maintained; American Indians would not enjoy equal rights; and the federal government's trust relationship with Native peoples and property would persist.[108]

That shift in attitude led to the passage of legislation and court rulings in the first quarter of the twentieth century that extended United States citizenship to various Native groups and individuals while allowing them to remain members of their tribes. Congress imposed citizenship upon tribes in the Indian Territory in 1901, but a subsequent act placed restrictions on the tribes' ability to dispose of their property. This indicated that lawmakers saw trusteeship and American citizenship as compatible.[109] In 1910, Congress passed the New Mexico Enabling Act, which stipulated that the Pueblo and their lands would be placed under federal trusteeship once New Mexico became a state. The Supreme Court affirmed the Pueblo peoples' dual citizenship in *United States v. Sandoval* in 1913.[110] Three years later, the Court ruled in *United States v. Nice* in 1916 that tribal citizenship, American citizenship, and federal guardianship could coexist.[111] In 1919, Congress passed legislation allowing Native American veterans of World War I to apply for American citizenship. Two years later, the House and Senate imposed U.S. citizenship upon the Osage.[112] The Citizenship Act of 1924 (described above) marked the culmination of federal officials' trend toward acceptance of dual citizenship. It declared, in effect, non–U.S. citizen Indians to be citizens of both the United States and their tribe.[113] Perhaps the clearest evidence that Congress only intended to extend partial citizenship is that the act's sponsor, Congressman Homer P. Snyder, stated that he did not intend that the law would "have any effect upon the suffrage qualifications [of Indians] in any State." Given that several states denied suffrage to all or at least some indigenous persons at that time (see below), Snyder's statement is telling.[114] It meant that the extension of United States citizenship did not mean Native Americans enjoyed equal rights with their fellow citizens.

Native American Views of United States Citizenship
In 1993, Wilma Mankiller, principal chief of the Cherokee Nation from 1985–95, described Native peoples' reaction to the Indian Citizenship Act of 1924:

Not all native people celebrated passage of the citizenship act. In fact, there was little lobbying for or against the measure, with one notable exception. Some of the Iroquois nations actively lobbied against the legislation, arguing that the citizenship act was being arbitrarily forced on them against their will. They contended it violated their own tribal citizenship and form of government. Their protests had little effect.[115]

Mankiller's statement reflects the fact that, historically, Native peoples had not favored becoming United States citizens. Most Cherokees, for example, rejected federal officials' offer that they surrender their tribal citizenship and accept individual land allotments in order to avoid removal to the Indian Territory in the 1830s.[116] Most Wyandots in Kansas strongly opposed the aforementioned Treaty of 1855, which made them U.S. citizens, dissolved their tribal ties, and allotted tribal lands.[117] In 1861, Chief Shahgwee objected when federal negotiators pushed the Prairie Band of Potawatomi to sign a treaty that would cede land but allow some tribal members to take up individual allotments and become American citizens. He argued that the agreement would allow land-hungry whites to strip his people of their property.[118] In a study commissioned by Congress, the Bureau of Municipal Research concluded in 1915 that with rare exceptions, the Native American "does not desire [non-tribal] citizenship."[119]

As noted above, the Iroquois Nations strongly opposed the Citizenship Act in the 1920s. As Tuscarora leader Clinton Rickard explained, his people feared:

> We would lose most of our independence. By our ancient treaties, we expected the protection of the government. The white man had obtained most of our land and we felt he was obliged to provide something in return, which was protection of the land we had left, but we did not want to be integrated and assimilated into his society. United States citizenship was just another way of absorbing us and destroying our customs and our government.[120]

That Iroquois opposition has persisted. Chief Irving Powless Jr. of the Onondaga Nation declared in 1998 that the Six Nations "have never accepted this law. [They] do not consider [themselves] as citizens of the United

States."[121] The following year, legal scholar Robert B. Porter of the Seneca described the 1924 act as "genocidal."[122]

Objections did not come from the Iroquois alone. In 1920 over half a dozen Pueblo nations told Congress that they did not wish to be made citizens because they believed it would lead to the loss of the trust relationship.[123] In 1976, Lakota elders Fools Crow and Charlie Red Cloud promulgated a "resolution of sovereignty" that affirmed their tribe's inherent sovereignty and rejected the Citizenship Act.[124] By the end of the twentieth century, a survey found that about 10 percent of all American Indians rejected United States citizenship and favored tribal citizenship exclusively.[125]

However, in the nineteenth century and early twentieth century, at least some tribal peoples sought or accepted American citizenship as a way of dealing with certain problems. As noted above, minorities among the Cherokee, Choctaw, Brothertown, Wyandot, and other tribes desired U.S. citizenship because they believed it would allow them to avoid being forced off their lands by the federal government. In the late 1830s, at least some Stockbridge–Munsee Mohicans in the Wisconsin Territory supported becoming United States citizens and severing their tribal relations because they believed their tribal government was unable to ensure law and order and wished to be under Wisconsin's jurisdiction.[126] Alaska Native organizations advocated for citizenship in the early 1900s to protect their land rights and to fight against racial discrimination.[127]

At least some Natives favored citizenship as a way to escape from the control of the OIA. The Office exercised extraordinary power over Indian Country by the early twentieth century. As historian Frederick Hoxie explained, "Individual Indians could be jailed without trial, barred from performing religious rituals, and removed from participating in the disposition of trust property assigned to them."[128] Hence, Luther Standing Bear (Lakota) wanted to become a United States citizen because it would allow him to control his own property and would free him from "the iron rule of the white agent" on the reservation.[129] Carlos Montezuma (Yavapai) agreed. He saw obtaining American citizenship as a way to liberate himself from the OIA's oversight and to exercise individual rights such as suffrage.[130] As noted above, he believed that U.S. citizenship was compatible with being a tribal member, as evidenced by his efforts to enroll at the San Carlos reservation.[131]

Not surprisingly, an organization Montezuma cofounded in 1911—the Society of American Indians (SAI)—advocated that American Indians be made U.S. citizens and maintain their tribal ties.[132] Those who organized the group felt that Native peoples had been "swallowed up by the United States" and turned into "an invisible minority."[133] As a result, tribal governments had been undercut by the OIA and individual Indians exploited by government agents and private citizens. Montezuma, attorney Thomas Sloan (Omaha), physician Charles Eastman (Dakota), and other SAI organizers believed U.S. citizenship would provide American Indians with the power they needed to force changes in destructive federal policies and practices. This would, in turn, allow for the preservation of tribes as politically and culturally distinct entities.[134] In other words, the SAI advocated for measured separatism.

Other Native Americans in the first part of the twentieth century endorsed the idea that Indians should be dual citizens of both their tribes and the United States. Richard C. Adams—a Delaware and founder of the short-lived Brotherhood of North American Indians in 1911—believed indigenous persons should have the same freedoms as other Americans, including the right to vote. At the same time, he called for the preservation of treaty rights, continuation of the reservation system, and authorization for Indians to send delegates to Congress.[135]

Robert Yellowtail echoed such sentiments. Yellowtail, a Crow political leader, urged Congress in 1919 to make American Indians citizens. This would recognize their service during World War I and afford them the same rights as other Americans. At the same time, he also favored the preservation of tribal citizenship by asserting that the Crow Reservation (and other reservations, by implication) stood out as "a separate semisovereign nation."[136] In other words, Montezuma and Yellowtail endorsed Duffy's concept of measured separatism.

United States Citizenship, Tribal Sovereignty, and Voting Rights

By 1924, the passage of the Citizenship Act showed that Congress had also accepted and formally codified the idea of dual citizenship for Indians.[137]

As noted, with a few exceptions, most Indian nations responded with indifference.[138] That stemmed from the fact that the act did little to change the lives of Native peoples, who continued to contend with various forms of paternalism, exploitation, and discrimination.[139] Over time, however, most American Indians would endorse the concept of dual citizenship and find ways to use their rights as American citizens to protect their tribal rights. Powerful examples of this include the work of individual Indians, tribes, and pan-Indian organizations like the National Congress of American Indians (NCAI) on behalf of Native voting rights and dual citizenship.

Citizenship without Rights

Despite the extension of citizenship to them, Native Americans continued to see their rights disregarded. Many states denied American Indians access to the ballot box, the courts, and public schools; public and private groups worked to separate Indians from their lands; and federal paternalism eroded the freedom of tribes and their members. As government attorney Nathan Margold put it in the early 1930s "The last noncitizen [Indians] were made citizens in 1924, but today Indians in Arizona, for instance, and in some other parts of the country, are not permitted to vote, and Indians are very largely excluded from juries and from local schools. Citizenship they have, but it is citizenship without the rights of citizens."[140] The experiences of the Pueblo Nations in Arizona and New Mexico during the 1920s and early 1930s illustrated Margold's point. The Pueblo continued to lose lands to non-Native squatters, often with the tacit or explicit support of public officials.[141] The OIA dictated which Pueblos would be allowed to travel to Washington to meet with federal officials, and it repeatedly attempted to ban Pueblo religious practices during the 1920s.[142]

Further, Pueblos and other Natives faced state restrictions on their right to vote, restrictions rooted in the idea that American citizenship and tribal citizenship were incompatible.[143] Arizona denied Indians suffrage based on a 1928 state-court decision—*Porter v. Hall*—that interpreted the trust doctrine to mean that Native Americans were under "guardianship." State officials interpreted the ruling to mean that all Indians, even those who lived off-reservation and had terminated their tribal ties, were "under guardianship" (that is, mentally incompetent) and thus ineligible to vote.[144] This reflected the conception, discussed earlier, that indigenous people could only partially be incorporated into American society. Neighboring New Mexico denied voting rights to "Indians not taxed." The phrase generally referred to Native Americans who continued to live as part of tribal societies but also to the fact that reservation lands were not taxable by the state. New Mexico was not alone in this; as late as 1940 the states of Idaho, Maine, Mississippi, and Washington all denied suffrage to "Indians not taxed."[145] In other words, in a paradigm reminiscent of earlier conceptions of American and tribal citizenship as mutually exclusive, Indians could only enjoy the same voting rights as other American citizens if they terminated their tribal ties.

Dual Citizenship and the Struggle for Native Voting Rights

It was in this context of discrimination against Indian citizens that a group of Native Americans formed the National Congress of American Indians (NCAI). The NCAI's struggle for indigenous voting rights illustrates the way that Native peoples used dual citizenship to empower Indian persons and nations. Founded by representatives of fifty tribes at a meeting in Denver in November 1944, the organization largely came into existence because of the work of three OIA employees: Archie Phinney (Nez Perce), D'Arcy McNickle (Flathead), and Charles E. J. Heacock (Rosebud Lakota). Heacock pieced together a network of Native American support for the new organization both inside and outside the Indian Affairs bureaucracy. McNickle utilized his close ties to the highest-ranking OIA officials to facilitate the NCAI's formulation. Phinney formulated the overarching vision for the group. It was to be a national organization that would, as anthropologist William Willard put it, "give Indians a voice not subject to the dictates of federal and state governments"—the organization would play a key role in revitalizing tribes.[146]

The NCAI's formation came at a critical time in the history of American Indians and federal Indian policy. By the early 1940s, a backlash had developed against the Indian New Deal, and that backlash took the form of an assimilationist policy that became known as "Termination." Termination's advocates envisioned liquidating tribes by stripping them of their unique legal status and legal rights by abolishing the federal trust doctrine, or guardianship.[147] Ultimately, advocates of Termination—which dominated Indian policy in the 1940s and 1950s—favored replacing dual citizenship with exclusively American citizenship. The policy reflected earlier conceptions of tribal and American identities as being incompatible, and its advocates proposed to resolve that supposed incompatibility by liquidating tribal ties. It was consistent with Duffy's category of co-opted or colonized citizenship, in which tribal membership is seen as valueless.

The NCAI responded by endorsing dual citizenship, which embodied Duffy's concept of measured separatism. The NCAI in the 1940s and 1950s defended the unique status of Indian tribes as well as the rights of Indians as United States citizens.[148] The organization's constitution pledged "to preserve Indian cultural values" and to protect "rights under Indian treaties or agreements with the United States."[149] At the same time, NCAI leaders stated that they were committed to securing and protecting "the rights and benefits to which [Natives] are entitled under the laws of the United States," along with "the Full Promise of Citizenship."[150] A clear illustration of this was the NCAI's position that state laws denying Native Americans the franchise violated the principles of democracy and the Fifteenth Amendment. The participants at the founding meeting voted unanimously to make protecting Native voting rights one of the organization's goals.[151]

To that end, in 1948 the organization supported lawsuits against Arizona and New Mexico brought by American Indians who had been prevented from voting. Frank Harrison (Mohave) and Harry Austin (Mohave) sued Arizona in *Harrison v. Laveen*, and Miguel Trujillo (Isleta Pueblo) sued New Mexico in *Trujillo v. Garley*. In both cases, the courts struck down the state laws that had barred Indians from the ballot box and affirmed dual citizenship. The judges acknowledged that Indians "occupy a peculiar and unique relationship to the federal government" (to quote *Harrison v. Laveen*), but that unique relationship was not changed by the extension of United States citizenship to Indians.[152] In other words, they were tribal citizens with a distinct relationship to the federal government as well as United States citizens with the same rights as non-Indian citizens.

Native peoples continued fighting against de jure voting discrimination after 1948 in other states such as Utah.[153] By the 1960s and 1970s, with the passage of the Voting Rights Act of 1965 and its application to Native Americans, overt suppression of Native American voting had largely ended. However, de facto discrimination persisted. Some states continued (and continue) to engage in practices that limit Native Americans' access to the ballot box or dilute Native American votes. Examples include drawing district lines in ways that limit the impact of Indian voters, failing to establish polling stations in areas accessible to reservation residents, and the like.[154] Those obstacles certainly stemmed from racism and a desire for partisan advantage. They also reflected hostility to dual citizenship. For example, officials in Big Horn County in Montana justified at-large elections, which diluted the Native vote, by arguing that as tribal citizens Indians did not wish to participate in mainstream elections. American Indians sued the county, and a federal judge struck down the at-large election system in *Windy Boy v. County of Big Horn* (1986). The judge ruled that dual citizenship did not justify the discriminatory practice.[155] South Dakota officials in the late twentieth and early twenty-first centuries have similarly objected to Indians voting unless they surrendered their dual citizenship.[156] This view is fundamentally at odds with that of most American Indians at the end of the twentieth century: roughly ninety percent of American Indians supported dual citizenship as well as voting in U.S. elections.[157]

In response, groups like the NCAI have not only challenged discriminatory practices through lobbying and litigation but actively encouraged Native Americans to exercise their rights as United States citizens by going to the polls.[158] The reason is that the actions of local, state, and federal officials can adversely affect tribes and their members by, among other things, limiting their rights of self-government. Therefore, voting stands out as a way by which Native Americans could defend the rights of their tribes. In other words, United States citizenship, which policymakers had seen as a way to detribalize Indians, has instead provided indigenous persons with a means of defending their tribal nations and tribal citizens alike. Helen Peterson, the NCAI's executive director for most of the 1950s, argued that voting allowed Indians to defend their interests and facilitated the continued existence of Indian nations.[159] Legal scholar John P. LaVelle (Santee Sioux) and former NCAI president Joe A. Garcia (Ohkay Owingeh) have found Native American voting to be critical to protecting and strengthening tribal sovereignty.[160] For example, the votes of indigenous persons played a key role in the election of officials sympathetic to tribal interests, such as Montana senator James Murray in 1954 and South Dakota senator George McGovern in 1962. Relatedly, a Native-led voter-mobilization campaign in the state of Washington led to the defeat of anti-Indian Senator Slade Gorton in 2000.[161]

Conclusion

Historian Linda K. Kerber described citizenship in the late twentieth century as "contested, variable, and fluid."[162] Such a conception could also apply to the history of the citizenship of American Indians, whether tribal or American. The history of Native American citizenship, at its essence, involved efforts by tribes to preserve a distinctive identity.

Different indigenous societies had different criteria for citizenship long before documented contact with Europeans, and that criteria typically included such factors as geography, culture, and kinship. Citizenship rules—and their associated rights, responsibilities, and identities—reflected and perpetuated a sense of distinction among different peoples. That distinction, in Diane Duffy's typology of Native American citizenship, falls into the category of indigenous nationalism, in which a Native individual's primary allegiance was to that individual's Native community.

Those tribes that fell under the rule of the United States found their citizenship affected. The federal government sought to formalize tribal membership and define the rights of those members as part of a larger campaign to exact land cessions and assimilate American Indians. For much of its history, United States policymakers sought to "terminate" tribes by breaking them up and "Americanizing" their members through measures such as the Dawes Act. American citizenship would supplant tribal citizenship, and distinctive tribal identities would be destroyed. Put another way, for much of the nineteenth and a significant portion of the twentieth centuries, most policymakers favored a conception of citizenship that Duffy referred to as assimilative and co-opted/colonized, in which tribal citizenship was inferior to U.S. citizenship.

By the early twentieth century, skepticism that American Indians had the capacity to assimilate fully into U.S. society led to the passage of the

Indian Citizenship Act of 1924. The law made Native Americans dual citizens of both the United States and their tribes. However, mainstream perceptions of Indians as inferior meant that they were citizens in name only and did not enjoy the same rights as non-Indian citizens in a variety of areas, including suffrage.

By the 1930s, federal policy shifted away from assimilation and toward the preservation of tribes as politically and culturally distinct entities. Tribes began to rebuild themselves by creating or strengthening federally recognized tribal governments and defining membership criteria. Tribes adapted seemingly "new" criteria such as blood quantum as a way to perpetuate older citizenship criteria like kinship.

Further, many Native Americans, such as the leaders of the SAI and NCAI in the twentieth century, fought for their rights as dual citizens—such as voting—in order to protect Indian nations against threats to their existence. Native peoples have continued to use their hard-fought access to the ballot box to help ensure the election of pro–tribal sovereignty candidates. Such efforts can be categorized in Duffy's citizenship typology as "measured separatism."

In the end, the ongoing effort by Native Americans to define tribal citizenship criteria and exercise their rights as U.S. citizens was and is part of a larger struggle—both pre- and postcontact—to ensure the survival of Indian tribes as politically and culturally distinctive entities. This effort reflects the core theme of *Rising from the Ashes*: the adaptability and resilience of Indigenous peoples.

NOTES

1. Gale Courey Toensing, "Nooksack Indian Tribe in Disenrollment Fight," *Indian Country Today*, April 11, 2013, https://newsmaven.io/indiancountrytoday/archive/nooksack-indian-tribe-in-disenrollment-fight-FqgzWQknlUasmo_7da9QZQ/; Liz Jones, "Nooksack Judge Halts Removal of 306 Tribal Members," KUOW.org, August 15, 2013, http://www.kuow.org/post/nooksack-judge-halts-removal-306-tribal-members.

2. A valuable study of tribal disenrollment is David Wilkins and Shelly Hulse Wilkins, *Dismembered: Native Disenrollment and the Battle for Human Rights* (Seattle: University of Washington Press, 2017). See also Alaina E. Roberts, "A Hammer and a Mirror: Tribal Enrollment and Scholarly Responsibility," *Western Historical Quarterly* 49, no. 1 (Spring 2018): 91–96.

3. The 2007 amendment reflected a long-standing effort by Cherokee leaders to exclude African Americans from full tribal citizenship. Matthew L. M. Fletcher, "On Black Freedmen," Legal Studies Research Paper Series, Research Paper no. 5–8, November 8, 2007, http://ssrn.com/abstract=1015282; William Loren Katz, *Black Indians: A Hidden Heritage* (New York: Aladdin, 1986), 135–48; Alex Kellogg, "Cherokee Nation Faces Scrutiny for Expelling Blacks," National Public Radio, September 19, 2011, http://www.npr.org/2011/09/19/140594124/u-s-government-opposes-cherokee -nations-decision; Tiya Miles, *Ties That Bind: The Story of an Afro-Cherokee Family in Slavery and Freedom* (Berkeley: University of California Press, 2005), 108–14; S. Alan Ray, "A Race or a Nation? Cherokee National Identity and the Status of Freedmen's Descendants," *Michigan Journal of Race and Law* 12, no. 2 (Spring 2007): 387–463; Circe Sturm, *Blood Politics: Race, Culture, and Identity in the Cherokee Nation of Oklahoma* (Berkeley: University of California Press, 2002), chapter 7; "Tribal Rights vs. Racial Justice," *New York Times*, September 15, 2011, http://www.nytimes.com /roomfordebate/2011/09/15/tribal-sovereignty-vs-racial-justice.

4. Peter Iverson, *Carlos Montezuma and the Changing World of the American Indians* (Albuquerque: University of New Mexico Press, 1982), 153–60; Olympia Sosange-lis, "'Something More Than an Indian': Carlos Montezuma and Wassaja, the Dual Identity of an Assimilationist and Indian Rights Activist" (Master's thesis, Simmons College, March 2008), 106–9.

5. Derek Heater, *Citizenship: The Civic Ideal in World History, Politics and Education*, 3rd ed. (Manchester UK: Manchester University Press, 2004), 187; John Scott and Gordon Marshall, *Oxford Dictionary of Sociology* (Oxford: Oxford University Press, 2009), 80–81.

6. On the complex, multifaceted, and evolving nature of citizenship, see Mehnaaz Momen, *The Paradox of Citizenship in American Politics: Ideals and Reality* (Cham CH: Palgrave Macmillan, 2018); Ayelet Shachar, Rainer Bauböck, Irene Bloemraad, and Maarten Vink, eds., *The Oxford Handbook of Citizenship* (Oxford: Oxford University Press, 2017); and the discussion that occurred on H-Net's H-Citizenship listserv in March 2008: H-Citizenship Discussion Logs, March 2008, http://h-net.msu.edu/cgi -bin/logbrowse.pl?trx=lx&list=H-Citizenship&month=0803&user=&pw=.

7. Scott and Marshall, *Oxford Dictionary of Sociology*, 80–81; Linda K. Kerber, "The Meaning of Citizenship," *Journal of American History* 84, no. 3 (December 1997): 835–36.

8. A few examples of recent works that focus on Native Americans and citizenship include Mikaëla M. Adams, *Who Belongs? Race, Resources, and Tribal Citizenship in the Native South* (New York: Oxford University Press, 2016); Jessica Leslie Arnett, "Unsettled Rights in Territorial Alaska: Native Land, Sovereignty, and Citizenship from the Indian Reorganization Act to Termination," *Western Historical Quarterly* 48, no. 3 (Autumn 2017): 233–54; Bethany R. Berger, "Race, Descent, and Tribal Citizenship," *California Law Review Circuit* 23, no. 4 (April 2013): 23–37; Kevin

Bruyneel, "Challenging American Boundaries: Indigenous People and the 'Gift' of U.S. Citizenship," *Studies in American Political Development* 18, no. 1 (Spring 2004): 30–43; Kevin Bruyneel, *The Third Space of Sovereignty: The Postcolonial Politics of U.S.-Indigenous Relations* (Minneapolis: University of Minnesota Press, 2007); Jill Doerfler, *Those Who Belong: Identity, Family, Blood, and Citizenship among the White Earth Anishinaabeg* (East Lansing: Michigan State University Press, 2015); Matthew L. M. Fletcher, "States and Their American Indian Citizens," *American Indian Law Review* 41, no. 2 (2017): 319–43; Eva Marie Garroutte, *Real Indians: Identity and the Survival of Native America* (Berkeley: University of California Press, 2010); Kirsty Gover, *Tribal Constitutionalism: States, Tribes, and the Governance of Membership* (Oxford: Oxford University Press, 2010); Alexandra Harmon, "Tribal Enrollment Councils: Lessons on Law and Indian Identity," *Western Historical Quarterly* 32 no. 2 (Summer 2001): 175–200; Norbert S. Hill Jr. and Kathleen Ratteree, *The Great Vanishing Act: Blood Quantum and the Future of Native Nations* (Golden CO: Fulcrum, 2017); Eric D. Lamont, ed., *American Indian Constitutional Reform and the Rebuilding of Native Nations* (Austin: University of Texas Press, 2006); Lucy Maddox, *Citizen Indians: Native American Intellectuals, Race, and Reform* (Ithaca NY: Cornell University Press, 2005); R. Warren Metcalf, *Termination's Legacy: The Discarded Indians of Utah* (Lincoln: University of Nebraska Press, 2002); Katherine M. B. Osburn, *Choctaw Resurgence in Mississippi: Race, Class, and Nation Building in the Jim Crow South, 1830–1977* (Lincoln: University of Nebraska Press, 2014); Roberts, "Hammer and a Mirror," 91–96; Deborah A. Rosen, *American Indians and State Law: Sovereignty, Race, and Citizenship, 1790–1880* (Lincoln: University of Nebraska Press, 2007); Paul C. Rosier, *Serving Their Country: American Indian Politics and Patriotism in the Twentieth Century* (Cambridge MA: Harvard University Press, 2009); Steve Russell, *Sequoyah Rising: Problems in Post-Colonial Tribal Governance* (Durham NC: Carolina Academic Press, 2010); Paul Spruhan, "A Legal History of Blood Quantum in Federal Indian Law to 1935," *South Dakota Law Review* 51, no. 1 (2006): 1–50, https://papers.ssrn .com/sol3/papers.cfm?abstract_id=955032; Paul Spruhan, "The Origins, Current Status, and Future Prospects of Blood Quantum as the Definition of Membership in the Navajo Nation," *Tribal Law Journal* 8, no. 1 (2007–8): 1–17; Sturm, *Blood Politics*; Brad Tennant, "'Excluding Indians Not Taxed': *Dred Scott, Standing Bear, Elk*, and the Legal Status of Native Americans in the Latter Half of the Nineteenth Century," *International Social Science Review* 86, no. 1–2 (2011): 24–43; Alan Trachtenberg, *Shades of Hiawatha: Staging Indians, Making Americans, 1880–1930* (New York: Hill and Wang, 2004); Kim Cary Warren, *The Quest for Citizenship: African American and Native American Education in Kansas, 1880–1935* (Chapel Hill: University of North Carolina Press, 2010); Wilkins and Wilkins, *Dismembered*. For a comparative analysis of indigenous citizenship in the United States, Canada, Australia, and New Zealand, see Kirsty Gover, "Indigenous Citizenship in Settler States," in *Oxford Handbook of Citizenship*, 453–77. For firsthand observations and assessments by scholars and tribal leaders, see the transcripts from "Who Belongs? From Tribal Kinship to Native National Citizenship to Disenrollment," a conference that took place on March 9–10, 2017, at the University of Arizona in Tucson; the transcripts are available at https://turtletalk.wordpress.com/2017/05/17/transcripts-of-who -belongs-from-tribal-kinship-to-native-nation-citizenship-to-disenrollment/.

9. "Who Belongs?," A.M. Session (transcript), March 9, 2017, p. 14, https://turtletalk .wordpress.com/2017/05/17/transcripts-of-who-belongs-from-tribal-kinship-to -native-nation-citizenship-to-disenrollment/.

10. Diane Duffy, "An Attitudinal Study of Native American Patriotism" (paper presented at the meeting of the International Society for Political Psychology Scientific Services, Krakow PL, July 22, 1997). This study relies on the extended summary and discussion of Duffy's work in Jeff Corntassel and Richard Witmer II, *Forced Federalism: Contemporary Challenges to Indigenous Nationhood* (Norman: University of Oklahoma Press, 2008), 64–65; see also David E. Wilkins and Heidi Kiiwetinepinesiik Stark, *American Indian Politics and the American Political System*, 4th ed. (Lanham MD: Rowman and Littlefield, 2018), 205–6. Duffy identified additional categories as well. One of these—"environmental allegiance"—essentially conceived of citizenship in a community as consisting of both humans and nonhumans. It reflected identification with the natural environment. Another entailed an essentially apolitical view of citizenship and patriotism.

11. A number of observers, including many Native people, question the characterization of indigenous societies as tribes or nations prior to contact with Europeans and Euro-Americans: the newcomers often imposed such characterizations for their own political advantage. Many Indians' primary allegiance was to their family or band, and they were not under the rule of a central government that could, among other things, cede land to the United States. See, for example, Nez Perce Tribe, *Treaties: Nez Perce Perspectives* (Lewiston ID: Confluence Press, 2003), 6; Roberta Connor and William L. Lang, "Early Contact and Incursion, 1700–1850," in *Wiyáxayxt/ Wiyáakaáawn/As Days Go By: Our History, Our Land, and Our People; The Cayuse, Umatilla, and Walla Walla*, ed. Jennifer Karson (Pendleton OR: Tamástslikt Cultural Institute, 2006), 24. At least some scholars question whether the concept of tribal citizenship had truly existed prior to contact with Europeans and Euro-Americans. See, for example, Lucy A. Curry, "A Closer Look at *Santa Clara Pueblo v. Martinez*: Membership by Sex, by Race, and by Tribal Tradition," *Wisconsin Women's Law Journal* 16, no. 2 (Fall 2001): 161–214.

Nevertheless, within the literature and in common parlance, Native American political communities, regardless of their level of centralization, are regularly referred to as "tribes" and "nations," and members of those communities commonly referred to as "citizens" or "members." Therefore, for consistency and convenience, that practice is followed here.

12. Russell, *Sequoyah Rising*, 110–11.

13. Jeffrey P. Shepherd, *We Are an Indian Nation: A History of the Hualapai People* (Tucson: University of Arizona Press, 2010), 19.

14. Allen V. Pinkham and Steven R. Evans, *Lewis and Clark among the Nez Perce: Strangers in the Land of the Nimiipuu* (Washburn ND: Dakota Institute Press, 2013), 8. See also Deward E. Walker Jr., in collaboration with Daniel N. Matthews, *Nez Perce Coyote Tales: The Myth Cycle* (Norman: University of Oklahoma Press, 1994), 9–11.

15. Ella Deloria, *Speaking of Indians* (New York: Friendship Press, 1944; reprint, Lincoln: University of Nebraska Press, 1998), 24–25. Citations refer to the 1998 edition.

16. Connor and Lang, "Early Contact and Incursion," 24.

17. Alan Gould Marshall, "Nez Perce Social Groups: An Ecological Interpretation" (Ph.D. diss., Washington State University, 1977), chapters 3 and 4; Nez Perce Tribe, *Treaties*, 4–6.

18. Marshall, "Nez Perce Social Groups," 77, 142. See also Alan G. Marshall, "Fish, Water, and Nez Perce Life," *Idaho Law Review*, 42, no. 3 (2006): 765.

19. Nez Perce Tribe, *Treaties*, 5–6; Alvin M. Josephy Jr., *Nez Perce Country* (Lincoln: University of Nebraska Press, 2007), 7–8. The right of being unbound by leaders' decisions endured after contact with the Americans. As one U.S. government agent observed in 1872, "If in council the tribe or band are pleased with the council and advice of their chiefs or headmen they follow it. If it does not accord with their feelings, it is disregarded." Monteith to Walker, August 31, 1872, John Monteith Letterbook, 134, Nez Perce National Historical Park Research Center, Lapwai ID.

20. Joe Sando, *Pueblo Nations: Eight Centuries of Pueblo Indian History* (Santa Fe NM: Clear Light, 1998), 22.

21. Sando, *Pueblo Nations*, 26.

22. Tessie Naranjo, "Thoughts on Migration by Santa Clara Pueblo," *Journal of Anthropological Archeology* 14, no. 2 (1995): 250.

23. Peter Iverson, "Taking Care of Earth and Sky," in *America in 1492: The World of the Indian Peoples before the Arrival of Columbus*, ed. Alvin M. Josephy Jr. (New York: Vintage Books, 1991), 95.

24. William B. Carter, *Indian Alliances and the Spanish in the Southwest, 750–1750* (Norman: University of Oklahoma Press, 2009), 75.

25. Peter Iverson, *Diné: A History of the Navajos* (Albuquerque: University of New Mexico Press, 2002), 16.

26. Colin G. Calloway, *One Vast Winter Count: The Native American West before Lewis and Clark* (Lincoln: University of Nebraska Press, 2003), 58–60.

27. Bethany R. Berger, "Red: Racism and the American Indian," *UCLA Law Review* 56, no. 3 (February 2009): 593; R. David Edmunds, "Native Americans, New Voices: American Indian History, 1895–1995," *American Historical Review* 100, no. 3 (June 1995): 733; Audrey Smedley, *Race in North America: Origin and Evolution of a Worldview* (Boulder CO: Westview Press, 1993), 85–89, 178–81.

28. Spruhan, "Legal History of Blood Quantum," 18; Wilkins and Wilkins, *Dismembered*, 27–28.

29. Paul Spruhan, "'Indians, in a Jurisdictional Sense': Tribal Citizenship and Other Forms of Non-Indian Consent to Tribal Criminal Jurisdiction," *American Indian Law Journal* 1, no. 1 (Fall 2012): 82–84, http://www.law.seattleu.edu/Documents/ailj/Fall%20issue/SpruhanConsentFinal.pdf.

30. Vine Deloria Jr., "A Better Day for Indians," 1977, box 123, folder 9, p. 21, Sol Tax Papers, Department of Special Collections, University of Chicago Library. For example, see "Acts of the Forty-Third Congress, Second Session," March 3, 1875, in *Indian Affairs: Laws and Treaties*, ed. Charles J. Kappler (Washington DC: USGPO, 1904), 1:24.

31. Treaty with the Winnebago, November 1, 1837, in *Indian Affairs: Laws and Treaties*, ed. Charles J. Kappler, 2:499 (Washington DC: USGPO, 1904); Treaty with the Sioux, September 29, 1837, in *Indian Affairs*, ed. Charles J. Kappler, 2:493; Spruhan, "Legal History of Blood Quantum," 10, 18–19.

32. Works on the Dawes Act include Emily Greenwald, *Reconfiguring the Reservation: The Nez Perces, Jicarilla Apaches, and the Dawes Act* (Albuquerque: University of New Mexico Press, 2002); Laurence M. Hauptman and L. Gordon McLester III, eds., *The Oneida Indians in the Age of Allotment, 1860–1920* (Norman: University of Oklahoma Press, 2006); John P. LaVelle, "The General Allotment Act 'Eligibility' Hoax: Distortions of Law, Policy, and History in Derogation of Indian Tribes," *Wicazō Śa Review* 14, no. 1 (Spring 1999): 251–302; Janet McDonnell, *The Dispossession of the American Indian, 1887–1934* (Bloomington: Indiana University Press, 1991); D. S. Otis, *The Dawes Act and the Allotment of Indian Lands* (Norman: University of Oklahoma Press, 1973); Kristin T. Ruppel, *Unearthing Indian Land: Living with the Legacies of Allotment* (Tucson: University of Arizona Press, 2008); Rose Stremlau, *Sustaining the Cherokee Family: Kinship and the Allotment of an Indigenous Nation* (Chapel Hill: University of North Carolina Press, 2011); Nicole Tonkovich, *The Allotment Plot: Alice C. Fletcher, E. Jane Gay, and Nez Perce Survivance* (Lincoln: University of Nebraska Press, 2012).

33. See, for example, Angie Debo, *And Still the Waters Run: The Betrayal of the Five Civilized Tribes* (Princeton NJ: Princeton University Press, 1940), 47; Doerfler, *Those Who Belong*, 2–3.

34. Doerfler, *Those Who Belong*, 3.

35. Wilkins and Wilkins, *Dismembered*, 35. See also Adams, *Who Belongs?*, 106–7.

36. Cohen to Bennett, August 4, 1944, 1–2; *Indian Wardship*, (New York: Home Missions Council of North America, 1944), 5. Both abovementioned documents are in series 1, box 2, folder 26, Felix S. Cohen Papers, Beinecke Rare Book and Manuscript Library, Yale University. Debo, *And Still the Waters Run*, 38–39; Doerfler, *Those Who Belong*, 4; Carole Goldberg, "Members Only? Designing Citizenship Requirements for Indian Nations," *Kansas Law Review* 50 (2002): 445–46; Gover, *Tribal Constitutionalism*,

110; Harmon, "Tribal Enrollment Councils," 184; Iverson, *Carlos Montezuma,* 153–60; LaVelle, "General Allotment Act," 258–59; Spruhan, "Legal History of Blood Quantum," 21–22, 24–25, 29.

37. Debo, *And Still the Waters Run,* 179–80; Spruhan, "Legal History of Blood Quantum," 40–42; Stremlau, *Sustaining the Cherokee Family,* 142–44.

38. Cato Sells, "Declaration of Policy," April 17, 1917, reprinted in *Indian Wardship,* 43–44, series 1, box 2, folder 26, Cohen Papers, Beinecke Rare Book and Manuscript Library, Yale University; Francis Paul Prucha, *The Great Father: The United States Government and the American Indian* (Lincoln: University of Nebraska Press, 1984), 2:882–83.

39. Rodney Frey, *Landscape Traveled by Coyote and Crane: The World of the Schitsu'umsh (Coeur d'Alene Indians)* (Seattle: University of Washington Press, 2001), 42, 95.

40. For dissatisfaction regarding allotment and related policies and programs, see, for example, Prucha, *Great Father,* vol. 2, chapter 31; Elmer R. Rusco, *A Fateful Time: The Background and Legislative History of the Indian Reorganization Act* (Reno: University of Nevada Press, 2000), chapter 3.

41. Works on the Indian New Deal and the IRA include Jon. S. Blackman, *Oklahoma's Indian New Deal* (Norman: University of Oklahoma Press, 2013); Vine Deloria Jr. and Clifford M. Lytle, *The Nations Within: The Past and Future of American Indian Sovereignty* (New York: Pantheon Books, 1984); Laurence M. Hauptman, *The Iroquois and the New Deal* (Syracuse NY: Syracuse University Press, 1981); Alice Beck Kehoe, *A Passion for the True and Just: Felix and Lucy Cohen and the Indian New Deal* (Tucson: University of Arizona Press, 2016); Lawrence C. Kelly, "The Indian Reorganization Act: The Dream and the Reality," *Pacific Historical Review* 45, no. 3 (August 1975): 291–312; Donald L. Parman, *The Navajos and the New Deal* (New Haven: Yale University Press, 1976); Kenneth R. Philp, *John Collier's Crusade for Indian Reform, 1920–1954* (Tucson: University of Arizona Press, 1977); Kenneth R. Philp, ed., *Indian Self-Rule: First-Hand Accounts of Indian-White Relations from Roosevelt to Reagan* (Logan: Utah State University Press, 1995), part 1; Paul C. Rosier, *The Rebirth of the Blackfeet Nation, 1912–1954* (Lincoln: University of Nebraska Press, 2001); Rusco, *Fateful Time;* Graham D. Taylor, *The New Deal and American Indian Tribalism: The Administration of the Indian Reorganization Act, 1934–1945* (Lincoln: University of Nebraska Press, 1980).

42. "Indian Reorganization Act," June 18, 1934, reprinted in *The Indian Reorganization Act: Congresses and Bills,* ed. Vine Deloria Jr. (Norman: University of Oklahoma Press, 2002), 23.

43. Margold to Secretary of the Interior, "Powers of Indian Tribes," October 25, 1934, reprinted in *Indian Affairs: Laws and Treaties,* ed. Charles J. Kappler, (Washington DC: USGPO, 1941), 5:778, 788–92; Spruhan, "Legal History of Blood Quantum," 47.

44. Some indigenous groups—such as the Cherokee and the Osage—had already developed constitutions prior to 1934. For a useful overview of the membership requirements in tribal constitutions, see Wilkins and Wilkins, *Dismembered,* 49–59.

45. Constitution and Bylaws of the Fort McDermitt Paiute and Shoshone Tribe, July 2, 1936, http://thorpe.ou.edu/constitution/pai-shoconst.html.

46. Constitution and By-Laws of the Papago Tribe, January 6, 1937 (Washington DC: USGPO, 1937), http://thorpe.ou.edu/ira/papcons.html.

47. Constitution and Bylaws of the Mississippi Band of Choctaw Indians, April 20, 1945, http://thorpe.ou.edu/ira/misschoccons.html.

48. Spruhan, "Origins, Current Status," 5.

49. Constitution and Bylaws of the Minnesota Chippewa Tribe, March 3, 1964 (revised 1972), http://thorpe.ou.edu/constitution/chippewa/. Citations refer to the 1972 edition.

50. Constitution of the Cherokee Nation of Oklahoma (1975), http://thorpe.ou.edu/constitution/cherokee/index.html; Constitution of the Cherokee Nation (1999), https://www.cherokee.org/media/abbelmas/constitution_english.pdf; Sharon O'Brien, *American Indian Tribal Governments* (Norman: University of Oklahoma, 1989), 200.

51. Constitution and Bylaws of the Nez Perce Tribe (1948), rev. September 2, 1999, http://thorpe.ou.edu/constitution/nezperce.html. Citations refer to the 1999 edition.

52. Gover, *Tribal Constitutionalism*, 113–15, 125; Harmon, "Tribal Enrollment Councils," 179, 186–87.

53. See, for example, Harmon, "Tribal Enrollment Councils," 191; Alison Maria Meadow, "The Legislation of Identity: 'I'll be Damned If I Let These People Take My Family's Heritage Away with the Stroke of a Pen'" (Master's thesis, University of Arizona, 1999), 51–53.

54. Harmon, "Tribal Enrollment Councils," 179, 183.

55. Spruhan, "Legal History of Blood Quantum," 45.

56. Goldberg, "Members Only," 446–47.

57. "Firsthand Accounts: Membership and Citizenship," in *American Indian Constitutional Reform*, 179; Spruhan, "Origins, Current Status," 5–6.

58. Jessica Bardill, "Tribal Sovereignty and Enrollment Determinations," National Congress of American Indians, 2011, http://genetics.ncai.org/tribal-sovereignty-and-enrollment-determinations.cfm.

59. Goldberg, "Members Only," 446–49.

60. Adams, *Who Belongs?*, 3.

61. Kimberly TallBear, "DNA, Blood, and Racializing the Tribe," *Wicazō Ša Review* 18, no. 1 (2003): 83.

62. Bardill, "Tribal Sovereignty and Enrollment Determinations"; Goldberg, "Members Only," 152–53.

63. Gover, *Tribal Constitutionalism*, 40.

64. See, for example, Lydia Edwards, "Protecting Black Tribal Members: Is the Thirteenth Amendment the Linchpin to Securing Equal Rights within Indian Country," *Berkeley Journal of African-American Law and Policy* 8, no. 1 (2013): 122–54; Hill and Ratteree, *Great Vanishing Act*; Russell, *Sequoyah Rising*, chapter 10; TallBear, "DNA, Blood, and Racializing," 81–107; Sturm, *Blood Politics*, chapter 7.

65. Roberts, "Hammer and a Mirror," 92.

66. See, for example, Bardill, "Tribal Sovereignty and Enrollment"; Fergus M. Bordewich, *Killing the White Man's Indian: Reinventing Native Americans at the End of the Twentieth Century* (New York: Anchor Books, 1995), 73; Osage Constitutional Reform Testimony, "'An Organization, a Club, or Is It a Nation?' (2007)," in *Say We Are Nations: Documents of Politics and Protest in Indigenous America since 1887*, ed. Daniel M. Cobb (Chapel Hill: University of North Carolina Press, 2015), 226–27; Russell, *Sequoyah Rising*, 115–23; "Who Belongs," A.M. Session (transcript), 10–11, 17.

67. Goldberg, "Members Only," 460.

68. Quotation from Gover, *Tribal Constitutionalism*, 156. See also Gover, "Indigenous Citizenship," 463–65, and Berger, "Race, Descent, and Tribal Citizenship."

69. Adams, *Who Belongs?*, 121–31; Osburn, *Choctaw Resurgence*, chapter 2; Katherine M. B. Osburn, "The 'Identified Full-Bloods' in Mississippi: Race and Choctaw Identity, 1898–1918," *Ethnohistory* 56, no. 3 (Summer 2009): 423–47.

70. On Flandreau, see TallBear, "DNA, Blood, and Racializing," 94; on Flathead, see Ronald L. Trosper, "Native American Boundary Maintenance: The Flathead Indian Reservation, Montana, 1860–1970," *Ethnicity* 3, no. 3 (1976): 256–74; on Navajo, see Spruhan, "Origins, Current Status," 1–17.

71. Spruhan, "Origins, Current Status," 8.

72. Spruhan, "Origins, Current Status," 8–10.

73. Harmon, "Tribal Enrollment Councils," 195.

74. Harmon, "Tribal Enrollment Councils," 194.

75. Harmon, "Tribal Enrollment Councils," 196.

76. "Firsthand Accounts," in *American Indian Constitutional Reform*, 181. The White Earth Anishinaabeg also manipulated federal agents' fixation on racial criteria in an effort to protect their rights and property; see Doerfler, *Those Who Belong*, 16–18.

77. Goldberg, "Members Only," 461.

78. "Firsthand Accounts: Membership and Citizenship," in *American Indian Constitutional Reform and the Rebuilding of Native Nations*, ed. Eric D. Lamont (Austin: University of Texas Press, 2006), 177.

79. Carol Berry, "Northern Ute Tribal Enrollment May Rise, Pending Election Could Lower Blood Quantum," April 9, 2013, *Indian County Today*, https://newsmaven.io/indiancountrytoday/archive/northern-ute-tribal-enrollment-may-rise-pending-election-could-lower-blood-quan-WNUSDINXnkWO5R2o9nr4uw/.

80. "Who Belongs," A.M. Session (transcript), p. 6.

81. Citizenship Act, reprinted in *Indian Affairs: Laws and Treaties*, ed. Charles J. Kappler (Washington DC: USGPO, 1929), 4:1165.

82. Jefferson to Hawkins, February 18, 1803, in *Jefferson: Political Writings*, ed. Joyce Appleby and Terrence Ball (Cambridge UK: Cambridge University Press, 1999), 522; Jefferson to Alexander von Humboldt, December 6, 1813, *The Writings of Thomas*

Jefferson, ed. Andrew A. Lipscomb, (Washington DC: Thomas Jefferson Memorial Association, 1904), 14:23. See also Robert J. Miller, *Native America, Discovered and Conquered: Thomas Jefferson, Lewis and Clark, and Manifest Destiny* (Westport CT: Praeger, 2006), 85–86; Anthony C. F. Wallace, *Jefferson and the Indians: The Tragic Fate of the First Americans* (Cambridge MA: Belknap Press of Harvard University Press, 1999).

83. "Report of the Commissioner of Indian Affairs," October 1, 1891, in *Report of the Secretary of the Interior; Being Part of the Message and Documents Communicated to the Two Houses of Congress at the Beginning of the First Session of the Fifty-Second Congress* (Washington DC: USGPO, 1892), 2:6.

84. On guardianship/trust doctrine, see D'Arcy McNickle, Mary E. Young, and W. Roger Buffalohead, "Captives within a Free Society: Federal Policy and the American Indian," n.d., box 14, D'Arcy McNickle Papers, Newberry Library, Chicago; Felix S. Cohen, *Handbook of Federal Indian Law* (Washington DC: USGPO, 1945), 172, 237–38, 306–9; Felix S. Cohen, "Indian Wardship: The Twilight of a Myth," in *The Legal Conscience: Selected Papers of Felix S Cohen*, ed. Lucy Kramer Cohen (New Haven: Yale University Press, 1960), 328–34, originally published in *American Indian* 6, no. 4 (Summer 1953): 8–14; David E. Wilkins and K. Tsianina Lomawaima, *Uneven Ground: American Indian Sovereignty and Federal Law* (Norman: University of Oklahoma Press, 2001), 64–97; S. James Anaya, "International Law and U.S. Trust Responsibility toward Native Americans," in *Native Voices: American Indian Identity and Resistance*, ed. Richard A. Grounds, George E. Tinker, and David E. Wilkins (Lawrence: University Press of Kansas, 2003), 155–85. On the Cherokee Cases, see Jonas Bens, "When the Cherokee Became Indigenous: *Cherokee Nation v. Georgia* and Its Paradoxical Legalities," *Ethnohistory* 65, no. 2 (April 2018): 247–67; Jill Norgren, *The Cherokee Cases: Two Landmark Federal Decisions in the Fight for Sovereignty* (Norman: University of Oklahoma Press, 2004).

85. Willard Hughes Rollings, "Citizenship and Suffrage: The Native American Struggle for Civil Rights in the American West, 1830–1965," *Nevada Law Journal* 5, no. 1 (Fall 2004): 130.

86. Treaty with the Choctaw, September 27, 1830, in *Indian Affairs*, ed. Charles J. Kappler, 2:313; Treaty with the Cherokee, December 29, 1835, in *Indian Affairs*, ed. Charles J. Kappler, 2:444; Ronald N. Satz, *American Indian Policy in the Jacksonian Era* (Lincoln: University of Nebraska Press, 1975), 83; Stremlau, *Sustaining the Cherokee Family*, 33.

87. Ronald H. Lambert Sr., *A History of the Brothertown Indians of Wisconsin* (Bloomington IN: AuthorHouse, 2010), 72; James W. Oberly, *A Nation of Statesmen: The Political Culture of the Stockbridge-Munsee Mohicans, 1815–1872* (Norman: University of Oklahoma Press, 2005), 63–66; Prucha, *Great Father*, 1:265–66.

88. Rosen, *American Indians and State Law*, 157.

89. Treaty with the Wyandot, January 31, 1855, in *Indian Affairs*, ed. Charles J. Kappler, 2:677–78; Treaty with the Ottawa of Blanchard's Fork and Roche de Boeuf, June

24, 1862, in *Indian Affairs*, ed. Charles J. Kappler, 2:830–31; Prucha, *Great Father*, 1:349–50.

90. Treaty with the Potawatomi, November 15, 1861, in *Indian Affairs*, ed. Charles J. Kappler, 2:825; Treaty with the Kickapoo, June 28, 1862, in *Indian Affairs*, ed. Charles J. Kappler, 2:836. See also Alexandra Witkin, "To Silence a Drum: The Imposition of United States Citizenship on Native Peoples," *Historical Reflections* 21, no. 2 (1995): 366–67. An 1871 federal law extended citizenship to those members of the Stockbridge and Munsee tribe in Wisconsin who wished to sever their tribal relations. "An Act for the Relief of the Stockbridge and Munsee Tribe of Indians," February 6, 1871, in *Indian Affairs*, ed. Charles J. Kappler, 2:130.

91. Rosen, *American Indians and State Law*, 157.

92. Fletcher, "States," 327–28; Alexander Keyssar, *The Right to Vote: The Contested History of Democracy in the United States*, rev. ed. (New York: Basic Books, 2009; New York: Basic Books, 2000), 134. Page references are to the 2009 edition.

93. Ann Marie Plane and Gregory Button, "The Massachusetts Indian Enfranchisement Act: Ethnic Contest in Historical Context, 1849–1869," *Ethnohistory* 40, no. 4 (Autumn 1993): 587–618; Rosen, *American Indians and State Law*, chapter 6.

94. Sando, *Pueblo Nations*, 86.

95. Deborah A. Rosen, "Pueblo Indians and Citizenship in Territorial New Mexico," *New Mexico Historical Review* 78, no. 1 (Winter 2003): 8. A revised version of this article appeared as chapter 7 in Rosen, *American Indians and State Law*.

96. United States v. Lucero, 1 NM 422 (N.M., 1869), http://www.waterbank.com/FTP/Tomah%20Valuation/Case%20Law/United%20States%20v%20Lucero%201%20NM%20422.pdf; the "wild, wandering savage" line is from page 9. Witkin, "To Silence a Drum," 368–70.

97. Rosen, "Pueblo Indians and Citizenship," 15–18.

98. Elliott West, *The Last Indian War: The Nez Perce Story* (New York: Oxford University Press, 2009), xviii–xxii, 318–19; Elliott West, "Reconstructing Race," *Western Historical Quarterly* 34, no. 1 (Spring 2003): 6–26.

99. See, for example, *Annual Report of the Commissioner of Indian Affairs to the Secretary of the Interior for the Year 1880* (Washington DC: USGPO, 1880), 133–35; *Fifty-Ninth Annual Report of the Commissioner of Indian Affairs to the Secretary of the Interior, 1890* (Washington DC: USGPO, 1890), 172–74. Donald L. Fixico, *The Invasion of Indian Country in the Twentieth Century* (Niwot: University of Colorado Press, 1998), 61–62. Witkin, "To Silence a Drum," 370.

100. Nor did tribal members become U.S. citizens under the Fourteenth Amendment to the U.S. Constitution. Ratified in 1868, the amendment extended citizenship to "All persons born or naturalized in the United States." However, the Senate Judiciary Committee concluded that the law did not apply to tribal members, because the federal government did not have exclusive jurisdiction over them. A federal court

affirmed that interpretation in 1871. Keyssar, *Right to Vote*, 133; Tennant, "'Excluding Indians Not Taxed,'" 32–33.

101. Witkin, "To Silence a Drum," 367–68.

102. Jeanette Wolfley, "Jim Crow, Indian Style: The Disenfranchisement of Native Americans," *American Indian Law Review* 16, no. 1 (1991): 177–78.

103. General Allotment Act, February 8, 1887, in *Indian Affairs*, ed. Charles J. Kappler, 1:35.

104. Tonkovich, *Allotment Plot*, 184.

105. Wolfley, "Jim Crow," 178; Indians also became citizens through other means, such as Indian children being born to parents who received citizenship through allotment, or Native women marrying white men; see "Indian Citizenship," in *Indian Affairs*, ed. Charles J. Kappler, 4:1165–66.

106. Charles M. Buchanan, "Report of the Superintendent of the Tulalip Agency," August 15, 1905, in *Annual Reports of the Department of the Interior for the Fiscal Year Ended June 30, 1905*, vol. 1, *Indian Affairs* (Washington DC: USGPO, 1906), 363.

107. Frederick E. Hoxie, *A Final Promise: The Campaign to Assimilate the Indians, 1880–1920* (Cambridge UK: Cambridge University Press, 1984), 230.

108. Bruyneel, "Challenging American Boundaries, 32–33; Hoxie, *Final Promise*, chapters 4 and 7. See also Kenneth W. Johnson, "Sovereignty, Citizenship and the Indian," *Arizona Law Review* 15, no. 4 (1973): 989–1003; Vine Deloria Jr. and David E. Wilkins, *Tribes, Treaties, and Constitutional Tribulations* (Austin: University of Texas Press, 1999), 146.

109. "Indian Citizenship," in *Indian Affairs*, ed. Charles J. Kappler, 4:1166; N. D. Houghton, "The Legal Status of Indian Suffrage in the United States," *California Law Review* 19, no. 5 (July 1931): 514.

110. G. Emlen Hall, *Four Leagues of Pecos: A Legal History of the Pecos Grant, 1800–1933* (Albuquerque: University of New Mexico Press, 1984), 202–6.

111. Witkin, "To Silence a Drum," 378–79. The case involved a non-Indian who provided alcohol to an American Indian in violation of federal law.

112. On citizenship for World War I veterans, see "An Act Granting Citizenship to Certain Indians," November 6, 1919, in *Indian Affairs*, ed. Charles J. Kappler, 4:232; Thomas A. Britten, *American Indians in World War I: At Home and at War* (Albuquerque: University of New Mexico Press, 1997), 178–79. On Osage citizenship, see "An Act to Amend Section 3 of the Act of Congress of June 28, 1906," March 3, 1921, in *Indian Affairs*, ed. Charles J. Kappler, 4:317.

113. Britten, *American Indians in World War I*, 179–81; Bruyneel, "Challenging American Boundaries," 31–32; Deloria and Wilkins, *Tribes, Treaties, and Constitutional*, 146; Gary C. Stein, "The Indian Citizenship Act of 1924," *New Mexico Historical Review* 47, no. 3 (1972): 260–63; Witkin, "To Silence a Drum," 377–79.

114. Stein, "Indian Citizenship Act," 259–60.

115. Wilma Mankiller and Michael Wallis, *Mankiller: A Chief and Her People* (New York: St. Martin's Press, 1993), 174.

116. William L. Anderson, introduction to *Cherokee Removal: Before and After* (Athens: University of Georgia Press, 1991), x; Stremlau, *Sustaining the Cherokee Family*, 33.

117. Treaty with the Wyandot, January 31, 1855, in *Indian Affairs*, ed. Charles J. Kappler, 2:677–78; John P. Bowes, *Exiles and Pioneers: Eastern Indians in the Trans-Mississippi West* (Cambridge UK: Cambridge University Press, 2007), 202–10.

118. An eyewitness account appears in "St. Mary's of the Potawatomi, II," reprinted in *The Jesuits of the Middle United States*, vol. 3, part 4, *Indian Missions*, ed. Gilbert J. Garraghan (Chicago: Loyola University Press, 1984), 27; Arthur T. Donohue, "The Effects of the Treaty of 1861 on the Cultural Life of the Pottawatomie Nation," *AKD Quarterly* 22, no. 2 (December 1951): 10.

119. Bureau of Municipal Research, *Administration of the Indian Office*, report 65, September 1915, 17.

120. Barbara Graymont, ed., *Fighting Tuscarora: The Autobiography of Chief Clinton Rickard* (Syracuse NY: Syracuse University Press, 1973), 53.

121. Quoted in Michael D. Oeser, "Tribal Citizen Participation in State and National Politics: Welcome Wagon or Trojan Horse?," *William Mitchell Law Review* 36, no. 2 (2010): 805.

122. Robert B. Porter, "The Demise of the Ongwehoweh and the Rise of the Native Americans: Redressing the Genocidal Act of Forcing American Citizenship upon Indigenous Peoples," *Harvard BlackLetter Law Journal* 15 (Spring 1999): 110, 126–27.

123. Porfirio Mirabel, "I Want to be Free," in *Say We Are Nations: Documents of Politics and Protest in Indigenous America since 1887*, ed. Daniel M. Cobb (Chapel Hill: University of North Carolina Press, 2015), 39–44.

124. Edward Lazarus, *Black Hills, White Justice: The Sioux Nation versus the United States, 1775 to the Present* (New York: HarperCollins, 1991), 349.

125. Corntassel and Witmer, *Forced Federalism*, 64.

126. Oberly, *Nation of Statesmen*, 56–57.

127. Arnett, "Unsettled Rights," 236.

128. Frederick E. Hoxie, *This Indian Country: American Indian Political Activists and the World They Made* (New York: Penguin Press, 2012), 273.

129. Luther Standing Bear, *My People the Sioux* (Lincoln: University of Nebraska Press, 1975), 278–81; quotation on p. 278.

130. Sosangelis, "'Something More Than an Indian,'" 102–3. See also Iverson, *Carlos Montezuma*, 113.

131. Iverson, *Carlos Montezuma*, 153–60; Sosangelis, "'Something More Than an Indian,'" 106–9.

132. For an overview and analysis of the SAI, see Hazel W. Hertzberg, *The Search for an American Indian Identity: Modern Pan-Indian Movements* (Syracuse NY: Syracuse University Press, 1971), part 1.

133. Hoxie, *This Indian Country*, 227.

134. Hoxie, *This Indian Country*, 225–29; Rosier, *Serving Their Country*, 43–44; Maddox, *Citizen Indians*, chapter 2.

135. Steven Crum, "Almost Invisible: The Brotherhood of North American Indians (1911) and the League of North American Indians (1935)," *Wicazō Ša Review* 21, no. 1 (Spring 2006): 3–4, 6.

136. "Address by Robert Yellowtail in Defense of the Rights of the Crow Indians, and the Indians Generally, before the Senate Committee on Indian Affairs," 66th Cong. 219, 1st sess., serial set vol. 7590 (September 9, 1919), in *U.S. Senate Report* (Washington DC: USGPO, 1919), 9–10 (quotation on page 9); Rosier, *Serving Their Country*, 55; Frederick E. Hoxie, ed., *Talking Back to Civilization: Indian Voices from the Progressive Era* (Boston: Bedford/St. Martin's, 2001), 133–38.

137. However, as noted above, federal officials' acceptance was not an endorsement of tribal identity; rather, it stemmed from a sense that Indians lacked the capacity to assimilate as quickly as expected. Further, Robert Porter and Gary C. Stein note that the 1924 act had less to do with a desire to "civilize" Indians than a political conflict between the legislative and executive branches of government. Specifically, many in Congress voted for the legislation because they wanted to limit the power of the Interior Department to extend to or withhold citizenship from Native Americans; see Porter, "Demise," 124–25; Stein, "Indian Citizenship Act," 266–70.

138. Rosier, *Serving Their Country*, 60; Mankiller and Wallis, *Mankiller*, 174.

139. Shepherd, *We Are an Indian Nation*, 121; Stein, "Indian Citizenship," 269.

140. "Draft of Address by Mr. Margold," n.d., series 1, box 10, folder 137, p. 3, Cohen Papers, Beinecke Rare Book and Manuscript Library, Yale University. The denial of Native voting rights in the twentieth century continued a trend from the nineteenth. In *Elk v. Wilkins* (1884), the Supreme Court ruled that John Elk, a detribalized Indian, did not have the right to cast a ballot even though he had consciously separated himself from his tribe. The court concluded that adopting the elements of mainstream American culture was not enough to make a Native American a U.S. citizen. Indigenous persons could only become citizens and voters through a specific Act of Congress. See Deloria and Wilkins, *Tribes, Treaties, and Constitutional*, 145–46.

141. "Minutes of All-Pueblo Council, Santo Domingo Pueblo," March 15, 1934, reprinted in *The Indian Reorganization Act: Congresses and Bills*, ed. Vine Deloria Jr. (Norman: University of Oklahoma Press, 2002), 197; Joe S. Sando, *Pueblo Profiles: Cultural Identity through Centuries of Change* (Santa Fe NM: Clear Light, 1998), 34, 38.

142. Sando, *Pueblo Profiles*, 37, 116.

143. Racial and cultural discrimination also motivated efforts to keep indigenous people away from the ballot box. Wilkins and Stark, *American Indian Politics*, 208–9.

144. Daniel McCool, Susan M. Olson, and Jennifer L. Robinson, *Native Vote: American Indians, the Voting Rights Act, and the Right to Vote* (Cambridge UK: Cambridge University Press, 2007), 15–16.

145. Margold to Secretary of the Interior and attachment, August 13, 1937, in *Opinions of the Solicitor of the Department of the Interior Relating to Indian Affairs* (Washington DC: Department of the Interior, 1974), 1:777–79; Daniel McCool, "Indian Voting," in *American Indian Policy in the Twentieth Century*, ed. Vine Deloria Jr. (Norman: University of Oklahoma Press, 1985), 109–11; McCool, Olson, and Robinson, *Native Vote*, 12–13. State literacy tests and poll taxes also disenfranchised many indigenous persons; see McCool, Olson, and Robinson, *Native Vote*, 18–19; Margold to Secretary of the Interior and attachment, in *Opinions of the Solicitor*, 778.

146. William Willard, "Archie Phinney and the Development of the National Congress of American Indians" (unpublished manuscript in the possession of Christopher K. Riggs), 203. See also chapter 5 in the present volume.

On the founding and development of the NCAI, see also Alison R. Bernstein, *American Indians and World War II: Toward a New Era in Indian Affairs* (Norman: University of Oklahoma Press, 1991), 112–21; Thomas W. Cowger, *The National Congress of American Indians: The Founding Years* (Lincoln: University of Nebraska Press, 1999), chapter 2; Hertzberg, *Search for an American Indian Identity*, 289–91; Rosier, *Serving Their Country*, 104–8.

147. On Termination see, for example, Arnett, "Unsettled Rights," 233–54; Laurie Arnold, *Bartering with the Bones of Their Dead: The Colville Confederated Tribes and Termination* (Seattle: University of Washington Press, 2012); Larry W. Burt, *Tribalism in Crisis: Federal Indian Policy, 1953–1961* (Albuquerque: University of New Mexico Press, 1982); Donald L. Fixico, *Termination and Relocation: Federal Indian Policy, 1945–1960* (Albuquerque: University of New Mexico Press, 1986); Larry J. Hasse, "Termination and Assimilation: Federal Indian Policy, 1943–1961" (PhD diss., Washington State University, 1974); Metcalf, *Termination's Legacy*; Nicholas C. Peroff, *Menominee Drums: Tribal Termination and Restoration, 1954–1974* (Norman: University of Oklahoma Press, 1982); Kenneth R. Philp, *Termination Revisited: American Indians on the Trail to Self-Determination* (Lincoln: University of Nebraska Press, 1999); Rosier, *Serving Their Country*.

148. "Transcript of National Congress of American Indians Convention," November 15–18, 1944, pp. 21–22, Colorado Historical Society, Denver CO; Helen L. Peterson, "American Indian Political Participation," *Annals of the American Academy of Political and Social Sciences* 311, no. 1 (May 1957): 116–17. See also "Archie Phinney: A Man Ahead of His Time," *Ta'c Tito'oqan*, June 2004, 1; Cowger, *National Congress*, 31–32, 110.

149. "Preamble," n.d., box 11, folder 12, Oklahoma Indian Rights Association, Western History Collections, University of Oklahoma, Norman; "Transcript of National Congress of American Indians," 12, 18, 55.

150. NCAI, *Minutes of Proceedings: Seventh Annual Convention*, August 28–31, 1950, 2, "Seventh Annual Convention, 1950" (folder), box 5, Helen L. Peterson Papers, National Anthropological Archives, Smithsonian Institution, Washington DC.

151. "Transcript of National Congress of American Indians," 48; NCAI, "The Indians of the United States Seek Together to Attain in Their Own Plans and Action the Full Promise of Citizenship," n.d., box 16, folder 6, William Zimmerman Papers, Center for Southwestern Research, University of New Mexico, Albuquerque.

152. On Harrison and Trujillo's suits, see Harrison v. Laveen (1948), 67 Ariz. 337; "Judge Phillips orally delivered the opinion of the court" (*Trujillo v. Garley*), n.d., "Trujillo vs. Garley" (folder), box 127, RG21, National Archives—Rocky Mountain Region, Denver CO; NCAI, *Minutes of Proceedings: Fifth Annual Convention*, December 13–16, 1948, pp. 27–28, Western History Collections, Denver Public Library, Denver CO; Henry Christman, "Southwestern Indians Win the Vote," *American Indian* 4 (September–October 1948), 6–10; Cowger, *National Congress*, 64–65; Sando, *Pueblo Profiles*, 57–62.

153. In 1957, Utah's legislature repealed an 1897 law that disenfranchised American Indians by effectively denying the right to vote to residents of a reservation. Keyssar, *Right to Vote*, 203–4; McCool, Olson, and Robinson, *Native Vote*, chapter 4.

154. On voting discrimination against American Indians, see, for example, Danna R. Jackson, "Eighty Years of Indian Voting: A Call to Protect Indian Voting Rights," *Montana Law Review* 65, no. 2 (Summer 2004): 269–88; Tanya Lee, "Supreme Court Upholds American Indian Voting Rights," *Indian Country Today*, June 18, 2013, https://newsmaven.io/indiancountrytoday/archive/supreme-court-upholds -american-indian-voting-rights-4yFYcTUNEkiH9puBQoXVpw/; McCool, Olson, and Robinson, *Native Vote*; Laughlin McDonald, *American Indians and the Fight for Equal Voting Rights* (Norman: University of Oklahoma Press, 2010); Rollings, "Citizenship and Suffrage," 126–40; Orlan J. Svingen, "Jim Crow, Indian Style," *American Indian Quarterly* 11, no. 4 (Fall 1987): 275–86; Wilkins and Stark, *American Indian Politics*, 209–10; Wolfley, "Jim Crow," 167–202; Stephanie Woodard, "The Missing Native Vote," *In These Times*, June 10, 2014, http://inthesetimes.com/article/16773/the _missing_native_vote.

155. Wolfley, "Jim Crow," 190–91; Svingen, "Jim Crow, Indian Style," 275–86.

156. Wolfley, "Jim Crow," 190; NCAI, "*Mark Wandering Medicine, et al. (Plaintiffs-Appellants) v. Linda McCulloch, et al. (Defendants-Appellees.)*—Brief of Amicus Curiae in Support of Plaintiffs—Appellants in Support of Reversal," March 26, 2013, 6, http:// www.ncai.org/resources/legal_briefing/mark-wandering-medicine-et-al-plaintiffs -appellants-v-linda-mcculloch-et-al-defendants-appellees-brief-of-amicus-curiae-in -support-of-plaintiffs-appellants-in-support-of-reversal.

157. Corntassel and Witmer, *Forced Federalism*, 64.

158. McCool, Olson, and Robinson, *Native Vote*, 177–79.

159. Peterson, "American Indian Political Participation," 123–26.

160. John P. LaVelle, "Strengthening Tribal Sovereignty through Indian Participation in American Politics: A Reply to Professor Porter," *Kansas Journal of Law and Public Policy* 10, no. 3 (Spring 2001): 538; Wilkins and Stark, *American Indian Politics*, 176.

161. Peterson, "American Indian Political Participation," 124; Corntassel and Witmer, *Forced Federalism*, 67–68; McCool, Olson, and Robinson, *Native Vote*, 177. Despite the small size of the Native American population, Native voting can have a decisive impact on close elections in those states or districts with a large enough number of Native residents, such as Alaska, Arizona, Minnesota, Montana, New Mexico, North Dakota, South Dakota, and Washington DC; see McCool, "Indian Voting," 129, and Jordy Yager, "Native American Tribes' Lawsuit Could Decide Who Controls Senate in 2015," *Hill* (Washington DC), July 16, 2013, http://thehill.com/homenews/senate/311199-tribes-lawsuit-could-decide-who-controls-senate-in-2015.

162. Kerber, "Meaning of Citizenship," 833.

7 Looking Back to the Future

The Emergence of Modern Jicarilla Apache
Leadership in the Twentieth Century

BRAD WAZANEY

Historical Background

The Jicarilla Apache are one of six Athapascan groups, that including
the Chiricahua, Navajo, Western Apache, Mescalero, Kiowa Apache, and
Lipan. Migration out of the Canadian Mackenzie Basin and settlement in
the American Southwest between 1300 and 1500 CE occurred during the
so-called Fremont Period (500–1700 BCE).[1]

Politically, the Jicarilla Apache were almost entirely democratic. No
Apache, regardless of rank, could speak for all of the Apache or even for all
of the people in that person's own band.[2] With the exception of hunting and
warfare (including raids), decisions reached by council rather than chiefs
governed the Jicarillas. During times of war or while hunting, headmen
were appointed to act as leaders.[3] Although in many bands leadership
was inherited, power could be rescinded at any time. Individual groups
acted independently of all others.[4] Since the Jicarilla were matrilocal,
women contributed their opinions regarding the welfare of the tribe, but
they usually relinquished the role of decision-making to the men of the
group.[5] Because children were important in Jicarilla society and women
were the primary caregivers, women were equally respected and held a
status equivalent to that of men.[6]

The Jicarilla utilized both the mountains (what we know today as the
Sangre de Cristo Mountains area) and the prairies (often more than a thousand miles north of New Mexico).[7] With a territorial range encompassing

two ecological zones, the Jicarilla sustained themselves through a mix of hunting, gathering, and horticulture. Taking advantage of Pueblo and Spanish practices, the Jicarilla irrigated crops such as corn, pumpkins, beans, and melons.[8] Given the fact that they lived in both mountainous and prairie locales, the Jicarilla developed a unique relationship with settled peoples such as the Pueblos and the Spaniards. Having few reasons to attack settled peoples eager to trade for meat and skins, and because they lived in territories outside of Spanish authority, the Jicarilla managed to escape mention in most Spanish reports, remaining relatively obscure during the sixteenth and seventeenth centuries.[9] Although each group depended upon each other for trade, the Jicarilla were able to maintain their autonomy by living outside Spanish-dominated areas. With the arrival of the Americans, however, the Jicarilla's autonomy ended and drastic changes began. With the signing of the Treaty of Guadalupe Hidalgo in 1848 (ratified by the United States on March 16, 1848), the Mexican–American War ended, and the United States gained control of the territory of New Mexico. According to Article 8 of the treaty, the United States had to recognize the rights of Mexicans living in the territory:

> Mexicans now established in territories previously belonging to Mexico, and which remain for the future within the limits of the United States, as defined by the present treaty, shall be free to continue where they now reside.

Although this treaty recognized the rights of Mexican land claimants who possessed clear title to the land, the Jicarilla lacked titular ownership. Failure to possess legal title created serious challenges for the landless Jicarilla. Before 1848, Mexican settlers had considered the Jicarilla's traditional homeland undesirable. The territory did not have a reputation for decent agricultural land, nor did it have an abundance of mineral wealth.[10] Therefore, the Jicarilla remained relatively isolated until the United States gained control of the land. Within two years of American occupation and settlement of their land, the Jicarilla became wanderers without a territory to call their own. As early as fall 1850, a group of Jicarillas traveled to the military post at Abiquiu (Rio Arriba County, New Mexico) and requested permission to settle there.

Subsequently, in 1854 famed scout Christopher "Kit" Carson was appointed United States Indian Agent to the Jicarilla.[11] Carson understood that the Jicarilla needed assistance, or they would be forced to return to raiding—an economic strategy they had previously employed—in order to support their families. Carson negotiated an arrangement with Lucien B. Maxwell, the current deeded owner of the Jicarilla's lands, to hire Jicarillas as hunters, herders, and artisans.[12] Thirteen years earlier in 1841, Mexican Governor Manuel Armijo had granted 1.7 million acres of land to Guadalupe Miranda and Carlos Beaubien. Following that, Beaubien's son-in-law Maxwell inherited and purchased all of the lands from the original Miranda–Beaubien grant. Consequently, Maxwell allowed the Jicarillas to live relatively undisturbed in this territory. While this minimized disruptions to Jicarilla lifeways, it also kept them from contesting Maxwell's land claim with the United States. By 1865 the Jicarilla were squatters on their own territory—the lands owned by Lucien B. Maxwell.[13] There had been federal attempts to settle the Jicarilla near Bosque Redondo, New Mexico, but Jicarilla chief Largo found those lands unsuitable.[14] Federal efforts had also been made to purchase lands in northern New Mexico for the Jicarilla, but this ended when Lucien B. Maxwell sold the subject land in 1870. The new owners viewed the Jicarilla as little more than trespassers, and the company attempted to have them removed.[15] In 1883, the federal government relocated 721 Jicarilla Apaches to the Mescalero Apache Reservation in southern New Mexico.[16]

The Jicarilla, conditioned to a repeated cycle of relocation and removal, remained hesitant to begin farming without clear title to their lands. William H. H. Llewellyn, the United States Indian Agent for the Mescalero Reservation, explained their apprehension:

> About three-fourths of the entire tribe say it is a waste of time for them to make permanent improvements so long as they have no guarantee of being allowed to remain here; and can regard the land as their own; that they might be moved again at any time, at the will of the Government. The fact that this last move from Amargo to this reserve is the fifth one within fifteen years rather demonstrates the truth of the sayings of these people.[17]

On February 11, 1887, President Grover Cleveland created a reservation for the Jicarilla Apaches via executive order. The northern New Mexico lands set aside for the Jicarilla totaled 415,000 acres.[18] Certain areas of the reservation rise to more than seven thousand feet above sea level. Although the Jicarillas finally had land of their own, their struggles continued. For the majority of Jicarillas, economic security remained unattainable. The sense of hopelessness that existed prior to settlement—though somewhat alleviated by the creation of the reservation—remained. Soon after the Jicarilla had received their lands, epidemic tuberculosis swept through the community. Federal authorities predicted that unless measures were taken to eliminate the disease among the Jicarilla, they would be extinct by 1932. Adding to the problem was the skewed birth-to-death ratio: from 1887 to 1920 there were fewer births than deaths, as multiple epidemics beleaguered the Jicarillas.[19] Tuberculosis was the principal cause of this decline, but other diseases such as trachoma, measles, and influenza took a similarly heavy toll. Though their numbers continued to fluctuate, the overall Jicarilla population suffered a steady decline: each decade brought a reduction from the previous decade. As the Jicarilla were struggling to survive, new policies were introduced that would impact not only the Jicarilla's future but those of all American Indian communities throughout the United States.

Three days before the Jicarilla Reservation was established, Congress enacted the General Allotment Act—also known as the Dawes Act, after the sponsoring Massachusetts senator Henry Dawes (Stats. 24, 388ff.). Intended to make Indians full United States citizens through individual ownership of land, the Act parceled tribal lands into sections of 160 and 320 acres. The Act required that individual allotments be held in trust for twenty-five years and momentarily delayed the transfer of Indian lands into the hands of white owners; however, all tribal lands deemed "surplus" were opened to white settlement.[20] After the reservation lands were partitioned to individual families, the remaining lands were considered excess and made available for non-Indian use. Ironically, one of the main provisions of the Act—fee-patented land under titled ownership—was exactly what the Jicarilla had been trying to achieve for decades. The movement to allot the Jicarilla Reservation had come not from the federal government but from the Jicarilla themselves.[21] As early as 1881, federal and state officials understood the Jicarilla's desire to obtain fee patents for their lands. For example, Edmund G. Ross, governor of New Mexico Territory, suggested that the Jicarillas "desired to break up their tribal relations, to separate themselves entirely from other Indians and take lands in severalty by families; in a word, as they expressed it, they 'wanted to be like white men and live as white men do.'"[22] While Ross's letter may have overstated the Jicarillas desire to "be like white men" by "breaking up their tribal relations," officials had warned the Jicarillas from the beginning that their reservation would be allotted. With passage of another executive order on July 2, 1887, the government authorized survey of the Jicarilla lands for allotment assignments; however, as of 1890, no actions had been taken.[23]

High-elevation lands provide little practical use: they are insufficient for substantial crop growth and are often inaccessible to livestock. Since the lands belonging to the Jicarilla Reservation post allotment were all high elevation, the environmental conditions on the Jicarilla Apache Reservation could potentially limit the Jicarilla's future growth. Following a new survey, the lands were determined to be inadequate and in violation of the mandates of the Dawes Act. Though there were few Jicarillas, there were still too many families to allot the reservation into the regulated parcels of 160 or 320 acres. Compliance with the Dawes Act required additional land, and as a result, the southern portion of the reservation was affixed in 1908.[24] The addition of this section, which almost doubled the size of the reservation and added twenty-five townships, continues to account for a significant portion of the Jicarilla economy. The affixed southern portion also acts as a grazing range for Jicarilla livestock during the winter.[25] Between 1912 through 1922, the federal government sold $242,152 worth of timber from the Jicarilla reservation. In 1920, that money was used to purchase sheep issued to individual Jicarilla Apaches in an effort to reduce the Jicarilla's dependency on federal rations. The southern addition contains most of the Jicarilla's oil and mineral reserves, which continue to provide a large portion of the Jicarilla's overall income since 1951.

While the introduction of livestock certainly increased the importance of pastoralism to the Jicarilla economy and altered their economic structure, its introduction had little negative impact on the Jicarilla's existing political structure. They fit this addition into their existing framework, once again adapting and modifying it to their new situation. Members of a camp grazed their herds together, the camp continuing to act as the center of distribution and production.[26] Table 1 demonstrates the increasing importance of pastoralism to the Jicarilla economy.[27]

That sheep surpassed cattle in relative importance on the Jicarilla Reservation is evident by the total figures for each animal. The federal

TABLE 1. Livestock counts in Jicarilla economy

Year	Total cattle	Total sheep
1932	154	22,000
1933	220	24,500
1934	465	23,359
1935	515	25,841
1936	862	22,889
1937	1,094	25,705
1938	1,403	27,512
1939	1,611	28,776
1940	1,471	32,319
1941	1,345	33,501
1942	1,372	36,001
1943	1,431	38,654
1944	1,559	37,312
1945	1,670	36,698
1946	1,729	33,614
1947	1,747	27,830
1948	2,099	25,549
1949	2,112	21,710
1950	2,091	20,617
1951	1,956	18,916
1952	1,845	15,690
1953	1,798	17,152
1954	1,155	17,480
1955	1,401	18,922
1956	1,100	15,988
1957	1,177	15,029
1958	1,226	15,144
1959	1,068	15,768

government encouraged the adoption of a pastoral economy through various herd-building projects, fiscal appropriations, and herd additions. Successive increases in Jicarilla livestock herd totals resulted from both the successful implementation and the Jicarilla's enthusiastic adoption of these livestock programs. Although livestock became the central component of their mid-century economic structure, the Jicarillas utilized the available resources collectively. By adhering to their traditional system of cooperation and allocation for livestock grazing, the Jicarilla maintained group solidarity. This cohesion would be vital to future Jicarilla successes.

The Emergence of Modern Jicarilla Leadership

Although the Jicarilla population declined during the first two decades of the twentieth century (reaching an all-time low of 588 in 1920), their numbers began to increase in the 1930s. The 1920 population of 588 had improved to 680 by 1934, a year that ushered in a new era of economic development that paralleled improving tribal health and populations.

After a century and a half of federal assimilation and acculturation, in 1934 Commissioner of Indian Affairs John Collier and the Franklin Delano Roosevelt administration implemented an abrupt departure from older policies of allotment and disenfranchisement. Recognizing that federal policies and the Bureau of Indian Affairs (BIA) had left widespread poverty and demoralization across Indian Country, Collier proposed an "Indian New Deal" aimed at improving the conditions of Indians throughout the United States. Collier, as head of the BIA, developed new policies that encouraged tribal efforts to maintain and restore Native languages, religious practices, social customs, economies, governments, and artistic forms.[28] Collier's efforts resulted in the 1934 Indian Reorganization Act (IRA), also known as the Wheeler-Howard Act (signed June 18, 1934). This new legislation stood in direct opposition to the previous 150 years of assimilation, segregation, disenfranchisement, and acculturation policies.

Even though some Native groups strongly opposed the IRA, only 78 of the 252 bands and tribes eligible to vote for the IRA rejected the Act.[29] Whatever the acknowledged shortcomings of the IRA were, the measure offered American Indians some control over their future. For the first time, Native Americans had the option to adopt or reject federal legislation.

Unlike the General Allotment Act—legislation enacted to forcefully assimilate Indians into the dominant society—the IRA afforded Indian communities the chance to decide their future by ballot, though somewhat awkwardly. Whereas earlier legislative acts provided opportunities for American Indian communities that wanted to assimilate, the IRA allowed for communities to return to self-governance. The Jicarilla were among the tribal groups that eagerly sought to approve the measure. They were one of the first tribes to adopt the IRA, accepting Collier's recommendation that they form a "cooperative commonwealth."[30] On August 4, 1937, the federal government approved the Jicarilla's new constitution and bylaws. Their constitution called for a tribal council consisting of eighteen members from the six reservation districts. On September 4, 1937, the Jicarilla Apaches formally adopted a corporate charter, officially naming themselves the Jicarilla Apache Tribe, with the tribal council acting as its governing body.[31]

A unique addition to the Jicarilla Apache constitution was the provision that the tribe maintain a flock of sheep "to care for the aged and incapacitated."[32] Known as the "Old People's Herd," the animals came from a federal sheep-flock issue in 1930.[33] The Tribal Council was responsible for the care of the herd. In addition, the Jicarillas voluntarily returned their allotted land to tribal control, including individual oil rights.[34] In exchange for returning their allotments, the Jicarillas received shares in the new tribal corporation. The rarity of this request was reflected in a comment made by Alan Harper, a coordinator for the BIA. Harper "wished more tribes saw the wisdom of such a course, instead of insisting on specific assignments of land in exchange for allotted land."[35] Among the Jicarilla, the successful implementation of the IRA resulted from their group solidarity. Arguably, their sustained communal usage of grazing lands aided this unity. The Jicarilla's collective history demanded adaptability and cooperation for survival. Even though the Jicarillas accepted the provisions of the IRA and elected leaders from each township, the Tribal Council did not immediately become a part of the internal political structure. Jicarillas continued to look for leadership at the local level. The reasons why the Jicarillas were slow to accept the new Tribal Council are many.

Examining the Jicarilla's economic structure in 1960, anthropologist H. Clyde Wilson found three causal factors. Wilson established several reasons for the Tribal Council remaining outside the Jicarilla's internal political structure:

> First, there was no historical precedent for a tribal governing body. Second, the Tribal Council was set up in such a way that it obviously could not function effectively as an administrative unit: the council was to meet only twice a year for one or two days and no permanent offices were maintained so tribal officials could be aware of and act upon tribal matters. Third, and most important for our discussion here, the Tribal Council was delegated power and responsibility at the tribal level while the allocation of goods and services existed at other levels.

Once again, the Jicarilla showed their aptitude for adapting and accepting the provisions required of them; nevertheless, they did fit the new system into their existing political framework without major cultural changes. The camp leader remained responsible for the needs of the group, retaining his position of authority at the local level. Because sheep were herded together collectively, the group—and its localized authority—remained intact. The influence of the Tribal Council did not surpass the influence of local leaders until new economic improvements developed.[36]

Because the IRA was also intended to revitalize Indian economies, loans were made available to invigorate Indian financial systems. The Jicarilla borrowed $85,000 from this fund, known as the revolving credit fund, to purchase the Wirt Trading Post.[37] Under Jicarilla ownership, the Wirt Trading Post—renamed the Jicarilla Apache Cooperative—became the first Indian-operated tribal store in 1937.[38] The loan greatly improved economic conditions on the reservation, and the Jicarilla were able to repay the loan within eight years.[39]

Economic growth continued through increases in livestock, a variety of investments, and, most important, the development of local resources. Preliminary mineral exploration was begun on the reservation in the 1940s. Full-scale oil drilling did not begin until the 1950s, but the Jicarilla had already demonstrated their willingness to diversify their economy. During this time, lumber sales accounted for a large portion of the Jicarilla's income, but the Bureau of Indian Affairs misused much of this money. As Montana Senator Burton K. Wheeler argued in 1933, "What has been done to these Indians is that the timber resources have been depleted and all that money has been spent practically for agency purposes."[40]

Wheeler contended that the money should have been spent on sheep and cattle rather than administrative costs, which would have allowed the Jicarilla to be self-sufficient. As soon as the Jicarilla were permitted to utilize the timber profits rather than spending the money on BIA expenditures, tribal income soared. Table 2, adapted from Wilson, illustrates the increase in profits for the tribe's timber, oil, and gas ventures.[41]

TABLE 2. Profits for the Jicarilla Apache

Year	Timber ($)	Oil and gas ($)	Total ($)
1947	12,640	57,751	70,391
1950	350	20,112	20,462
1951	. . .	1,125,110	1,125,110
1952	. . .	. . .	. . .
1953	. . .	3,357,892	3,357,892
1954	2,167	1,812,874	1,815,038
1955	. . .	1,128,416	1,128,416
1956	23,787	534,144	557,931
1957	109,380	496,371	605,751
1958	44,124	3,020,971	3,065,095
1959	80,266	1,716,175	1,796,441
1960	. . .	1,330,881	1,330,881

Individual Jicarilla families also experienced increases in personal wealth. In turn, the rising incomes allowed for improvements in other areas. Table 3 shows the overall gains made in individual—as opposed to tribal—earnings for the Jicarilla Apache.[42] During this time, more children were enrolled in school, health conditions improved greatly, and, most important, the Jicarilla Apache population steadily increased. These changes certainly improved the morale of the Jicarillas.[43]

TABLE 3. Jicarilla Apache individual earnings, 1920–60

Year	Livestock ($)	Wages ($)	Unearned ($)	Year	Livestock ($)	Wages ($)	Unearned ($)
1920	18,290	34,777	16,650	1941	149,701	. . .	. . .
1921	16,814	24,260	8,720	1942	183,369	35,040	. . .
1922	36,707	23,338	11,726	1943	208,677	37,333	. . .
1923	50,309	14,812	2,524	1944	193,683	34,558	. . .
1924	58,948	14,574	. . .	1945	214,810	41,086	. . .
1925	76,456	22,738	. . .	1946	197,375	. . .	. . .
1926	68,058	23,332	. . .	1947	234,833	. . .	. . .
1927	63,517	19,567	. . .	1948	309,106	. . .	. . .
1928	80,999	31,784	. . .	1949	271,533	. . .	. . .
1929	61,783	24,887	. . .	1950	281,502	. . .	. . .
1930	33,920	20,724	. . .	1951	403,341	. . .	. . .
1931	. . .	. . .	. . .	. . .	. . .	. . .	. . .
1932	32,467	. . .	2,150	1952	157,316	. . .	299,500
1933	43,034	. . .	. . .	1953	166,974	154,202	515,000
1934	21,609	. . .	1,200	1954	148,820	155,331	538,000
1935	47,599	. . .	. . .	1955	149,563	181,541	550,000
1936	66,342	55,636	. . .	1956	150,133	193,836	857,250
1937	79,524	42,730	. . .	1957	188,693	. . .	583,000
1938	67,950	446,020	3,600	1958	175,999	248,501	598,000
1939	79,374	81,127	. . .	1959	212,549	360,512	499,200
1940	114,224	79,127	. . .	1960	. . .	. . .	. . .

Figures for unearned income from 1952 to 1959 are before deductions.

An additional piece of legislation that increased the Jicarilla's economic prospects was the Indian Claims Commission Act (60 Stat. 1049, Chap. 959) adopted in 1946. The Indian Claims Commission (ICC) was created to adjudicate all legitimate American Indian claims against the United States.[44] The ICC allowed any identifiable group of American Indian claimants living in the United States or Alaska to seek compensation from the federal government for past injustices. Upon passage of the ICC, the Jicarilla Apache Tribal Council secured an attorney to manage the Jicarilla Apache Tribe's litigation against the United States. Robert J. Nordhaus (an attorney from Albuquerque, New Mexico) as well as Richard M. Davis and Robert O. Harry (attorneys from Denver, Colorado) were hired to present the Jicarilla's land claim to the Indian Claims Commission. The first step required authentication of the assertion that the lands claimed as stolen from the Jicarillas had been, in fact, utilized "exclusively" and from "time immemorial" by them.[45] Employing anthropological, archaeological, and historical data, the Jicarilla and their attorneys proved that the lands they used prior to conquest—more than 72,000 square miles—should be considered by the ICC for damages. The ICC denied liability for 4,859,576.23 acres that were part of the original Spanish and Mexican land grants, and they appraised and considered the value for 9,218,532.77 additional acres.[46] The Jicarilla were awarded $9,950,000 (less $800,000 deducted for federal expenditures on behalf of their claim).[47]

Despite steady improvements in their tribal wealth, many Jicarilla families still found financial security elusive. Some of the lingering personal financial problems resulted from an economic environment that did not foster self-improvement. For example families without access to credit in the 1940s were denied one essential way to support themselves: lacking credit for basic start-up costs, they could not establish gardens or purchase livestock for ranching. Much of the economic distress this created continued Jicarilla dependency on government assistance, which could have been alleviated by tribal or federal policy changes such as allowing or providing family-based credit.

In an effort to alleviate individual financial burdens, the Tribal Council approved per-capita payments to individual tribal members in 1952. Tribal per-capita payments of $300 per person were made that year ($299,500 in total), including half of the per-capita payment for children under the age of eighteen, which was deposited in their name in a trust fund. As of 1958, the fund was earning about 3 percent interest per year.[48] This money becomes available to minors in four equal payments after their eighteenth birthdays.

A portion of the money used for the per-capita payments came from lease sales to oil and gas corporations from 1951, the first significant year for earnings generated by this new tribal venture. The Jicarilla Apache earned $2,000,000 in 1951. Through 1957, earnings of additional "bonus money" from oil and gas revenues totaled $6,121,573.13, and the yearly rentals rose to about $500,000.[49]

By 1960, annual production from more than fifty natural gas wells and eighty oil wells on the Jicarilla Apache Reservation exceeded $5,000,000. Operating expenses also grew proportionally as the Tribal Council realized more profits. Within an eleven-year period, Council expenditures went from $200 per year to more than $3,000,000 per year. Table 4 highlights the dramatic rise in expenditures for 1942 and over the 1947–60 period.

There was also an exciting rise in the complexity of tribal business during the 1950s and early 1960s. The Tribal Council's relative responsibility

TABLE 4. Corporate expenditures, 1942, 1947–60

Fiscal year	Per capita payments ($)	Special funds ($)	Operating expenses ($)	Total ($)
1942	. . .	. . .	200	200
1947	. . .	. . .	11,030	11,030
1948	. . .	. . .	35,537	35,537
1949	. . .	. . .	50,023	50,023
1950	. . .	. . .	51,126	51,126
1951	. . .	*20,000	105,020	125,020
1952	299,500	†218,515	260,274	778,289
1953	515,000	‡3,051,716	137,713	3,704,429
1954	538,000	. . .	204,423	742,423
1955	550	. . .	209,959	759,959
1956	857,250	. . .	274,893	1,132,143
1957	583,000	. . .	266,044	849,044
1958	598,000	. . .	520,221	1,118,221
1959	499,200	. . .	434,956	934,156
1960	390,000	. . .	498,263	888,263

* This amount was placed in the Tribal Revolving Stock Fund.

† Of this amount, $188,515 was loaned to the cooperative store, and $30,000 was loaned to the Soil Conservation Fund.

‡ Of this amount, $2,501,116 was used for the purchase of Treasury Bonds, and $555,000 was used to establish the Tribal Loan Fund.

increased as it replaced leadership at the local level, but it did not achieve complete autonomy from the federal government. The government maintained veto power over tribal affairs through the Secretary of the Interior. Any expenditure approved by the Tribal Council was first subjected to federal scrutiny.[50]

By the 1950s, the Jicarilla Apache population had reached 1060 enrolled members, 628 of whom were under the age of twenty-one. Appreciating the importance of an education, the Tribal Council established the Chester E. Faris Scholarship Fund in 1955. Named for an early reservation Indian agent, the $1,000,000 scholarship fund—the equivalent of $833 from each enrolled Jicarilla member at the time—was created to help any Jicarilla who wanted to attend college or vocational school.[51] In 2002, the name of the fund was changed in honor of a venerated elder. Now known as the Norman TeCube Sr. Scholarship Fund, the scholarship money continues to encourage Jicarilla youth to obtain advanced degrees and helps defray the costs of leaving the reservation to attend school. The Jicarilla have also planned other measures for their future generations in addition to this form of educational assistance; improving the lives of enrolled members and leaving a legacy for future generations are of great concern to Jicarilla leaders. In 1994, profits were used to increase Jicarilla tribal landholdings by more than 94,000 acres, enlarging the reservation's boundaries by nearly 12 percent.[52]

Jicarilla Apache tribal investments have resulted in a diversified financial portfolio. Through sound investments and astute fiscal management, they have become involved in a wide array of business ventures. The Tribal Council began financing private Jicarilla enterprises when it passed two resolutions in 1983. The first was to allow market principles to govern economic development; the second provided economic support for any tribal member wishing to go into business. For tribal entrepreneurs who need a large loan that must go through a bank or lending institution, the Tribal Council guarantees the loan. Consequently, a profit-sharing arrangement is usually established between the borrower and the tribe. The Tribal Council has in this way financed many business loans for tribal members deemed as sound investments "in the best interests of the tribe."[53]

The Council finances private businesses in an effort to generate tribal jobs and services. Because the Tribal Council provides loans that are nearly interest free, there are no banks on the reservation. It is often difficult, if not impossible, for residents of reservations to obtain bank loans. Because Jicarilla land is held in trust, banks are unable to seize an individual's land if they default on a loan. Since a bank can only attach the personal assets of a person who defaults on a loan, many lending institutions baulk at making loans to American Indians living on trust lands. Banks or lending institutions are unwilling to make loans without the Tribal Council's guarantee.[54]

Much of the revenue from tribally owned natural resources has financed the Jicarilla Apache's enterprises. The Jicarilla Apache Reservation sits on what is known as the San Juan Basin, considered by many fossil-fuel experts to be one of North America's largest sources of natural gas.[55] Natural gas and petroleum reserves exist in the southern and central sections of the reservation. Billions of cubic feet of gas and hundreds of thousands of barrels of oil are produced annually from these sources.[56] Annual revenues from these natural resources topped the $1,000,000 mark for the tribal government in the late 1940s and early 1950s.[57] These reserves rapidly accounted for a larger proportion of tribal revenue. Table 5 highlights the revenues received from oil and gas from 1951 to 1960.[58]

TABLE 5. Oil and gas revenues, 1951–60

Year	Oil and gas revenues ($)
1951	1,125,110
1952	. . .
1953	3,357,892
1954	1,812,874
1955	1,128,416
1956	534,144
1957	496,371
1958	3,020,971
1959	1,716,175
1960	1,330,881
Total	14,522,834

In comparison to revenues generated between 1951 and 1960, earnings for the years 1971–75 emphasize the rising value of petroleum and natural gas. For example, the Jicarilla Apache tribe received $8.7 million in royalties from oil and gas from 1971 through 1975. Of this amount, $6.86 million, or 78.7 percent, came from natural gas.[59] Whereas the tribe earned $14,522,834 during the 1950s, in the four years between 1971 and 1975 the Jicarilla earned $8,657,118 from royalties. Tables 6 and 7 show royalty and production earnings by the Jicarilla from petroleum and natural gas between 1971 and 1975.[60]

TABLE 6. Petroleum production and royalties, 1971–75

Year	Production (42 gal. barrels)	Royalties ($)
1971	722,626.07	262,844.51
1972	780,400.09	293,556.81
1973	514,800.11	252,671.62
1974	786,505.35	609,834.29
1975	411,752.52	414,823.28
Total	3,216,084.14	1,833,739.51

With the exception of royalties earned for 1974 ($609,834.29), annual earnings were higher in 1951–60 than in 1971–75. If the earnings for 1974 were to be held alongside annual earnings in 1951–60, forming a nonconsecutive eleven-year period, the 1974 royalties would be the third lowest in the period. This follows the predicted peak in U.S. oil production in 1970 and the subsequent shift in the importance of natural gas to the Jicarilla's royalties.[61] The reduction in annual earnings can be more accurately observed by examining the average price per barrel that the Jicarilla earned in 1971–75; the price per barrel declined with each subsequent year. In 1971 the Jicarilla received $2.79 per barrel; the per-barrel price fell to $2.65 in 1972, $2.03 in 1973, and $1.28 in 1974, plummeting further to $0.99 in 1975.

As United States oil production peaked and declined, so did the importance the Jicarilla placed on the resource. Table 7 highlights the royalties received by the Jicarilla from natural gas leases, illustrating the increased importance of natural gas on Jicarilla Apache earnings in 1971–75.[62]

TABLE 7. Natural gas production and royalties, 1971–75

Year	Production (Mcf.)*	Royalty ($)
1971	51,330.95	945,728.14
1972	54,676.14	1,238,078.66
1973	44,073.75	1,299,947.80
1974	45,679.71	1,762,790.20
1975	36,715.92	1,576,833.86
Total	232,476.47	6,823,378.66

* The unit "Mcf." represents a thousand cubic feet.

Natural gas production during this five-year period earned the Jicarilla $6.8 million, or 78.7 percent of their revenue.[63] The production of natural gas shows the opposite trend occurring during the first half of the 1970s. In 1971 royalties received for a thousand cubic feet of natural gas was $18.42; that value rose to $22.64 in 1972 and even higher to $29.49 in 1973. Royalties earned per thousand cubic feet of natural gas reached $38.59 in 1974, rising once again to $42.94 in 1975. Oil exploration on the Jicarilla Apache Reservation reached a frantic pace during these years. During 1970–75, a total of 276,118 acres, or roughly 37 percent of the reservation, was leased for oil and gas development.[64]

In addition to royalty payments by oil and natural gas companies, a standard usage fee was assessed for American Indian reservation lands leased for other purposes. The value of these leases was standard for all reservations and continues to be determined by the Bureau of Indian Affairs (BIA). In the 1970s, royalties earned for mineral production varied depending on the mineral. For minerals other than oil, gas, and natural gas, the minimum royalty was 10 percent of the value of the mineral from its nearest shipping point. Royalties for oil, gas, and natural gas were set at a minimum of 16.67 percent.[65]

A global shortage in petroleum production during the 1970s resulted in reduced royalties per barrel. This was counterintuitive to the laws of supply and demand: less supply generally results in higher prices due to limited availability. The Tribal Council understood this, alleging that the federal government—acting as federal guardian for the Jicarilla Apache

Tribe—had failed to adequately serve the Jicarilla's financial interests. Concerned that the tribe was not being paid sufficient royalties for the minerals extracted from reservation lands, Tribal President Hubert Velarde wrote to Secretary of Interior Rogers Morton on March 23, 1973.[66] Velarde alleged that the tribe was not being paid royalties based on the true value of the oil and gas produced from the leases. He argued that certain purchasers had plotted an illegal restraint of trade to maintain artificially low prices for natural gas produced in the San Juan Basin, that Morton had made no effort to verify the amount of oil and gas reportedly produced from reservation lands, and that the tribe had been grossly underpaid for the entire lease period as a result. Morton did not respond to the letter until September 4, 1975, nearly seventeen months later.[67]

Throughout the 1970s, the Jicarilla were involved in legal actions against various oil companies; they even brought a suit against Secretary of Interior Morton. While many of the oil companies quickly settled, the federal government did not reach an agreement with the Jicarilla Apache. In retaliation, the Secretary of Interior refused to sign any new leases (a process required for their validation) unless the Jicarilla agreed to abandon the lawsuit. Morton's threat made it impractical for Jicarilla leaders to pursue legal action against the federal government, and the Jicarilla Apache eventually withdrew their claim. Although the Jicarilla were forced to capitulate, this episode signaled a new relationship between the Jicarilla and the federal government. From now on, Jicarilla leadership would take the initiative in brokering increasingly sophisticated agreements with industry partners.[68]

The Jicarilla's ever-increasing desire for self-rule may have been spurred by the diminishing royalties. In 1976, the Jicarilla Apache tribe entered into a contract with the Palmer Oil Company of Billings, Montana, for oil and gas development. But one year later, Palmer was selling off its leases and planning to remove from the reservation. At that time in 1977, the Tribal Council arranged to purchase the lease rights from the Palmer Oil Company and became the first American Indian tribe in the United States to own and operate its own oil and gas wells.[69] Unlike the diminishing profitability of petroleum production, the value of natural gas continued to rise. This too must have factored into the Jicarilla's decisions regarding the acquisition of Palmer Oil Company's interests on the reservation. The Tribal Council, increasingly more astute at self-governance and certainly aware of oil profits, realized that the surest means of providing security for tribal members was to operate the wells without the oil corporations.

The Jicarilla Apache sought additional ways to raise capital beyond fossil fuels. With the passage of the Indian Tribal Governmental Tax Status Act (1983), made permanent in 1985, American Indian communities could issue municipal bonds. Through this Act (26 U.S. Code § 7871), tribes attained the equivalent status of states and their political subdivisions. The Act enabled tribal governments to issue tax-exempt bonds either to finance the exercise of an essential governmental function or to build a manufacturing facility on tribal trust lands. Municipal bonds enabled many tribes to raise money for a variety of business and non-business-related enterprises, and the Jicarilla were at the forefront of this new opportunity.

The Jicarilla raised the revenue needed to purchase 55,000 acres adjoining the Jicarilla Apache Reservation partially through the issuance of a tribal revenue bond. The Jicarilla were the first American Indian tribe to offer the bond in 1985, after the 1983 federal tax law permitted tribes to enter the municipal market.[70] The tax-exempt bonds, which carried interest rates of 9.125 percent and 9.625 percent for bonds maturing in twelve and twenty years, respectively, were backed by revenue from Jicarilla oil and gas wells.[71] In 1983, the annual revenue from the Jicarilla's oil and gas wells was valued at $20 million, and it was estimated that annual tribal revenue beyond oil and gas revenue exceeded $108 million. The bond, which raised $30.2 million, afforded the Jicarilla an opportunity to address problems on the reservation without assistance from the federal government. Tribal President Leonard Atole remarked, "We desired this fertile land [the 55,000 acres] for future economic development and for the housing needs of our people. The bond issue allows us to manage our financing needs without relying on the Federal Government."[72]

Revenue from local and off-reservation business ventures has allowed the Jicarilla Apache Tribe to serve as employer for many of its members. Tribal enrollment for 2002 was 3,403 persons, with 900 members living off of the reservation. According to the Four Corners Regional Study of 2003, approximately 50 percent of the enrolled Jicarilla Apache members were under the age of twenty-four (as of 2002). Of those Jicarilla Apaches living in the area, the Jicarilla Apache Tribe employed 902 people. As of the year 2000, 14.3 percent of the Jicarilla Apache population was unemployed. Table 8, adapted from the Four Corners Regional Study, illustrates the areas of employment made available by the Jicarilla Apache Nation for the year 2000.

TABLE 8. Jicarilla Apache Nation employment statistics, 2000

Employment	Jobs (no.)	Jobs (%)
Agriculture, forestry, fishing/hunting, and mining	81	9
Construction	91	10
Manufacturing	16	2
Information	9	1
Wholesale trade	9	1
Retail trade	32	4
Transportation and warehousing, and utilities	11	1
Finance, insurance, real estate, and rental and leasing	18	2
Services		
Professional, scientific, management, administrative, and waste management services	26	...
Educational, health, and social services	251	...
Arts, entertainment, recreation, accommodation, and food services	61	...
Other services	42	...
Public administration	255	28
Total	902	100

Though somewhat dated, these employment data figures—along with the creation of a new health-care facility—demonstrate the Jicarilla Apache's commitment to its members. Reviewing the numbers above gives a clearer image of how many Jicarilla are employed by the Jicarilla Apache tribal corporation. The Jicarilla population residing on the reservation numbered 2,500 in 2000. Though more than 50 percent of the population was under twenty-four at the time, 66.6 percent was over the age of eighteen, and 10 percent was over the age of sixty-two. If an age restriction for full-time employment were established at nineteen, for the earliest age one may begin working, and if sixty-two were held as the retirement age, there would have been 1,499 Jicarillas eligible for employment, according to this data from 2000. Including the fifty new employees created by the construction of the new Jicarilla Apache tribal health-care facility highlighted below, the Jicarilla Apache Corporation employed 952 Jicarillas, or 64 percent of the local population.

While the Jicarilla Apaches have been able to utilize their resources, this became possible only after numerous legal actions in federal and state courts. Although the Jicarilla became involved in these court proceedings partly out of necessity, the opportunity to expand and assert their autonomy from federal control must have factored into their decision to seek legal redress. Indeed, in 1998 they demonstrated their desire to display their sovereignty as an independent nation living within the borders of the United States: they officially changed their name from the "Jicarilla Apache Tribe" to the "Jicarilla Apache Nation."[73]

Even though the Jicarilla did not officially change their name until 1998, they had been attempting to assert their autonomy from federal governmental interference for a long time. A prime example was the abovementioned lawsuit brought against Secretary of Interior Morton. The Jicarilla Apache Nation reasoned that since they were an independent nation, they should have the right to set their own tax rates apart from established state or federal amounts. The Jicarilla wanted the ability to tax all natural-resource products (oil, coal, lumber, etc.) on their reservation. Taking on the fight for other Indian governments as well as their own to do so, the Jicarilla filed a lawsuit in 1982. Consequently, the Supreme Court ruled in *Merrion v. The Jicarilla Apache Tribe* (102 S. Ct. 894 [1982]) that the Jicarilla had the right to impose a severance tax on mining activities conducted on the reservation. The Court held that the tribe could impose this tax as part of its power to govern and help defray the costs of self-government. The Court argued that Congress had never divested Indian nations of the power to impose a tax, and therefore the Jicarilla Apaches could exercise their "inherent powers" by taxing mining companies that operated on their lands.[74]

Increased profits have enabled the Tribal Council to improve members' lives in many areas. In 2002 the Jicarilla Apache Nation completed a joint venture with the Indian Health Service (IHS), an agency of the Department of Health and Human Services (HHS). The two collaborated on a new $10.5 million replacement health-care facility to serve those living in Dulce in New Mexico as well as its surrounding areas. The 65,000-square-foot health center is the first replacement facility owned by a tribal entity in the United States. Named the Dulce Health Center, the facility offers ambulatory services, primary care, dental care, optometry services and urgent care. Special clinics are held for childcare, women's health, and diabetes care. Dr. Charles W. Grim, director of the Indian Health Service, summed up this accomplishment: "This facility demonstrates the successful exercise of self-determination by the Jicarilla Apache Nation and their dedication of improving the quality of health care services provided to their members." In addition to the improvements in available health services, the new facility will add an additional forty positions to the current staff of fifty people already employed in health care.[75]

In conclusion, in employment, healthcare, education, business loans, economic development, and land repatriation, the Jicarilla Apache have developed a system that ensures their tribal members' basic needs. According to some economists, however, the actions of the tribal leadership—in effect, a corporate board of directors—are in conflict with what is considered sound business practice. Economic philosophers often view corporations as vehicles created to generate revenue with. According to these economists, the correct course for improving American Indian economies emphasizes the individual over the group.[76] The economists implant the values of dominant society and the corporate world into the schema of small-scale societies such as the Jicarilla Apache. But the Jicarilla Apache Nation's method of governance benefits a larger number of people due, in large part, to its smaller size. A small-scale system of governance that emphasizes the group rather than the individual ensures that more people's needs are met and that the allocation of benefits occurs more evenly and fairly.

Collectively held lands and resources, say many economists, result in struggling economies. The lack of institutional change—tribes holding on to notions of common property, for instance—contributed to the inability to produce economic solvency on reservations throughout the country. Economist Terry Anderson maintains that agricultural output on reservations was 85 percent higher on lands held individually in comparison to lands held collectively.[77] While alarming, this statistic is nonetheless incomplete. Collectively held lands may pose a liability for some people, but the decisions of enrolled Jicarilla members to turn their allotments over to Tribal Council control has proven a major factor in the Jicarilla's economic gains. For the Jicarilla, communally held property has enabled the Jicarilla Apache Nation to bargain from a position of united strength that would not have existed if reservation lands had been held individually.

The General Allotment Act was designed as an agent of change to create individual allotments from communally held lands. Once tribal lands were divided and owned independently, many American Indians lost their allotments. Prior to the Act, tribes could offer a united effort against land cessation, but after lands were lost, stolen, or sold in fee title, white ranchers, farmers, and land speculators found it much easier to take lands away from individual Indian families than from the tribe as a whole.[78] The Jicarilla's political system, though imposed upon them through IRA legislation, was modified to fit within existing cultural frameworks. While the IRA legislation required a leadership structure with more permanence than the Jicarilla had previously recognized, placing the needs of the people before the individual remained a key value. Again, economist Terry Anderson argues that only by abandoning their collectivist approach to governance would tribes achieve self-sufficiency:

> To develop collective sovereignty, Indians will have to return to the basics of individual sovereignty and build from the ground up . . . [T]his approach . . . may seem inimical to the accepted mind set of Indians as communal societies. However, assuming that a particular set of communal institutions should govern individual relationships is, once again, imposing a set of rules from the top down. In contrast, self-determination begins with the individual, as it did prior to European contact.

It is entirely possible that the Jicarilla would have achieved the same level of success had they accepted that "self-determination begins with the individual" and had their lands remained individually owned.[79] What is certain, however, is that collectively held lands have enabled the Jicarilla leadership to negotiate the most evenhanded lease agreements with corporations possible. If lands had been held individually, the oil fields would have been fractured. Those families fortunate enough to hold mineral-rich lands as a result of receiving a favorable allotment rather than through any of their own efforts would be the sole beneficiaries of royalties. Because lands are held collectively, all profits generated from those lands benefit the tribe as a whole. Moreover, without the tribally owned oil and natural gas fields to act as collateral, the Jicarilla Apache Nation could not have issued their revenue-generating municipal bonds. The purchase of additional land acquired with a portion of the bond revenues would not have been realized.

Perhaps the most important decision made by the Jicarilla was one that resulted in the emergence of the modern Jicarilla Apache method of governance: the acceptance of the IRA. The willingness to put the group first by relinquishing individual allotments was one of the most important decisions made in the history of the Jicarilla Apache Nation. That unselfish act, combined with astute decisions made by Jicarilla leadership, provided benefits for all enrolled members that continue today. Despite early and erroneous predictions of their extinction as a tribal entity, the Jicarilla Apaches have defied the odds—they continue to flourish today.

NOTES

1. Tiller, *Jicarilla Apache Tribe*, 4; Haskell, *Southern Athabaskan Migration*, 51.
2. Terrell, *Apache Chronicle*, 90.
3. Goddard, *Indians of the Southwest*, 174.
4. Terrell, *Apache Chronicle*, 90.
5. Tiller, *Jicarilla Apache Tribe*, 16.
6. Tiller, *Jicarilla Apache Tribe*, 16.
7. Paul Weideman, "Weaving an Origin Story: The Jicarilla Apache at Home," *Pasatiempo*, August 29, 2016, Santa Fe Art Museum, Santa Fe NM, http://www.santafenewmexican .com/pasatiempo/art/museum_shows/weaving-an-origin-story-the-jicarilla-apache -at-home/article_16627ca3-5722-5840-8371-4e08bfb9a8bf.html.
8. Greenwald, *Reconfiguring the Reservation*, 97.
9. Gunnerson, *Jicarilla Apaches*, 11.
10. Tiller, *Jicarilla Apache Tribe*, 29.
11. Worcester, *Apaches*, 61.
12. Haley, *Apaches*, 114.

13. Greenwald, *Reconfiguring the Reservation*, 98.
14. Tiller, *Jicarilla Apache Tribe*, 61.
15. Greenwald, *Reconfiguring the Reservation*, 99.
16. Greenwald, *Reconfiguring the Reservation*, 102; VanRoekel, *Jicarilla Apaches*, ii.
17. Greenwald, *Reconfiguring the Reservation*, 103.
18. Worcester, *Apaches*, 339.
19. Stanley, *Jicarilla Apaches*, 233.
20. Lazarus, *Black Hills White Justice*, 124.
21. Greenwald, *Reconfiguring the Reservation*, 107.
22. Territorial Archives of New Mexico (TANM), 101, 995.
23. Greenwald, *Reconfiguring the Reservation*, 107.
24. Tiller, *Jicarilla Apache Tribe*, 10.
25. Tiller, *Handbook of North American Indians*, 453.
26. Wilson, *Jicarilla Apache*, 352–53.
27. Wilson, *Jicarilla Apache*, 342.
28. Deloria and Lytle, *American Indians, American Justice*, 99.
29. Dippie, *Vanishing Indian*, 318.
30. Philp, *John Collier's Crusade*, 169.
31. Tiller, *Tiller's Guide*, 456. *Handbook*, op cit, 456.
32. Philp, *John Collier's Crusade*, 169.
33. Tiller, *Jicarilla Apache Tribe*, 177.
34. Philp, *John Collier's Crusade*, 169.
35. Taylor, *New Deal*, 123.
36. Wilson, *Jicarilla Apache*, 353.
37. Tiller, *Tiller's Guide*, 456.
38. Philp, *John Collier's Crusade*, 169.
39. Tiller, *Tiller's Guide*, 456.
40. Tiller, *Jicarilla Apache Tribe*, 115.
41. Wilson, *Jicarilla Apache*, 345.
42. Wilson, *Jicarilla Apache*, 347.
43. Tiller, *Tiller's Guide*, 457.
44. Nordhaus, *Tipi Rings*, 10.
45. Nordhaus, *Tipi Rings*, 2.
46. Tiller, *Tiller's Guide*, 457.
47. Nordhaus, *Tipi Rings*, 205.
48. Southwestern Association on Indian Affairs (SAIA), collection no. 1976-037, no. 26.
49. SAIA, collection no. 1976-037, no. 26.
50. Wilson, *Jicarilla Apache*, 334.
51. Tiller, *Jicarilla Apache Tribe*, 191.
52. Casaus, Phill, "Jicarilla Indians Expand Their Reservation," *High Country News*, accessed November 21, 2019.

53. Hay, "On the Jicarilla Reservation," 1.

54. Hay, "On the Jicarilla Reservation," 1.

55. Tauli-Corpuz, "Energy Development Impacts."

56. Segerstrom and Henkes, "Status of Mineral Resource," 10.

57. Tiller, *Jicarilla Apache Tribe*, 184.

58. Wilson, *Jicarilla Apache*, 14.

59. Segerstrom and Henkes, "Status of Mineral Resource," 11.

60. Segerstrom and Henkes, "Status of Mineral Resource," 15.

61. Deffeyes, *Hubbert's Peak*, 15.

62. Segerstrom and Henkes, "Status of Mineral Resource," 15.

63. Segerstrom and Henkes, "Status of Mineral Resource," 16.

64. Tiller, *Jicarilla Apache Tribe*, 234.

65. Segerstrom and Henkes, "Status of Mineral Resource," 10.

66. Tiller, Jicarilla Apache Tribe, 234.

67. Tiller, *Jicarilla Apache Tribe*, 234.

68. Tiller, *Jicarilla Apache Tribe*, 444.

69. Tiller, *Jicarilla Apache Tribe*, 444.

70. "Investments: Apaches on the Bond Path," *Time Magazine*, July 15, 1985, http:// content.time.com/time/magazine/article/0,9171,959631,00.html.

71. Tiller, *Jicarilla Apache Tribe*, 244.

72. "Investments: Apaches on the Bond."

73. Velarde, *Cultre and Customs*, 124.

74. Deloria and Lytle, *American Indians, American Justice*, 55.

75. "Jicarilla Apache Nation Opens New Health Center." Indianz.com, December 1, 2014, https://www.indianz.com/News/2004/005561.asp.

76. Anderson, *Sovereign Nations*, 121–31.

77. Anderson, *Sovereign Nations*, 121–31.

78. Frazier, *On the Rez*, 40.

79. Anderson, *Sovereign Nations*, 170–71.

BIBLIOGRAPHY

ARCHIVES

Southwestern Association on Indian Affairs, collection no. 1976-037. State Archives of New Mexico, Santa Fe, New Mexico. (SAIA)

Territorial Archives of New Mexico. State Archives of New Mexico, Santa Fe, New Mexico. (TANM)

PUBLISHED WORKS

Anderson, Terry L. *Sovereign Nations or Reservations? An Economic History of American Indians*. San Francisco: Pacific Research Institute for Public Policy, 1995.

Deffeyes, Kenneth S. *Hubbert's Peak: The Impending World Oil Shortage*. Princeton NJ: Princeton University Press, 2001.

Deloria, Vine, Jr., and Clifford M. Lytle. *American Indians, American Justice*. Austin: University of Texas Press, 1983.

Dippie, Brian W. *The Vanishing Indian: White Attitudes and U.S. Indian Policy*. Middletown CT: Wesleyan University Press, 1982.

Frazier, Ian. *On the Rez*. New York: Farrar, Straus and Giroux, 2000.

Goddard, Pliny Earle. *Indians of the Southwest*. Handbook Series 2. New York: American Museum of Natural History Press, 1931.

Greenwald, Emily. *Reconfiguring the Reservation: The Nez Perces, Jicarilla Apaches and the Dawes Act*. Albuquerque: University of New Mexico Press, 2002.

Gunnerson, Dolores A. *The Jicarilla Apaches: A Study in Survival*. DeKalb: Northern Illinois University Press, 1974.

Haley, James L. *Apaches: A History and Culture Portrait*. Garden City NY: Doubleday, 1979.

Haskell, Loring J. *Southern Athabaskan Migration: A.D. 200–1750*. Tsaile AZ: Navajo Community College Press, 1987.

Hay, Andrew. "On the Jicarilla Reservation, Capitalism Is Not a Dirty Word; the Tribe Is Encouraging Entrepreneurs and Partnerships with Private Industry." *New Mexico Business Journal*, June 1996.

Lazarus, Edward. *Black Hills White Justice: The Sioux Nation Versus the United States: 1775 to the Present*. New York: HarperCollins, 1991.

Nordhaus, Robert J. *Tipi Rings: A Chronicle of the Jicarilla Apache Land Claim*. Albuquerque NM: BowArrow, 1995.

Philp, Kenneth R. *John Collier's Crusade for Indian Reform: 1920–1954*. Tucson: University of Arizona Press, 1977.

Segerstrom, Kenneth, and W. C. Henkes. "Status of Mineral Resource Information for the Jicarilla Indian Reservation, New Mexico." Administrative Report, U.S. Geological Society and U.S. Bureau of Mines, BIA-25, 1977.

Stanley, F. *The Jicarilla Apaches of New Mexico 1540–1940*. Pampa TX: Pampa Print Shop, 1962.

Tauli-Corpuz, Victoria. "Energy Development Impacts on Indigenous Peoples." Report for the Rights of Indigenous Peoples Hearing, February 25, 2017 Albuquerque NM. http://lawschool.unm.edu/events/united-nations/docs/energy-development-impact -on-indigenous-peoples-final-report.pdf. Taylor, Graham D. *The New Deal and American Indian Tribalism*. Lincoln: University of Nebraska Press, 1969.

Terrell, John Upton. *Apache Chronicle: The Story of the People*. New York: Thomas Y. Crowell, 1974.

Tiller, Veronica E. Velarde. *The Jicarilla Apache Tribe: A History*. Albuquerque NM: BowArrow, 2000.

———. "Jicarilla Apache." In *Southwest*, edited by Alfonso Ortiz, 440–62. Vol. 10 of *Handbook of North American Indians*, edited by William C. Sturtevant. Washington DC: Smithsonian Institution, 1983.

―――. *Culture and Customs of the Apache Indians*. Culture and Customs of the World. Santa Barbara CA: Greenwood, 2011.

―――, ed. *Tiller's Guide to Indian Country: Economic Profiles of American Indian Reservations*. Albuquerque NM: BowArrow, 1996.

Van Roekel, Gertrude B. *Jicarilla Apaches*. San Antonio TX: Naylor, 1971.

Wilson, H. Clyde. *Jicarilla Apache Political and Economic Structures*. Vol. 48, no. 4 of *University of California Publications in American Archaeology and Ethnology*, edited by R. L. Beals, J. B. Birdsell, and Harry Hoijer, 297–360. Berkeley: University of California Press, 1964.

Worcester, Donald E. *The Apaches: Eagles of the Southwest*. Norman: University of Oklahoma Press, 1979.

8 Salmon Nation Building
Globalization and the Future
BENEDICT J. COLOMBI

The primary aim of this paper is to explore the evolution of a globalizing economy and Nez Perce adaptive strategies of salmon nation building. Thus, to understand globalization in both its colonial and contemporary forms is to suggest that there is "one dominant global system structured around transnational corporations, a transnational capitalist class and the culture-ideology of consumerism."[1] With that in mind, the effort of incorporating Nez Perce land, people and resources into a global system began with the arrival of Lewis and Clark and the Corps of Discovery to the Nez Perce watersheds of the Snake and Columbia rivers in 1805. For millennia, the Nez Perce had interacted with their tribal neighbors from the Plains, Northwest Coast, and Great Basin; they lived in a world of complex human interactions that were in some ways like the present-day global system. Nez Perce power in the region was noteworthy and formidable, and as the sociologists Christopher Chase-Dunn and Kelly M. Mann suggest, tribal relationships before European and American contact were in many ways a "very small world-system."[2] Even so, the earliest encounters between the Nez Perce and Lewis and Clark marked something entirely new and different—that is, for the first time the Nez Perce confronted a government-sponsored strategy to bring nonstate people and spaces under the firm control of the larger nation-state.

So, what is salmon nation building? Salmon nation building is about

Nez Perce survival and is built on the adaptive capacity of the Nez Perce to maintain themselves as an autonomous tribal nation in light of the apparent and opaque pressures of globalism and American statecraft.[3] In this way, Nez Perce governance challenges external forms of development through a deliberate policy of nation building through salmon. The foundations of salmon nation building include assertions from below, advocacy networks, and a legal framework of reserved rights and sovereignty in developing competing forms of indigenous self-governance and economic development. In sum, for the Nez Perce, salmon nation building posits the survival of a salmon-based culture, environmental sustainability, and the resiliency of ecosystems.

The Origins of Salmon Nation Building

Salmon and water are the foundation from which the Nez Perce built their indigenous culture. Without these, Nez Perce creation would be nonexistent. Thus, the Nez Perce respond to these traditional (*walíim*) resources with prayer and contemporary reverence. The Creator (*haniyawáat*), for instance, fashioned both the world and humanity, and the foundations for life express a particular history in environment and place. Nez Perce interactions are therefore a matrix of labor, ceremony, and place, told in terms of salmon (*léwliks*) and water (*kúus*).[4]

Nez Perce stories and the history of their kin relations and community are also tied to salmon and water, with individual and collective identities vested in symbolic and material sources of salmon, places to fish for salmon, and water in the Columbia and Snake River drainages. Nez Perce develop relations and identity in regard to family, band, tribe, and their relation to land, water, and salmon. Social cohesion and basic values are enhanced and governed by these aforementioned relations.

Fish and water are widely used in important ways in Nez Perce daily life and ceremony, and both are necessary for the fulfillment of individual and community life. For the Nez Perce these events include: births, funerals, testimonial "giveaways" for the first anniversary of an individual's death, weddings, "name-giving" ceremonies, "first salmon," "first kill," "first roots" ceremonies marking adulthood, "pow-wows," and other celebrations, including "dinners" conducted to share and give thanks to the joy of life. The "dinners," which are both ritual "feasts" and non-ritual meals ideally include items unavailable for purchase in supermarkets, including "water" (*kúus*), "Chinook salmon" (*nacóʔox*), "meat" (elk, deer, moose, and bison) (*núukt*), "roots" (*qáaws*), and "huckleberries" (*cemíitx*). The capture of all these traditional foods is thought of as a gift (*pínitiní*) by the Creator, because these living beings gave up their lives so that Nez Perce can continue to prosper.

For fish, Nez Perce prefer salmon: Chinook in first place, then sockeye, and silver last. Nez Perce also use other fish species, including eels (*hésú*), sturgeon (*qîilex*), and steelhead trout (*héyey*), all anadromous fish, and other native fish including cutthroat (*wawáalam*) and bull (*ʔíislam*) trout, northern pikeminnows, suckers, and chiselmouths. Nonnative fish species such as carp, walleye, and bass are rarely used, if ever; they are regarded as either culturally insignificant or unimportant. Store-bought fish is unacceptable. Chinook salmon from hatcheries is acceptable but not preferred. Fish other than Chinook salmon is generally disliked.

Water, just like fish, has ideological and material importance to Nez Perce cosmology and everyday survival. From an ideological perspective, water is home to powerful spirits; materially, water is used for medicinal and healing purposes. According to Nez Perce cosmology, the eddies and confluences of free-flowing rivers and waterfalls are thought of as the homes of spirits. Similar to fish, not all water sources are considered the same or equal in both importance and preference by Nez Perce. Springs possess the purest, strongest, and most spiritually powerful water, and spring water is used in the ritual sweathouse and poured on hot rocks. Cold, flowing water from high-mountain streams is less preferred than spring water but considered "better" than water that runs at lower elevations, with less velocity, and at higher temperatures.

Water and salmon are essential to everything that is Nez Perce, and they are found in streams and rivers of great cultural importance. Basic values and beliefs in water and salmon are evident as moral instruction in Nez Perce traditional stories, such as "Coyote Breaks the Fish Dam at Celilo," "The Maiden and the Salmon," "How Salmon Got Over the Falls," and "Coyote and Salmon."[5] These stories illuminate the creation of the world and the beings that inhabit it, and include places in the Columbia and Snake River drainages, from Celilo Falls on the mid-Columbia to the tributaries of the Snake River, including the Palouse, Tucannon, Clearwater, Grande Ronde, Salmon, Weiser, and Payette Rivers in the Snake River Basin. Except the waterway before the lower falls on the Palouse River, all of these rivers and streams supported annual returns of salmon, and all of the subbasins, including the Palouse River, flourished with abundant springs, cold running water, waterfalls, and deep holes and eddies.

Encounters with Globalization

Lewis and Clark and the Nez Perce met in the upper reaches of the Clearwater River drainage in 1805. This encounter signaled the beginnings of globally integrated world economy in the Nez Perce homeland. For example, by 1813 the Nez Perce were actively trading furs with the North West Company, resulting in considerable change to Nez Perce social and economic systems. Fur trading companies encouraged Nez Perce men to marry more wives and become "chiefs." Institutional shifts increased the pace with which pelts could be trapped, processed, bought from Native producers, and sold for greater profit to non-Native consumers. The fur industry depleted vast populations of fur-bearing animals, and by the mid-1840s there were few beavers remaining in the region. The fur trade also brought relative prosperity to a minority of Nez Perce, but it was also indirectly responsible for an unprecedented depopulation of Nez Perce people. Epidemics brought in by non-Native trappers ravaged various villages of Nez Perce, and by 1841 population estimates had dwindled to two thousand against the 1805 estimate of six thousand people.[6]

Not surprisingly, the missionaries found relatively eager converts among ailing Nez Perce Indians. Throughout the early nineteenth century, many Nez Perce died as a result of disease. Missionaries provided food and medical care to sickly Nez Perce Indians and in turn successfully converted large numbers of the Nez Perce to Christianity. By the 1830s, the Presbyterian missionaries Henry Harmon Spalding and Asa Bowen Smith had established successfully operating missions along the confluence of Lapwai Creek and the Clearwater River, as well as farther upstream on the Clearwater River in Kamiah, Idaho. The Christian missions strongly prohibited religious converts from engaging in any forms of Nez Perce traditional culture or religion:

> The following customs were proscribed by missionaries: polygyny; gambling; shamanism; tutelary spirit seeking; warfare; stealing; most ceremonials with their attendant drumming, dancing, singing, and costumes, especially the cults, which were regarded as devil inspired; and sex outside monogamous marriage. In their place the missionaries taught the tenets of Protestant theology, Christian marriage, attendance during religious instruction and on holy days, adoption of horticulture, sedentary living, literacy, and Bible reading.[7]

As a result, many traditional bands of Nez Perce opposed and resisted religious conversion and continued to practice ancient lifeways.

Increasing pressure for Nez Perce land in the 1850s prompted the U.S. government to respond with policies of removal and treaty agreements. The treaties of 1855, which were later ratified in 1863 and 1868, established legal ties between the United States and the Nez Perce. The territorial governor, Isaac Stevens, guaranteed the Nez Perce ownership of a large and contiguous reservation as well as off-reservation rights to hunt, fish, and gather at usual and customary places. Many Nez Perce were cognizant of the dilemma they faced: non-Natives would continue to settle their homeland, and due to the impending reality, the Nez Perce ceded large portions of their traditional territory while retaining reserved rights in salmon and other critical resources. Article 3 of the 1855 Treaty states:

> The right of taking fish in all the streams where running through or bordering said reservation is further secured to said Indians; as also the right of taking fish at all usual and accustomed places in common with citizens of the Territory; and of erecting temporary buildings for curing, together with the privilege of hunting, gathering roots and berries, and pasturing their horses and cattle upon open and unclaimed land.[8]

Subsequently, Idaho became a territory in 1863, and U.S. officials renegotiated the 1855 treaty with a ratification that substantially reduced the 1855 treaty of almost 5 million acres to roughly 800,000 acres.[9] In addition to a reduction of Nez Perce land, the second treaty produced a schism within

Nez Perce tribal community.[10] Pro-Christian tribal members were pitted against non-Christian traditional factions. Acculturated forces decisively split the Nez Perce into antagonistic and polarized entities.

Native and non-Native hostilities continued to escalate, and by 1877 the Nez Perce War had emerged as a weapon to "root-out" all nontreaty, nonacculturated factions of Nez Perce resistance. Battles were fought at Whitebird near the Salmon River and across the Bitterroot Mountains in the Valley of the Big Hole. U.S. military policy was to kill all Indians—including women and children. This strategy appalled Nez Perce warriors, since traditional warfare strategy never involved the direct killing of civilian lives. Chief Joseph realized his people could fight no more and surrendered forty miles from the Canadian border at the Bear Paw Battle-field in northern Montana. The survivors of Joseph's Band were eventually detained in Oklahoma, and more lives were lost due to the extreme heat of a foreign climate.[11] It was not until 1885 that Chief Joseph and his people were permitted to return to the Nez Perce homeland and reservation.[12]

With most Nez Perce now confined to federal oversight and reservation life, the U.S. government found a highly effective strategy for reducing communally owned Indian land. Designed by federal policymakers, the Dawes Severalty Act of 1887 allotted each head of an Indian household 160 acres of land; individuals over eighteen years of age 80 acres; and those under eighteen, who were mostly orphans, 40 acres. The Dawes Act, or "Allotment," was a carefully crafted policy aimed at dividing and destroying communally owned land and traditional tribal relations.

During this period, Nez Perce populations were at an all-time low; large portions of communally owned reservation land thus became available to non-Native individuals. Before 1800, the Nez Perce had successfully managed nearly 28 million acres. However, after Allotment, the Nez Perce received a monetary sum of $1,626,222 in exchange for roughly 500,000 acres of unallotted land, or nearly 75% percent of the reservation. More-over, of the 800,000 acres of total reservation land, the Nez Perce were left with a staggering 204,587 acres, or 27.4 percent, of the land base within the reservation after Allotment.[13] By 1975, Indian-owned land on the Nez Perce Reservation was down to a meager 80,000 acres. Within a period of only a few generations, Nez Perce land considered too sacred to be bought and sold was now mostly in the hands of non-Native individuals and federal oversight.

Globalization and the Agricultural Economy

Christian converts were the first Nez Perce to engage in an agricultural economy. Henry Harmon Spalding's ambitious and sometimes cruel driving of the Nez Perce to secure his own "civilized" ends" had successfully turned Christianized Nez Perce into Euro-American agriculturalists.[14] The new work ethos of domestication and sedentary living fueled the production of Nez Perce garden vegetables, eggs, cattle, and horses. Gardens were located along the fertile bottoms of the Clearwater, Salmon, and Snake Rivers. Domesticated food products were not only consumed in communion at various missions but also sold to non-Native settlers, mostly miners, who began trespassing through the Nez Perce Reservation in large numbers after the Treaty of 1855. With the barter and sale of tribally produced agrarian products, the Nez Perce became quite astute at acquiring specific articles of the non-Native global economy—for example, alcohol, guns, and tobacco. At present-day Lewiston, Idaho, the Nez Perce managed several garden plots, domesticated animal pastures, and feed lots. Moreover, the Nez Perce exacted tolls along all major migratory routes leading to illegal gold mines and non-Native settlements. Natural crossings of fallen logs were destroyed and replaced with Nez Perce–controlled toll bridges.[15] For roughly the next thirty years, the Nez Perce increasingly traded in non-Native commodities and began to farm at a more intensive, commercial level.

With Nez Perce social conditions worsening, large numbers of non-Natives began farming on the reservation. Archie Phinney notes by stating, "This region, once abundant with wild game, fish, berries and roots, had been transformed into a settled territory, dotted with white town sites and farmsteads."[16] Most farms cultivated several varieties of wheat without irrigation. The Nez Perce began farming, along with their non-Native neighbors, and emulated the agricultural techniques employed by the white farmers. Governmental policies of turning the Nez Perce into individual farmers temporarily succeeded. Farming technologies of the late nineteenth century included the widespread use of large draft horses and the McCormick Harvester to plow the ground and harvest the grain. The Nez Perce were quite successful in using these animals to increase the productivity of their small-scale farms. Energy inputs for small-scale farming were relatively self-sufficient. Locally produced grain as well as grazing on open pastures fed the horses, and farm machinery was relatively simple. In essence, small farms not only were energy efficient but also generated sufficient income and supported local communities for the maximum number of Nez Perce after the Dawes Act.

The productivity of non-Native farmers, however, began to outcompete that of Nez Perce farmers in both capital and land. In the 1930s Archie M. Phinney (Nimiipuu) commented on post–Dawes Act policies, suggesting, "The efforts of the government to induce the Indians to participate in the industrial life of white men failed."[17] Thus, non-Native agriculturalists acquired greater concentrations of land and capital and developed technologies that improved the profitability of their farms. The Dawes Act failed to facilitate the participation of Indians in the industrial matrix of the dominant culture.

Settlement by non-Natives in the Nez Perce homeland in the twentieth century continued to increase at an unprecedented scale. Even so, many Nez Perce resisted the dominant cultural ideologies of individualism and salvation through labor in a capitalist system. Many Nez Perce remained fixated on collective participation and traditional community life. The Nez Perce, who saw little value in doing farming themselves, transformed their individually allotted land into a cash-generating system of market sale and leasing.

The Bureau of Indian Affairs handled all trust land owned by individual Indians and tribal collectives by leasing agricultural properties to non-Native farmers. This situation provided the Nez Perce with short-lived economic gains and, in many cases, represented the only source of income for many individual Nez Perce Indians. The money allowed Nez Perce individuals to purchase consumer goods and participate in a modern global economy. Items for purchase included imported food commodities and manufactured goods. Phinney, in his 1937 article, "Numipu among the White Settlers," reported that in essence, "the Numipu [Nez Perce] had become 'agency' Indians."[18]

By the early twentieth century the Dawes Act proved to be a complete failure on three levels. First, the federal government could not effectively transcend traditional Indian values of group collectivity and community. Many Nez Perce were not enticed by concepts of individualism and European-American efforts to make land more productive and ultimately more profitable through capital-intensive agriculture. Second, the leasing of individual trusts and the eventual sale of land in fee title enabled the Nez Perce to relinquish remaining reservation lands and become a new class of land-poor Indians. The third level was the great harm directly inflicted on the environment through the rapid development of an agricultural economy. Phinney reflected on the relationship between environmental degradation and Dawes Act policy, stating,

> White Men exploited the territory with a vengeance. Pasturelands were overgrazed, forests were clear-cut by lumber companies with no thought of reforestation, agricultural lands were wastefully farmed out, particularly Indian lands, for the leaseholder had no interest in maintaining the fertility of, or building up, the soil of lands that were his only temporarily. Lack of fertilization and proper summer fallowing soon decreased the productivity of farmlands and resulted in the decrease[d] rental value of Indian lands. On the other hand, the cycles of depression of a capitalistic economy brought hard times for the white farmers. This meant that in some years the Indians received irregular and diminished payments of lease money or they could not rent their lands at all.[19]

As a result of worsening nationwide conditions on U.S. Indian reservations, the Institute for Government Research under chairman Robert S. Brookings instigated a comprehensive survey of the economic and social conditions of American Indians. Along with Secretary of the Interior Hubert Work, Brookings and colleagues selected Lewis Meriam and nine specialists to conduct an independent investigation of the alleged conditions.[20] The published findings appeared in the 1928 book *The Problem of Indian Administration* and included eight sections spanning the state of American Indian economies, with a particularly focus on agriculture and even far-ranging practices such as missionary activities among Indians.

Meriam and his associates commented on "several past policies . . . which, if long continued, would tend to pauperize any race. They continued, "Part of the plan was to instruct and aid them in agriculture, but this vital part was not pressed with vigor and intelligence. It almost seems as if the government assumed that some magic in individual ownership of property would in itself prove an educational civilizing factor, but unfortunately this policy has for the most part operated in the opposite direction."[21] In fact, the agriculture specialist for the Meriam Report was the agricultural economist William J. Spillman. He held an academic post with the State College of Washington (the present-day Washington State University) and headed the College's Department of Agriculture from 1896 to 1902. The Washington State College campus was and still is located within the Nez Perce 1855 treaty boundary. By the late 1900s, this region, commonly referred to as the Palouse, became one of the nation's largest producers of dryland wheat. Spillman developed, through a process of breeding and selection, wheat seeds that were optimally adapted to the dry-farming technique, and his "Hybrid, 128" seed became a standard crop throughout eastern Washington and north-central Idaho.[22]

The Meriam Report concluded that the best economic opportunities for American Indians lay in some form of agriculture, that their greatest economic asset was their ownership of land, and that a substantial majority pursued agriculture as an occupation. The Meriam survey staff collected occupational information cards from Indian children attending Indian boarding schools. The results were startling: of the 16,720 cards collected nationwide, 12,353 recorded their father's occupation as "farmer." The next most frequent occupation was "rancher," and together both farming and ranching accounted for 81 percent of all Indian occupations nationwide.[23] The Nez Perce had failed to achieve the same occupational status as other U.S. Indian populations. In the American West, most Indian reservations were situated on extremely arid land and were not considered very attractive or productive agricultural lands by the non-Native agricultural majority. On the contrary, the Nez Perce Reservation included some of the richest nonirrigated wheat land found in the Pacific Northwest, and its real estate became an increasingly desirable commodity throughout the late nineteenth and twentieth centuries.

The Dawes Act produced an aftermath that stripped the Nez Perce of any real possibility of being large-scale landowners or viable commercial agriculturalists. For example, by 1937, Nez Perce Indian–owned land was down to a mere 70,600 acres from the roughly 800,000 acres reserved in the 1863 treaty.[24] By the advent of World War II, this demographic situation had left the Nez Perce land poor while the non-Native population grew land rich. Of the 800,000 reservation acres recognized in 1937, non-Natives owned over 90 percent, or 729,400 acres; in addition, they leased the remaining portions of Nez Perce–owned agricultural land held in trust or fee title.

Globalization and Dam Building

The social and economic consequences of the late nineteenth and twentieth centuries produced the rise of factory farming and large dams. The incentive to radically transform the Nez Perce homeland from a small-scale agrarian society to large-scale agribusiness was an issue of economic growth and national defense. The key technological changes after 1940 were to replace naturally reproducing, self-sufficient farm-inputs (human labor and horses) with fossil-fuel-powered farm machinery, along with agricultural chemicals. Factory farming technologies produced higher yields and tremendous surpluses. For example, the Eastern Washington portion of the Nez Perce homeland experienced a tripling of wheat yields per acre from 1910 to 1987.[25] This farmland intensification destroyed over two-thirds of the small-scale farms and replaced them with fewer and more powerful large-scale farms. Economies of scale removed roughly fourteen thousand people away from small-scale farming and damaged the economic self-sufficiency and viability of many small towns throughout the region.

To be sure, many Nez Perce suffered from the economic disparities produced during World War II and the post-war modernization process. By the mid-twentieth century, the Nez Perce faced an overwhelming presence of non-Natives who owned and controlled most reservation land. The Nez Perce lacked the financial muscle to compete with the capital-intensive requirements of factory farming. Large-scale agribusiness required the use of fossil fuels and globally manufactured products. The costs of fossil-fuel-consuming farm machinery and the increasing use of chemical fertilizers and pesticides made them an economic impossibility for individual Nez Perce. In southeast Washington and north-central Idaho, for example, the use of chemical fertilizers and fossil fuels had been nonexistent in 1910; by 1940 they comprised 31 percent of total farm inputs.[26]

World War II also generated new demands for national defense and hydroelectricity. Before the war, the lower Snake River remained dam free, and railroads provided farmers with the primary mode of transporting grain to international ports at the mouth of the Columbia River in Portland, Oregon. The lower Snake River was beginning to face its ultimate demise. In the mid-1940s Congress appropriated the funds to begin the Lower Snake River Project.[27] In 1947 the U.S. Army Corps of Engineer's North Pacific Division formed the largest construction district in the entire Corps bureaucracy. The Walla Walla District in southeast Washington would erect and manage all the dams on the lower Snake River. Non-Native actors opportunistically worked through the Army Corps' institutional structures; taming the lower Snake River would provide growth in two economic sectors: commercial shipping and farming. Lewiston, Idaho, would soon become the Pacific Northwest's first inland seaport, and an emerging agricultural elite would gain more profitable methods and associated wealth with transporting agriculture commodities downriver to newly expanding national and global markets.

During the postwar years, Congress was slow to appropriate the funds to build dams. Proponents argued that building more dams would stimulate the economy. They also pleaded that dams were in the interest of national defense, because the United States was engaged in defending the nation against the perceived threats of communism and the Cold War. The Atomic Energy Commission's Hanford Plant lobbied for more energy and increased production. An aggressive campaign was launched. Hanford's supporters agreed that Ice Harbor Dam would solve Hanford's growing energy needs. By 1955, after a long-winded political battle, Congress appropriated a modest $1 million to begin constructing Ice Harbor Dam. Money continued to flood in, and by November 1961 the Army Corps had begun filling in the dam's pool. By December of the same year, Ice Harbor generated its first hydroelectric power.

On the lower Snake River, the next two dams were relatively easy to build compared to Ice Harbor. Lower Monumental, located thirty miles upstream, began producing energy in 1969. The next dam, Little Goose, was constructed an additional thirty miles upstream. The Walla Walla District signed their largest civil-works contract in Corps of Engineers history, with nearly $72 million allocated to a private construction company to begin building Little Goose Dam. Workers completed the dam in 1970. The concrete structure, 2,600 feet long, caused enough backwater to flood over Little Goose Island, thereby giving the dam its name. The Lower Monumental and Little Goose Dams came to fruition within only two years of each other, but the fourth and final dam, Lower Granite, would take an additional five years to complete.

Lower Granite was built during a time of heightened national and regional environmental consciousness. Protesters questioned the long-term survivability of salmon in the Pacific Northwest. Concerned citizens pointed to the harmful effects of the three lower–Snake River dams, all built within a period of ten years. The acute trauma to the lower Snake River was at an all-time high. Never before had the lower Snake suffered from such a rapid alteration of its main-stem watershed. Even so, dam opponents could not stop Lower Granite from being completed, and in 1975 Lower Granite began generating electricity. At last, Lewiston had realized its coveted status as an inland seaport. Idaho Governor Cecil Andrus commented somberly at the three-day festival celebrating the completion of Lower Granite, "Before I accept this structure, I want to point out that the cost of this system has been horrendous, both in dollars and in cost to our natural resources."[28] Dam proponents reveled in the fact that the lower Snake had finally been tamed, and many non-Native commercial activities benefited from the newly transformed watershed.

On the contrary, the four lower–Snake River dams were a significant obstacle to Nez Perce sovereignty and well-being. Since time immemorial the Nez Perce have revered salmon and healthy watersheds as paramount symbols of their cultural and religious identity. This ancient relationship was built upon three main elements: salmon as food, salmon as an object of trade, and salmon as a necessary representative component of traditional religious expression. After 1975, the Nez Perce began to push for the removal of the four lower–Snake River dams. This fulfilled a larger Nez Perce public-policy campaign based on treaty rights and twentieth-century legal precedents to restore salmon and other endangered fishes to the entire Columbia and Snake River drainage. The Treaty of 1855 guaranteed the Nez Perce and other Columbia Basin tribes the "right of taking fish" at their "usual and accustomed" fishing sites. Roughly a century later, the U.S. Supreme Court (*Washington v. Washington State Commercial Passenger Fishing Vessel Ass'n., 443 U.S. 658*) ruled in 1979 that the original treaties entitled Northwestern tribes to half of the total Columbia Basin salmon harvest and approved the use of modern fishing equipment:

> Without this technology, the rulings recognizing treaty fishing rights would have been hollow victories: in these times of intensified fishing pressure and dwindling runs of fish due to dams and other developments in the watersheds, modern gear is a necessity if the tribes are to obtain the amount of fish to which they are entitled under court-ordered apportionment.[29]

Ultimately, Nez Perce fishery policies are based on the belief that restoring salmon to harvestable stocks is the best solution to federal treaty obligations and, more important, to maintaining tribal identity and culture. The Nez Perce realized that if harvestable stocks were not restored, the federal government and its taxpayers may ultimately be obligated to compensate the tribes for lost cultural and legal rights to harvest salmon.

More recently, Columbia Basin Tribes have refused, on religious grounds, to estimate an appropriate monetary amount, but the dollar value of reparations may be between $6 billion and $12 billion. The Institute for Fisheries Resources's 1996 study *The Cost of Doing Nothing* determined this figure.[30] The report used widely accepted economic methods to calculate a net asset value of $13 billion for Columbia Basin salmon. Historically, Snake River salmon has accounted for half of total Columbia Basin salmon and, therefore, the net asset value for Snake River salmon has been pegged at $6.5 billion. Columbia Basin tribal claims could also include lost land value; by the late 1800s, Northwest Indian tribes had ceded over six million acres of communally managed land to the United States. The Institute for Fisheries Resources valued that land at $2,000 per acre and estimated the value of tribal land cessations at an additional $12 billion. In short, if harvestable stocks were not restored, the federal government and its taxpayers could be responsible for roughly $23 billion in compensation to the tribes.

The Nez Perce Tribe set a legal precedent in their fight for healthy watersheds. According to recent estimates, the Nez Perce and the federal government have "spent $10 million preparing their water case for trial and will spend an additional $2 million per year in the years ahead."[31] The two major legal battles currently facing the Nez Perce tribe are securing adequate flows of water in the Snake River drainage and upholding a duty of fiduciary trust on behalf of the U.S. government. The Nez Perce support free-flowing rivers because without the adequate habitat salmon and other anadromous fishes fail to successfully reproduce and survive. Furthermore, the federal government has violated its responsibilities as a benevolent guardian to the Nez Perce Tribe. The damming of the Snake River watershed disregarded several promises legally supported by the Treaty of 1855. If necessary, the Nez Perce Tribe will pursue a legal campaign to litigate the federal government for a breach of trust. Tribal leaders conclude that the federal Snake River management plan is geared to protect dams and the status quo, not salmon.

Meanwhile, the Nez Perce continue to witness the collapse of a once-plentiful Columbia Basin anadromous fishery. Prior to Euro-American settlement, ten to sixteen million adult salmon entered the river each year.[32] Of those, roughly eight to ten million were adult Chinook. In the early summer large runs of eighty-pound Chinook salmon, appropriately named "June Hogs" by early Euro-American settlers, would enter the Snake River each year. For countless generations the Nez Perce had fished for these giant salmon, but now the June Hogs have vanished from the Nez Perce watersheds of the Snake and Columbia Rivers. Fishery biologists failed to acquire hatchery stocks prior to the June Hogs' total disappearance from the Columbia and Snake River drainages. In 1993, counts of the remaining Chinook salmon were at an all-time historical low. That year, only 450,000 fish returned to the Columbia River Basin and roughly 250,000 Chinook salmon, or half of the total run, were harvested.

As a result, large sums of money are being invested in restoring salmon throughout the Pacific Northwest. In the Columbia Basin this type of policy has resulted in skyrocketing costs with few tangible results. Well-intentioned fishery managers have relied on hatcheries and fish passage systems to solve the problem of declining salmon. However, neither hatcheries nor fish-bypass systems are solving the salmon crises. A retired Army Corps of Engineers fishery biologist recently stated that roughly $8 to 10 billion has already been spent to improve fish passages on the lower Snake River.[33] A fish screen was put in at McNary Dam to facilitate juvenile salmon's returning to the Pacific Ocean. This improvement cost the federal government and U.S. taxpayers roughly $18 million.

So, who benefits from the maintenance and perpetuation of large dams in the Nez Perce homeland? To be sure, a few individual actors and the institutions they direct are benefiting exponentially from the dams, while the majority pays enormous costs for the perceived benefits derived from dam development. Agribusinesses, large-scale industry, electricity-generating corporations, and resource-management institutions derive increased revenues and social power that, in turn are deciding the fate of salmon in the Nez Perce homeland.

Moreover, dam building in the Nez Perce watersheds of the Snake and Columbia Rivers have enabled a transnational river-barge industry to ship wheat and other agricultural commodities to international markets. Of the total amount of grain produced on the Nez Perce Reservation, more than 90 percent is globally exported to East Asia, much of it going to China. Furthermore, the dilemma of dam removal on the lower Snake River considers the increases in the cost of shipping grain by railroad and highway. This would raise the price per bushel of wheat, for example, by 8 to 10 percent. Unless the federal government subsidizes these costs, farmers will resort to paying higher prices to ship their commodities to the consumer. Powerful agricultural individuals and corporations have transformed the regional farming industry by purchasing or leasing most small-scale farms. Large-scale farmers, who profit enormously from the building of the lower Snake dams, have therefore resisted dam removal on the lower Snake River.

In addition to the agricultural economy, several federal agencies, including the Bonneville Power Administration, have an interest in maintaining the Columbia Basin dams. The Columbia and Snake River drainages produce more hydroelectricity than any other river system in the United States and likely the world over. In the 1930s, Roosevelt's New Deal administrators struggled with whether the Army Corps of Engineers, the Bureau of Reclamation, or an independent agency would be the sole marketers of energy produced from Columbia Basin hydroelectric dams—they eventually settled on the Bonneville Power Administration. Since the late 1930s, the Bonneville Power Administration has marketed all electricity produced by federal dams in the Pacific Northwest. This monopoly includes the management of hydropower produced from the four lower–Snake River dams. In sum, the combined monopoly of powerful actors through dam building endangers not only salmon but also Nez Perce attempts to building a viable salmon nation in the twenty-first century.

Salmon Nation Building as Adaptive Strategy

In building a salmon nation, the Nez Perce and other indigenous nations actively seek a more sustainable future. Native nations are developing alternative systems to external policies of assimilation and global-scale development. Salmon nation building utilizes indigenous adaptive strategies in the formation of policy and restores and implements those decisions in Native homelands.[34] The goal in salmon nation building is to develop comprehensive and collective strategies in rebuilding societies and eco-systems that are more sustainable, equitable, and resilient.

Salmon nation building, therefore, proposes creative solutions to the current salmon crisis and may also have the capacity to countervail the negative effects of critical environmental problems such as global climate change and large dams. Drawing on the 1855 Treaty and a system of reserved rights, the Nez Perce operate several large natural-resource programs, including a well-established fisheries program.[35] In this regard, the Nez Perce are effectively building a strong sovereign nation while shaping a vigorous future economy that fits their own circumstances and specific tribal culture. The primary goal for the Nez Perce fisheries program is to recover and restore all species of anadromous fish in the Nez Perce homeland. Under the Treaty of 1855, the Nez Perce achieved the goals of protection, restoration, and enhancement using a culturally driven, holistic approach to salmon management. This includes a focus on the entire watershed and utilizing a ridgetop-to-ridgetop approach, thereby managing all of the drainage rather than taking a piecemeal approach to fisheries management. Furthermore, nation building through salmon draws from the ideological and material aspects of Nez Perce salmon cosmology, described earlier in this chapter.

Beyond the individual and tribal levels, indigenous fishery managers are working together through the Columbia River Inter-Tribal Fish Commission (CRITFC). The Columbia Basin salmon-treaty tribes (the Nez Perce Tribe, Umatilla Tribes, Warm Springs Tribes, and Yakama Nation) established CRITFC in 1977 to counteract the effects of nearly two hundred years of large-scale, external development (e.g., dams and agribusiness) as well as protect treaty-reserved rights and a sacred salmon heritage.[36] In sum, CRITFC engages in salmon nation building by exercising the inherent sovereign powers of the tribes as fishery managers in the Columbia River Basin.

At the local level, each CRITFC tribe operates its own fishery programs and regional fish hatcheries. This means that the salmon treaty tribes extend their jurisdictional boundaries far beyond the reservation to include hatchery programs and restoration projects at "usual and accustomed places." For example, the Nez Perce operate a total of six anadromous fish hatcheries located on the Clearwater, Salmon, Snake, Imnaha, Grande Ronde, and Wallowa Rivers; they also comanage several salmon projects with the U.S. Fish and Wildlife Service at the Dworshak National Fish Hatchery Complex, located just below Dworshak Dam on the lower North Fork of the Clearwater River. Furthermore, the Nez Perce, in combination with the other CRITFC tribes, monitor the harvest of 50 percent of the available adult salmon migrating in the Columbia River drainage each year. Beyond that, CRITFC makes recommendations for the protection and restoration of critical salmon habitats listed under the federal Endangered Species Act.[37] Thus, consultation between CRITFC and federal agencies results in the issuance of biological opinions for the survival and recovery of listed salmon species. Most biological opinions arose in response to a federal action directly or indirectly related to the alteration of critical habitat. Consequently, the Nez Perce and other salmon treaty tribes generally oppose large dams and other development projects that negatively impact overall water quality and therefore also the survival of salmon.

In salmon nation building, the idea that salmon need cold, clean water is a paramount concern. For instance, in 2005 the Nez Perce formed an agreement between non-Native water users, the Idaho State Senate, and the U.S. Congress in the Snake River Basin Adjudication (SRBA)—a water rights case introduced in 1986 to settle more than 150,000 outstanding claims to water in the Snake River drainage. The Nez Perce, in turn, drew from their cultural connections to salmon and water to form an agreement in which the Bureau of Reclamation may lease up to 427,000 acre-feet of water from the state to increase flow augmentation in the Snake River drainage and help endangered salmon. Additional water will flow down the Snake River, aid salmon migration, and improve Nez Perce fish and habitat projects. In doing so, the Nez Perce use their reserved rights to salmon and water, self-determination, and autonomous self-governance to build a salmon nation and reduce internal and external conflicts from globalization and other external forms of development.

Ultimately, then, the greatest potential conflict to Nez Perce environment and society stems from the projected impacts of climate change and its associated consequences to salmon and water. In the Pacific Northwest, tribal nations are reacting to climate change with novel and innovative policies.[38] The adjudication of water rights for salmon is a powerful tool in an environment of increasing demand and declining supply. The federal Endangered Species Act is a valuable legal strategy for salmon tribes aiming to protect fish populations from extinction, and additional legal structures—such as contract law—may provide another means by which tribes might attempt to secure in-stream flows to protect migrating salmon. Furthermore, in the protection of salmon, indigenous policies aim to designate wild and scenic rivers as public lands in national parks and monuments.

The formation of intergovernmental and intertribal cooperation has resulted in collaborations with various federal agencies such as the National Oceanographic and Atmospheric Administration (NOAA) and the National Fish and Wildlife Service (NFWS). In salmon restoration, these partnerships are effective in comanaging hatchery programs and in developing long-range management strategies. Salmon tribal nations develop and implement strong policies on the future of dams and related irrigation projects. Tribes, for instance, might seek to enforce the release of more water by dam operators to improve fish passage when necessary, as well as litigate for the decommissioning of dams as a measure of last resort.

Regarding climate change, salmon nation building for the Nez Perce includes on- and off-reservation carbon sequestration. The Nez Perce has committed to twenty-nine forest-restoration projects and about 5,000 acres to carbon sequestration; plantings of Douglas fir and ponderosa pine saplings are projected to absorb a year's worth of carbon dioxide from nearly five hundred thousand cars, trucks, and SUVs.[39] The Nez Perce not only aim to have corporations offset their greenhouse gas emissions by paying to keep trees growing but also advocate for forests to remain intact. Presently, few American companies are mandated to curb greenhouse emissions with carbon sequestration, but tribal efforts are models that demonstrate for others that the real value in forests lies in keeping them both alive and in place. In short, twenty-first century (social and environmental) realities have led the Nez Perce to generate policies that focus on healthy ecosystems and rebuilding a vibrant and strong salmon nation.

Challenges to Salmon Nation Building

Continuing stress from nearly two centuries of external growth is rapidly transforming tribal homelands. For example, at the beginning of the twenty-first century there were over ten million inhabitants in the greater Pacific Northwest, which is three orders of magnitude greater than the indigenous population in 1750.[40] By the late nineteenth century the immigrant population had exceeded the Native population, and by the early twentieth century the total population was more than one million people. Shortly before World War II economic expansion and population growth fueled the construction of large dams, with the state-sponsored completion of the Bonneville and Grand Coulee dams in 1938 and 1942, respectively. After World War II per-capita energy consumption increased dramatically, and between 1985 and 2003 the economy nearly doubled in size. A century of commercial growth in the global system has degraded ecosystems, diminished the opportunities available to many ranching, farming, and forest-based communities, and destroyed the great Columbia River salmon fishery.[41] Massive change in historical ecosystems has removed 80 to 90 percent of the old-growth coniferous forests. Timber cutting, grazing, and fire suppression have made the remaining forests prone to disease and fire. Ninety percent of the sagebrush steppe in Idaho and 99 percent of the Palouse Prairie steppe, a unique ecosystem in the Nez Perce homeland, has been removed, mostly for urban and agricultural development. Dramatic human changes to the environmental habitat have led to the extinction of fourteen bird and mammal species from Washington and Oregon; the State of Oregon lists forty-two additional mammals and birds as "species of concern."[42] Researchers predict that in coming decades the resiliency of the entire region, including salmon-based ecosystems, will be additionally challenged by the combined effects of water shortages, global climate change, and increasingly severe streamflow fluctuations.[43]

For Nez Perce, salmon ecosystems define cosmology, labor, energy, and economy. Moreover, salmon link biodiversity and productivity because they are "transport vector[s]" of key processes in the movement of "materials, and energy and nutrients between marine, aquatic, and terrestrial ecosystems."[44] Spawning salmon in the Columbia River drainage have historically transported over one hundred million kilograms of nutrients gained from marine to terrestrial ecosystems annually in the form of ten to sixteen million fish, making the drainage the world's richest inland fishery.[45] Before the arrival of Europeans these rich ecosystems supported some two hundred thousand indigenous peoples diversified into forty-seven cultural subareas and representing eleven language families.[46] Allowing for the impact of European disease, the precontact population may have been twice this size.[47] Indigenous peoples in the Columbia River drainage consumed nearly thirty-six billion kilocalories in returning salmon.[48] The five species of Pacific Northwest salmon (*Oncorhynchus*) have existed in their present form for six million years, and they have been a food source for indigenous peoples for millennia. Now in the Columbia Basin, salmon runs measure at roughly 20 percent of their historical levels of ten to sixteen million before 1805, with as few as two hundred thousand fish returning annually.[49] The current decline in Columbia Basin salmon can be attributed to the impact of hydroelectric dams, irrigation projects, and overall habitat loss.[50]

It is projected that global climate change will spatially redistribute streamflow scenarios and reduce the amount of annual freshwater cycling.[51] Sharp variations in water are affected by the reduction in annual snowpack. Average annual air temperatures in the Pacific Northwest warmed between 0.7 and 0.9 degrees Celsius in the twentieth century, and climate models suggest that by the mid-twenty-first century additional increases of between 1.5 and 3.2 degrees Celsius will occur.[52] These higher air temperatures could harm salmon during their spawning, incubation, and rearing life stages. Warmer temperatures create earlier snowmelt and less moisture falling as snow. Increases in rain as opposed to snow lead to increased peak flows during winter, which scour stream and riverbeds and obliterate salmon eggs. A reduction in snowpack results in diminished flows in summer and fall, decreasing the availability of suitable spawning habitats and expediting further increases in water temperatures.

Little is known about the ability of salmon to adjust to global climate change. The negative effects of climate change, however, are projected to be most pronounced in the higher and more pristine tributaries of major river systems. In the Nez Perce homeland, rivers and streams are markedly cooler, higher, and more suitable as habitats for spawning salmon than the warmer, lower-elevation streams located farther downstream in the lower Columbia River basin. Perturbations in climate and increases in average temperatures will likely challenge the remaining salmon stocks in the next fifty to hundred years. Recent research in the Pacific Northwest on Chinook salmon populations suggests a decline of 20–40 percent by 2050.[53] The Nez Perce and other Columbia Basin tribal peoples depend on Chinook salmon due to the fish's large size and high fat content. A significant decline in Chinook salmon threatens indigenous livelihoods and sociocultural sustainability. I use the term "sustainability" here to refer to the ability of the members of any human society to acquire the energy and materials needed for the successful cross-generational maintenance and reproduction of individual households, society, and culture.

Conclusion

Salmon nation building emphasizes the sustainability advantages of smaller-scale tribal nations in challenging the negative effects of roughly two centuries of unprecedented growth in the region. Salmon nation building also addresses creative strategies for a changing climate, the problems presented by large dams, and other critical environmental problems of the twenty-first century. In short, salmon nation building and this collection of essays in *Rising from the Ashes* are about tribes increasing their capacity for autonomous self-governance and sustainable community development.[54]

On the other hand, globalization is not a new phenomenon but rather a process with roots, origins, and a trajectory. In the Nez Perce homeland the globalization of land, resources, and people commenced with the immigration of settler Americans into the region throughout the nineteenth and twentieth centuries. A much older process, globalization is not something new, with its roots in Europe beginning in the fifteenth century and perhaps even before that, with intercontinental trade occurring between the regions of Eurasia and the African continents since biblical times.[55]

To be sure, the capitalist world economy has profited enormously from the opening of the Pacific Northwest and Native homelands. As world-systems theorist Immanuel Wallerstein suggests:

> A capitalist world-economy is a collection of many institutions, the combination of which accounts for its processes, and all of which are intertwined with each other. The basic institutions are the market, or rather the markets; the firms that compete in the markets; the multiple states, within an interstate system; the households; the classes; and the status-groups (to use Weber's term, which some people in recent years have renamed the "identities" . . .).[56]

Even so, salmon nation building is a tool that the Nez Perce and Columbia Basin Tribes are using to push back against and redefine relationships within the larger global system.[57] No longer are Native nations "subordinate" to the U.S. system; rather, Indigenous salmon nations today are "making new assertions of sovereignty."[58] These nations are "shifting from what they can persuade government to do to rebuilding their own capacities for organized, sustained, goal oriented action."[59]

Furthermore, in *The State of Native Nations*, Kalt and colleagues describe current American Indian economic development strategies as follows: "Tribes around the country are investing in their ability to get things done for their citizens, in ways previously rendered impossible by federal paternalism, red tape, off-reservation special interests, and a lack of resources. Importantly, these investments account for a growing number of tribal successes—tribes are overcoming long-standing challenges and creating new opportunities, addressing a wide range of socioeconomic and cultural concerns. Nevertheless, the challenge of increasing both the breadth and depth of governing capacity is paramount to furthering tribal development."[60]

In conclusion, salmon nation building is a process by which indigenous nations use tribally specific, cultural solutions to solve external problems of growth-oriented development. In the Nez Perce watersheds of the Snake and Columbia Rivers, solutions to rebuilding the resiliency of salmon-based systems will be cultural ones and will require, in part, a cultural paradigm shift that embraces past lessons and indigenous cultural understandings of society and environment. This is especially important in a time of declining resources and an uncertain future. Salmon nation building, therefore, is an opportunity to invest in the next generation, to rethink development and economic patterns, and to put salmon nations on a course for a better tomorrow.

NOTES

1. Sklair, *Globalization*, 1.
2. Chase-Dunn and Mann, *Wintu and Their Neighbors*.
3. Colombi, "Salmon and the Adaptive," 75–97; Colombi and Smith, "Adaptive Capacity," 13; Colombi and Smith, "Insights on Adaptive Capacity," 189–202.
4. Marshall, "Fish, Water," 763–93.
5. Phinney, "Numipu among the White"; Spinden, "Nez Perce Indians"; Walker, *Nez Perce Coyote Tales*.
6. Walker, "Nez Perce," 420–38.
7. Walker, "Nez Perce," 433–34.
8. Axtell et al., *Treaties*, 117.
9. Phinney, "Numipu among the White," 21–42.
10. Walker, *Conflict and Schism*.
11. Pearson, *Nez Perces in the Indian Territory*.

12. Slickpoo and Walker, *Nu Mee Poom.*
13. Greenwald, *Reconfiguring the Reservation.*
14. Morrill and Morrill, "Pioneer Portraits," 4–24.
15. Wells, "Farmers Forgotten," 28–32.
16. Phinney, "Numipu among the White," 22.
17. Phinney, "Numipu among the White," 24.
18. Phinney, "Numipu among the White," 25.
19. Phinney, "Numipu among the White," 26.
20. Lewis Meriam (1883–1972), a government bureaucrat and graduate of Harvard University, served as technical director of the survey report, more commonly referred to as the "Meriam Report." His nine associates comprised Ray A. Brown, Henry Roe Cloud, Edward Everett Dale, Emma Duke, Herbert R. Edwards, Fayette Avery McKenzie, Mary Louise Mark, W. Carson Ryan Jr., and William J. Spillman. Meriam et al., *Problem of Indian Administration.*
21. Meriam et al., *Problem of Indian Administration,* 7–8.
22. Meriam et al., *Problem of Indian Administration.*
23. Meriam et al., *Problem of Indian Administration.*
24. Phinney, "Numipu among the White."
25. Bodley, *Power of Scale.*
26. Bodley, *Cultural Anthropology.*
27. Petersen, *River of Life.*
28. Peterson, *River of Life,* 147.
29. Wilkinson, *American Indians,* 73.
30. Radtke and Davis, *Cost of Doing Nothing.*
31. McCool, *Native Waters,* 79.
32. Lichatowich, *Salmon without Rivers,* 180.
33. Personal communication with the author, 2003.
34. Native Nations Institute, "What Is Native Nation Building?"
35. Wilkins and Lomawaima, *Uneven Ground.*
36. "Columbia River Inter-Tribal."
37. Solomon, "Winters in Salmon Country," 238–57.
38. Hanna, "Native Communities."
39. Zaffos, "Tribes Look to Cash In," 5.
40. Bodley, "Scale, Power, and Sustainability."
41. Augerot and Foley, *Atlas of Pacific Salmon.*
42. Iten et al., "Extirpated Species," 452–73.
43. Parson et al., "Potential Consequences of Climate," 247–80.
44. Cederholm et al., "Pacific Salmon," 628–84.
45. Lichatowich, *Salmon without Rivers,* 180.
46. Kroeber, *Cultural and Natural Areas.*
47. Boyd, "Introduction of Infectious Diseases."

48. Bodley, "Scale, Power, and Sustainability."
49. Augerot and Foley, *Atlas of Pacific Salmon.*
50. Blumm, *Sacrificing the Salmon*; Lichatowich, *Salmon without Rivers.*
51. Parson et al., "Potential Consequences of Climate," 247–80.
52. Battin et al., "Projected Impacts of Climate," 6720–25.
53. Battin et al., "Projected Impacts of Climate."
54. Cornell and Kalt, "Sovereignty and Nation-Building," 187–214.
55. Wallerstein, *Modern World-System I*; Wolf, *Europe and the People.*
56. Wallerstein, *World-Systems Analysis*, 24.
57. Colombi and Brooks, *Keystone Nations.*
58. Kalt et al. *State of Native Nations*, 10.
59. Cornell and Kalt, "Processes of Native Nationhood," 20.
60. Kalt et al. *State of Native Nations*, 10.

BIBLIOGRAPHY

Augerot, Xanthippe, and Dana Foley. *Atlas of Pacific Salmon: The First Map-Based Status Assessment of Salmon in the North Pacific.* Berkeley: University of California Press, 2005.

Axtell, Horace, Kristie Baptiste, Dave Cummings, Rick Eichstaedt, Carla HighEagle, Dave Johnson, Julie Kane, Diane Mallickan, Allen Pinkham, Julie Simpson, et al. *Treaties: Nez Perce Perspectives.* Lewiston ID: Confluence Press, 2003.

Battin, James, Matthew W. Wiley, Mary H. Ruckelshaus, Richard N. Palmer, Elizabeth Korb, Krista K. Bartz, and Hiroo Imaki. "Projected Impacts of Climate Change on Salmon Habitat Restoration." *Proceedings of the National Academy of Sciences of the United States of America* 104, no. 16 (2007): 6720–25.

Blumm, Michael. *Sacrificing the Salmon: A Legal and Policy History of the Decline of Columbia Basin Salmon.* Den Bosch NL: BookWorld, 2002.

Bodley, John H. *Cultural Anthropology: Tribes, States, and the Global System.* Boston: McGraw Hill, 2005.

———. *The Power of Scale: A Global History Approach.* New York: M. E. Sharpe, 2003.

———. "Scale, Power, and Sustainability in the Pacific Northwest." Paper presented at the annual meeting for the Society for Applied Anthropology, Vancouver BC, Canada, March 27, 2006.

Boyd, Robert T. "The Introduction of Infectious Diseases among the Indians of the Pacific Northwest 1774–1874." PhD diss., University of Washington, 1985.

Cederholm, C. Jeff, David H. Johnson, Robert E. Bilby, Lawrence G. Dominguez, Ann M. Garrett, William H. Graeber, Eva L. Greda, Matt D. Kunze, Bruce G. Marcot, John F. Palmisano, et al. "Pacific Salmon and Wildlife-Ecological Contexts, Relationships, and Implications for Management." In *Wildlife-Habitat Relationships in Oregon and Washington*, edited by David H. Johnson and Thomas A. O'Neil, 628–84. Corvallis: Oregon State University, 2001.

Chase-Dunn, Christopher, and Kelly M. Mann. *The Wintu and Their Neighbors: A Very Small World-System in Northern California*. Tucson: University of Arizona Press, 1998.

Colombi, Benedict. "Salmon and the Adaptive Capacity of Nimiipuu (Nez Perce) Culture to Cope with Abrupt Change." *American Indian Quarterly* 36, no. 1 (Winter 2012), 75–97.

Colombi, Benedict J., and Courtland L. Smith. "Adaptive Capacity as Cultural Practice." *Ecology and Society* 17, no. 4, (2012), art. 13. http://dx.doi.org/10.5751/ES-05242-170413.

———. "Insights on Adaptive Capacity: Three Indigenous Pacific Northwest Historical Narratives." *Journal of Northwest Anthropology* 48, no. 2 (2014), 189–202.

Colombi, Benedict J., and James F. Brooks. *Keystone Nations: Indigenous Peoples and Salmon across the North Pacific*. Santa Fe NM: School for Advanced Research Press, 2012.

Cornell, Stephen. "Processes of Native Nationhood: The Indigenous Politics of Self-Government." *International Indigenous Policy Journal* 6, no. 4 (2015): 1–30.

"Columbia River Inter-Tribal Fish Commission" (web page). Accessed August 25, 2010. http://www.critfc.org/.

Cornell, Stephen, and Joseph P. Kalt. "Sovereignty and Nation-Building: The Development Challenge in Indian Country Today." *American Indian Culture and Research Journal* 22, no. 3 (1998): 187–214.

Greenwald, Emily. *Reconfiguring the Reservation: The Nez Perces, Jicarilla Apaches, and the Dawes Act*. Albuquerque: University of New Mexico Press, 2002.

Hanna, Jonathan M. "Native Communities and Climate Change: Protecting Tribal Resources as Part of National Climate Policy." (Boulder CO: Natural Resources Law Center, Colorado Law School, University of Colorado, 2007).

Iten, Constance, Thomas A. O'Neil, Kelly A. Bettinger, and David H. Johnson. "Extirpated Species of Oregon and Washington." In *Wildlife-Habitat Relationships in Oregon and Washington*, edited by David H. Johnson and Thomas A. O'Neil, 452–73. Corvallis: Oregon State University, 2001.

Kalt, Joseph P., Stephen Cornell, Catherine E. A. Curtis, Kenneth W. Grant II, Eric C. Henson, Miriam R. Jorgensen, Harry Nelson, and Jonathan B. Taylor. *The State of Native Nations: Conditions under U.S. Policies of Self-Determination*. Oxford: Oxford University Press, 2008.

Kroeber, Alfred L. *Cultural and Natural Areas of Native North America*. Berkeley: University of California Press, 1939.

Lichatowich, Jim. *Salmon without Rivers: A History of the Pacific Salmon Crisis*. Washington DC: Island Press, 1999.

Marshall, Alan G. "Fish, Water, and Nez Perce Life." *Idaho Law Review* 42 (2006): 763–93.

Meriam, Lewis, et al. *The Problem of Indian Administration: Report of a Survey Made at the Request of Honorable Hubert Work, Secretary of the Interior, and Submitted to Him, February 21, 1928/Survey Staff: Lewis Meriam . . . [et al.]*. Baltimore MD: Johns Hopkins University Press, 1928.

Morrill, Allen, and Eleanor Morrill. "Pioneer Portraits: J. P. Vollmer & James S. Reuben." *Idaho Yesterdays* 18, no. 4 (1975): 4–24.

Mote, Philip W., Edward A. Parson, Alan F. Hamlet, William S. Keeton, Dennis Lettenmaier, Nathan Mantua, Edward L. Miles, David W. Peterson, David L. Peterson, Richard Slaughter, et al. "Preparing for Climatic Change: The Water, Salmon, and Forests of the Pacific Northwest." *Climatic Change* 61, nos. 1–2 (2003): 45–88.

Native Nations Institute. "What is Native Nation Building?" Accessed October 17, 2007. https://nni.arizona.edu/programs-projects/what-native-nation-building.

Parson, Edward A., Phillip W. Mote, Alan Hamlet, Nathan Mantua, Amy Snover, William Keeton, Ed Miles, Douglas Canning, and Kristyn Gray Ideker. "Potential Consequences of Climate Variability and Change for the Pacific Northwest." In *Climate Change Impacts on the United States: The Potential Consequences of Climate Variability and Change*, edited by National Assessment Synthesis Team, 247–80. Cambridge UK: Cambridge University Press, 2001.

Pearson, J. Diane. *The Nez Perces in the Indian Territory: Nimiipuu Survival.* Norman: University of Oklahoma Press, 2008.

Petersen, Keith C. *River of Life, Channel of Death: Fish and Dams on the Lower Snake.* Lewiston ID: Confluence Press, 1995.

Phinney, Archie. "Numipu among the White Settlers." *Wicazō Śa Review* 17, no. 2 (2002): 21–42.

———. *Nez Perce Texts.* New York: Columbia University Press, 1934.

Radtke, Hans D., and Shannon W. Davis. *The Cost of Doing Nothing: The Economic Burden of Salmon Declines in the Columbia River Basin.* Eugene OR: Institute of Fisheries Resources, 1996.

Sklair, Leslie. *Globalization: Capitalism and Its Alternatives.* Oxford: Oxford University Press, 2002.

Slickpoo, Allen P., Sr., and Deward E. Walker, Jr. *Nu Mee Poom Tit Wah Tit: Nez Perce Legends.* Illustrated by Leroy L. Seth. Lapwai ID: Nez Perce Tribe of Idaho, 1972.

Solomon, Mark. "Winters in Salmon Country: The Nez Perce Tribe Instream Flow Claims." In *The Future of Indian and Federal Reserved Water Rights: The Winters Centennial*, edited by Barbara Cosens and Judith V. Roysten, 37–43. Albuquerque NM: University of New Mexico Press, 2012.

Spinden, Herbert Joseph. "The Nez Perce Indians." In Vol. 2, part 3 of *Memoirs of the American Anthropological Association*, 165–72. Lacaster PA: New Era, 1908.

Walker, Deward E., Jr. *Conflict and Schism in Nez Perce Acculturation: A Study of Religion and Politics.* Pullman: Washington State University Press, 1968.

———. *Nez Perce Coyote Tales: The Myth Cycle.* In collaboration with Daniel N. Mathews, illustrations by Marc Seahmer. Norman: University of Oklahoma Press, 1998.

———. "Nez Perce." In *Handbook of North American Indians*, edited by Deward E. Walker, Jr. Washington DC: Smithsonian Institution, 1998.

Wallerstein, Immanuel. *The Modern World-System I: Capitalist Agriculture and the Origins of the European World-Economy in the Sixteenth Century.* New York: Academic Press, 1974.

———. *World-Systems Analysis: An Introduction.* Durham NC: Duke University Press, 2004.

Wells, Donald N. "Farmers Forgotten: Nez Perce Suppliers of the North Idaho Gold Rush Days." *Idaho Yesterdays* 2, no. 5 (1958): 28–32.

Wilkins, David E., and K. Tsianina Lomawaima. *Uneven Ground: American Indian Sovereignty and Federal Law*. Norman: University of Oklahoma Press, 2001.

Wilkinson, Charles F. *American Indians, Time, and the Law: Native Societies in a Modern Constitutional Democracy*. New Haven: Yale University Press, 1987.

Wolf, Eric. *Europe and the People without History*. Berkeley: University of California Press, 1987.

Zaffos, Joshua. "Tribes Look to Cash In with 'Tree-Market' Environmentalism." *High Country News* 13, no. 5 (2006): 5.

9 Sovereignty as Accountability
Theorizing from the Osage Nation
JEAN DENNISON

The inaugural Osage Sovereignty Day took place on the Osage campus in Pawhuska, Oklahoma, on an unseasonably warm February day in 2005. It was held to celebrate the passage of Public Law 108-431, which sought "to reaffirm the inherent sovereign rights of the Osage Tribe to determine its membership and form of government" and had just been enacted into United States law. Following a signing of the Osage Declaration of Sovereignty and Independence, which states that the inherent sovereign rights of the Osage Nation not only existed prior to the United States Constitution but continues to exist today, a large crowd gathered for the rest of the day's events in an enormous white pavilion tent. Before the processional began, the lead singer stood up, thanked his fellow singers for joining him at the drum, and quietly remarked to them, "Today is a big day for our people here. All of our ancestors were up on this hill just like we are doing now. We want these people to get that feeling today. When you are singing today bring that feeling in here." Sitting back down, he nodded, and the drumming began.

While not referencing sovereignty directly, the singer's short speech reflected the theme of Sovereignty Day as much as the many longer formal speeches to follow. Because the Osage had existed as a political body prior to the American Constitution, Osage sovereignty is understood here as a feeling that needs to be brought forward. The authority of the past must be enacted to further the future. As this singer's comments signal, sovereignty is understood here as a mental framework that must be harnessed and enacted. The question remains, however, as to what exactly "that feeling" is.

Pulling from the speeches of Osage Nation government officials over the last ten years as well as Osage citizen responses, this chapter highlights Osage theories of sovereignty. This focus on Osage theoretical perspectives is intentional: it seeks to build on Indigenous thinkers within the academy who disrupt the centrality of universal European theories by privileging theories derived from and serving the interests of Indigenous peoples.[1] Theorizing from Indigenous perspectives is certainly nothing new in the academy, but it has taken on new forms as more Indigenous peoples have themselves become recognized authors and scholars.

One of the many examples of theorizing from Indigenous perspectives is Renya Ramirez's *Native Hubs*. In the book's introduction, the central tenant (the hub) is described as coming directly from Laverne Roberts, a Paiute and a founder of the nonprofit American Indian Alliance based in San Jose, California. Such nonexoticized usage of Indigenous perspectives as theory serves to destabilize elitist notions of what theory is and where it comes from. It also fundamentally shifts not only the perspectives theory can provide but also the structures of power in knowledge itself. By focusing on Indigenous theories, I similarly seek to continue this work of *indigenizing the academy*—that is, making academia a place where more Native American and Indigenous peoples can thrive and work toward building a stronger future for our communities.

An indigenizing approach to scholarship attempts to articulate theory as it emanates from a wide variety of sources rather than articulating only what Anaheed Al-Hardan describes as theory with a capital "T": "the practice of referring to and paying homage to what are usually dead European men." Al-Hardan argues that "theory used in this gate-keeping way is not an apolitical or distant intellectual exercise, but a way to reinforce an intellectual class hierarchy in the academy, and with it, a colonial and Eurocentric 'ego-politics of knowledge.'"[2] Indigenizing theory means challenging its Eurocentric origins and applicability. It also means discrediting limited Eurocentric models and privileging the general applicability of differently situated theories.

Sovereignty in the Osage context is most often theorized as a tool for increasing accountability. In the wake of a hundred years of direct federal control over Osage governance, Osage officials in the early 21st century frequently make the case that the federal government has not looked after Osage interests and that a sovereign Osage government could be more accountable to Osage needs. Positioning sovereignty as accountability is an intentional move by officials to bring into question settler claims to authority over Osage bodies and territories as well as to assert that if Osage people assert sovereignty, they can better serve Osage interests. While these officials are primarily focused on what sovereignty should mean in local contexts, they are also intentionally insisting on a connection between sovereignty and accountability writ large. Following a discussion of some of the prominent theories of sovereignty among non-Indigenous and Indigenous scholars, this chapter turns to Osage oratory as a tool for indigenizing theories of sovereignty.

Sovereignty as a State of Exception

Linking sovereignty to accountability is quite different from how sovereignty is most frequently discussed in academic literature today. Giorgio Agamben's understanding of sovereignty, which derives directly from Carl Schmitt and other Western thinkers, has now become ubiquitous within scholarly debates.[3] Agamben's work has served as an important space from which to critique settler-colonial assertions of sovereignty.[4] This focus on sovereignty as a "state of exception" assumes that sovereign governance is, at its core, outside the rules of society and thus unable to be held accountable.[5] Such definitions of sovereign power fit within longstanding understandings of sovereignty as an attribute of statehood and statehood as unique to European styles of governance.[6]

In English language texts, sovereignty is usually given a European origin. One popular narrative—forwarded by political scientist Robert Jackson, among others—is that seventeenth-century European rulers claimed sovereignty in moments of political crisis as a means of asserting their supreme authority over their territory, against the authority claimed by the Pope as well as other rival rulers.[7] Other treatments of sovereignty cite sixteenth-century French jurist Jean Bodin and seventeenth-century philosopher Thomas Hobbes, who both argued that rulers of states should have absolute authority within their own realms.[8] Still others, such as Michel Foucault, take the idea back further to ancient Roman times, when emperors claimed sovereign authority in moments of emergency.[9] Whatever its origin story, "modern" sovereignty is too often seen as rooted in the European nation-state system and tied to the absolute authority of a ruler.

Such stories about sovereignty are never neutral; they do work in the world. These stories tie legitimate territorial authority to state governments, particularly European nation-states, and even, or perhaps especially, when these governments represent colonial forces that are subjugating Native populations. They also serve to discredit Indigenous forms of governance. Much has been made of Hobbes's contrast of the state of nature, in which violence predominates, with civil society, in which authority has been surrendered to a sovereign ruler. *Johnson v. McIntosh*, a unanimous United States Supreme Court ruling in 1823, justified European conquest of the land in these terms: "The Tribes of Indians inhabiting this country were fierce savages whose occupation was war, and whose subsistence was drawn chiefly from the forest. To leave them in possession of their country, was to leave the country a wilderness."[10] In this context indigeneity and sovereignty are constructed as mutually exclusive categories, which clearly serves to justify colonization.

While European nations, and later the United States, recognized Indigenous nations' territorial authority through treaties, laws, court decisions, and in practice, they have attempted to reserve full sovereignty for settler nation-state governments. In 1831 the Courts of the United States recognized American Indian nations as "domestic dependent nations," generally meaning that they are subject to U.S. federal law but not state law.[11] Popular representations of Indigenous peoples as part of nature, as less evolved "kinship-based" polities, as a dying race, and as a disappearing culture all contribute to discrediting Indigenous sovereignty today; these thus serve the ongoing colonial process.

While it is important to understand sovereignty as a term with its own history, it must also be understood that these are never simply academic arguments.[12] These debates take place within larger colonial struggles over authority and power, where there is a lot at stake in claiming or denying sovereignty. Perhaps even more dangerous, they also run the risk of reifying colonial sovereignty in ways that further contribute to the solidifying of the settler state's authority. In turning to Indigenous definitions of sovereignty, there is the possibility of not only understanding the broader set of meanings that surround the term but also reworking the power structures that terms like "sovereignty" sustain.

Indigenous Theories of Sovereignty

This chapter builds on a rich debate among Indigenous scholars about the usefulness of sovereignty in our scholarship and to Indigenous peoples. Perhaps most notorious, Gerald Taiaiake Alfred (Kahnawake Mohawk) goes as far as to argue that "'sovereignty' is inappropriate as a political objective for Indigenous peoples."[13] While he and others offer a vital critique of the ways that the current system of federal recognition is limiting, his assumptions about what sovereignty is and can be are both inadequate and dangerous.[14] Alfred frames sovereignty and indigeneity as having "two fundamentally opposed value systems," thus perpetuating essentialist settler-colonial binaries and limiting possibilities for Indigenous futures.[15] He also sees current Indigenous politicians as using sovereignty to create "a zero-sum contest for power," which, as the Osage case illustrates, is not always the reality.[16]

In his discussion of what a postsovereignty approach should look like, Alfred does offer some useful ways to go about repatriating theories of sovereignty to serve Indigenous nations. Notably, he argues that "the reification of sovereignty in politics today is the result of a triumph of a particular set of ideas over others—no more natural to the world than any other man-made object." This is a helpful reminder to pay close attention to the values contained and perpetuated within our notions of sovereignty and how the term is being deployed. He also argues for moving past the view "that there is only one right way to see and do things," which can be dangerous in limiting the ways that sovereignty is sometimes understood. Finally, as Alfred argues, "in the last two or three generations, there has been movement for the good in terms of rebuilding social cohesion, gaining economic self-sufficiency, and empowering structures of self-government within Indigenous communities."[17] I contend that as Native communities are defining it, sovereignty is often understood as playing a central role in these movements.

To address some of Alfred's concerns, Indigenous scholars have developed the concept of "cultural sovereignty," which is understood as a definition of sovereignty that is "generated within our tribal communities, rather than as a defensive response to attacks from the outside."[18] While this is a productive step away from an overly settler state–based definition of sovereignty, cultural sovereignty too has some serious dangers. First, such an approach plays into existing popular representations of Indigenous peoples as cultures first and foremost rather than as polities. Rarely within mainstream media representations are Indigenous peoples referred to as nations, but almost all such representations contain imagery of Indigenous people dancing, beating drums, or playing flutes. Even the common political terms used to describe Indigenous peoples (such as "member," "tribe," and "chief") work to downplay the political nature of these groups.[19]

Joanne Barker (Lenape) writes about how Indigenous peoples have been denied sovereignty through various processes of depoliticization, including a focus on "cultural authenticity, racial purity, and traditional integrity" rather than the political aspects of these peoples. While her deep skepticism of the term "sovereignty" is clear throughout her writing, she does usefully position sovereignty as best theorized by Indigenous peoples themselves. She writes, "The challenge to understand how and for whom sovereignty matters is to understand the historical circumstances under which it is given meaning."[20] Turning to Osage theories of sovereignty in the second half of this chapter, I attempt to demonstrate not only for whom sovereignty matters but also what it is understood as mattering for.

Another peril of the cultural-sovereignty approach is how its focus on culture and tradition creates dangerous notions of authenticity. In the settler-colonial process, wherein the colonizers have come to stay, the "logic of elimination" functions as one of the primary tactics of colonization. Settlement requires territory, therefore necessitating the elimination of others' claims to the land.[21] While the intentional erosion of American

Indian cultural ways is a central part of this logic, settler colonialism also works by denying American Indians the ability to change by insisting on their unbroken connections to a static notion of culture and creating generalized stereotypes about what constitutes an American Indian. Living up to the standards of authenticity set by the settler state—standards too often internalized within our own communities—proves an almost impossible task, which in turn furthers the logic of elimination.[22]

Finally, such a focus on the "difference" of Indigenous sovereignty creates a dangerous and inaccurate definition of Indigenous sovereignty as an exception to the unmarked or unqualified sovereignty of the settler state. For example, Kevin Bruyneel talks of Indigenous sovereignty as existing within a "third space." Stemming from the work of Homi Bhabha and other postcolonial theorists, the "third space" is an attempt to move away from the authority of binaries.[23] For Bruyneel, this concept describes the way American Indian sovereignty occupies territory neither strictly inside nor outside the American political system; it instead relies on historical ambivalence to open possibilities for self-determination.[24]

While a useful tool for critiquing colonial narratives that attempt to entirely erase Indigenous authority from their territory, the "third space" fails to account for the ways in which sovereignty across the globe is always contingent. Rather than seeing American Indian sovereignty as fundamentally different—and thus too easily reading it as lesser than the sovereignty of settler states—it is more productive to use Indigenous-settler disputes over authority to expand our understanding of sovereignty more generally.

Valerie Lambert (Choctaw) writes, "The Choctaws and other Indian tribes in the United States are not alone in having to negotiate certain aspects of their sovereignty. All nations must (and do)."[25] Lambert goes on to explain that in the American Indian context, sovereignty is a set of inherent rights. These include the ability to "elect their own leaders, determine their own membership, maintain tribal police forces, levy taxes, regulate property under tribal jurisdiction, control the conduct of their members by tribal ordinances, regulate the domestic relations of their members, and administer justice." These inherent rights, however, are not without contestation by either the State of Oklahoma or the United States government, which have "overlapping and competing sovereignties."[26] Sovereignty here is understood as the right of a group of people to control their own affairs and make decisions on the issues that affect their lives.

Within the United States, the relationships between governments, including establishing exact jurisdiction, is still quite dynamic—as is the case with, for example, the legalization of marijuana in several states or the debt owed by the United States to China. Additionally, the continued existence of Indigenous populations brings all claims of complete and justified sovereignty into question.[27] Rather than a kind of fixed authority over a territory, sovereignty must instead be understood as a series of power-laden entanglements that are neither straightforward nor consistent through time.[28]

Jodi Byrd (Chickasaw) also outlines many of these same efforts to theorize sovereignty within current Indigenous studies, speaking directly to the dangers and possibilities of Indigenous articulations of sovereignty. She eloquently concludes, "In the context of Indigenous studies, we cannot not want sovereignty. However, we must remain vigilant as a matter of methodology to maintain the persistent critiques that will disrupt the hegemonies that have naturalized sovereignty as the only difference that matters."[29] This dual goal of articulating Indigenous authority as existing in the same realm as other claims to authority, while also maintaining a critical eye for the entanglements of these articulations, must be the primary project of indigenizing sovereignty.

Like Audra Simpson, I argue that the term "sovereignty" is useful for its ability to insist on the legitimacy of self-governance within a territory, which continues to be of deep importance to many Indigenous peoples today.[30] Osage sovereignty, like other Indigenous sovereignty, is inherent in that it existed before the colonial process and continues to exist through and outside colonial recognition. This is, however, a political sovereignty, not unlike that claimed by other nations across the globe; it therefore comes into conflict with other sovereign claims, creating realms of contention. If sovereignty cannot be understood as fixed, in terms of either a rigid territorial authority or even an exact meaning, then our understanding of sovereignty will benefit a great deal from looking at how it is actually articulated in context.

From 2005 to 2015 Osage Nation officials talked at length about the significance of Osage sovereignty as a tool of accountability. This strong connection between accountability and sovereignty no doubt serves to give sovereignty, and by extension these government officials, validity and importance in the minds of the general Osage population. While there is always a danger that this connection is mere political rhetoric, this chapter explores how this link between sovereignty and accountability can also be a tool for people to discredit what they see as unaccountable settler practices. As David Wilkins (Lumbee) usefully argues, "sovereignty does not mean that leaders are above the people. Sovereignty means leaders have a profound responsibility to the people. It is up to the people to hold their leader accountable for their words and deeds."[31] Once the link between sovereignty and accountability has been made, officials must, at the very least, prove they are accountable prior to the next election. In the Osage context, indigenizing sovereignty means creating a government that is more accountable to the Osage people than to the colonial government they have been under for the past hundred years.

"Self-Governance Will Make Us More Accountable"

Following the inaugural Osage Sovereignty Day processional and several other shorter speeches, Chief Gray rose to give his official Sovereignty Day address. In his speech he discussed his understanding of what sovereignty means to the Osage:

> Over a hundred years ago, a man named Wa-Ti-a-kah, my forefather, was sent to this land, and he said, "There is something in the land that will ensure that our children will never starve." Many of us thought that to be oil. Today, I know what he meant—the sovereignty of the Osage Nation, and that is what will sustain us . . . Exercising our tribal sovereignty in the areas of self-governance will make us more accountable to our people and make us more informed to make better decisions as a nation . . . For after today, the Osage themselves must move back and take their sovereignty.

Chief Gray here connects sovereignty to oil, a key metaphor for many Osage, whose primary income has been based on oil revenues for over a century. In doing so, Gray defines the power of sovereignty in positive terms, as something that "will sustain us." He also relates sovereignty to self-determination and informed decision-making. Perhaps most telling, Gray defines sovereignty as something that will bring about accountability.

This act of taking sovereignty back is seen as a vital part of the indigenizing process. Over the last hundred years the Osage Nation has faced extreme mismanagement by the U.S. government. The United States has insisted that the Osage operate under a limited tribal-council structure, in which corruption was rampant and only a fraction of Osage could vote. Furthermore, the Bureau of Indian Affairs (BIA) has been successfully sued in federal courts for mismanagement, including a $380 million settlement for the mismanagement of the Osage Mineral Estate. Given the extreme nature of these failures, it is little wonder that many Osage would find the concept of self-control appealing and more likely to lead to greater accountability.

The connection between sovereignty and accountability not only shifts the focus of current discussions of sovereignty but also challenges current theories of accountability. In much of the contemporary literature on "audit cultures" across the globe, practices of accountability are seen as part and parcel of neoliberal governmentality or the proliferations of NGOs.[32] As Andrew Kipnis points out, however, this assumes that these practices can only ever be derivative of the West.[33] It is certainly true that systems of accountability contain and promote a variety of ideals, with chain of command and individual responsibility no doubt being the most deep-seated. The danger with this literature, particularly in the context of historical and ongoing colonization, is that it assumes a unidirectional flow between "center" and "periphery," as if theories, values, and practices can only move from an imagined core out to the margin and never be reimagined or retooled.

Accountability is certainly not a new concept within Osage governance. As Mary Joe Webb, Osage elder and one of the writers of the 2006 Osage Nation Constitution, describes, accountability was at the core of the oldest known Osage structure of governance. Drawing both from her family's oral history and Garrick Bailey's writings on Francis La Flesche,

Webb describes a structure made up of the "sky people" and the "earth people," each with their own high chief and lesser chiefs. Meeting yearly in the fall, it was only possible for the Osage nations to come together if all the representatives were there, as representatives had their own part to contribute, which only they knew. If there were any disharmony in the tribe, they would have to work it out before the meeting. This, Webb argued, was the people's way of ensuring harmony within the nation and holding everyone accountable.[34]

This chapter understands Osage desires for accountability not as fundamentally "Western" in origin or inherently oppressive in nature but as a potential tool for building a stronger Osage future. In challenging the failures of settler governments to meet the needs of Indigenous populations, and in asserting the desire to maintain governance structures in which Indigenous people are the sole electorate, these calls for accountability fundamentally challenge the ongoing settler-colonial process. This does not mean that all implemented accountability practices are inherently good or without their own challenges and power dynamics. Instead, accountability must be seen as entangled in this settler-colonial moment, in which Indigenous populations are seeking to weave their own futures out of the various materials they have available to them.[35] More research is needed to understand exactly what these calls for accountability are creating in the Osage and in other contexts.

"It's Yours to Determine What Your Government Wants to Be"

Following the Osage Nation Sovereignty Day in 2005, the Osage Tribal Council appointed ten Oklahoma Osages to the Osage Government Reform Commission (OGRC) and tasked them with reforming the Osage government, including the Osage's citizenship criteria. Throughout this process, sovereignty was a word frequently deployed in calls for increased accountability, sustainable economic development, and cultural revitalization. All of these calls for improvement were seen as dependent on increased Osage control. In order for an Osage government to be accountable, it was argued, the Osage Nation had to assert sovereignty.

Shortly after the OGRC had been appointed, Leonard Maker, the head of planning for the tribe, addressed the new commissioners and spoke of the commission's job in educating the public about sovereignty: "Most of our people don't understand sovereignty; it's not part of their daily life. They say, It's a nice phrase but what does it mean to me? . . . I think that's one of the tasks of the commission, to make sure that people are aware of what sovereignty is and why it's important."[36] Maker then went on to describe the tangible results of "enacting sovereignty," such as the tribe's status as the largest employer in the area, the opening of the new casino, and the administration of tribal programs in areas such as education, health, and housing. He frequently asked what the current Osage government had done for the Osage people, and he wanted to build a nation that would better provide for Osage needs through services and economic development. Whether or not Maker had been correct in his assessment of the Osage public, it was clear that he felt the central goal of the reform process was not only to further assert Osage authority but also help the Osage people understand the connection between sovereignty and directly serving Osage needs.

In an interview I conducted with him a year earlier, Maker also emphasized the people's lack of knowledge about the meaning of sovereignty; he concluded by saying that sovereignty was ultimately "the ability of our tribe to meet the needs of our own people in a way that is special to us."[37] Here, Maker is not just arguing for the rights of the Osage Nation but also for the Nation's obligation to meet the needs of its people. In the first round of community meetings, Maker further explained his understanding of sovereignty in relation to the bill recently passed by the U.S. government recognizing the Osage right to determine their own affairs:

> "Congress hereby reaffirms the inherent sovereign right of the Osage Tribe to determine its own form of government," which is as broad a statement as you can make in terms of federal law as to what this tribe's right is. That means we can do whatever we want. We don't need the Secretary to approve it; we don't need the President to approve it; it's ours; it's yours to determine what your government wants to be. It is also an idea that this is an expression of Osage sovereignty. It's up to us to not have other people telling us what to do.[38]

This understanding, that the Osage people have not just the right but also the obligation to take this moment and make something out of it, was central to Maker's theory of sovereignty.

One young Osage said of the recent law in another community meeting, "[It] basically takes all the handcuffs and all the shackles off us as a tribe . . . We're creating a government; a new one. We get to pick it; we get to decide what it is. It is our decision, nobody else's . . . and I think we're more than capable of handling it."[39] Such theories of sovereignty during the reform process can be seen as a call to action. Because the Osage tribal government had been focused almost exclusively on the Mineral Estate for close to a hundred years, some Osage hoped that the 2004–6 reform process would be a conduit for change that would, once again, privilege the needs and desires of all Osage people in areas far beyond the extraction of natural resources. Sovereignty in this context meant that the Osage themselves needed to take control over their own affairs, which was seen as the first and most essential step in creating accountable governance.

"You Have to Have Faith in Yourself"

Not all Osage were in support of the passage of the 2006 Osage Constitution or the assertion of full Osage sovereignty. The Osage Shareholders Association (OSA) took the most vocal stand against the 2006 Constitution, led initiatives against its passage, and advocated for its reform.[40] The OSA is a group of Osage annuitants who organized in 1994 in Pawhuska, Oklahoma, for the purpose of protecting the federal trust relationship with the Mineral Estate and encouraging better management of the Mineral Estate by the BIA. While certainly not representative of a majority of Osage, the group is made up of the most vocal and politically active of the Osage citizens and has therefore continued to play a formidable role in Osage politics for most of the ten years following the passage of the Constitution.

The August 2005 OSA meeting was held at the Dave Landrum Community Center in Pawhuska, Oklahoma, a neutral space outside the control of the Osage Nation. Most of those in attendance were women over the age of sixty, and they sat at the round tables that filled the room, some joking and laughing while others engaged in intense conversation. Jim Gray,

Chief of the Osage Nation, was scheduled to give a talk on the importance of entering into self-government compacts with the federal government.

In 1975 the U.S. Congress adopted the Indian Self-Determination and Education Assistance Act, which enabled the transference of resources from the BIA to the nations themselves. Rather than having the BIA oversee all the programs, services, functions, and activities of each nation, interested American Indian nations negotiated with the BIA to establish the roles and responsibilities each government would have in running various programs. This transference allowed nations to have far greater representation in how programs, ranging from health care to mineral leasing, would serve national needs as well as how federal funds would be used. Chief Gray, hoping to build a stronger and larger Osage Nation, argued that the compacting process would lead to a greater ability to meet Osage needs.

Chief Gray opened with a discussion about the responsibilities of getting ready for the new governing structure and the excitement of this moment in Osage history. He asserted that sovereignty through self-governance would improve Osage lives and the economy of the area, and he cited the Harvard Project's research on economic development to argue that everyone would benefit from an Osage takeover of more control from the BIA. Focusing much of his attention on the Osage Mineral Estate, he argued that compacting would increase accountability and allow the Osage to better monitor the oil at each stage, putting an end to the theft and mismanagement that had plagued the Osage Mineral Estate for a hundred years. After talking for approximately thirty minutes about the benefits of self-governance, he opened the floor to questions.

Those in attendance eagerly asked pointed questions for the next forty minutes, which, while all very critical of Gray's plans, continued to make strong connections between sovereignty and accountability. One of the first to speak asked, "According to the article that came out in the Tulsa paper, the Osage Tribe is not really in compliance with [the National Indian Gaming Commission (NIGC)] on some things. If they're not capable of handling this and getting all their ducks in a row, why should we trust the Council now to manage the minerals?"[41] While Chief Gray responded that the arguments by the NIGC were "just part of the process" and that the Osage were doing exactly what needed to be done, concerns that the Osage were unprepared for increased authority could not be assuaged.

Others at the meeting continued this line of argument by saying that the Nation was losing money on many of their enterprises, most notably the Palace Grocery store, and should not yet be expanding its authority over the Mineral Estate. The concern that the Osage Nation was overextending itself did have some legitimacy. Over the last hundred years the United States and the State of Oklahoma had limited the scope of the Osage Nation so that it did not have in place the complete infrastructure necessary for immediate expansion. For example, the Osage Nation did not yet have in place the environmental laws needed to regulate mineral extraction. In the case of the grocery store, although it did temporarily turn a profit, the Nation was ultimately forced to sell it. In these conversations there was still a clear link between sovereignty and accountability, but this manifested as a concern that given the ongoing colonial impediments, the Osage did not yet have the infrastructure or experience needed to succeed at sovereignty. Sovereignty should not be exercised, it was argued, until it was truly possible for the government to be accountable to the Osage people.

These interrogations signal the tenuous position of the Osage Nation in this moment of ongoing settler colonialism, but they must also be read in their political context. The act of creating a larger constitution-style government would inevitably shrink the authority of headright holders. The Osage that filled this room had the most to lose with the upcoming reform process, and the timing of compacting, along with Chief Gray's speech linking the two efforts, did little to garner their support for the process. Having battled the federal government for the last hundred years to extend the life of the Mineral Estate, it is little wonder that these Osage annuitants would now decide that the safest road was to maintain the status quo, especially when they felt that their quarterly payments from the Osage Mineral Estate were at stake. In this way it is possible to see the two primary concerns for annuitants: the right to profit from their shares in the Mineral Estate and the right to exclusive governance of Osage national affairs.

There was, however, a third aspect to their resistance to the constitutional process. Many of the members of the OSA worried that any assertion of Osage sovereignty would weaken the accountability of the United States government to Osage affairs. This concern surfaced when a woman asked, "If you take the contract from the BIA, what protection do we still have that it is still in restricted funds? Because, once you take it out of the BIA, it loses all restrictions."[42] Her primary concern here was whether the government reform was going to threaten the trust relationship of the Mineral Estate, which she and other OSA members worried would end the United States government's protection of Osage interests—or worse, that the communal resource would be distributed to the individual surface owners instead of Osage annuitants.

Again, we see within these OSA concerns a direct connection between sovereignty and accountability. As the United States asserted sovereignty over the territory, it tried to establish itself as "protector" of American Indian nations.[43] The 1808 and subsequent Osage treaties are riddled with such phrases. For example, Article 10 of the 1808 Osage treaty reads, "The United States receives the Great and Little Osage nations into their friendship and under their protection; and the said nations, on their part, declare that they will consider themselves under the protection of no other power whatsoever."[44] The Supreme Court first suggested the existence of a trust relationship in the 1831 case *Cherokee Nation v. Georgia.* Chief Justice John Marshall's majority opinion characterized the Cherokee Nation as "a domestic dependent nation . . . in a state of pupilage . . . [t] heir relation to the United States resembles that of a ward to his guardian."[45] This language of "ward," "pupil," and "protection" are all, despite their problematic infantilizing of Indigenous people, different ways of referring to a kind of accountability.

In 1942 the United States Supreme Court held that this promised protection created a unique bond between the United States and each recognized American Indian nation, imposing on the federal government "moral obligations of the highest responsibility and trust."[46] Although treaty making ended in 1871, another Supreme Court case held that laws could also create a trust responsibility, since they would be used to fulfill treaty obligations and stipulate further fiduciary responsibility.[47] Since the Congress has plenary power, which allows it to change or negate any of its trust responsibilities, these are moral obligations rather than any genuine guarantee of accountability.[48] Here again there is a clear link between assertions of sovereignty and accountability. As the United States has attempted to assert sovereign authority over Indigenous lands and bodies, it has done so by insisting, at least in its words, that it is responsible for the welfare of Indigenous peoples.

The Osage Nation has long used its relationship with other nations, including the United States government, to establish its authority. As Kathleen DuVal writes, the Osage historically placed great value on their relations with European nations: "The Osage took advantage of French exchange to build their own trading empire, expanding onto new lands, and casting out native rivals . . . Rather than weakness, interdependence was a form of power. A people with no links of interdependence could be in trouble, as Europeans quickly discovered."[49] American paternalism, in the form of the management of Osage funds from oil proceeds, is likewise perceived by many Osage annuitants as part of this legacy of responsibility as well as one of the obligations the federal government owes the Osage people in exchange for all of the lands and resources that have been extorted from the latter. While all nations strive to form alliances with other nations, this relationship with the United States has been more paternalistic than mutually interdependent. The trust relationship thus functions to bolster United States sovereignty claims through the appearance of accountability over the Osage Mineral Estate.

Chief Gray responded to OSA members' concerns by saying, "The law of self-governance has been on the books for decades. Over the years, tribes have engaged in taking over these BIA programs. Part of the critical elements of this bill ever getting passed to begin with, and a significant issue for all the tribes who have compacted over half of the BIA budget now, is that the trust relationship has not changed. This is a negotiated management agreement between the tribe and the federal government. . . . The benefits of self-governance are not fear, but hope. You have to have faith in yourself and faith in your other tribal members to assume that we can bring the tools and resources together." Throughout his tenure as chief of the Osage, Gray argued adamantly for building a powerful Osage Nation. Drawing on the tools and tactics of other successful American Indian nations, Gray hoped to strengthen accountability through an assertion of Osage Nation sovereignty.

Members of the OSA, however, did everything in their power to block these efforts, convincing the Osage government for at least the next ten years that compacting the Mineral Estate was not a good political strategy. For these Osage annuitants, assertions of sovereignty through self-governance were dangerous because the Osage government was not ready to be fully accountable. This sense of Osage deficiency was clearly a result of ongoing colonialism, both in the sense that the United States government had limited the structure and scope of Osage governance for a hundred years and in the sense that these Osage felt the United States government would be more accountable than any Osage administration could be at this time. Despite this skepticism of the Osage Nation's abilities, sovereignty was still linked directly to accountability. For these OSA members, asserting Osage sovereignty was dangerous not only because the Osage were unequipped to be fully accountable but also because the United States would no longer be held accountable in the same way.

"The Nation's Expression of Its People's Values"

Ten years after the inaugural Osage Sovereignty Day, Osage leaders, now operating under the 2006 Osage Constitution, once again gathered to reflect on what sovereignty meant to the nation. Filling the platform at the front of the Osage Congressional Chambers, each leader stood and talked about the ongoing projects they were involved in. They addressed Osage programs that protected the land, taught the Osage language, and educated Osage children. While an event like this was clearly an act of self-promotion for these government officials, it also provides important examples of how sovereignty is theorized. Congressional Speaker Maria Whitehorn described sovereignty as "an idea put into action" and talked about how Osage laws, programs, and daily practices continued to enact Osage sovereignty on a daily basis.[50] Through these discussions, sovereignty was envisioned as enabling Osages to develop these programs but also as strengthened through the enactment of laws and programs for the Osage, by the Osage.

Assistant Chief Raymond Red Corn outlined a new program that would create a space for Osages to grow their own food. He argued that Osages needed to "once again feed ourselves, that is a fundamental right, that is a fundamental obligation and nothing secures our futures more than that ability."[51] As articulated in earlier Osage discussions of sovereignty, accountability was seen to be a key element. Here articulated as a "fundamental obligation," Osage sovereignty was tied directly to its ability to feed its people. This is, significantly, not a sovereignty based on partial authority alone but one based on taking care of and meeting the needs of future Osage generations.

Another key aspect of sovereignty as envisioned during the 2015 Osage Sovereignty Day was creating a government accountable to Osage values. Supreme Court Justice Meredith Drent talked about sovereignty as "the Nation's expression of its people's values—they're reflected in our actions, in our politics, priorities, and in our views." She said sovereignty also shows itself in several ways: "The way we govern our resources, how we manage our assets, how we raise our children, care for our elders and our sick, how we honor those who came before us and remember those who have passed."[52] Unlike theorizations of sovereignty as something that is inherently Western and thus non-Indigenous, Osage leaders clearly articulated the ways in which they saw sovereignty as distinctly serving Osage values, and, in fact, stemming from these values themselves.[53] This move at once challenges the dangerous binary between "Western/ political" and "Indigenous/cultural," and it illustrates the fluidity of the concept of sovereignty.

Critiquing the temptation to "equate the freedom struggles of subaltern 'peoples' with the establishment of some form of sovereignty," Alvaro Reyes and Mara Kaufman draw upon several European scholars to argue that sovereign power will by definition always define the norms, foreclosing any possibility that sovereign power can itself be defined by, or even held accountable to, existing community values.[54] In direct contradiction to this theorization of sovereignty, here we see Osage leaders arguing for just the opposite, saying that the values of the people are at the core of how sovereignty is being enacted in the Osage Nation today. The danger remains, however, in whether these values, even if truly derived from the people, will then work to further entrench existing power structures.

Judge Drent's connection between sovereignty and Osage values did not adopt the sometimes-static quality of "culture"; it was instead theorized as something inherently fluid.[55] As Judge Drent went on to say, "Sovereignty is a moving target, we must move with it as the rest of the world changes . . . sovereignty is our way to show the world we are here, we have a voice, we have strength, we learn, we grow and we change, we have a place in this community, in this county and this country, in this state, and the world at-large."[56] Here, Judge Drent theorizes that sovereignty is foundational yet flexible enough to address the people's current needs. Sovereignty also signals that the Osage as a nation has carved out a space in the world. Unlike other available tools for defining who the Osage people are (a unique culture, a separate race of people, or shareholders in the Osage Mineral Estate, for instance), sovereignty provides the most potential for imagining a strong national future.[57]

These visions of sovereignty can perhaps be best visualized as a bridge, whereby each support beam enables the bridge to last longer and carry greater weight. The more that is put into sovereignty—envisioned here as happening both through everyday Osage practice and these government-sponsored programs—the stronger the bridge becomes. Sovereignty simultaneously serves as a flexible structure whose foundation needs proper support and an escort for moving between the past and the future. As special guest speaker Erin Casoose, a senior from a local high school, outlined, this bridge acts as a means of transporting Osage values. She explained her own meaning of sovereignty: "[It means] culture, community, and family . . . I know where I'm going, I know who I am, and I know where I come from."[58] More than merely a connection between past and present, sovereignty offers direction and support. Sovereignty facilitates movement with the changing world but in ways that continue to allow the Osage people to tread their own path.

Conclusion: Accountability in Practice

As the Osage Nation has continued to build a governing structure in the twenty-first century that can assert more authority over Osage affairs, various structures of accountability have been implemented. With the passage of the 2006 Osage Nation Constitution, the Osage have shifted from a single ten-member council to a constitutional government with legislative, executive, and judicial branches, as well as a constitutionally mandated board structure, creating an intricate system of checks and balances. During the same period, the Osage moved from a funding structure limited to $1 million in mineral extraction proceeds and various federal and nonprofit grant funds to an escalating enterprise, along with tax revenue that today totals over $80 million. These changes have led to a vast bureaucratic expansion, which now includes over five hundred employees and fifty programs.

Shifting from a sparsely funded, colonially imposed, structurally limited government with a deeply unengaged polity is no easy task, but it is one the current Osage administration has taken up with great zeal. In 2016 Osage theories of accountability manifest daily in the questions of government officials over whom exactly the government should be accountable to (those living within the Nation's jurisdiction or all voters), how it should be held accountable, and by whom. For example, in 2015 the Osage Nation compacted the Indian Health Clinic from the United States government and now runs it themselves. In addition to a director, the organization is currently accountable to a division leader, the independent Health Authority Board, the Osage chief and his immediate staff, the HR office (including a self-, supervisor-, and peer-merit review), the accounting office, the Congress, the Accreditation Association for Ambulatory Health Association, and the clinic's service population. Each of these groups has different processes and expectations around accountability; at times these conflict, and they often lead to substantial reporting and other bureaucratic work. The question remains as to what impacts these manifold practices of accountability will have on Native nations such as the Osage Nation.

The Osage are hardly unique in this push for accountability. In spite of, and in part because of, global neoliberal trends, many American Indian nations have been vastly expanding the services they offer their citizens in the twenty-first century. Several factors, including shrinking state and federal service programs, the development of other sources of revenue generation (primarily gaming), and U.S. policies of "self-determination" (whereby American Indian nations are encouraged to manage their own welfare programs) have all contributed to the unprecedented growth in American Indian bureaucratic structures over the last fifty years. This growth has led to a flurry of internal concerns over how these governments are operated and whether the money is being put to the best possible use. Given this growth and the long legacy of failed federal governance, many Indigenous nations are calling for accountability, which they see as a solution to many of the problems their nations face. More research is needed to better understand whether these attempts to indigenize sovereignty can in fact lead to governments that are more accountable to the needs of their service populations, whether the framework of accountability can be utilized to serve Native nations, and what role the ongoing colonial process plays in disrupting these efforts.

NOTES

1. Smith, *Decolonizing Methodologies.*
2. Al-Hardan, "Decolonizing Research," 64.
3. Jennings, "Sovereignty and Political Modernity."
4. Rifkin, "Indigenizing Agamben"; Bruyneel, "Exiled, Executed, Exalted"; Morgensen, *Spaces between Us.*
5. Agamben, *Homo Sacer.*
6. For further discussion of sovereignty's link to European governments, see Hannum, *Autonomy, Sovereignty*; Mair, *Primitive Government*; Gledhill, *Power and Its Disguises.*
7. Jackson, *Sovereignty.*
8. Hoffman, *Sovereignty.*
9. Foucault, *Power/Knowledge.*
10. 21 U.S. 8 Wheat. 543 (1823).
11. 30 U.S. 5 Pet. 1 (1831).
12. See Smith, *Ethnic Origins of Nations.*
13. Alfred, "Sovereignty," 464.
14. Wilkins, *American Indian Sovereignty.*
15. Alfred, "Sovereignty," 466; Dennison, *Colonial Entanglement.*
16. Dennison, *Colonial Entanglement.*
17. Alfred, "Sovereignty," 469, 471, 473.
18. Coffey and Tsosie, "Rethinking the Tribal Sovereignty," 192.
19. Dennison, *Colonial Entanglement.*
20. Barker, *Sovereignty Matters,* 17, 21.

21. Wolfe, "Settler Colonialism."

22. Smith, *Everything You Know*.

23. Bhabha, *Location of Culture*; Routledge, "Third Space as Critical"; Bruyneel, *Third Space of Sovereignty*.

24. Bruyneel, *Third Space of Sovereignty*.

25. Lambert, *Choctaw Nation*, 18.

26. Lambert, *Choctaw Nation*, 17.

27. Dennison, "Entangled Sovereignties."

28. For more on the history of American Indian sovereignty in the United States, see Mason, *Indian Gaming*; Bruyneel, *Third Space of Sovereignty*; Wilkins and Lomawaima, *Uneven Ground*; Cattelino, *High Stakes*; Lambert, *Choctaw Nation*.

29. Byrd, "Indigeneity's Difference," 136.

30. Simpson, *Mohawk Interruptus*.

31. David E. Wilkins, "The Sovereignty of Everything, the Power of Nothing," *Indian Country Today Media Network*, May 12, 2015, https://newsmaven.io/indiancountrytoday/archive/the-sovereignty-of-everything-the-power-of-nothing-7q5bRXaa0k2aPilRJ_mX9A/.

32. Power, *Audit Society*; Shore and Wright, "Coercive Accountability"; Strathern, *Audit Cultures*.

33. Kipnis, "Audit Cultures."

34. Mary Jo Webb, Tulsa University Law School Training Session for the OGRC, Tulsa OK, May 19, 2005.

35. Dennison, "Stitching Osage Governance."

36. Leonard Maker, OGRC Business Meeting, Pawhuska OK, March 21, 2005.

37. Leonard Maker, personal communication with the author, July 20, 2004.

38. Leonard Maker, interview by the author, Tulsa OK, May 05, 2005.

39. Anonymous, personal communication with the author, Skiatook OK, May 12, 2005.

40. During the reform process, OSA meetings were attended by about thirty individuals and generally occurred once a month, depending on current issues of concern.

41. Anonymous, Osage Shareholders Association Meeting, Pawhuska OK, August 29, 2005.

42. Anonymous, Osage Shareholders Association Meeting, Pawhuska OK, August 29, 2005.

43. Tsosie, "Conflict between the Public."

44. "Treaty with the Osage, 1808," 7 Stat. 107 (1808).

45. Cherokee Nation v. Georgia, 30 U.S. 5 Pet. at 17, 20 (1831).

46. Seminole Nation v. United States, 316 U.S. 286, 296–97 (1942).

47. United States v. Mitchell, 463 U.S. 206 (1983).

48. See Lone Wolf v. Hitchcock, 185 U.S. 553 (1903) for a full description of Congress's plenary power.

49. DuVal, *Native Ground*, 8.

50. Polacca, "Osage Dignitaries Share What 'Sovereignty' Means to Them," *Osage News* (Pawhuska OK), March 14, 2015, http://osagenews.org/en/article/2015/03/14/osage-dignitaries-share-what-sovereignty-means-them/.

51. Polacca, "Osage Dignitaries Share."
52. Polacca, "Osage Dignitaries Share."
53. Alfred, "Sovereignty."
54. Reyes and Kaufman, "Sovereignty, Indigeneity, Territory," 507.
55. Dennison, *Colonial Entanglement*.
56. Polacca, "Osage Dignitaries Share."
57. Dennison, *Colonial Entanglement*.
58. Horsechief-Hamilton, "Osage Leadership Talks Sovereignty."

BIBLIOGRAPHY

Agamben, Giorgio. *Homo Sacer*. Stanford CA: Stanford University Press, 1998.

Alfred, Gerald. "Sovereignty." In *A Companion to American Indian History*, edited by Phil Deloria and Neal Salisbury, 460–76. New York: Blackwell, 2002.

Al-Hardan, Anaheed. "Decolonizing Research on Palestinians: Towards Critical Epistemologies and Research Practices." *Qualitative Inquiry* 20, no. 1 (January 1, 2014): 61–71.

Barker, Joanne. *Sovereignty Matters: Locations of Contestation and Possibility in Indigenous Struggles for Self-Determination*. Lincoln: University of Nebraska Press, 2005.

Bhabha, Homi. *The Location of Culture*. London: Routledge, 1994.

Bruyneel, Kevin. "Exiled, Executed, Exalted: Louis Riel, *Homo Sacer* and the Production of Canadian Sovereignty." *Canadian Journal of Political Science* 43, no. 03 (2010): 711–32.

———. *The Third Space of Sovereignty: The Postcolonial Politics of U.S.–Indigenous Relations*. Minneapolis: University of Minnesota Press, 2007.

Byrd, Jodi. "Indigeneity's Difference: Methodology and the Structures of Sovereignty." *J19: The Journal of Nineteenth-Century Americanists* 2, no. 1 (2014): 137–42.

Cattelino, Jessica. *High Stakes: Florida Seminole Gaming and Sovereignty*. Durham NC: Duke University Press, 2008.

Coffey, W., and R. Tsosie. "Rethinking the Tribal Sovereignty Doctrine: Cultural Sovereignty and the Collective Future of Indian Nations." *Stanford Law and Policy Review* 12 (2001): 191–221.

Dennison, Jean. *Colonial Entanglement: Constituting a Twenty-First-Century Osage Nation*. Chapel Hill: University of North Carolina Press, 2012.

———. "Entangled Sovereignties." *American Ethnologist* 44, no. 4 (2017): 684–96.

———. "Stitching Osage Governance into the Future." *American Indian Culture and Research Journal* 37, no. 2 (2013): 115–28.

DuVal, Kathleen. *The Native Ground: Indians and Colonists in the Heart of the Continent*. Philadelphia: University of Pennsylvania Press, 2007.

Foucault, Michel. *Power/Knowledge: Selected Interviews and Other Writings, 1972–1977*. 1st Am. ed. New York: Pantheon Books, 1980.

Gledhill, John. *Power and Its Disguises: Anthropological Perspectives on Politics*. 2nd ed. London: Pluto Press, 2000.

Hannum, Hurst. *Autonomy, Sovereignty, and Self-Determination: The Accommodation of Conflicting Rights.* Rev. ed. Philadelphia: University of Pennsylvania Press, 1996.

Hoffman, John. *Sovereignty.* Minneapolis: University of Minnesota Press, 1998.

Horsechief-Hamilton, Geneva. "Osage Leadership Talks Sovereignty." *Osage Nation,* March 18, 2015. https://www.facebook.com/osagenation/posts/972924966051146.

Jackson, Robert H. *Sovereignty: Evolution of an Idea.* Malden MA: Polity Press, 2007.

Jennings, R. C. "Sovereignty and Political Modernity: A Genealogy of Agamben's Critique of Sovereignty." *Anthropological Theory* 11, no. 1 (2011): 23–61.

Kipnis, Andrew B. "Audit Cultures: Neoliberal Governmentality, Socialist Legacy, or Technologies of Governing?" *American Ethnologist* 35, no. 2 (2008): 275–89.

Lambert, Valerie. *Choctaw Nation: A Story of American Indian Resurgence.* Lincoln: University of Nebraska Press, 2007.

Mair, Lucy. *Primitive Government.* Bloomington: Indiana University Press, 1977.

Mason, W. Dale. *Indian Gaming: Tribal Sovereignty and American Politics.* Norman: University of Oklahoma Press, 2000.

Morgensen, Scott Lauria. *Spaces between Us: Queer Settler Colonialism and Indigenous Decolonization.* Minneapolis: University of Minnesota Press, 2011.

Power, Michael. *The Audit Society: Rituals of Verification.* Reprint, Oxford: Oxford University Press, 2010.

Reyes, Alvaro, and Maria Kaufman. "Sovereignty, Indigeneity, Territory: Zapatista Autonomy and the New Practices of Decolonization." *South Atlantic Quarterly* 110, no. 2 (April 1, 2011): 505–25.

Rifkin, Mark. "Indigenizing Agamben: Rethinking Sovereignty in Light of the 'Peculiar' Status of Native Peoples." *Cultural Critique* 73 (2009): 88–124.

Routledge, Paul. "The Third Space as Critical Engagement." *Antipode* 28, no. 4 (1996): 399–419.

Shore, Chris, and Susan Wright. "Coercive Accountability: The Rise of Audit Culture in Higher Education." In *Audit Cultures: Anthropological Studies in Accountability, Ethics, and the Academy,* edited by Marilyn Strathern, 21–54. London: Routledge, 2000.

Simpson, Audra. *Mohawk Interruptus: Political Life across the Borders of Settler States.* Durham NC: Duke University Press, 2014.

Smith, Anthony D. *The Ethnic Origins of Nations.* Oxford: Basil Blackwell, 1988.

Smith, Linda Tuhiwai. *Decolonizing Methodologies: Research and Indigenous Peoples.* London: Zed Books, 1999.

Smith, Paul Chaat. *Everything You Know about Indians Is Wrong.* Minneapolis: University of Minnesota Press, 2009.

Strathern, Marilyn, ed. *Audit Cultures: Anthropological Studies in Accountability, Ethics, and the Academy.* European Association of Social Anthropologists. London: Routledge, 2000.

Tsosie, Rebecca T. "Conflict between the Public Trust and the Indian Trust Doctrines: Federal Public Land Policy and Native Indians." *Tulsa Law Review* 39 (Winter 2003): 271–312.

Wilkins, David E. *American Indian Sovereignty and the U.S. Supreme Court: The Masking of Justice.* Austin: University of Texas Press, 1997.

Wilkins, David E., and K. Tsianina Lomawaima. *Uneven Ground: American Indian Sovereignty and Federal Law.* Norman: University of Oklahoma, 2001.

Wolfe, Patrick. "Settler Colonialism and the Elimination of the Native." *Journal of Genocide Research* 8, no. 4 (2006): 387–409.

CONTRIBUTORS

Benedict J. Colombi (PhD, Washington State University) is faculty director of the University of Arizona's Graduate Interdisciplinary Programs as well as acting head and associate professor of the American Indian Studies Department. His work focuses on the interface of human–environmental problems. He is the author of *Keystone Nations: Indigenous Peoples and Salmon across the North Pacific*.

Jean M. Dennison (PhD, University of Florida) is codirector for the Center for American Indian and Indigenous Studies and associate professor of American Indian Studies at the University of Washington. She is a member of the Osage Nation. Her book *Colonial Entanglement: Constituting a Twenty-First-Century Osage Nation* (University of North Carolina Press, 2012) speaks directly to national revitalization, one of the most pressing issues facing American Indians today. The primary goal of her academic endeavor is to explore how indigenous peoples negotiate and contest the ongoing settler-colonial process in areas such as citizenship, governance, and sovereignty.

Alan G. Marshall's (PhD, Washington State University) doctoral thesis focused on historical Nez Perce environmental relations. He taught at Lewis-Clark State College, where he developed programs in Native Studies and the Nez Perce language. He has retired from teaching but continues consulting for the Nez Perce Tribe.

J. Diane Pearson (PhD, University of Arizona) has taught Native American Studies at UC Berkeley and is author of *The Nez Perces in the Indian Territory: Nimiipuu Survival* (University of Oklahoma Press, 2008). She has also performed public-service work for the Hopi Nation and the Navajo Nation for the Office of Community Development at the University of Arizona and participated in a Violence against (American Indian) Women Project.

Christopher Riggs (PhD, University of Colorado at Boulder) is professor of history and chair of the Social Sciences Division at Lewis-Clark State College in Lewiston, Idaho.

Bradford D. Wazaney (PhD, Washington State University) is an applied anthropologist who focuses on cultural resource and environmental compliance for the Federal Energy Regulatory Commission. He has worked with environmental and cultural protection laws for numerous federal agencies and tribes throughout the United States.

INDEX

Page numbers in italics refer to illustrations or tables.

BIA (Bureau of Indian Affairs): under
Collier, 133–34; funding termination for Reorganization Division,
144, 145; involvement in Nez Perce
relocations, 41, 47, 48–49, 65, 72;
overview of, 127n104; and Phinney's
Constitution proposals for Nez Perce,
137–40, 148–51; and Phinney's NCAI
involvement, 142–43; and Phinney's
superintendent appointments, 145,
146–47; reduction in oversight of,
292, 294; suits against, 288; suspected of communism, 154–56;
and U.S. citizenship, 196–97; USSR
minority policy as potential model
for, 105–6, 114–15, 135. See also IRA
Blackeagle, Joseph, 81, 148
Bland, M. Cora, 64
blood quantum, 178, 179–80, 181, 182–
83, 184–87
Boas, Franz: correspondence with
Phinney, 106–7, 110–15, 125n79;
criticism of Collier, 134; involvement
in American–Russian scholarly
exchanges, 100–101, 102–4, 121n33;
Phinney as student of, 98–100; support for Phinney's BIA appointment,
105–6, 107, 134–35, 136–37
Bodin, Jean, 282
Bogoraz, Vladimir, 100–102, 105, 110,
112, 115–16, 121nn34–35
Bond, Trevor, 80
Bonnin, Gertrude, 142
Bonnin, Raymond, 142
Bronson, Ruth, 154
Brookings, Robert S., 257
Brothertown Indians, 190, 196
Brown, Ray A., 273n20
Bruner, Joseph, 155
Bruyneel, Kevin, 285
buffalo, xvi–xvii, 9–10, 69, 74–75, 78

Burke Act (1906), 179–80
Butler, Benjamin, 51
Buzzard, Frank, 66
Byrd, Jodi, 286
Byrne, Cornelius E., 91

Captain Jack, 74
captivity. See prison camps
Carson, Christopher "Kit," 223
Casoose, Erin, 298
Cataldo, Joseph, 99
Cayuse people, 63, 65, 68, 175–76
ceremonies: attire for, 69–70; federal
bans on, 72–73, 77–78; memorial,
45–47; and significance of horses, 46,
53; Sun Dances, 54, 66–73, 74–75,
77–78; winter, 39–40, 43–45
Chapman, Ad, 51
Chase-Dunn, Christopher, 249
Chattopadhyaya, Virendranath, 112, 117,
118, 125n85, 126n95, 127n116, 127n120
Chavez, Dionisio "Dennis," 154
Chavis, Ben, 32
Chee Dodge, Henry, 148
Cherokee Nation: federal allotment
offers, 190, 195, 196; tribal citizenship, 169, 182, 186–87; and Willard's
ancestral stories, xvi–xvii
Cherokee Nation v. Georgia (1831), 189,
294
Cheyenne people, 67, 74–75, 77
Chippewa people, 181–82
Choctaw people, 181, 185, 190, 196
Christianity, 6, 72, 74, 76–77, 137,
252–54
Cihu, 11
citizenship: defined, 170, 202
citizenship, tribal: and blood quantum
requirement, 178, 179–80, 181, 182–
83, 184–87; expanded requirements
for, 186–87; federal influence on

requirements for, 182–83; overview of, 171–72, 174–75; post-1934 requirements for, 180–82; pre-1934 U.S. conceptions of, 177–80; residency requirement for, 183, 185–86; traditional practices regarding, 175–77, 206n11

citizenship, U.S.: American Indian views of, 194–97; and nineteenth-century requirements for American Indians, 188–93, 213–14n100, 214n105; overview of, 171–72, 187–88; and twentieth-century requirements for American Indians, 193–94, 216n137; and voting rights, 194, 198–202, 216n140, 218n153, 219n161

Cleveland, Grover, 224

Coeur d'Alene tribe, 151–52, 180

Cohen, Felix S., 134, 139–40, 155

Collier, John: appointing Phinney to BIA, 134–37; appointment as BIA Commissioner, 105, 133–34, 227; assignments for Phinney, 140, 142, 145; criticism of, 145–46, 154–55

Collins, Rob, xv

Colombi, Ben, xix, xx, xxiv–xxv

Columbia University, 98–100

Colville, Washington Territory, 76–77, 78–80, 186

Communism in United States, 152–59. *See also* USSR

Communist International, 112, 126n92, 127n116

Conner, Roberta, 175

The Cost of Doing Nothing (Institute for Fisheries Resources), 262–63

Cox, Eugene A., 158

Craig, William, 98, 120n17

CRITFC (Columbia River Inter-Tribal Fish Commission), 266

Crow Blanket, 74

Dakota Sioux, 175

Dale, Edward Everett, 273n20

dam building, 259–65

dances. *See* ceremonies

Davis, Richard M., 232

Dawes, Henry, 178

Dawes Act (1887), 137, 178–79, 193, 224–25, 254, 256–57

Deloria, Ella, 175

Dennison, Jean, xix, xx, xxv

Dies, Martin, Jr., 155

Diné (Najavo) people, 177

Drent, Meredith, 297, 298

dual citizenship, 187–88, 194, 197, 200–201

Duffy, Diane, 172, 206n10

Duke, Emma, 273n20

DuVal, Kathleen, 295

Dyer, Daniel B., 72, 75, 77

Eastman, Charles A., 148, 197

economic development practices. *See* Jicarilla Apache people; salmon nation building

education, American Indian, 95–96, 147–48, 234

Edwards, Herbert R., 273n20

Elk, John, 216n140

Elk v. Wilkins (1884), 216n140

environmental sustainability. *See* salmon nation building

Es-pow-yes (Light in the Mountain), 74, 80

ethnology. *See* anthropology and ethnology

Evans, Steven, 34, 44, 49–50, 56n49

exile. *See* prison camps

Farver, Peru, 159, 160

FBI (Federal Bureau of Investigation), 149, 152–53, 156–57

Indian Citizenship Act (1924), 187, 194–95, 197–98
Indian Health Service (IHS), 242
Indian Self-Determination and Education Assistance Act (1975), 292
Indian Service. *See* BIA
Indian Territory: federal regulation of ceremonies in, 72–73, 77–78; Nez Perce removal from, 76; Quapaw Reservation, 47–51, 53–54, 63; and U.S. citizenship policy, 190. *See also* Oakland Sub-Agency, Indian Territory
Indian Tribal Governmental Tax Status Act (1983), 239
indigenization in academia, 280–81
indigenous nationalism, 172, 174. *See also* citizenship, tribal
Ingold, Tim, 26n2
Institute for International Education, 111
intertribal communication, 65–66
IPIN (Institute for the Study of the Peoples of the USSR), 102
IRA (Indian Reorganization Act, 1934): American Indian rejection of, 137, 138, 140–41, 227; Jicarilla Apache implementation of, 227–29; overview of, 133, 180, 227–28; Senate criticism of, 154; and tribal citizenship, 180–81, 182–83
Iroquois Nations, 195–96
Iverson, Peter, 177

Jackson, Robert, 281
Jefferson, Daniel, 74
Jennings, Joe, 136, 153
Jennison, Guy, 53
Jicarilla Apache people, 221–44; customs, 221–22; economic diversification and growth, 229–35, *230, 231, 233, 235*; employment statistics, 239–41, *240*; health services, 242; implementation of IRA, 227–29; introduction of livestock economy, 225–27, *226*; land ownership, 222–25, 228, 242–44; royalty earnings, *236,* 236–39, *237*; taxation rights, 241
Johnson v. McIntosh (1823), 282
Jones, Hiram W., 47, 48, 52
Joseph, Chief, senior (Tuekakas), 35, *36,* 38
Joseph, Chief, younger (Hinmátoon-yalatkáykt): Anderson on, 78; death and burial, 80; education, 56n49; guardian spirit quest, 16; homeland, affection for and visual record of, 25, 41–42; horse of, 53–54, 66; Meacham on, 64, 75; and memorial ceremony, 45–46; participation in ceremonial dances, 67, 70, 74; resistance to captivity and relocations, 38–39, 47–49, 50–52, 65, 76, 79–80, 81; surrender to U.S. Army, 31, 254; as teamster, 66

Kabardins, 114
Kalt, Joseph P., 272
Kan, Sergei, xxi
Kansa people, 177
Kaufman, Mara, 297
Kelly, Lawrence, 140
Kerber, Linda K., 202
Kickapoo people, 190
Kingsley, E. W., 49
Kinkade, M. Dale, 5
kinship, 13–15, 17–19, 175, 176
Kiowa people, 67, 69, 71, 74–75, 78
Kipnis, Andrew, 288
Kirov, Sergei Mironovich, 112, 118, 126n91
Kootenai people, 185
Korenizatsiya, 101, 105, 132
Kutenai tribe, 151

La Flesche, Francis, 288

Laguna, Frederica de, 100

Lakota people, 196

Lamar, Lucius Q. C., 75

Lambert, Valerie, 285

land: allotment policies, 178–80, 186–87, 190, 193, 224–25, 254; financial restitution for stolen, 145, 146, 147, 151, 164n60, 232; geographic diversity of Nez Perce, 6–8; Jicarilla Apache ownership approach to, 222–25, 228, 242–44; maps of Nez Perce homeland, 41–42; plants and wildlife in Nez Perce, 8–10; spiritual dimension of, 10–12, 39–41, 49–50; U.S. reduction of Nez Perce, 31–32, 35–39, 253–55. *See also* Indian Territory

landscape: as concept, 26n2

Lang, William L., 175

language: American Indian sign, 66; Nimiipuutímt, 4–5, 98–100, 107; Phinney's study of, 98–100, 108–10; Russian, 108–10, 112–13, 117–18; and sacred histories, 39–40

Lapwai, Idaho, 76–77, 78

Latham, Edward, 79

LaVelle, John P., 201–2

Lawyer, Archie, 35–38

Lee, J. M., 77

Leeds, William, 48

Lenin, Vladimir, 101, 105, 121n37, 131–32

Lewis and Clark expedition, 2, 7, 249, 252

Light in the Mountain (Es-pow-yes), 74, 80

Lincoln, Robert, 75

Lipps, Oscar, 96, 136, 162n13

Little Bluff, 71

Llewellyn, William H. H., 223

Looking Glass, senior (Apash Wyakaikt), 31, 35, *37*, 38

Looking Glass, younger (Allalimya Takanin), 38

Lott, Sam, 56n49

MacMurray, Junius W., 44

MAE (Museum of Anthropology and Ethnology)/IAE (Institute of Anthropology and Ethnography), 94–95, 100, 102–4, 106–7, 110, 112, 118, 119n7

Major Crimes Act (1885), 178

Makarov, M. V., 118

Maker, Leonard, 289–90

Manjapra, Kris, 127n120

Mankiller, Wilma, 194–95

Mann, Kelly M., 249

Margold, Nathan, 155, 198

Mark, Mary Louise, 273n20

Marr, Nicolai Yakovlevich, 122n43

marriage customs, 17–19, 24–25

Marshall, Alan, xviii–xx, xxiv, 26n3, 33, 40, 46, 50, 63, 66, 70, 176

Marshall, John, 294

Martinez, Maria, 148

Marx, Karl, 107, 118

Massachusetts Citizenship Act, 190–91

Mathew, John Joseph, 143

Matorin, Nikolai Mikhailovich, 102–4, 107, 112, 122n42, 126n93, 152–53

Maxwell, Lucien B., 223

McCarran, Patrick, 154–55

McClellan, Catherine, 100

McConville, James, 149

McCreery, Thomas Clay, 48

McGovern, George, 202

McKenzie, Fayette Avery, 273n20

McNickle, D'Arcy, 135–36, 142–43, 145, 159, 166n92, 199

Meacham, Alfred B., 51, 64, 75–76

Meany, Edmond, 79

measured separatism, 172, 188, 197, 200. *See also* citizenship, tribal medicine dances, 54, 66–73, 74–75, 77–78

memorial ceremonies, 45–47

Meriam, Lewis, 257–58, 273n20

Meriam Report (*The Problem of Indian Administration*), 103, 257–58, 273n20

Merrion v. The Jicarilla Apache Tribe (1982), 241

Mexico: and citizenship, 191–92; and land ownership, 222–23

Michelson, Truman, 98

Miles, Nelson A., 31–32, 51, 54

Miranda, Guadalupe, 223

Montezuma, Carlos, 169–70, 196–97

Morgan, Lewis Henry, 106–7, 118

Morton, Rogers, 238

Moses, Charley (Sup-poon-mas), 66, 67, 71–72, 74

Murray, James, 202

Muskrat Bronson, Ruth, 148

Naranjo, Tessie, 176

National Council of American Indians, 142

Native Hubs (Ramirez), 280

Navajo people and Nation, 113–14, 177, 181, 182–83, 185–86

Nazis, 154–55

NCAI (National Congress of American Indians): criticism of, 154; dual citizenship and voting rights advocacy, 199–201; establishment, 142–43; goals, 143–44, 159–60

Neiberding, Velma, 52, 53

Newman, George H., 79

New Mexico Enabling Act (1910), 194

Nez Perce Business Committee, 137–40, 163n36

Nez Perce people: and Christianity, 76–77, 137, 252–54; circumstances of captivity, 31–32, 35–39, 41, 254;

culture, 1–3; intertribal communication, 65–66; land, geographic diversity of, 6–8; land, human-built places in, 12–13; land, maps of, 41–42; land, plants, and wildlife, 8–10; land, spiritual dimension of, 10–12, 39–41, 49–50; lands restored to, 80; language, 4–5, 98–100, 107; leadership customs, 22–24, 176, 207n19; maintenance of spirituality during captivity, 33, 43–47, 52–53, 66–73, 74–75, 79; name customs, 15–16, 46; oral traditions, 1, 10–11, 175, 251–52; and Phinney as BIA superintendent, 145, 146–47; and Phinney's Constitution proposals, 137–40, 148–51; region, 4–5; relationship customs, 13–15, 16–22, 24–25, 176; resistance to relocations, 47–49, 50–52, 54, 78–81. *See also* salmon nation building; spirituality

Nez Perce Tribal Executive Committee (NPTEC), 93

Nick-co-lo-clum, 74

Nier, Albert O., 148

Nimiipuu. *See* Nez Perce people

NKVD (Soviet People's Ministry of Internal Affairs), 110, 118

Nooksack tribe, 169

Nordhaus, Robert J., 231–32

Oakland Sub-Agency, Indian Territory: federal regulation of ceremonies in, 72–73; intertribal communication in, 65–66; Nez Perce relocation to, 63–64; Sun Dances in, 66–73, 74–75

Obama, Barack, 145

OIA (Office of Indian Affairs). *See* BIA

Oirat Mongols, 113–14

Ollokot, 31, 38, 42, 45

Olsen, Loran, 71

Omaha people, 177

OSA (Osage Shareholders Association), 291–96, 301n40

Osage Mineral Estate, 288, 291–96

Osage Nation: citizenship, 177, 194; government reform, 289–91, 298–99; opposition to full self-governance, 291–96; Sovereignty Day, 279–80, 287, 296–98; view of accountability, 287–89, 294–95, 299

Osborne, E. C., 77–78

Ottowa people, 190

Owhi, 74

Pahalawasheschit (Star Doctor), 71, 83n43

Paiute people, 181

Palmer Oil Company, 238–39

Palus people, 63, 65, 71

Parker, Arthur C., 141–42, 143

Parsons, James, 148

Patterson, John J., 50

Pearson, Diane, 32, 164n60

peoplehood: as model of identity, 32–34; and resistance to captivity and relocation, 47–49, 50–52, 54, 78–81; spiritual and ceremonial expressions of, 43–47, 52–54, 67–73, 74–75, 77–79; visualization of, 41–43

Peterson, Helen, 201

Philips, Luke, 35–38

Phinney, Archie M., 91–119, 97, 109, 131–61, 149; on agricultural economy, 255, 256, 257; on American Indian education, 95–96, 147–48; BIA appointments, 134–37, 145, 146–47; challenges in USSR, 110–13; on Chief Joseph, 81; Constitution proposals for Nez Perce, 137–40, 148–51; death and burial, 91, 161; dissertation, 117–18; education and degrees in

U.S., 96–100; education and degrees in USSR, 102–4, 106–10, 116–17, 131; golf hobby, 160, 166n92; legacy, 91–92; NCAI involvement, 142–44, 159, 199; research on USSR minority policy, 113–16, 117, 157; on sacred histories and ceremonialism, 39–40, 45; study of tribal government, 140–41; suspected as communist, 152–54, 156–59

Phinney, Ellen French, 165n84

Phinney, Fitch, 160

Phinney, George, 137

Phinney, Mary Lily, 160, 165–66n84

Pinkham, Allen, 34, 44, 49–50

Pole Cat (Tisca), 67, 74

Ponca people, 77–78, 177

Porter, Robert B., 196, 216n137

Porter v. Hall (1928), 198–99

Potawatomi people, 190, 195

Powaukee, Amos, 137

Powder Horn Owl, 66

Powless, Irving, Jr., 195–96

Pratt, Richard Henry, 41

Price, David, 149, 154, 159

Price, Hiram A., 72

prison camps: circumstances of Nez Perce captivity in, 31–32, 35–39, 41, 254; continued exile for non-Christians in, 76–77, 78–80; federal regulation of ceremonies in, 72–73, 77–78; maintenance of spirituality during, 33, 43–47, 52–53, 66–73, 74–75, 79; and Nez Perce resistance to relocations, 47–49, 50–52, 54, 78–81; poor conditions in, 47, 57n66, 63–64

The Problem of Indian Administration (Meriam Report), 103, 257–58, 273n20

Public Law 280 (1953), 164n53

Pueblo people, 176, 191–92, 194, 196, 198, 222

Quapaw Reservation, Indian Territory, 47–51, 53–54, 63

race and blood quantum, 178, 179–80, 181, 182–83, 184–87
Ramirez, Renya, 280
Red Cloud, Charlie, 196
Red Corn, Raymond, 297
Red Elk, 67, 74
Red Wolf, 74
Reeves, Floyd, 148
religion. See ceremonies; Christianity; spirituality
reservations: for Jicarilla Apache, 223–24. See also Indian Territory
Reuben, James, 31, 35–38, 67, 74
Reyes, Alvaro, 297
Rhoads, Charles J., 105–6
Rickard, Clinton, 195
Riggs, Chris, xix, xxii
Riggs, Patricia, 171
Riley, Robert, 140, 148, 150
Rivers, Henry, 74
Roberts, Alaina E., 184
Roberts, Laverne, 280
Roe Cloud, Henry, 143, 273n20
Roosevelt, Franklin D., 133, 155, 227
Rose Bush (Tim-sus-sle-wit), 67, 74
Ross, Edmund G., 225
Russia. See USSR
Ryan, W. Carson, Jr., 273n20

Salish people, 185
salmon nation building, 249–72; as adaptive strategy, 265–68; vs. agricultural economy, 255–59; challenges, 268–70; vs. dam building, 261–65; and prominence of salmon

in Nez Perce diet, 9, 251; spiritual origins, 250–52; and U.S. reduction of Nez Perce lands, 253–55
Sapir, Edward, 103
Schmitt, Carl, 281
Scott, Cyrus M., 67–68, 74
Scott, John W., 73, 76
self-governance and self-determination: and attempts to create national American Indian organization, 141–42; and financial restitution, 145, 146, 147, 151, 164n60, 232; and IRA, 133, 136–37, 138, 140, 141, 227–28; and Jicarilla Apache implementation of IRA, 227–29; Phinney's Constitution proposals for Nez Perce, 137–40, 148–51; and trust doctrine, 189, 198–99, 200, 294–95; in USSR minority policy, 105, 131–32. See also Jicarilla Apache people; NCAI; salmon nation building; sovereignty
Sells, Cato, 180
Set-t'an calendar, 69, 71
Shahgwee, Chief, 195
Sharp, Peter B., xvii, xviii
Sheridan, Philip, 54
Shingoitewa, LeRoy, 187
Shoshone people, 181
sign language, American Indian, 66
Silver Horn calendar, 69–70, 71
Simpson, Audra, 286
Skvirsky, Boris Evssevich, 103–4, 122n45
Slickpoo, Allen P., Sr., 93, 119n4
Sloan, Thomas, 197
Smedley, Agnes, 108, 111, 113, 125n85
Smith, Asa Bowen, 252
Smohalla (Wanapum Dreamer Prophet), 39, 44, 68, 76
Snake River Basin Adjudication (SRBA), 267
Snyder, Homer P., 194

Society of American Indians (SAI), 142, 197

"Solitoso," 66

sovereignty, 279–300; and accountability, 287–89, 294–95, 299; European theories of, 281–83; Indigenous theories of, 280–81, 283–87; and Osage government reform, 289–91; and Osage opposition to full self-governance, 291–96; Osage reflections on, 279–80, 287–88, 296–98. *See also* citizenship; citizenship, tribal; citizenship, U.S.; self-governance and self-determination

Spalding, Henry Harmon, 6, 252, 255

Spicer, Edward H., xx, 32

Spier, Leslie, 68

Spillman, William J., 258, 273n20

Spining, George, 73

spirituality: and ancestors, 22; federal criticism and suppression of, 72–73, 76, 77–78; of graveyards and markers, 73–74, 79; and spiritual dimension of land, 10–12, 39–41, 49–50; and spiritual dimension of water, 49–50, 250–52; and Sun Dances, 54, 66–73, 74–75, 77–78; and *wéeyekin*, 12, 20–21; and winter ceremonials, 39–40, 43–45

Sprague, Roderick, 73–74

Spruhan, Paul, 185

Stalin, Joseph, 101, 105, 112, 121n37, 131–32

Standing Bear, Luther, 196

Star Doctor (Pahalawasheschit), 71, 83n43

Starkay, Frank P., 148

Stein, Gary C., 216n137

Stevens, Isaac, 253

Stickney, William, 47–48

Stockbridge–Munsee Mohican people, 196, 213n90

Stranahan, C. T., 76–77

St. Regis Mohawk Reservation, 141

Strong, Anna Louise, 114, 126–27n102

suffrage, 194, 198–202, 216n140, 218n153, 219n161

summer villages, 13

Sun Dances, 54, 66–73, 74–75, 77–78

Sup-poon-mas (Charley Moses), 66, 67, 71–72, 74

survival. *See* prison camps

Swimmer, Ross, 186

Taylor, Robert, 120n9

Teamster Act (1877), 65–66

Termination policy, 189, 199–200

territory. *See* land

Thomas, Robert K., xx, 32, 33

Thompson, Frank (Feathers around the Neck), 66, 74

Three Eagles, 74

Throessell, Henry, 143

Tim-sus-sle-wit (Rose Bush), 67, 74

Tisca (Pole Cat), 67, 74

Tohono O'odham people, 181

Tonkovich, Nicole, 193

Toohoolhoolzote, 31, 35

Towa people, 176

Towner, Elwood A., 155

Trafzer, Cliff, 79

Treaty of Guadalupe Hidalgo (1848), 191–92, 222

Trotsky, Leon, 112

Trujillo, Miguel, 200

Trujillo v. Garley (1948), 200

Truman, Harry S., 146, 147

trust doctrine, 189, 198–99, 200, 294–95

Tuekakas (Chief Joseph, senior), 35, 36, 38

Tuk-te-tna-tu-kayet, 74

Umatilla people, 175–76

United States v. Lucero (1869), 191–92

United States v. Nice (1916), 194

United States v. Rogers (1846), 177

United States v. Sandoval (1913), 192, 194
University of Kansas (KU), 98
U.S. government. See BIA; citizenship;
citizenship, tribal; citizenship, U.S.;
IRA; prison camps; self-governance
and self-determination
U.S.-Mexican War (1846–48), 191, 222
USSR: American-Russian anthropological
cooperation, 100–101, 122n45; anthropology ideology, 101–2, 106–7, 110,
118, 122n43; and Communist International, 112, 126n92, 127n116; economic
policy in, 101, 121n37, 123n49; Great
Purge, 110, 111–12, 118, 122n42, 124n77,
126n93, 127n120, 132; MAE (Museum
of Anthropology and Ethnology),
94–95, 100, 102–4, 106–7, 110, 112, 118,
119n7; minority policy in, 104–5, 108,
113–15, 117, 122n38, 122n40, 131–32, 135;
and Phinney suspected as communist,
152–54, 156–59; U.S. relations, 125n81
Ute people, 187

Velarde, Hubert, 238
Voth, Henry R., 77
voting rights, 194, 198–202, 216n140,
218n153, 219n161
Voting Rights Act (1965), 201

Walker, Deward, 39, 68
Walker, John (Yellow Head), 66, 74
Walla Walla people, 175–76
Wallerstein, Immanuel, 271
war and warfare, 31, 254
Washington v. Washington State Commercial Passenger Fishing Vessel Ass'n.,
443 U.S. 658 (1979), 262
water, spiritual dimension of, 49–50,
250–52. See also salmon nation
building
Watkins, Arthur V., 154

Watters, Samuel M., xix, xx, 11–12, 26n3,
27n6, 54
Wazaney, Brad, xix, xx, xxii–xxiv
Webb, Mary Joe, 288–89
wéetes (the land), 5
wéeyekin (guardian/tutelary/spirit or
genius), 12, 20–21
West, Elliott, 192
Wheeler, Burton K., 154, 230
Wheeler, Harry, 148
Wheeler-Howard Act. See IRA
White Bird, 31, 35
Whitehorn, Maria, 296
Whitfield, Mat, 74
Wilkins, David, 287
Wilkinson, Charles F., 92
Willard, William "Bill," xxiii; Cherokee
ancestral stories, xvi–xvii; on NCAI,
199; research on Phinney, xviii, 92–
95, 118, 125n79
Williamson, Nakia, 53, 120n9
Wilson, H. Clyde, 229
Wilson, Woodrow, 125n81
Windy Boy v. County of Big Horn (1986),
201
winter ceremonials, 39–40, 43–45
winter villages, 12–13, 39–41
Wolf Head, 67, 74
Worcester v. Georgia (1832), 189
Work, Hubert, 257
Wyandot people, 190, 195, 196

Yellow Bear, 49, 74
Yellow Bull, 31, 51, 66, 67, 70, 74, 76, 77,
80, 85n80
Yellow Head (John Walker), 66, 74
Yellow Robe, Evelyn, 148
Yellowtail, Robert, 197
Yellow Wolf, 35, 76–77
Yelvington, Kevin, xxi
Ysleta del Sur Pueblo people, 183, 187